MESSENGER:

THE LEGEND OF MUHAMMAD ALI

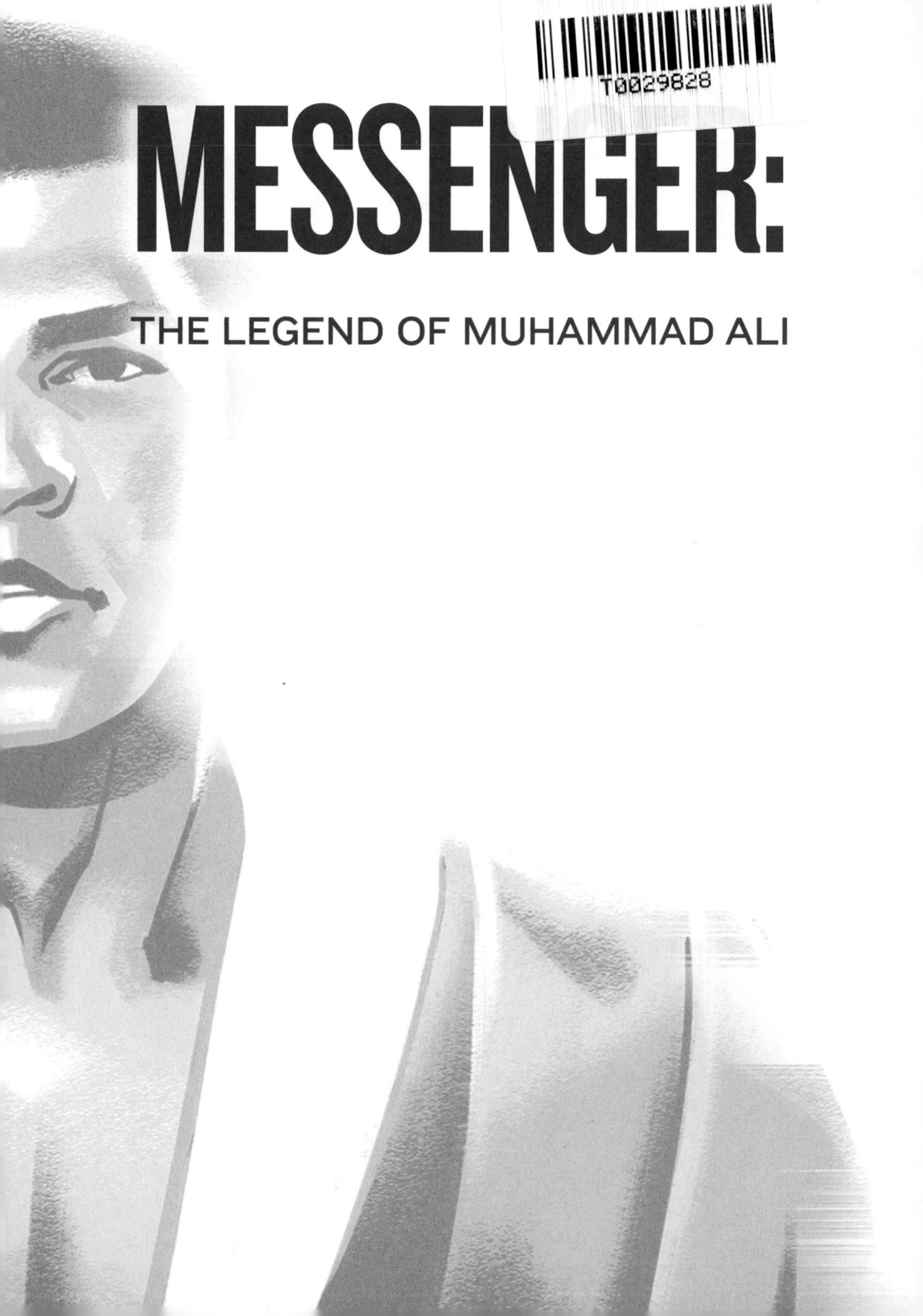

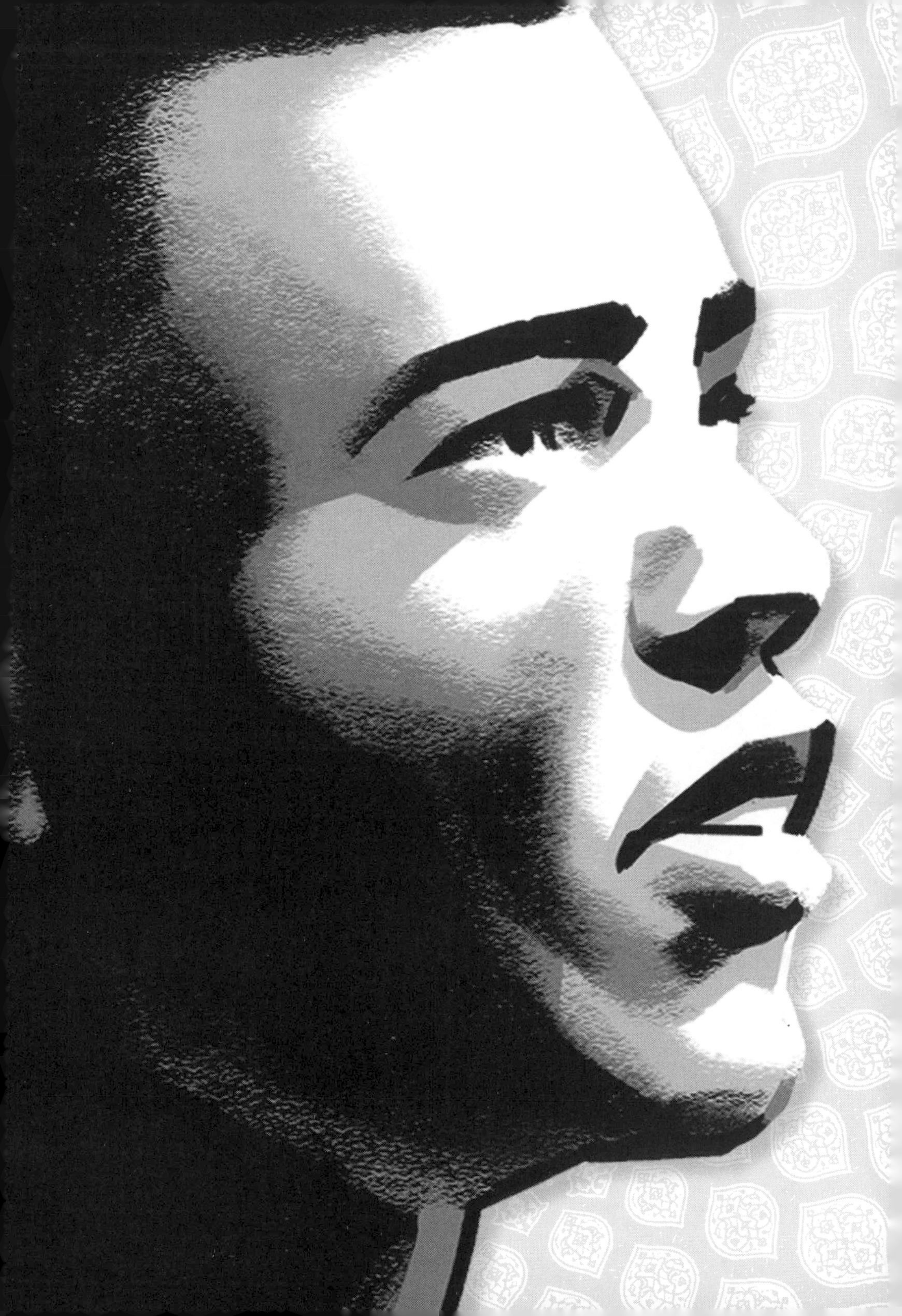

MESSENGER:

THE LEGEND OF MUHAMMAD ALI

Written by
MARC BERNARDIN

Art by
RON SALAS

:01

First Second
NEW YORK

First Second

PUBLISHED BY FIRST SECOND
FIRST SECOND IS AN IMPRINT OF ROARING BROOK PRESS,
A DIVISION OF HOLTZBRINCK PUBLISHING HOLDINGS LIMITED PARTNERSHIP
120 BROADWAY, NEW YORK, NY 10271
FIRSTSECONDBOOKS.COM

TEXT © 2023 BY MARC BERNARDIN
ILLUSTRATIONS © 2023 BY RON SALAS

LIBRARY OF CONGRESS CONTROL NUMBER: 2022920054

OUR BOOKS MAY BE PURCHASED IN BULK FOR PROMOTIONAL, EDUCATIONAL, OR BUSINESS
USE. PLEASE CONTACT YOUR LOCAL BOOKSELLER OR THE MACMILLAN CORPORATE AND
PREMIUM SALES DEPARTMENT AT (800) 221-7945 EXT. 5442 OR BY EMAIL AT
MACMILLANSPECIALMARKETS@MACMILLAN.COM.

FIRST EDITION

FIRST EDITION, 2023
EDITED BY CALISTA BRILL, CASEY GONZALEZ, AND MICHAEL MOCCIO
COVER DESIGN BY KIRK BENSHOFF
INTERIOR BOOK DESIGN BY SUNNY LEE AND YAN L. MOY
PRODUCTION EDITING BY HELEN SEACHRIST
COPY EDITING BY ELIZABETH MAZER
PROOFREADING BY HAYLEY JOZWIAK
ARABIC TRANSLATION BY SPECTRUM TRANSLATION

THE ILLUSTRATIONS FOR THIS BOOK WERE DONE IN CLIP STUDIO PAINT WITH A ROUGH BRUSH
AND RON CHAN SIDE PENCIL BRUSH. LETTERS, BALLOONS, AND SOUND EFFECTS WERE ADDED IN
ILLUSTRATOR AND INDESIGN. THE LETTERING WAS DONE IN SMACK ATTACK BY BLAMBOT.

PRINTED IN THE UNITED STATES OF AMERICA

ISBN 978-1-59643-971-9 (HARDCOVER)
10 9 8 7 6 5 4 3 2 1

ISBN 978-1-250-88163-2 (PAPERBACK)
10 9 8 7 6 5 4 3 2 1

DON'T MISS YOUR NEXT FAVORITE BOOK FROM FIRST SECOND! FOR THE LATEST UPDATES
GO TO FIRSTSECONDNEWSLETTER.COM AND SIGN UP FOR OUR ENEWSLETTER.

For Luc, who'll have plenty of fights to fight.

—**MARC**

To Barb and Ewan, for always showing me what love is each and every day. You make it all worth it.

—**RON**

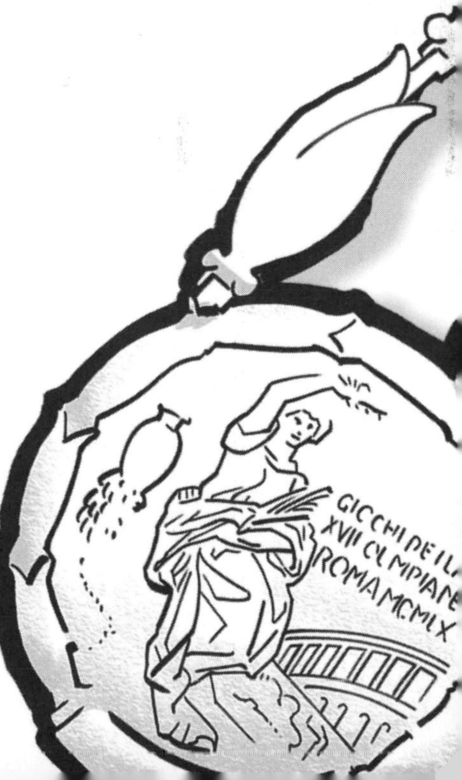
ROMA MCMLX

FOREWORD

Heroic poems: a storytelling style used to recount the exploits of "real" people and events with grandiosity and flair—used to be all the rage. Homer was a big fan. There seems to have been a place called Troy, and there might have been a war there, but the details that we think we know appear to come entirely from his accounts. Inspired by the truth and truth itself aren't exactly the same thing, but they both aim to land in the same place. The *Iliad, Paradise Lost, Gilgamesh*. Heroes and stories too big for the constraints of convention.

Muhammad Ali's life was just as big.

As formidable a warrior as Achilles, as steadfast a leader as Odysseus, as deft a slayer of monsters as Beowulf, Ali remains a singular figure—in many ways, his story is the story of the twentieth century in America. Race, class, sports, politics, religion, war, injustice, health care—all of which he faced and faced down while being, perhaps, the most famous man in the world.

I first heard about Muhammad Ali as a child growing up in the late 1970s. He was still fighting but was on the downward slope. When I asked my parents and grandparents why they were glued to the TV every time he strapped on his gloves, the only answer I'd get was "Because he was the greatest."

I did my research over the years because I wanted to understand why. I did even more once this book became a possibility. And sitting down to write about the life of Muhammad Ali—even thinking about it—was frightening. There's so, so much to that life. Maybe even too much to squeeze into a single graphic biography.

So I decided not to even try. Instead, I, along with my editors at First Second—Calista Brill and Casey Gonzalez—set our sights on the legend of Muhammad Ali.

Some of what you're about to read in these ten rounds, or chapters, is absolutely, verifiably true. But other parts . . . feel true. Maybe some time lines are smushed together. Maybe meetings and conversations are taking place in the "wrong" places. Maybe no one ever said these things in exactly these ways.

In other words, you are 100 percent going to fail a test on Muhammad Ali if this is your only resource. (The bookshelves are filled with other fantastic cradle-to-grave biographies out there, some of which helped inform this book.)

In trying to wrap our arms around everything that Muhammad Ali was, we decided that liberties could be taken with time, place, and point of view. Maybe even *should* be taken.

What we wanted to do was attempt to embody the essence of Muhammad Ali. What made him a hero, a rebel, an icon, a champion, a survivor? What made him so much larger than life?

What made Ali . . . Ali?

—MARC BERNARDIN
Los Angeles, June 2022

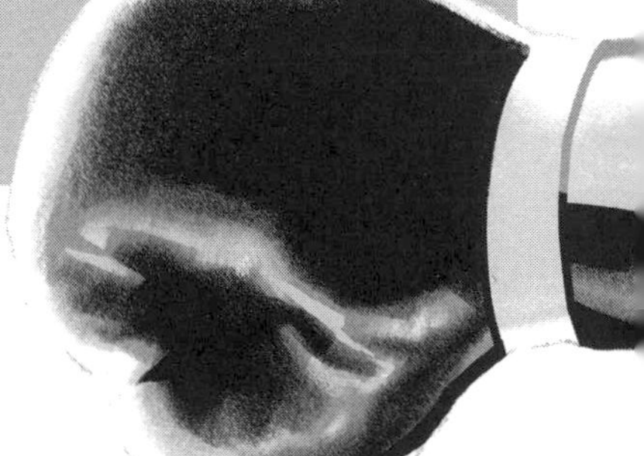

PROLOGUE: 1996.

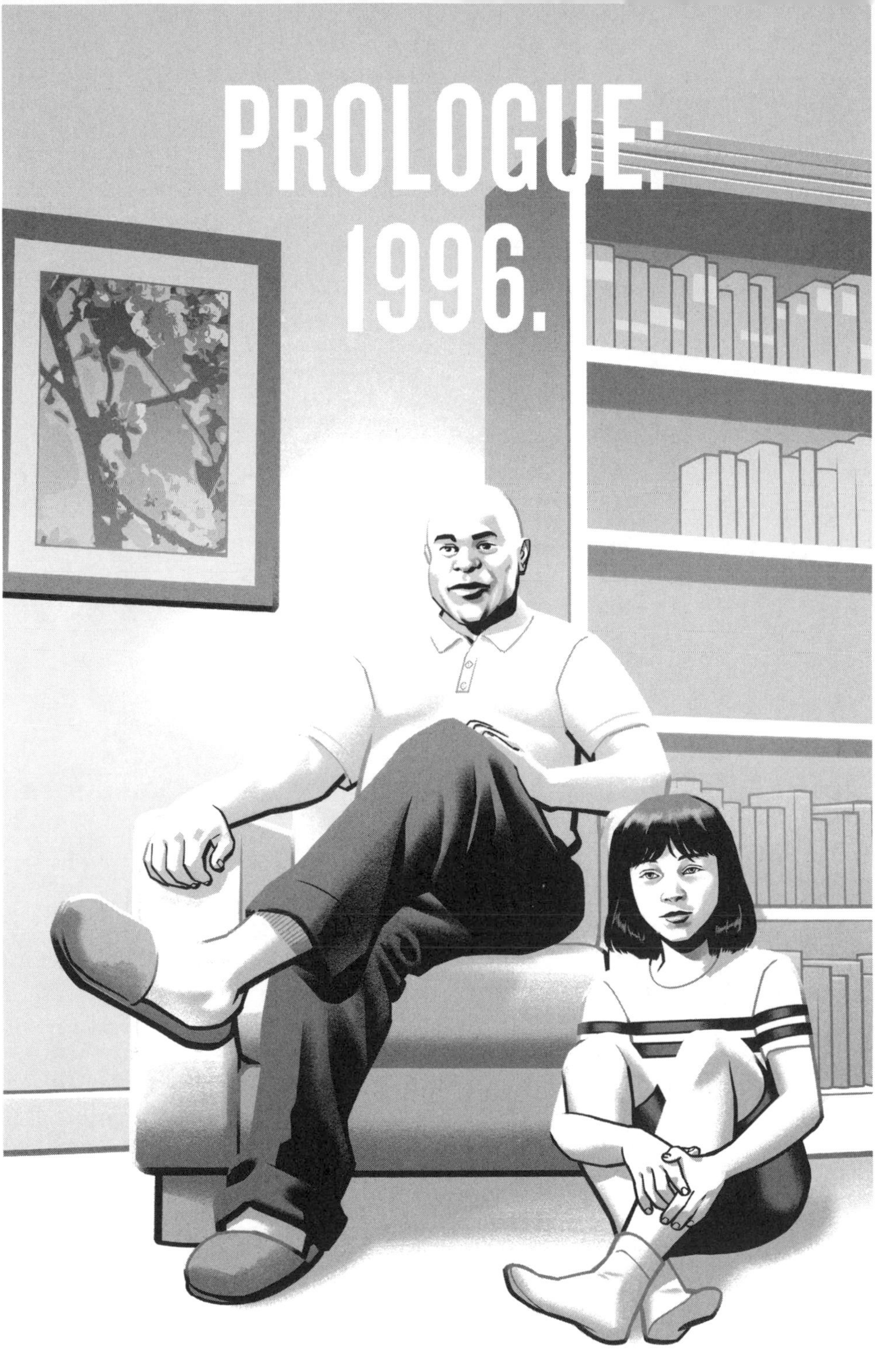

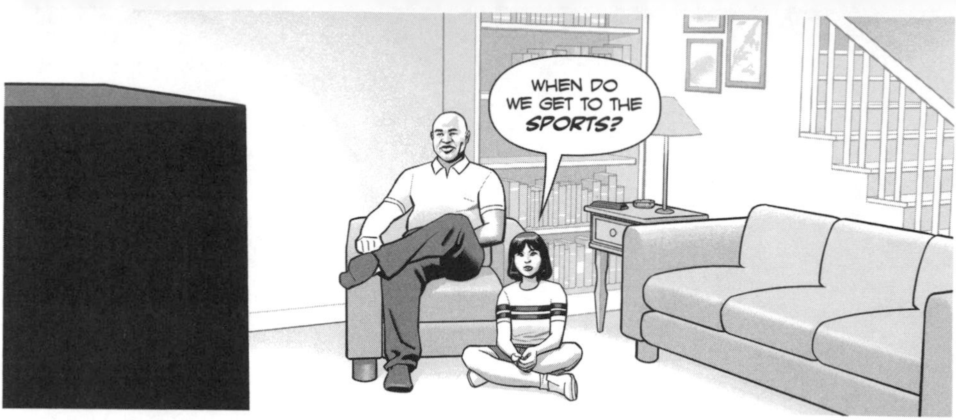
WHEN DO WE GET TO THE SPORTS?

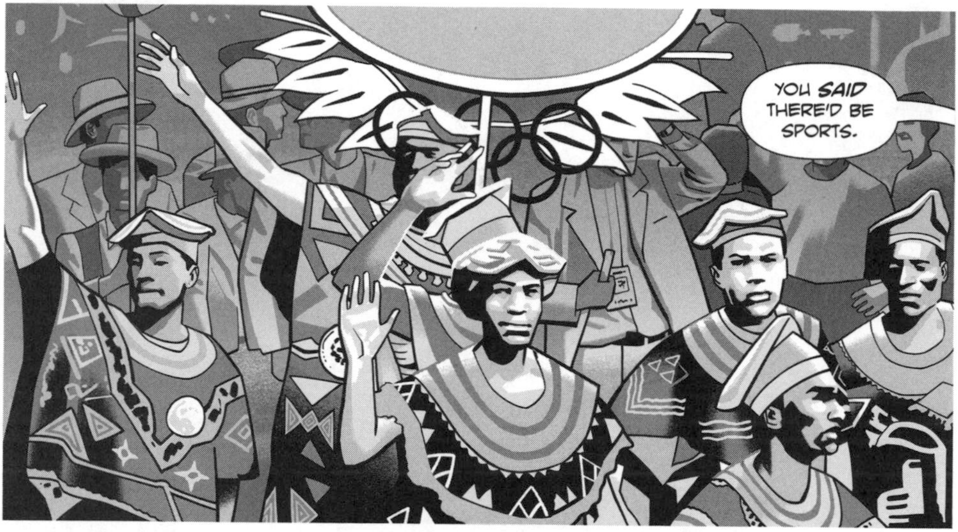
YOU SAID THERE'D BE SPORTS.

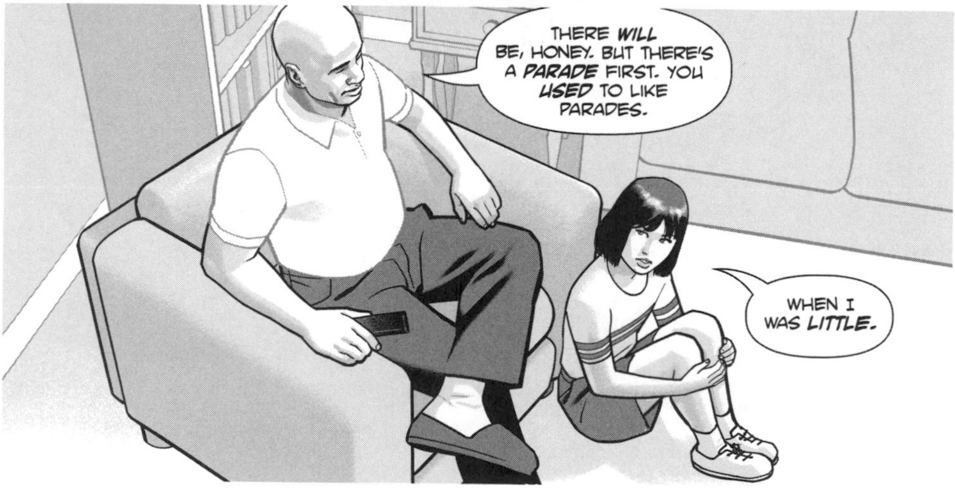
THERE WILL BE, HONEY. BUT THERE'S A PARADE FIRST. YOU USED TO LIKE PARADES.
WHEN I WAS LITTLE.

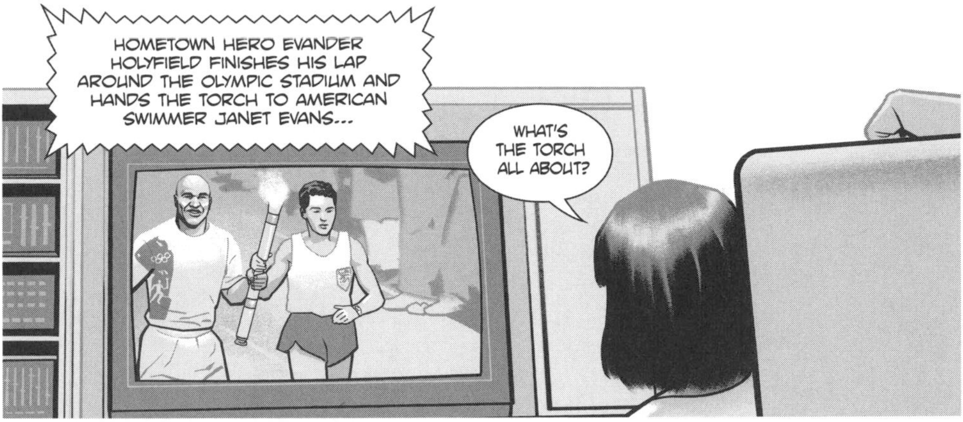
HOMETOWN HERO EVANDER HOLYFIELD FINISHES HIS LAP AROUND THE OLYMPIC STADIUM AND HANDS THE TORCH TO AMERICAN SWIMMER JANET EVANS...
WHAT'S THE TORCH ALL ABOUT?

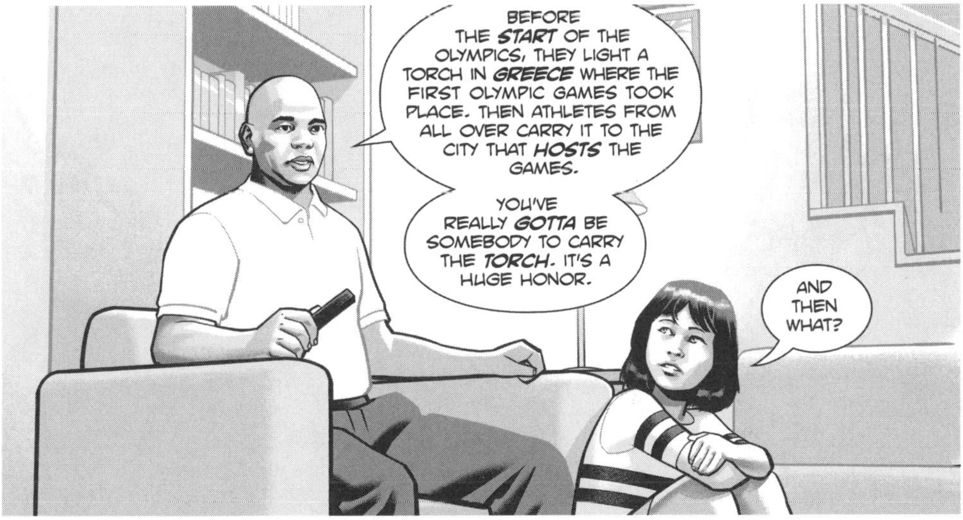
BEFORE THE START OF THE OLYMPICS, THEY LIGHT A TORCH IN GREECE WHERE THE FIRST OLYMPIC GAMES TOOK PLACE. THEN ATHLETES FROM ALL OVER CARRY IT TO THE CITY THAT HOSTS THE GAMES.
YOU'VE REALLY GOTTA BE SOMEBODY TO CARRY THE TORCH. IT'S A HUGE HONOR.
AND THEN WHAT?

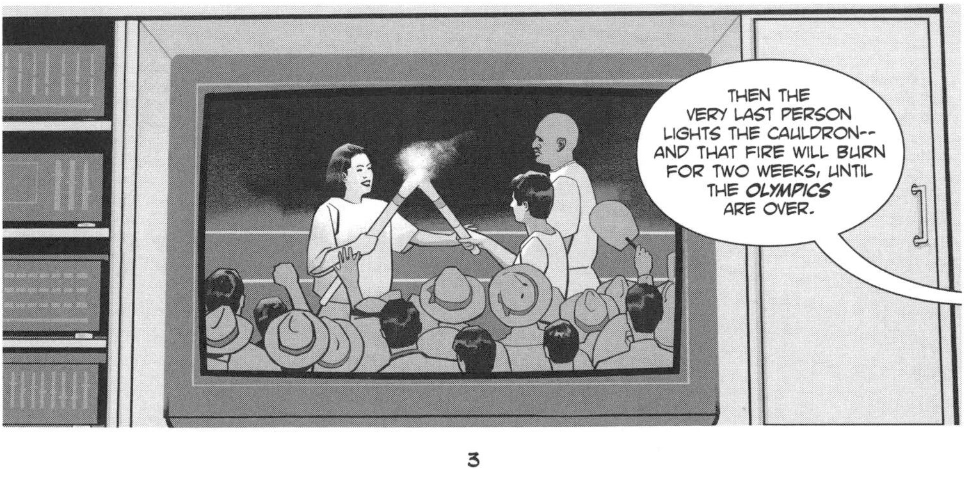
THEN THE VERY LAST PERSON LIGHTS THE CAULDRON--AND THAT FIRE WILL BURN FOR TWO WEEKS, UNTIL THE OLYMPICS ARE OVER.

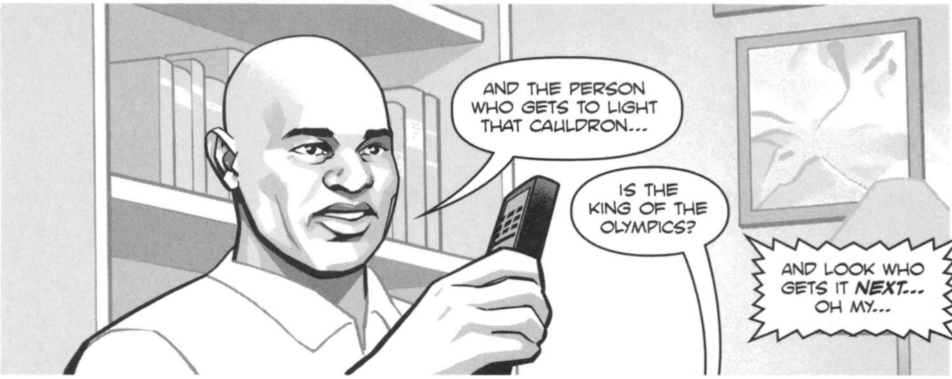
AND THE PERSON WHO GETS TO LIGHT THAT CAULDRON...
IS THE KING OF THE OLYMPICS?
AND LOOK WHO GETS IT *NEXT*... OH MY...

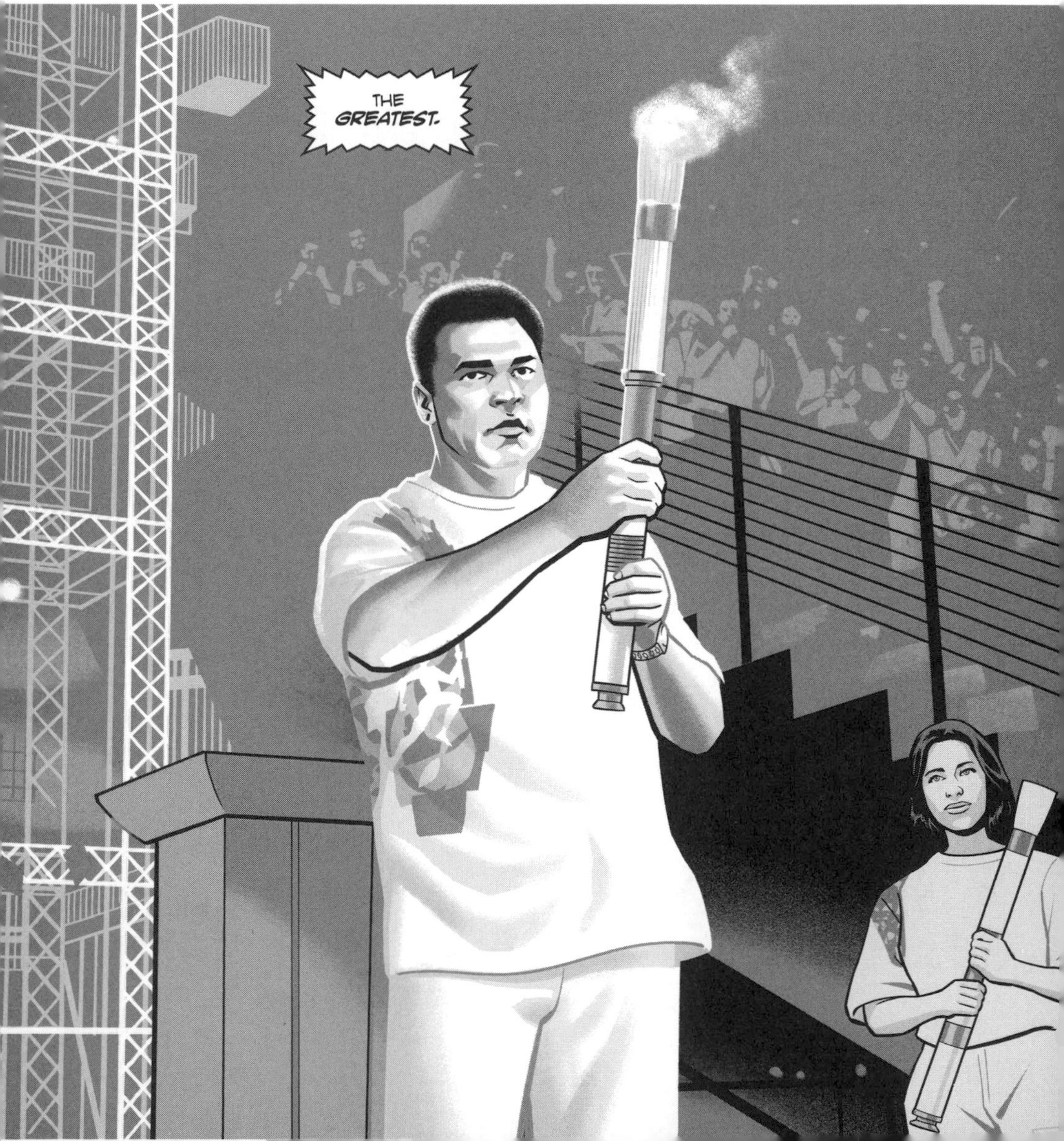
THE *GREATEST.*

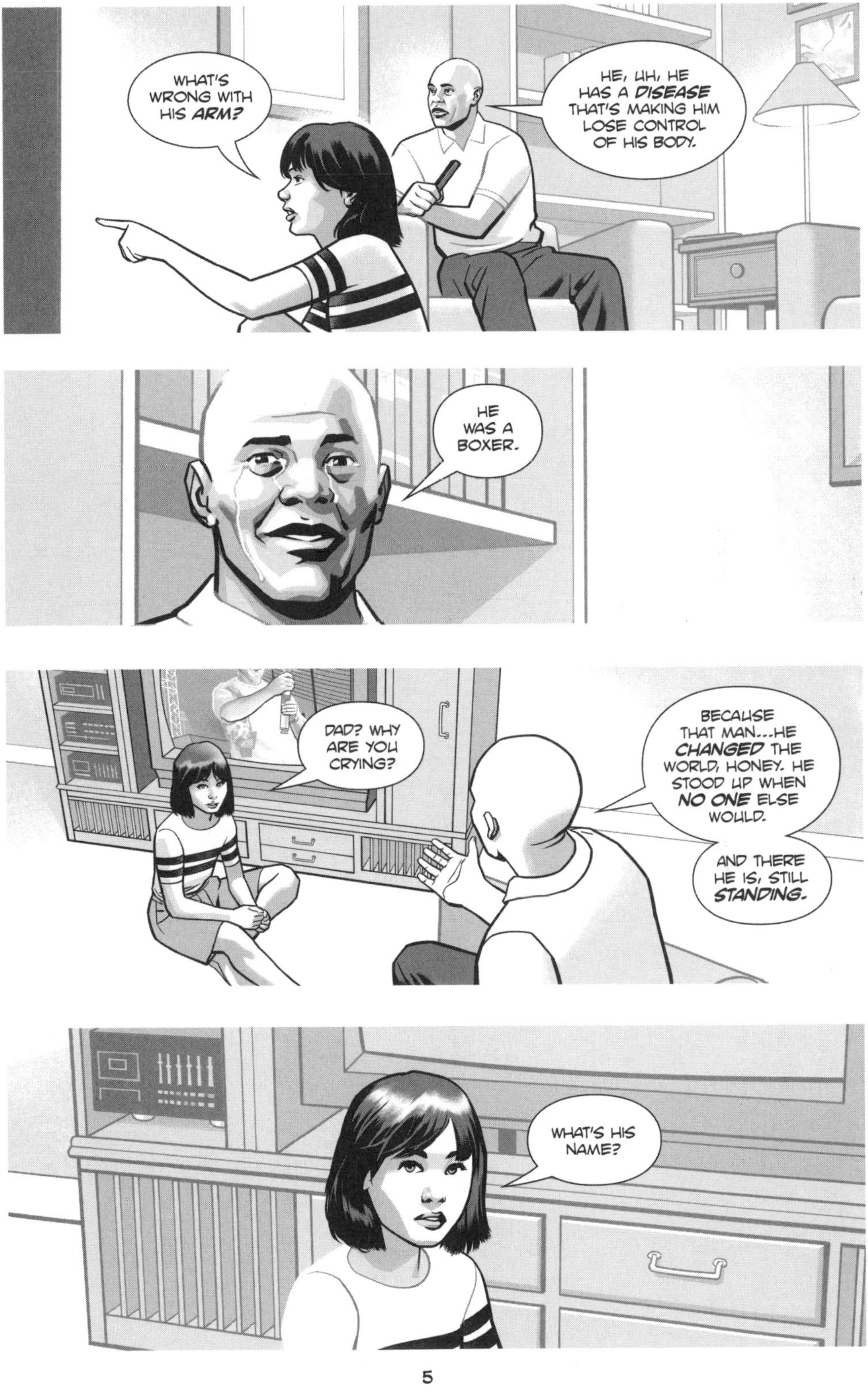
WHAT'S WRONG WITH HIS ARM?
HE, UH, HE HAS A DISEASE THAT'S MAKING HIM LOSE CONTROL OF HIS BODY.
HE WAS A BOXER.
DAD? WHY ARE YOU CRYING?
BECAUSE THAT MAN...HE CHANGED THE WORLD, HONEY. HE STOOD UP WHEN NO ONE ELSE WOULD.
AND THERE HE IS, STILL STANDING.
WHAT'S HIS NAME?

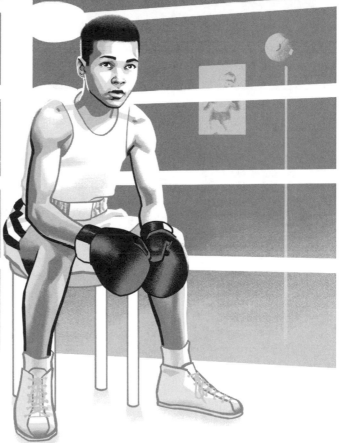

ROUND ONE:
SCHWINN. 1954

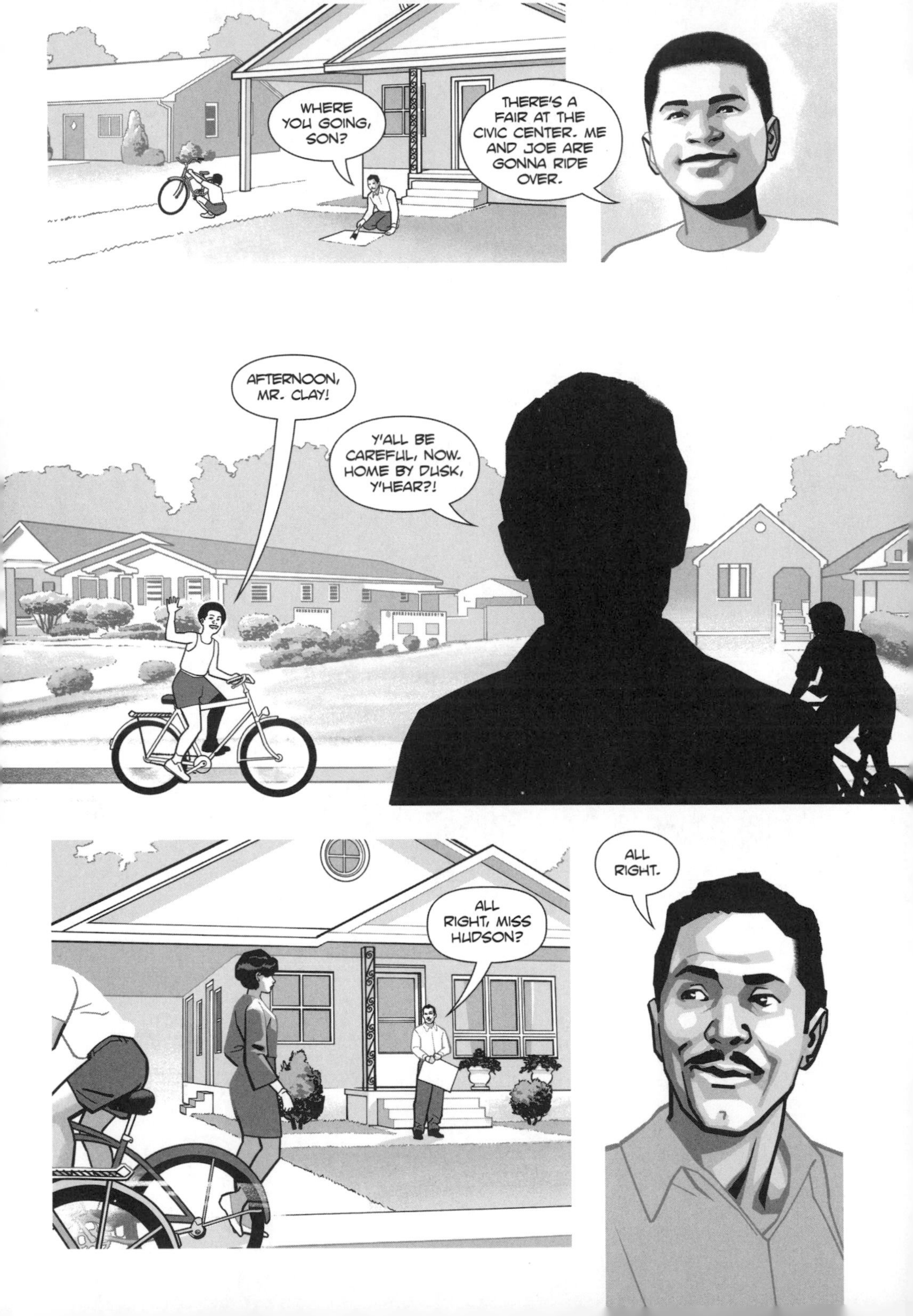
WHERE YOU GOING, SON?
THERE'S A FAIR AT THE CIVIC CENTER. ME AND JOE ARE GONNA RIDE OVER.
AFTERNOON, MR. CLAY!
Y'ALL BE CAREFUL, NOW. HOME BY DUSK, Y'HEAR?!
ALL RIGHT, MISS HUDSON?
ALL RIGHT.

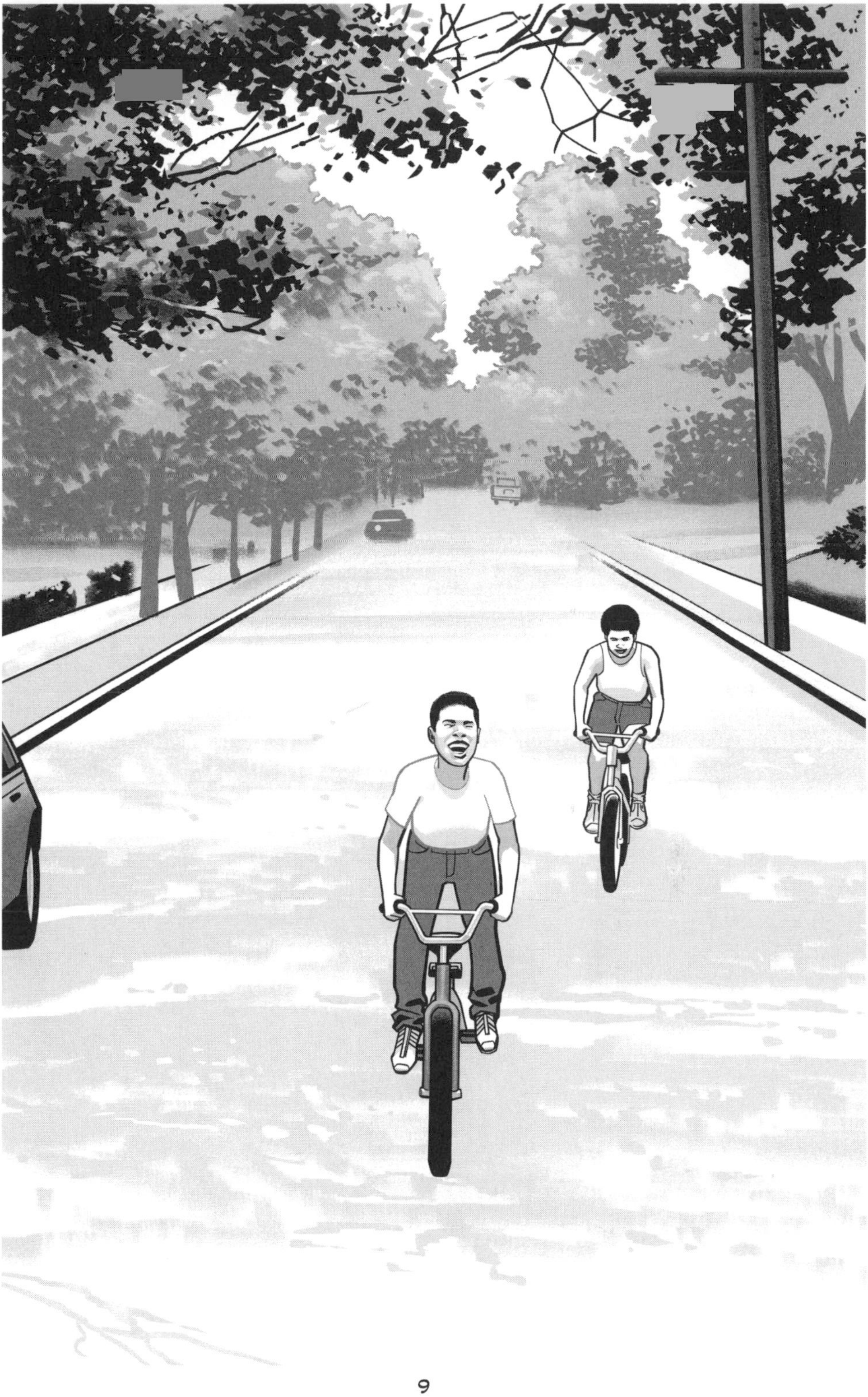

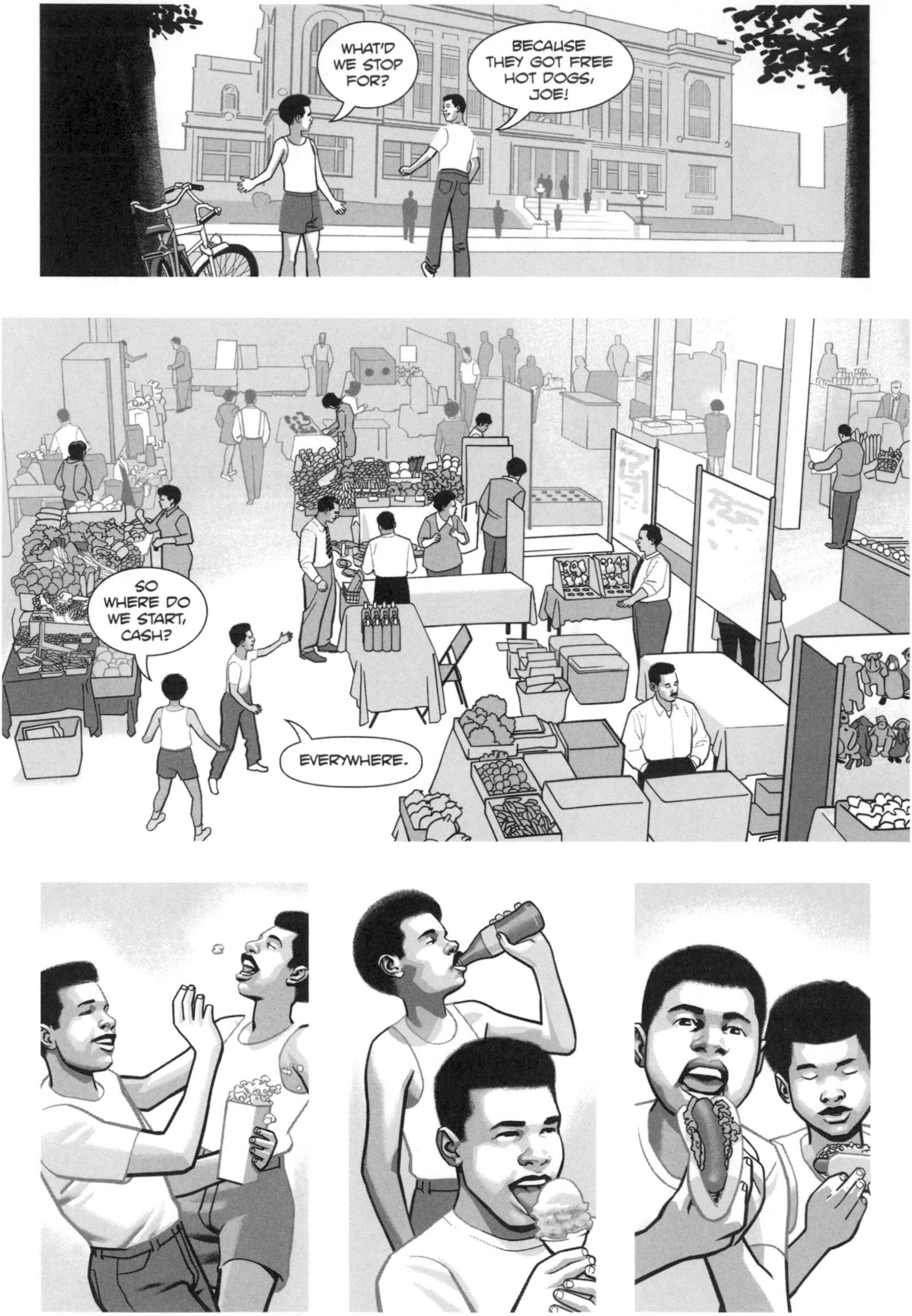
WHAT'D WE STOP FOR?
BECAUSE THEY GOT FREE HOT DOGS, JOE!
SO WHERE DO WE START, CASH?
EVERYWHERE.

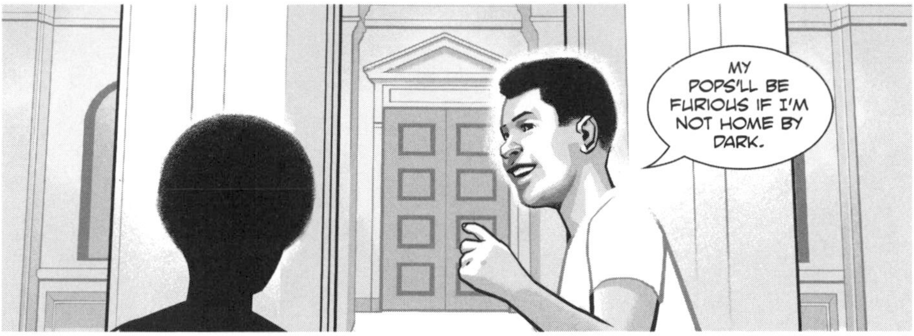
MY POPS'LL BE FURIOUS IF I'M NOT HOME BY DARK.

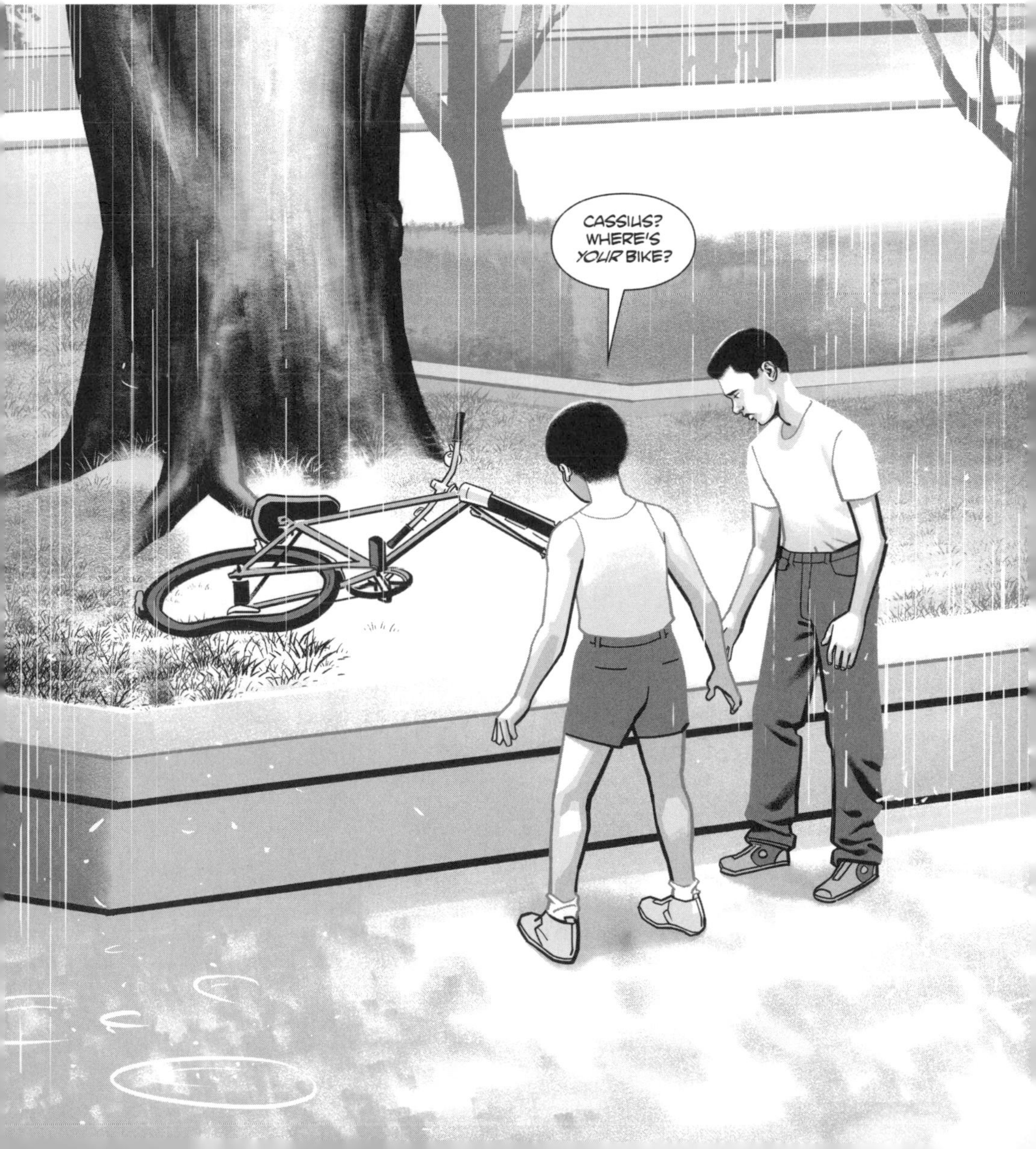
CASSIUS? WHERE'S *YOUR* BIKE?

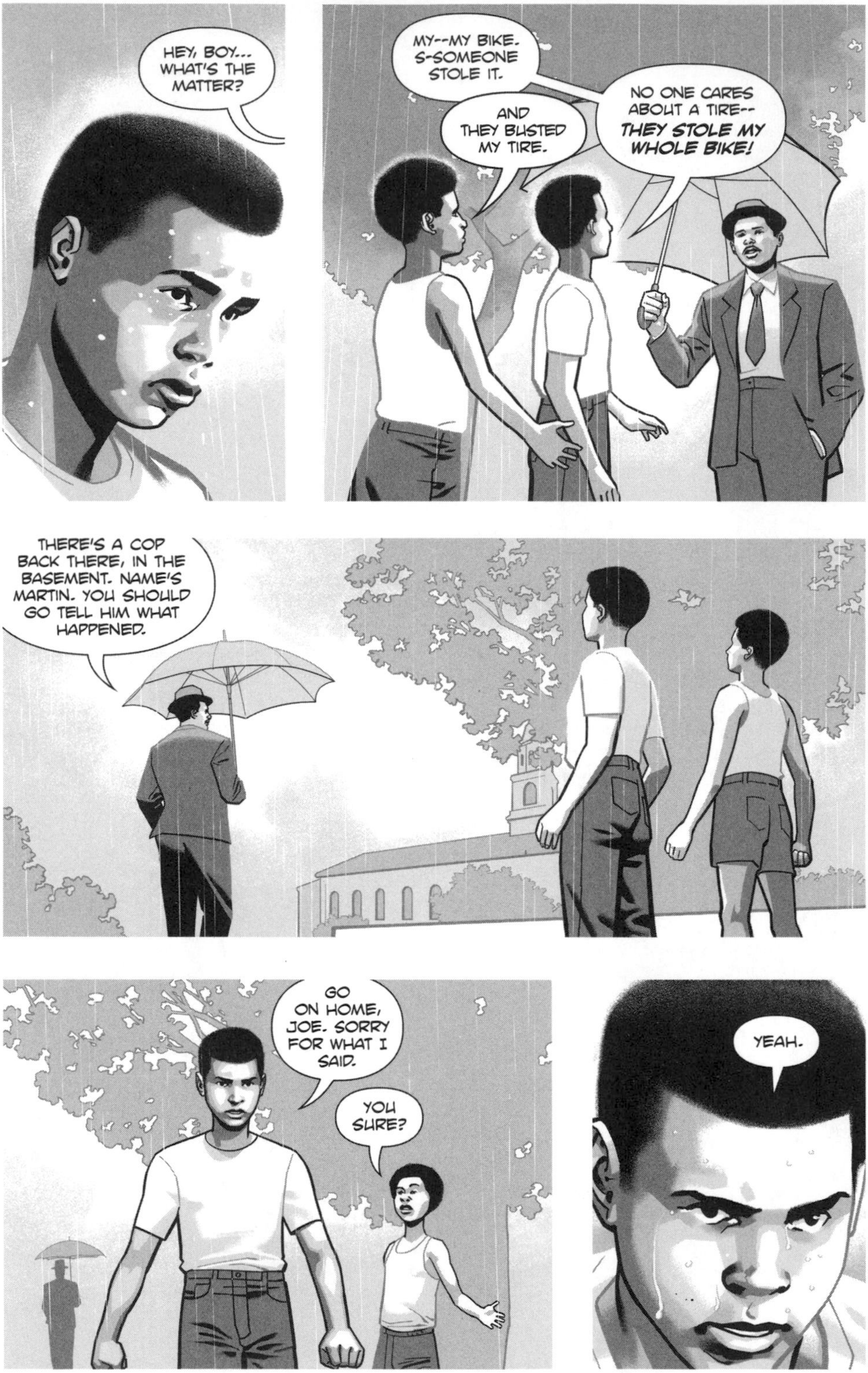
HEY, BOY... WHAT'S THE MATTER?
MY--MY BIKE. S-SOMEONE STOLE IT.
AND THEY BUSTED MY TIRE.
NO ONE CARES ABOUT A TIRE-- THEY STOLE MY WHOLE BIKE!
THERE'S A COP BACK THERE, IN THE BASEMENT. NAME'S MARTIN. YOU SHOULD GO TELL HIM WHAT HAPPENED.
GO ON HOME, JOE. SORRY FOR WHAT I SAID.
YOU SURE?
YEAH.

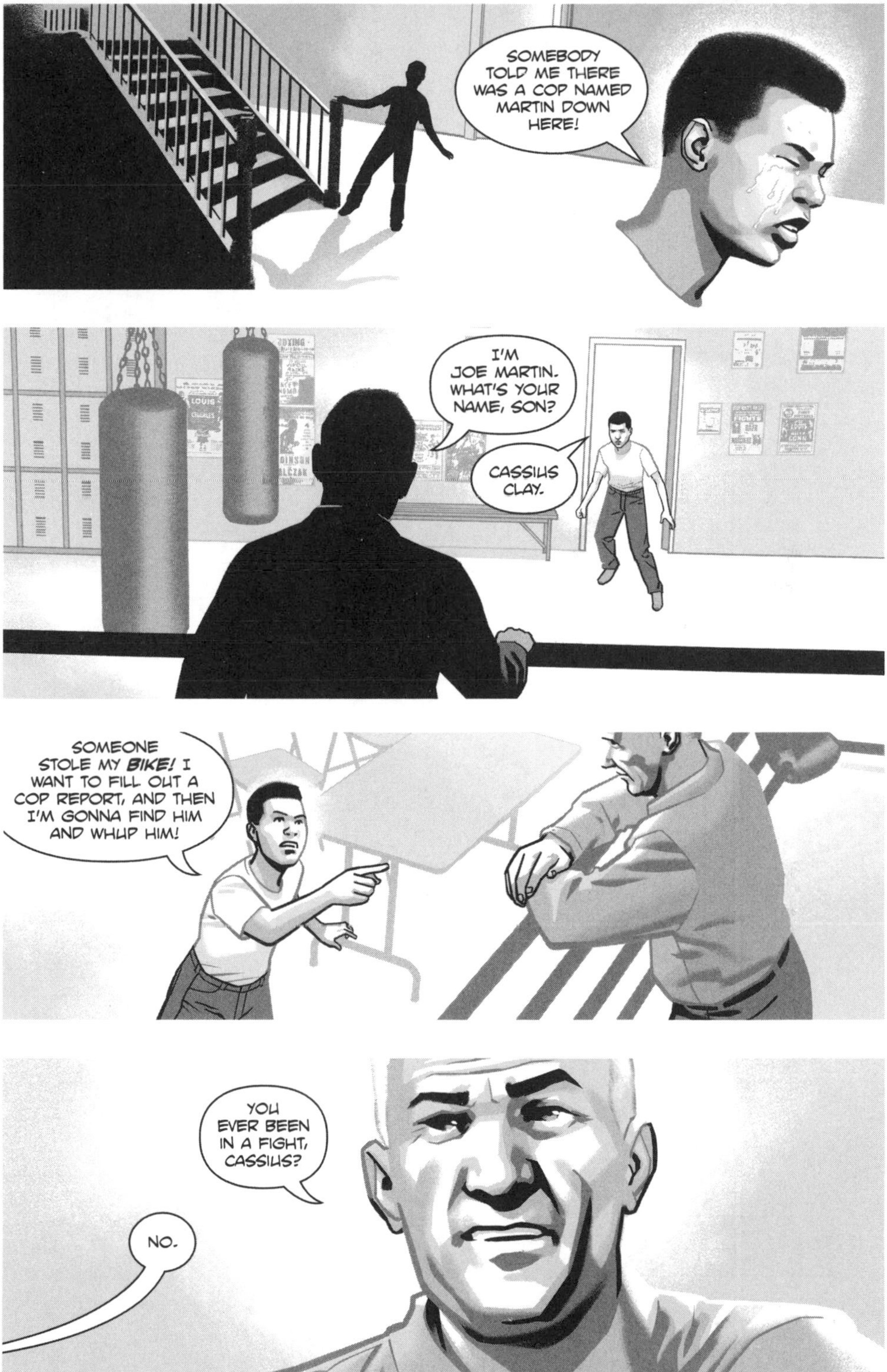
SOMEBODY TOLD ME THERE WAS A COP NAMED MARTIN DOWN HERE!
I'M JOE MARTIN. WHAT'S YOUR NAME, SON?
CASSIUS CLAY.
SOMEONE STOLE MY *BIKE!* I WANT TO FILL OUT A COP REPORT, AND THEN I'M GONNA FIND HIM AND WHUP HIM!
YOU EVER BEEN IN A FIGHT, CASSIUS?
NO.

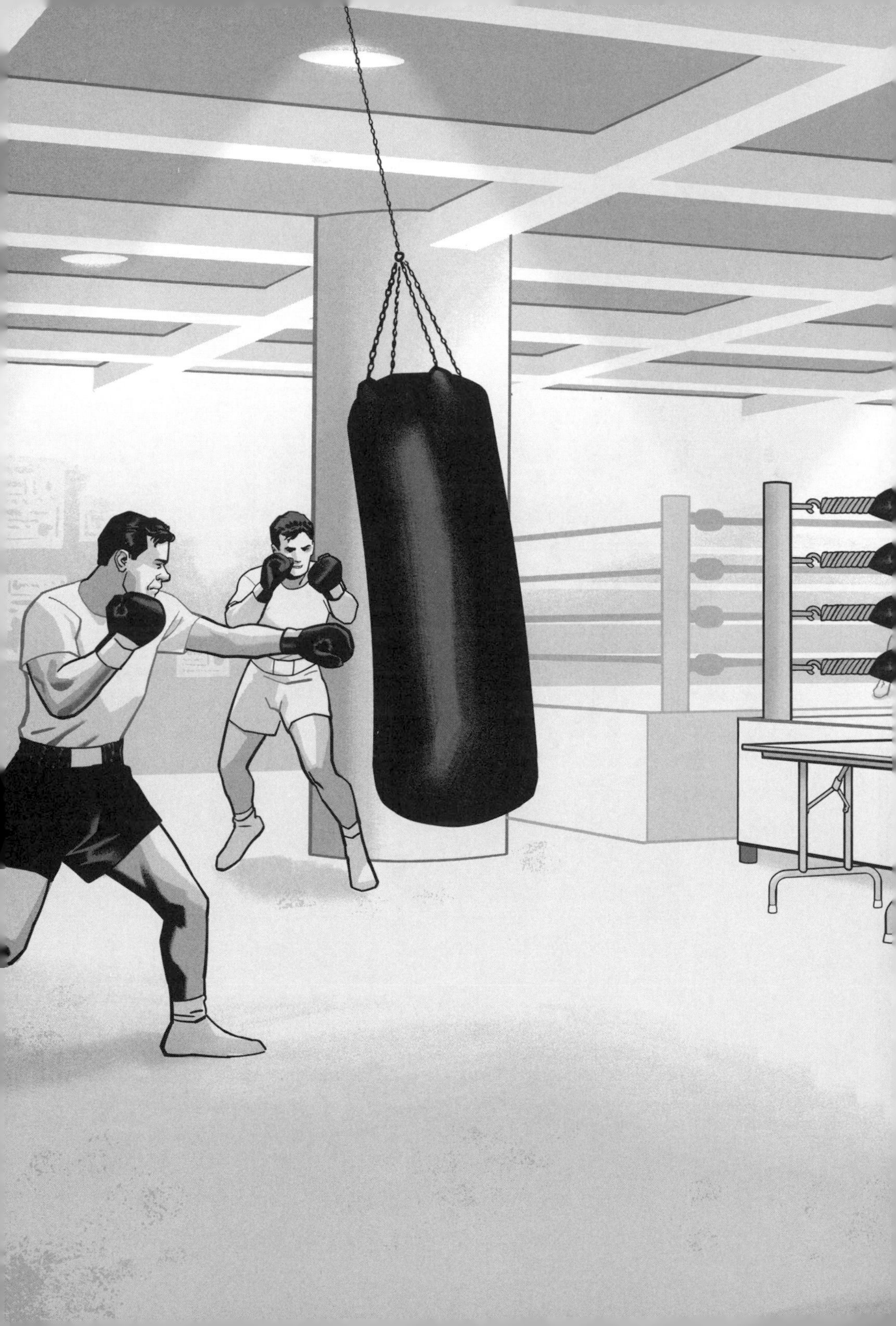

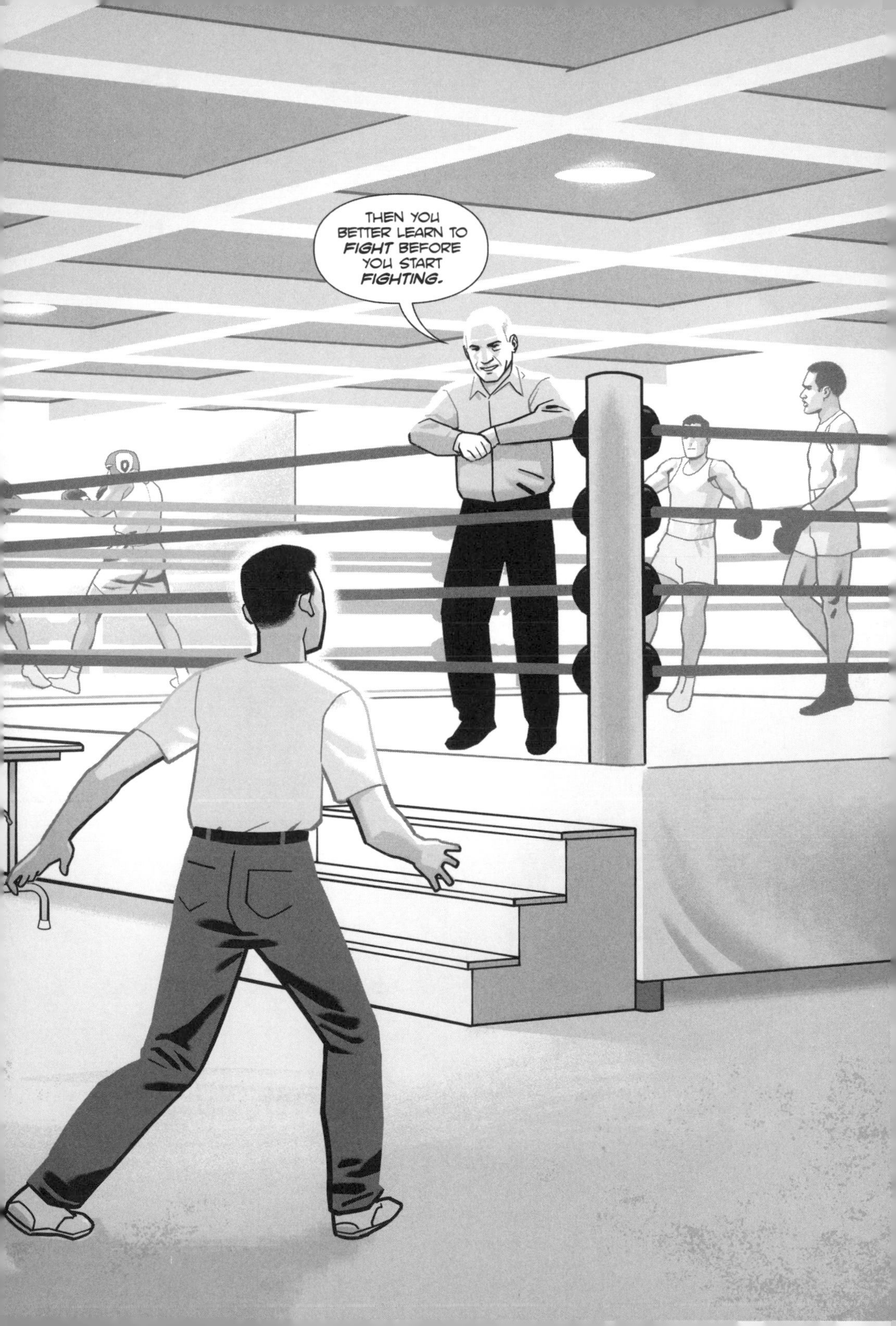
THEN YOU BETTER LEARN TO *FIGHT* BEFORE YOU START *FIGHTING.*

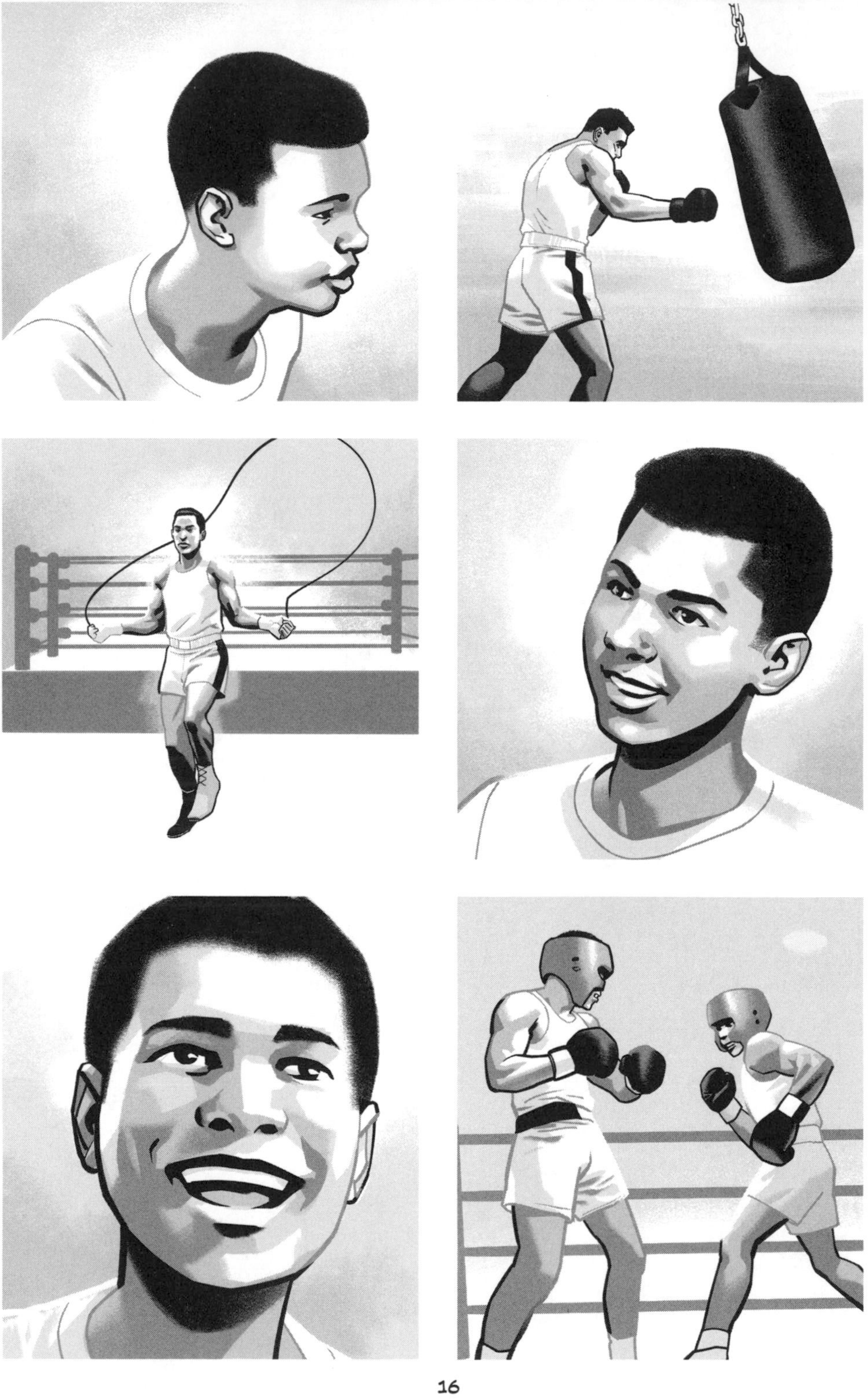

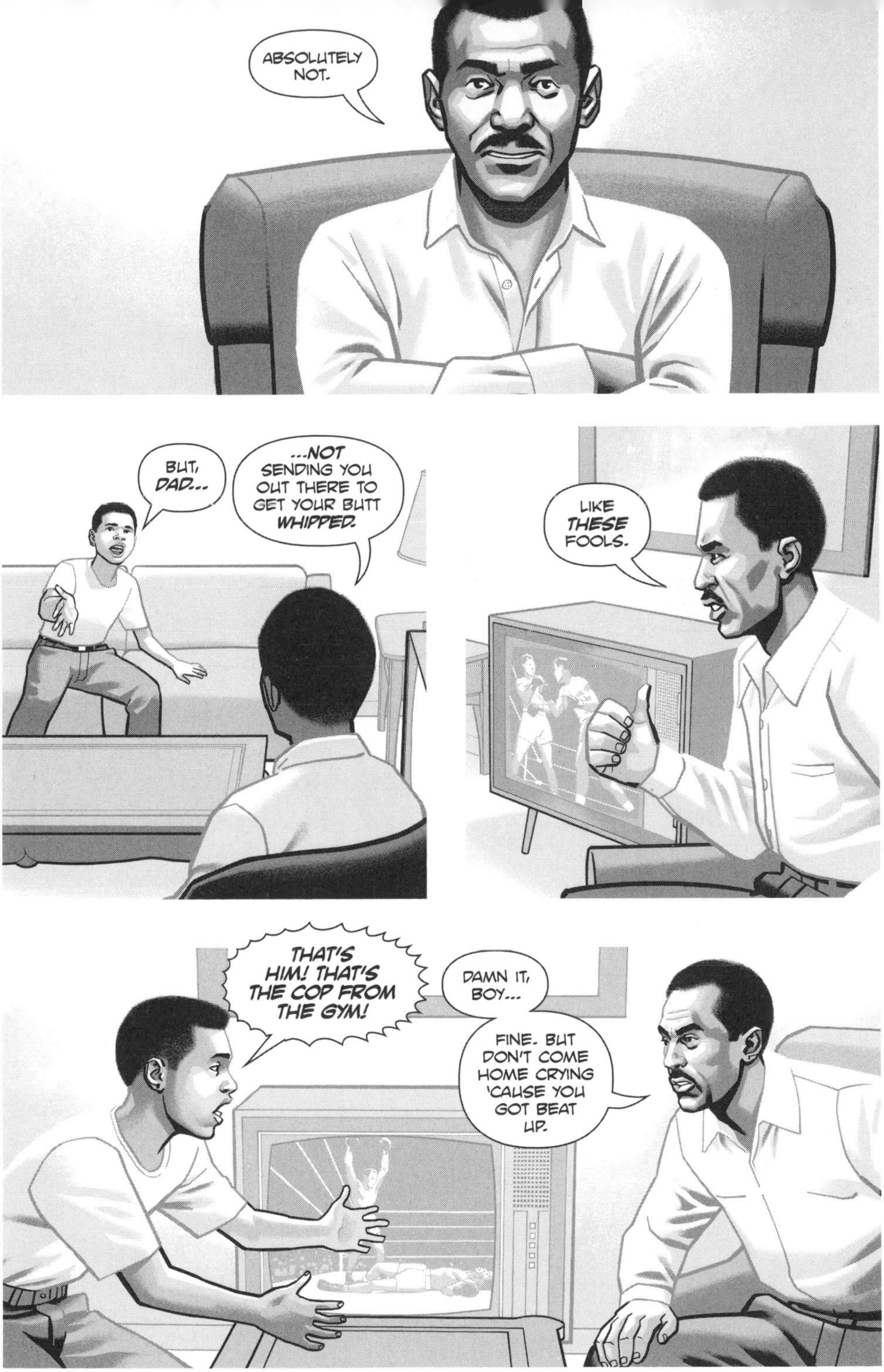
ABSOLUTELY NOT.
BUT, *DAD...*
...*NOT* SENDING YOU OUT THERE TO GET YOUR BUTT *WHIPPED.*
LIKE *THESE* FOOLS.
THAT'S HIM! THAT'S THE COP FROM THE GYM!
DAMN IT, BOY...
FINE. BUT DON'T COME HOME CRYING 'CAUSE YOU GOT BEAT UP.

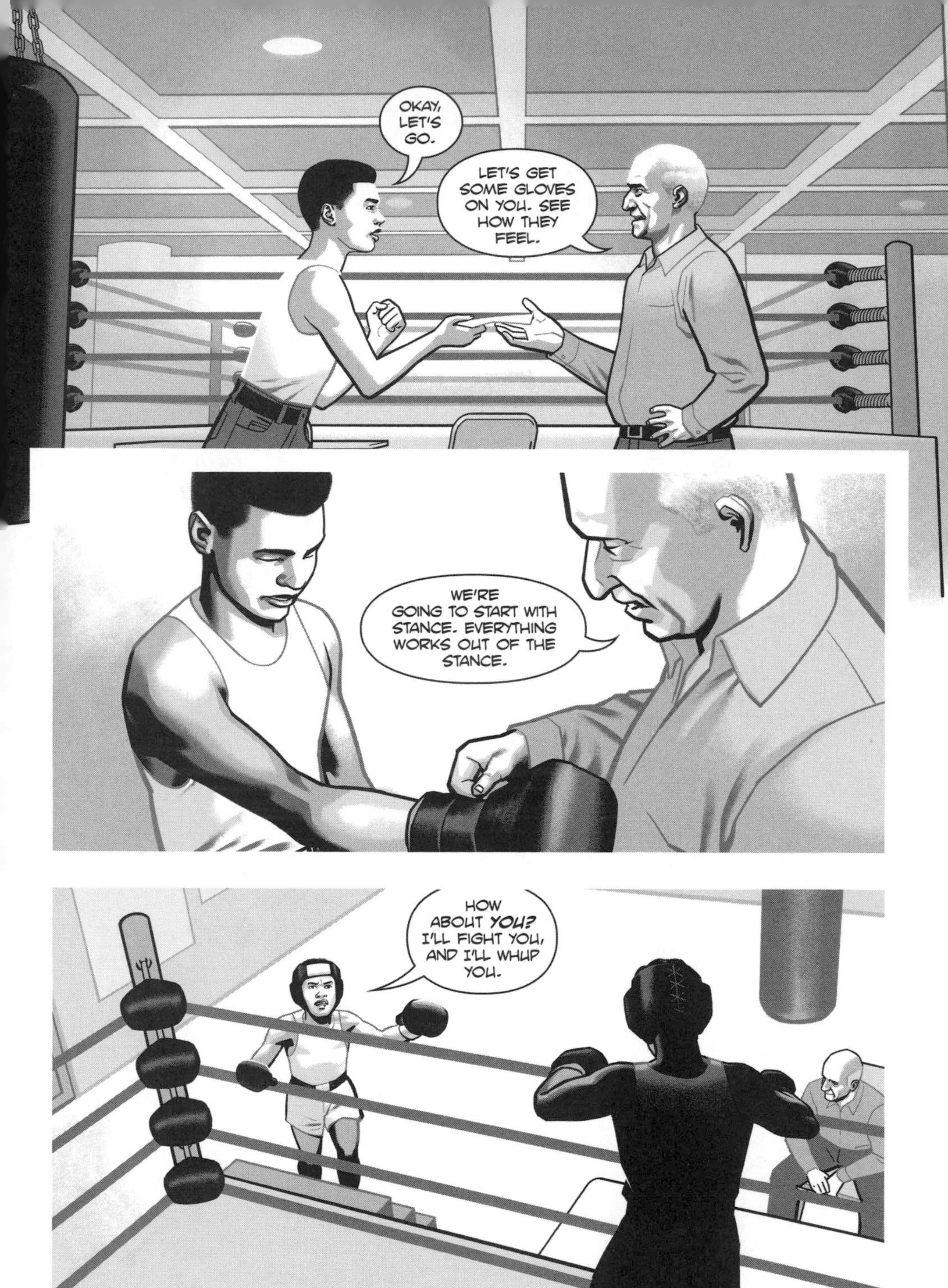
OKAY, LET'S GO.
LET'S GET SOME GLOVES ON YOU. SEE HOW THEY FEEL.
WE'RE GOING TO START WITH STANCE. EVERYTHING WORKS OUT OF THE STANCE.
HOW ABOUT *YOU?* I'LL FIGHT YOU, AND I'LL WHUP YOU.

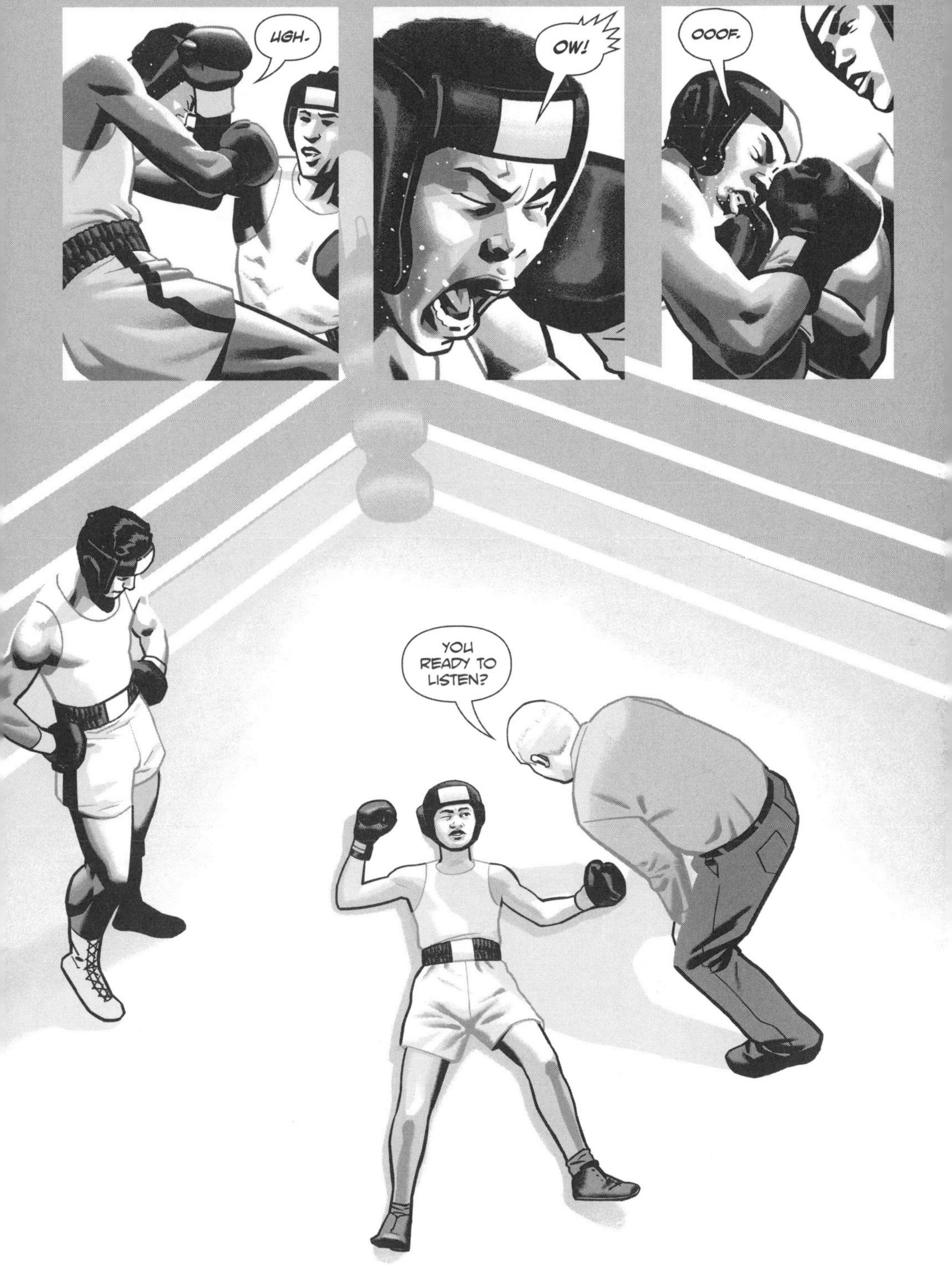
UGH.
OW!
OOOF.
YOU READY TO LISTEN?

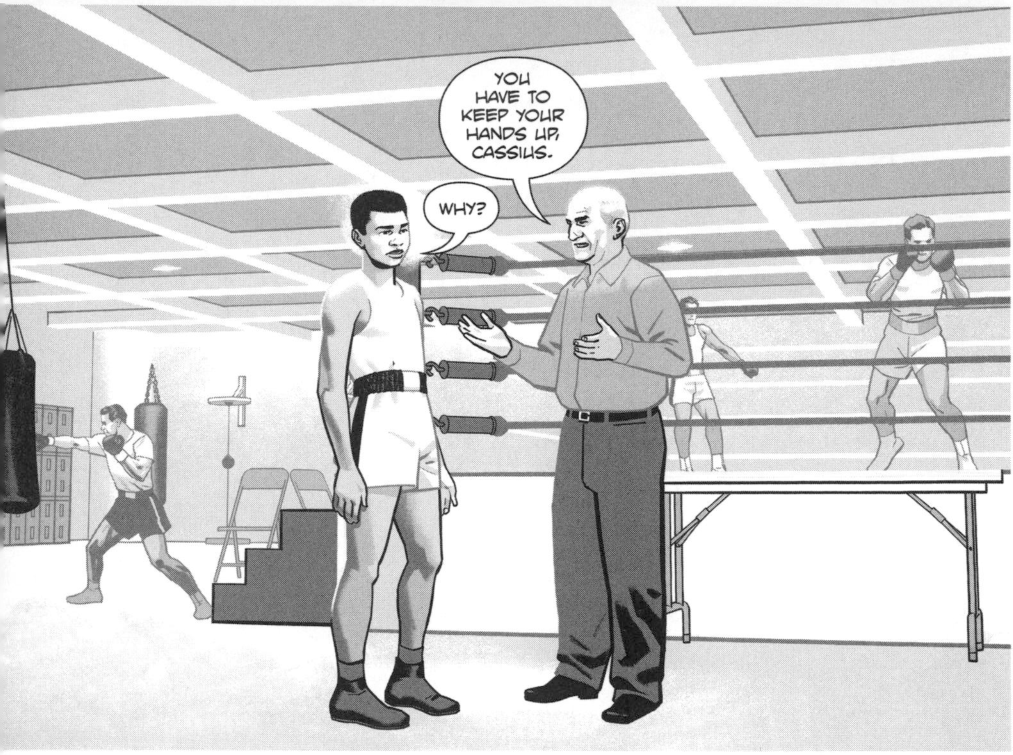
YOU HAVE TO KEEP YOUR HANDS UP, CASSIUS.
WHY?

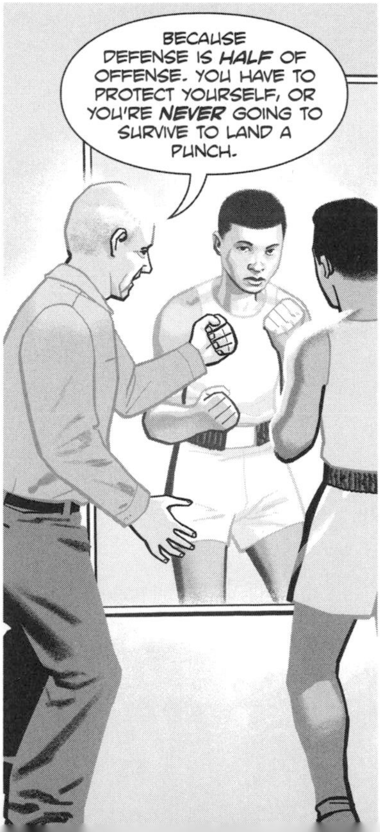
BECAUSE DEFENSE IS HALF OF OFFENSE. YOU HAVE TO PROTECT YOURSELF, OR YOU'RE NEVER GOING TO SURVIVE TO LAND A PUNCH.

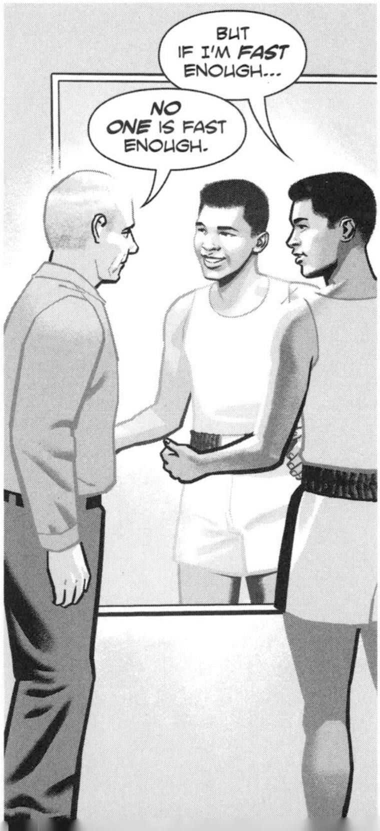
BUT IF I'M FAST ENOUGH...
NO ONE IS FAST ENOUGH.

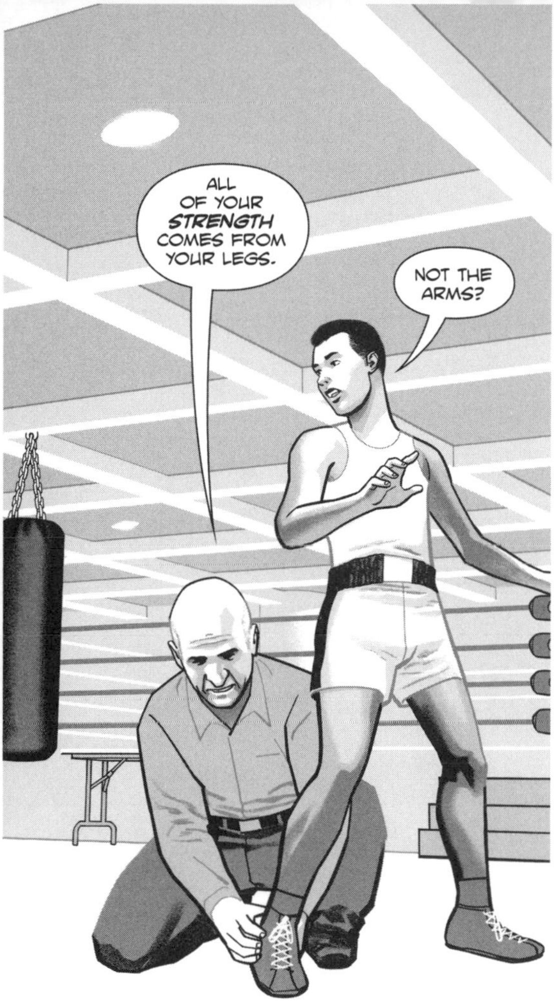
ALL OF YOUR **STRENGTH** COMES FROM YOUR LEGS.
NOT THE ARMS?

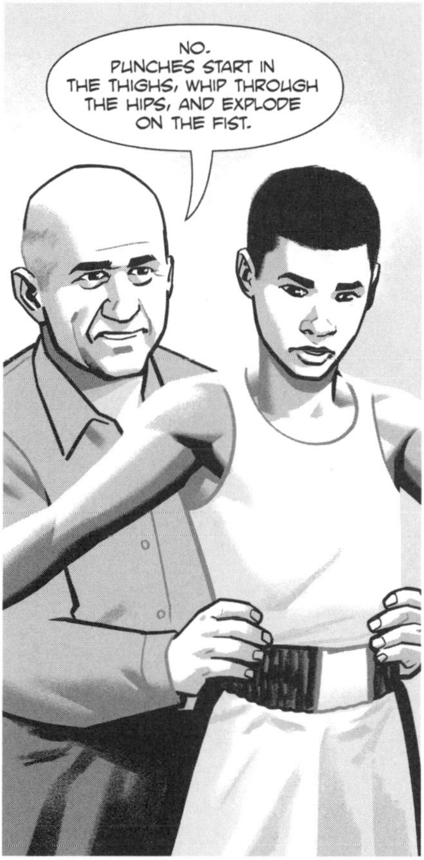
NO. PUNCHES START IN THE THIGHS, WHIP THROUGH THE HIPS, AND EXPLODE ON THE FIST.

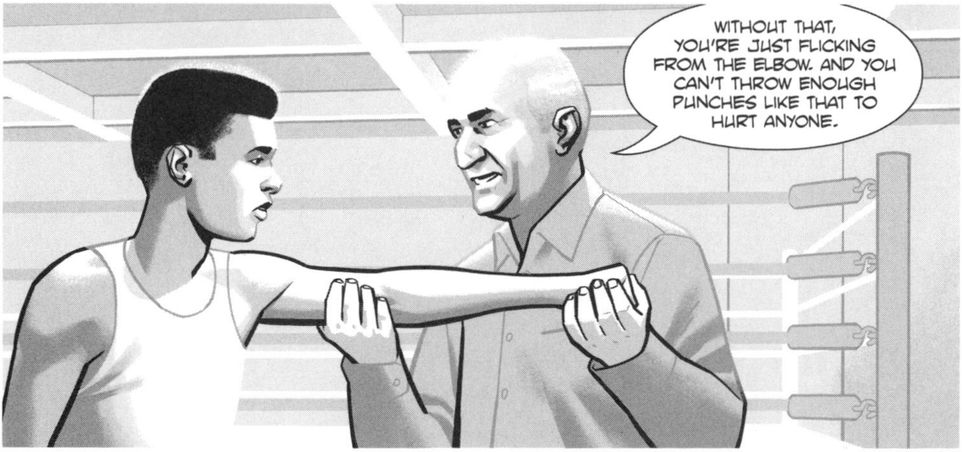
WITHOUT THAT, YOU'RE JUST FLICKING FROM THE ELBOW. AND YOU CAN'T THROW ENOUGH PUNCHES LIKE THAT TO HURT ANYONE.

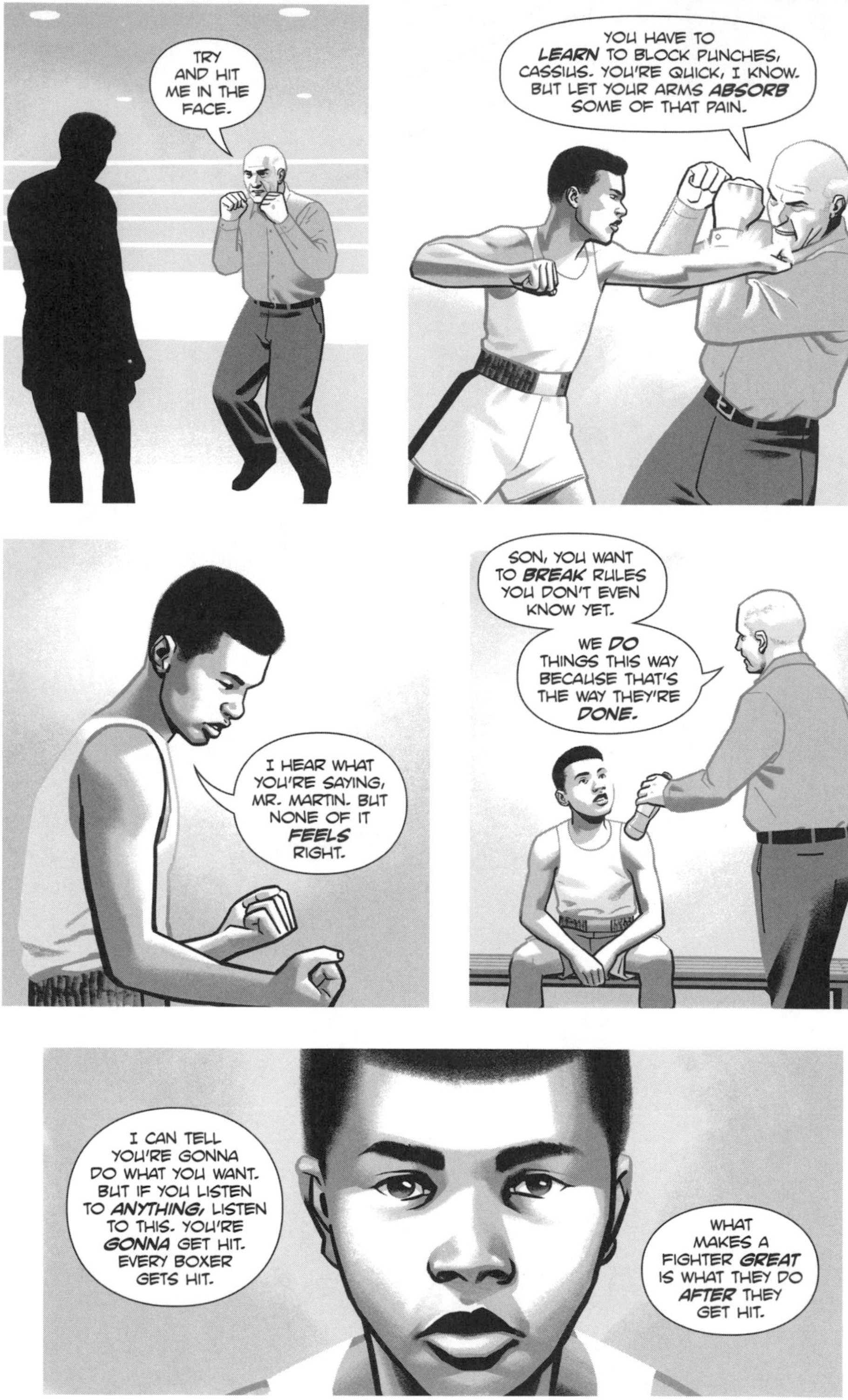
TRY AND HIT ME IN THE FACE.
YOU HAVE TO LEARN TO BLOCK PUNCHES, CASSIUS. YOU'RE QUICK, I KNOW. BUT LET YOUR ARMS ABSORB SOME OF THAT PAIN.
I HEAR WHAT YOU'RE SAYING, MR. MARTIN. BUT NONE OF IT FEELS RIGHT.
SON, YOU WANT TO BREAK RULES YOU DON'T EVEN KNOW YET.
WE DO THINGS THIS WAY BECAUSE THAT'S THE WAY THEY'RE DONE.
I CAN TELL YOU'RE GONNA DO WHAT YOU WANT. BUT IF YOU LISTEN TO ANYTHING, LISTEN TO THIS. YOU'RE GONNA GET HIT. EVERY BOXER GETS HIT.
WHAT MAKES A FIGHTER GREAT IS WHAT THEY DO AFTER THEY GET HIT.

ROUND TWO: OLYMPIAN. 1960.

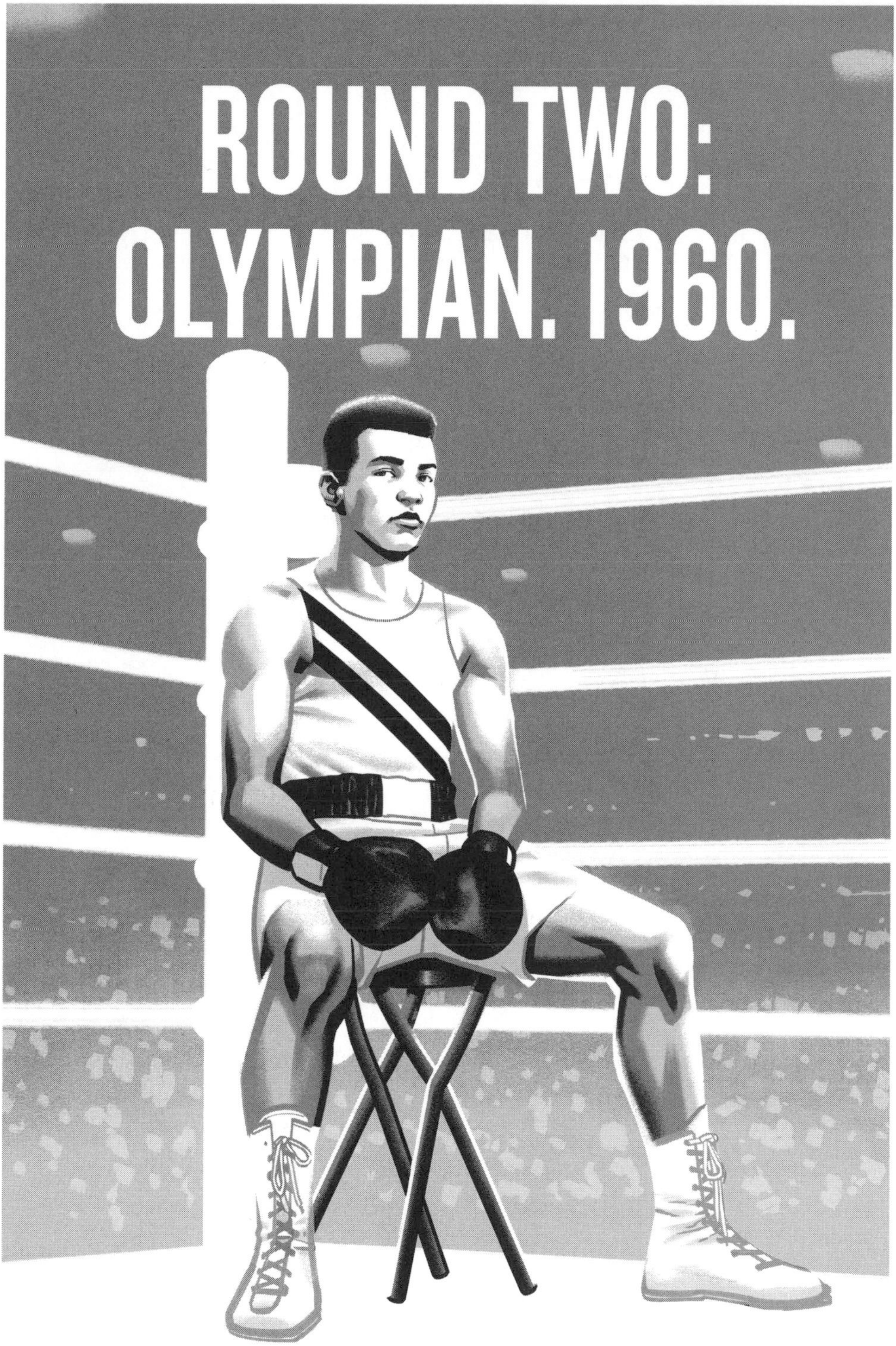

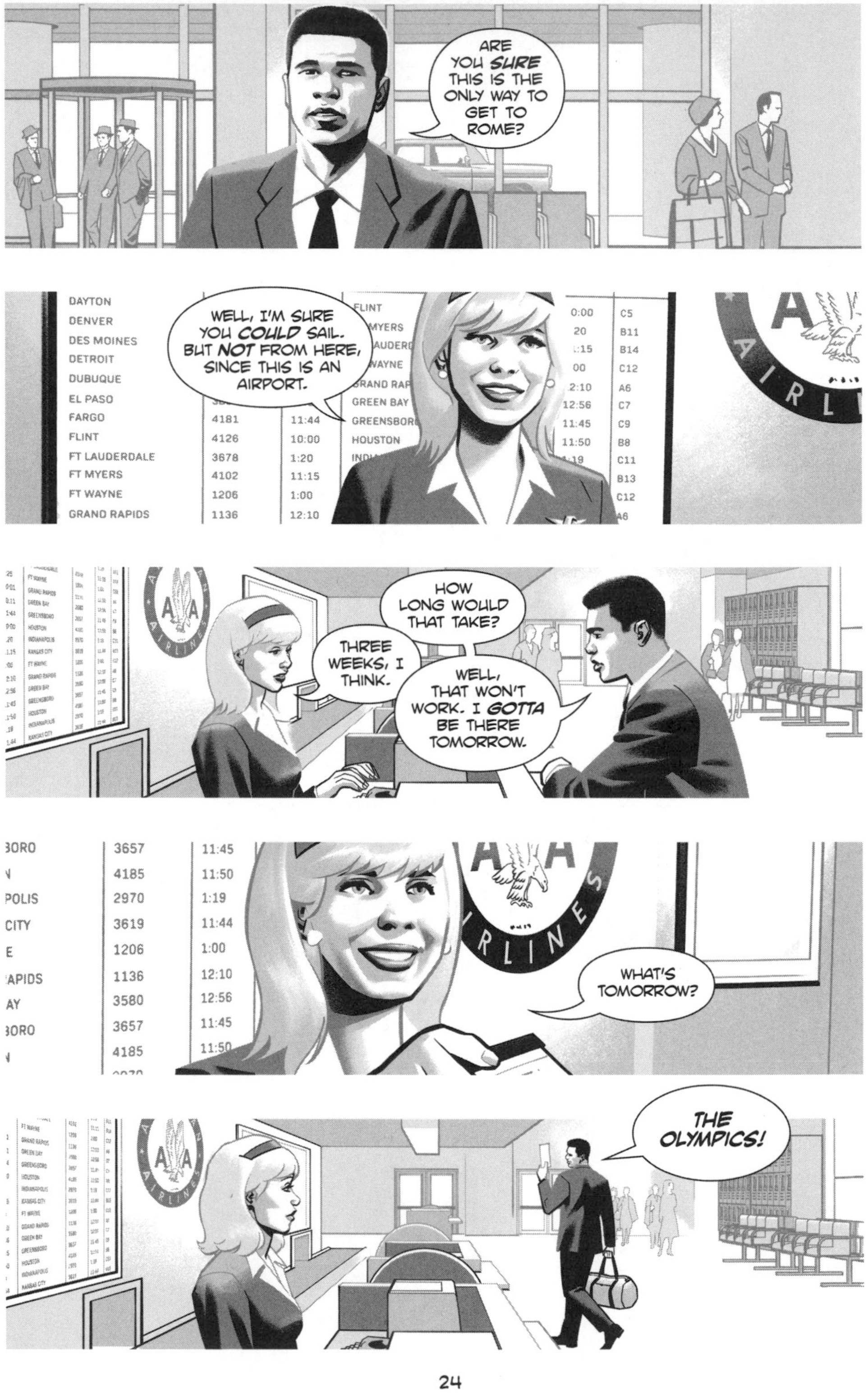
ARE YOU SURE THIS IS THE ONLY WAY TO GET TO ROME?
WELL, I'M SURE YOU COULD SAIL. BUT NOT FROM HERE, SINCE THIS IS AN AIRPORT.
HOW LONG WOULD THAT TAKE?
THREE WEEKS, I THINK.
WELL, THAT WON'T WORK. I GOTTA BE THERE TOMORROW.
WHAT'S TOMORROW?
THE OLYMPICS!

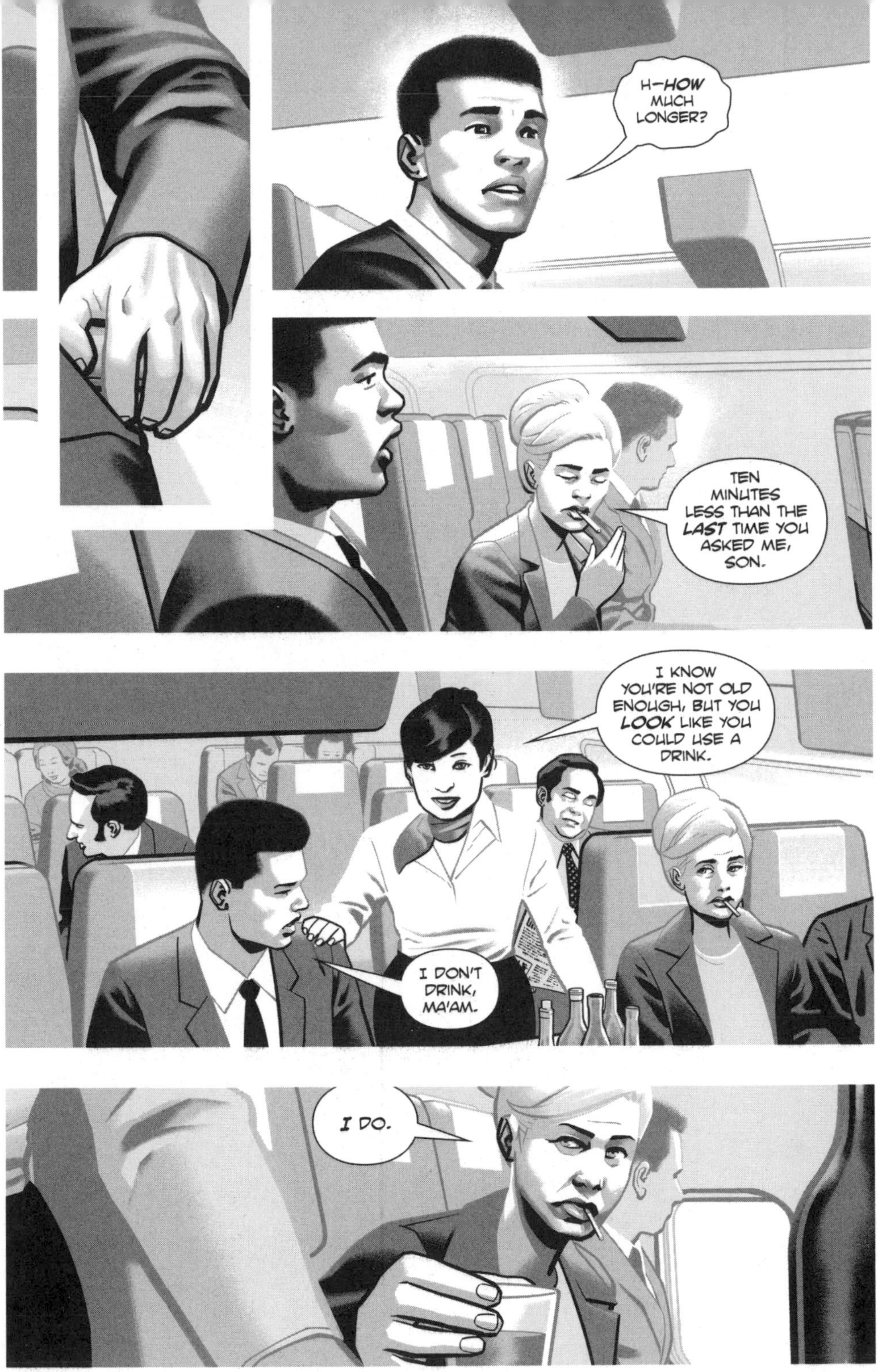
H–HOW MUCH LONGER?
TEN MINUTES LESS THAN THE LAST TIME YOU ASKED ME, SON.
I KNOW YOU'RE NOT OLD ENOUGH, BUT YOU LOOK LIKE YOU COULD USE A DRINK.
I DON'T DRINK, MA'AM.
I DO.

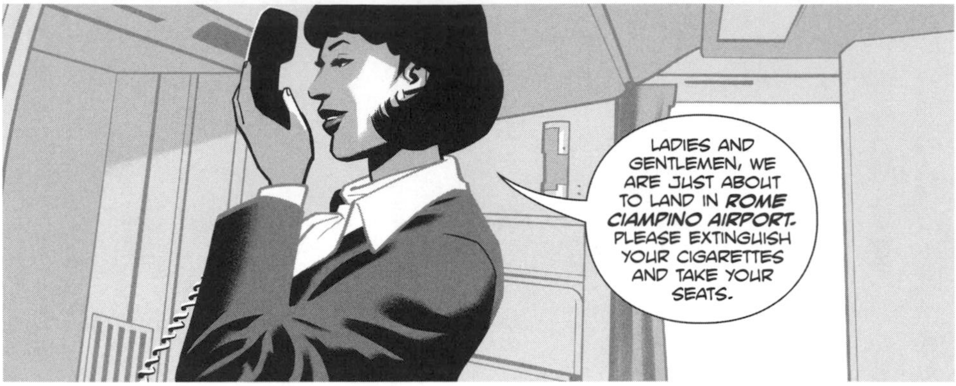
LADIES AND GENTLEMEN, WE ARE JUST ABOUT TO LAND IN ROME CIAMPINO AIRPORT. PLEASE EXTINGUISH YOUR CIGARETTES AND TAKE YOUR SEATS.

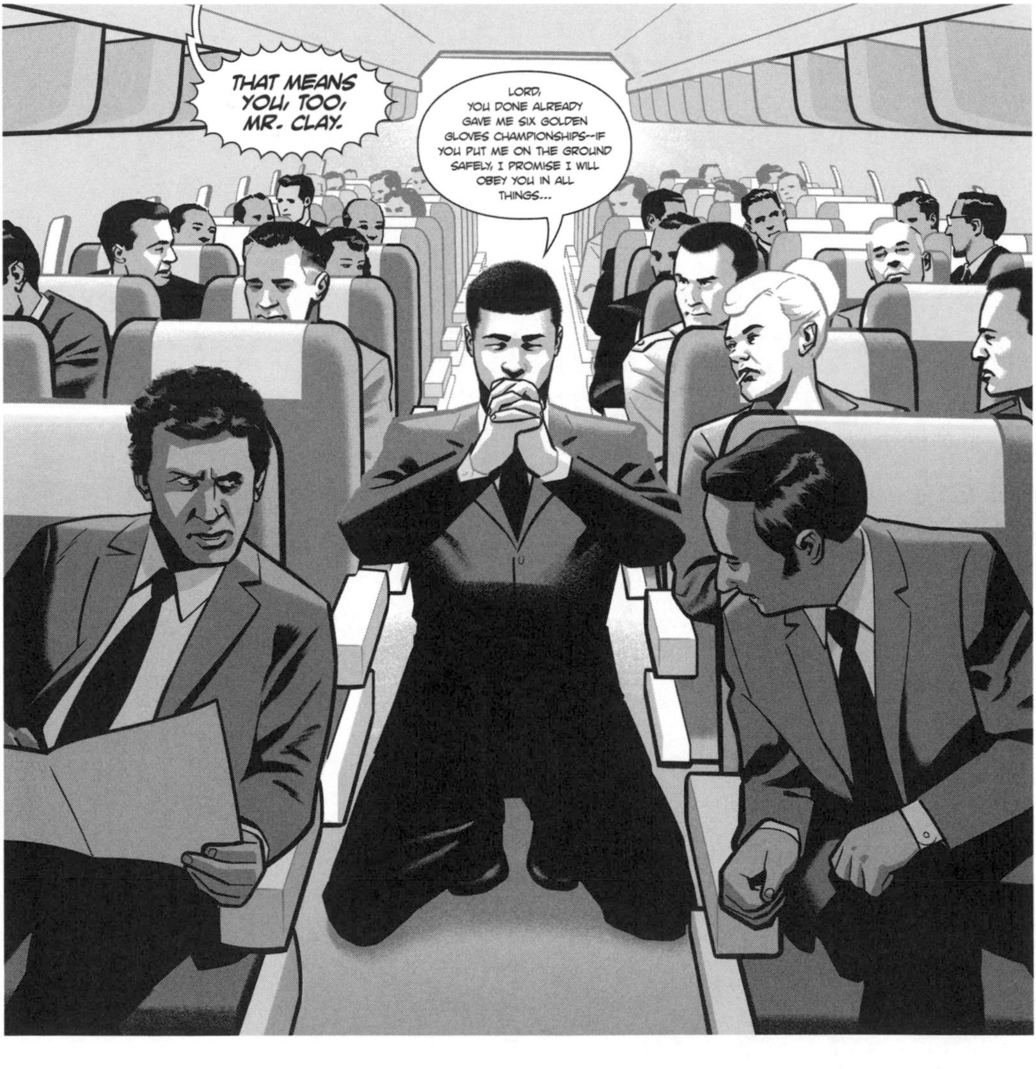
THAT MEANS YOU, TOO, MR. CLAY.
LORD, YOU DONE ALREADY GAVE ME SIX GOLDEN GLOVES CHAMPIONSHIPS--IF YOU PUT ME ON THE GROUND SAFELY, I PROMISE I WILL OBEY YOU IN ALL THINGS...

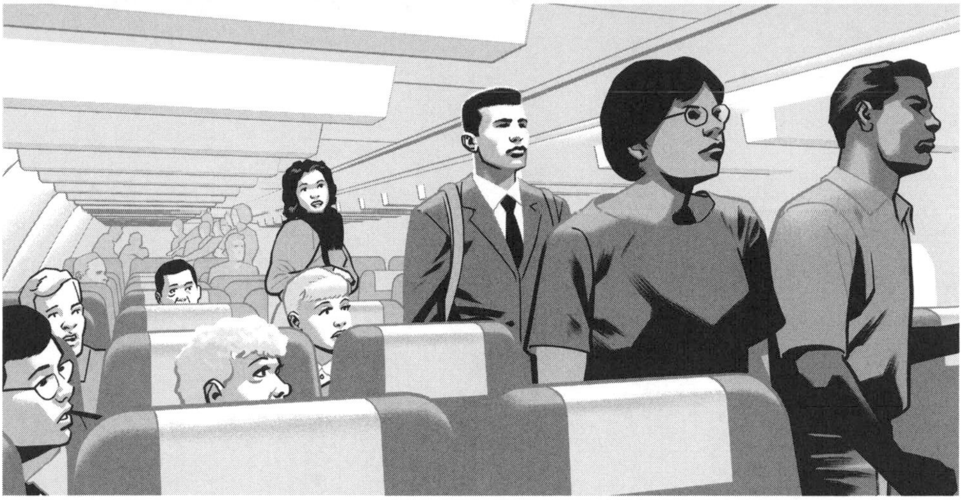

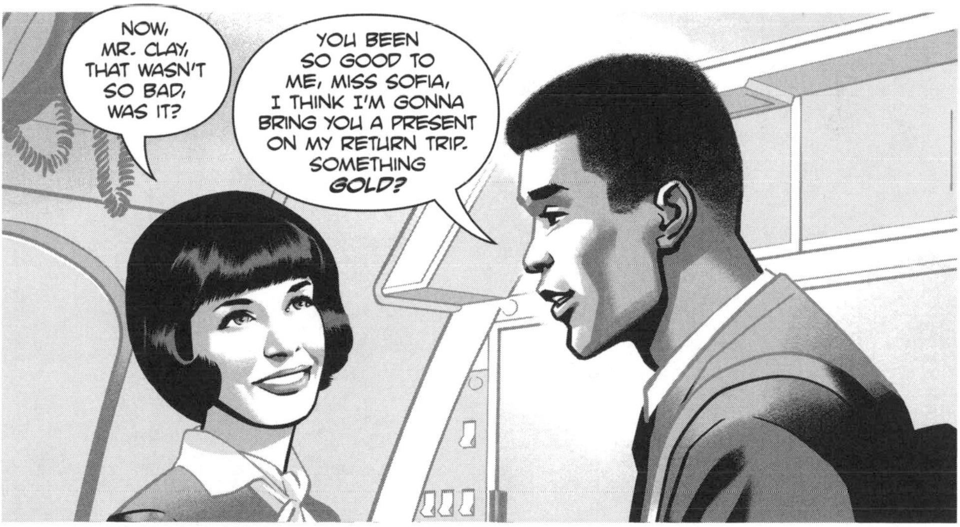
NOW, MR. CLAY, THAT WASN'T SO BAD, WAS IT?
YOU BEEN SO GOOD TO ME, MISS SOFIA, I THINK I'M GONNA BRING YOU A PRESENT ON MY RETURN TRIP. SOMETHING *GOLD?*

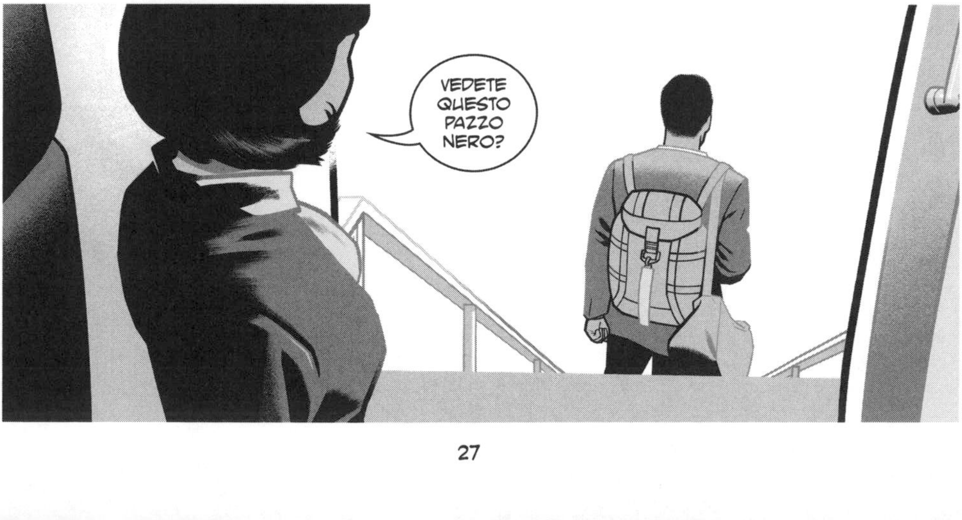
VEDETE QUESTO PAZZO NERO?

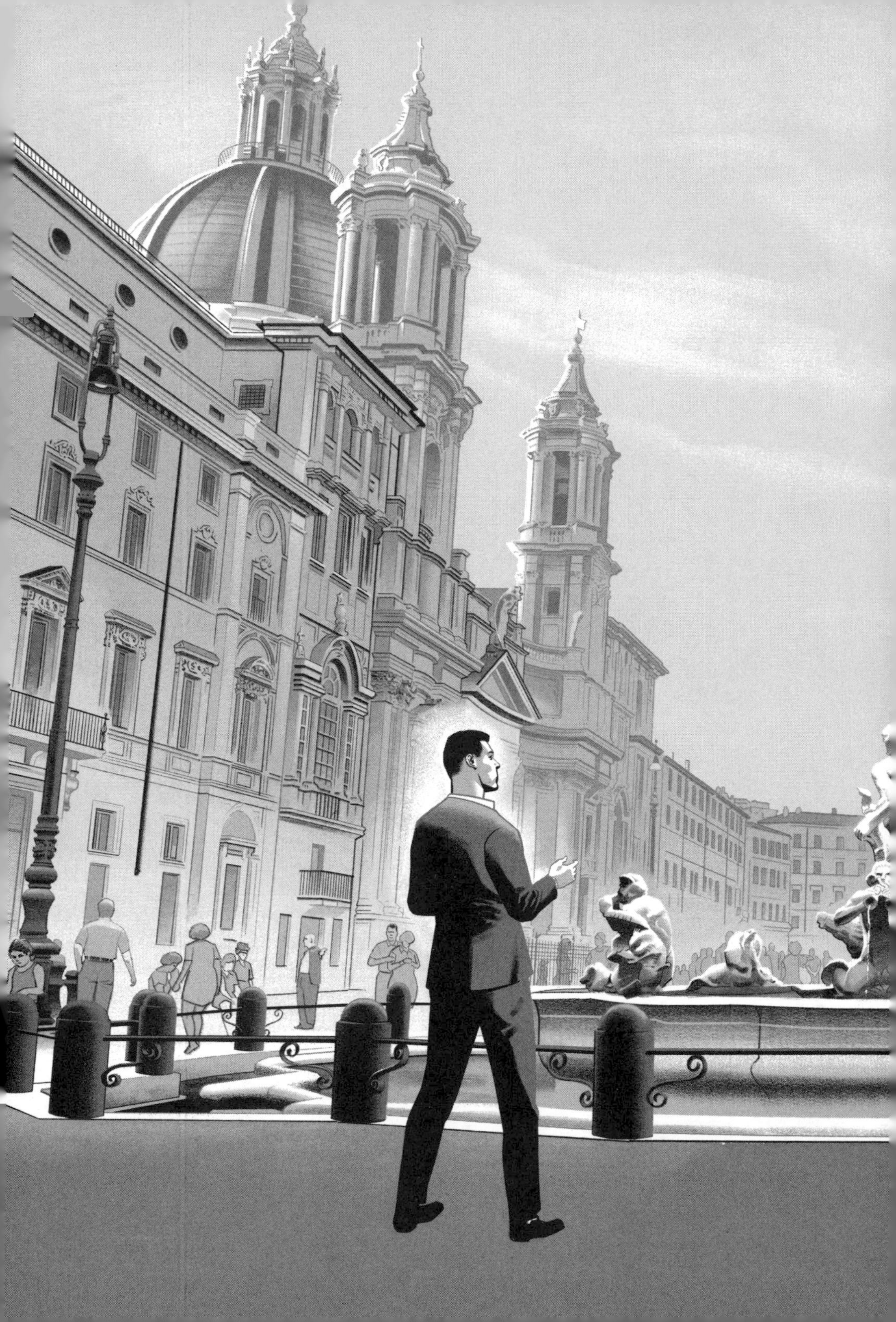

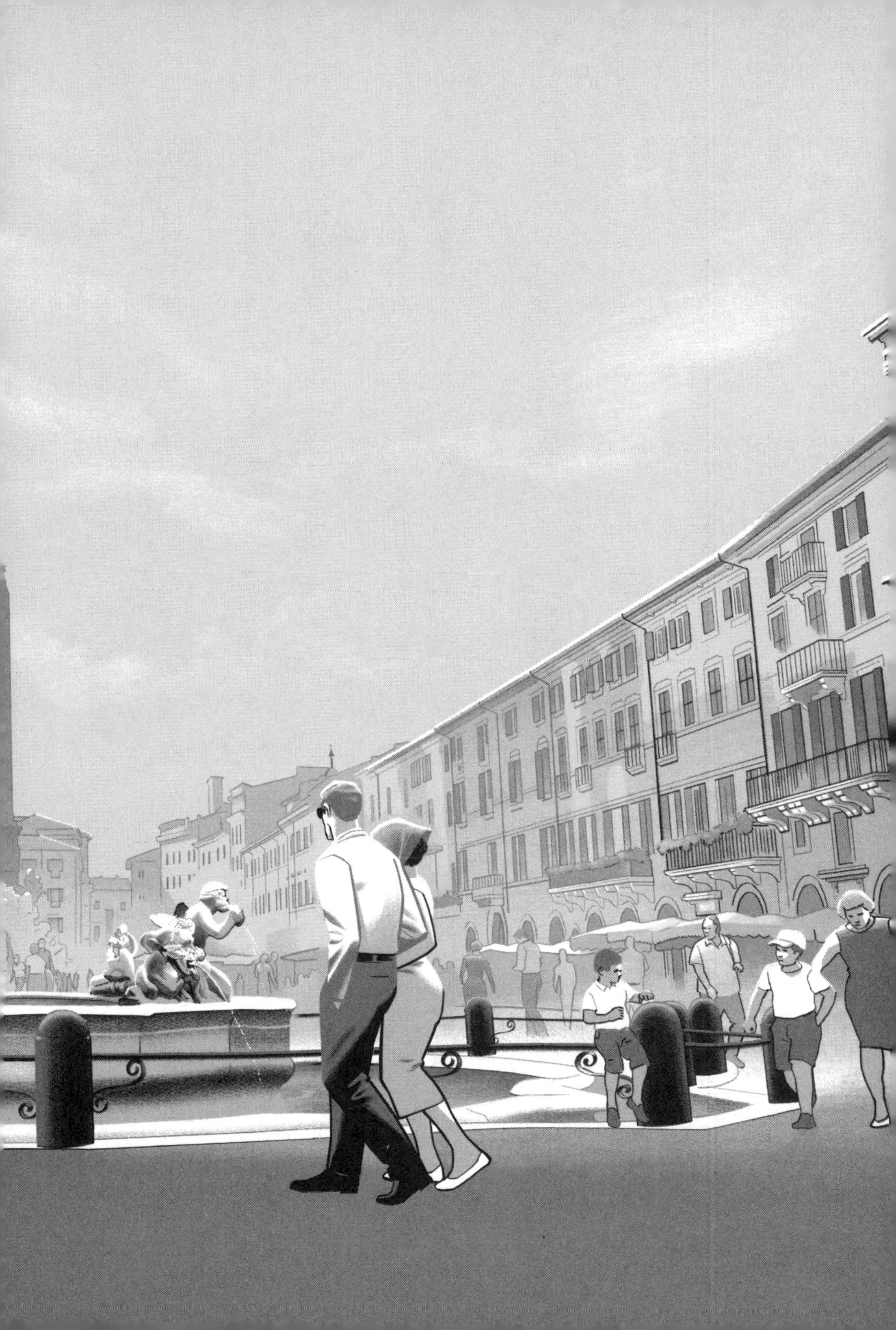

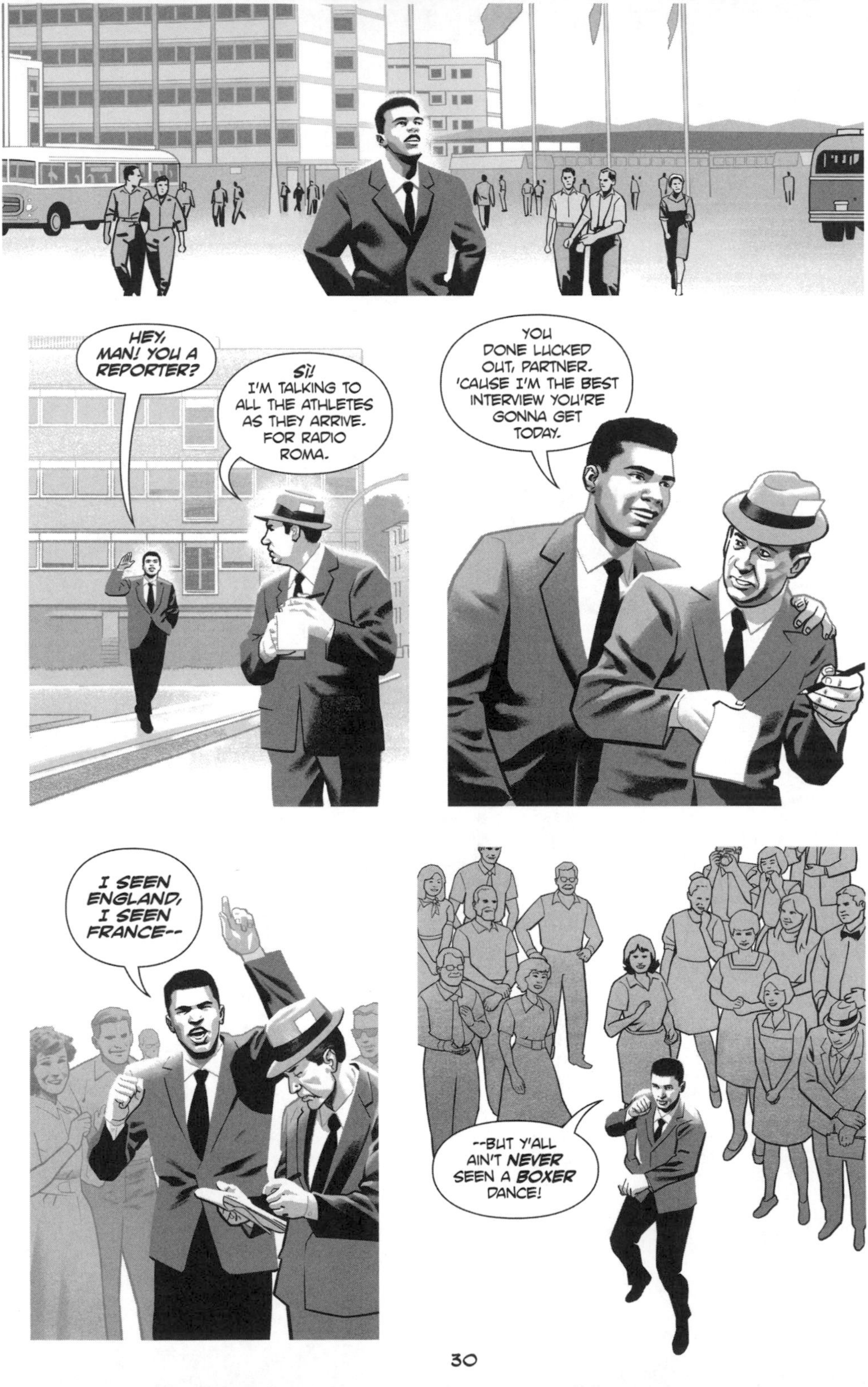
HEY, MAN! YOU A REPORTER?
SÌ! I'M TALKING TO ALL THE ATHLETES AS THEY ARRIVE. FOR RADIO ROMA.
YOU DONE LUCKED OUT, PARTNER. 'CAUSE I'M THE BEST INTERVIEW YOU'RE GONNA GET TODAY.
I SEEN ENGLAND, I SEEN FRANCE--
--BUT Y'ALL AIN'T NEVER SEEN A BOXER DANCE!

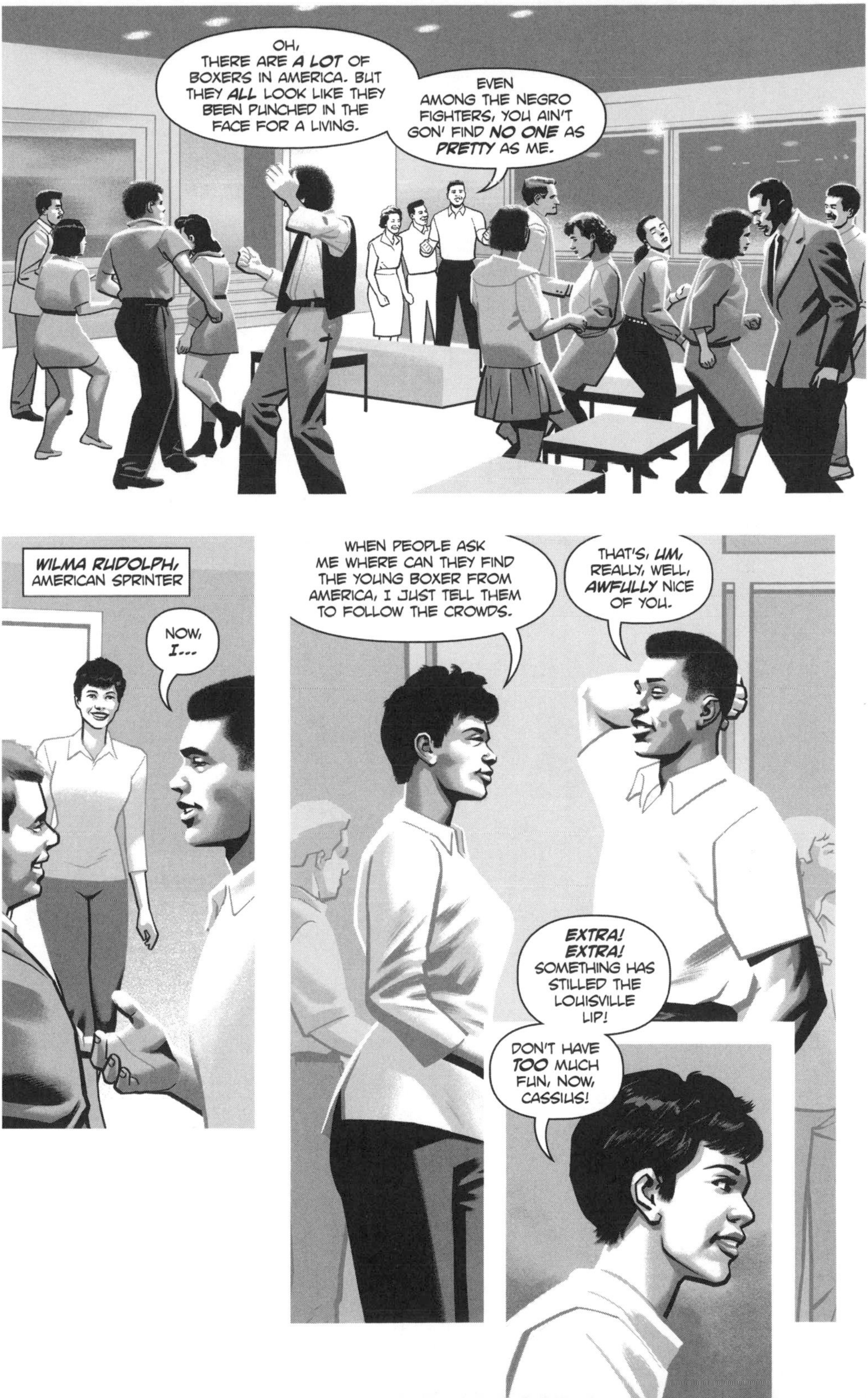
OH, THERE ARE A LOT OF BOXERS IN AMERICA. BUT THEY ALL LOOK LIKE THEY BEEN PUNCHED IN THE FACE FOR A LIVING.
EVEN AMONG THE NEGRO FIGHTERS, YOU AIN'T GON' FIND NO ONE AS PRETTY AS ME.
WILMA RUDOLPH, AMERICAN SPRINTER
NOW, I...
WHEN PEOPLE ASK ME WHERE CAN THEY FIND THE YOUNG BOXER FROM AMERICA, I JUST TELL THEM TO FOLLOW THE CROWDS.
THAT'S, UM, REALLY, WELL, AWFULLY NICE OF YOU.
EXTRA! EXTRA! SOMETHING HAS STILLED THE LOUISVILLE LIP!
DON'T HAVE TOO MUCH FUN, NOW, CASSIUS!

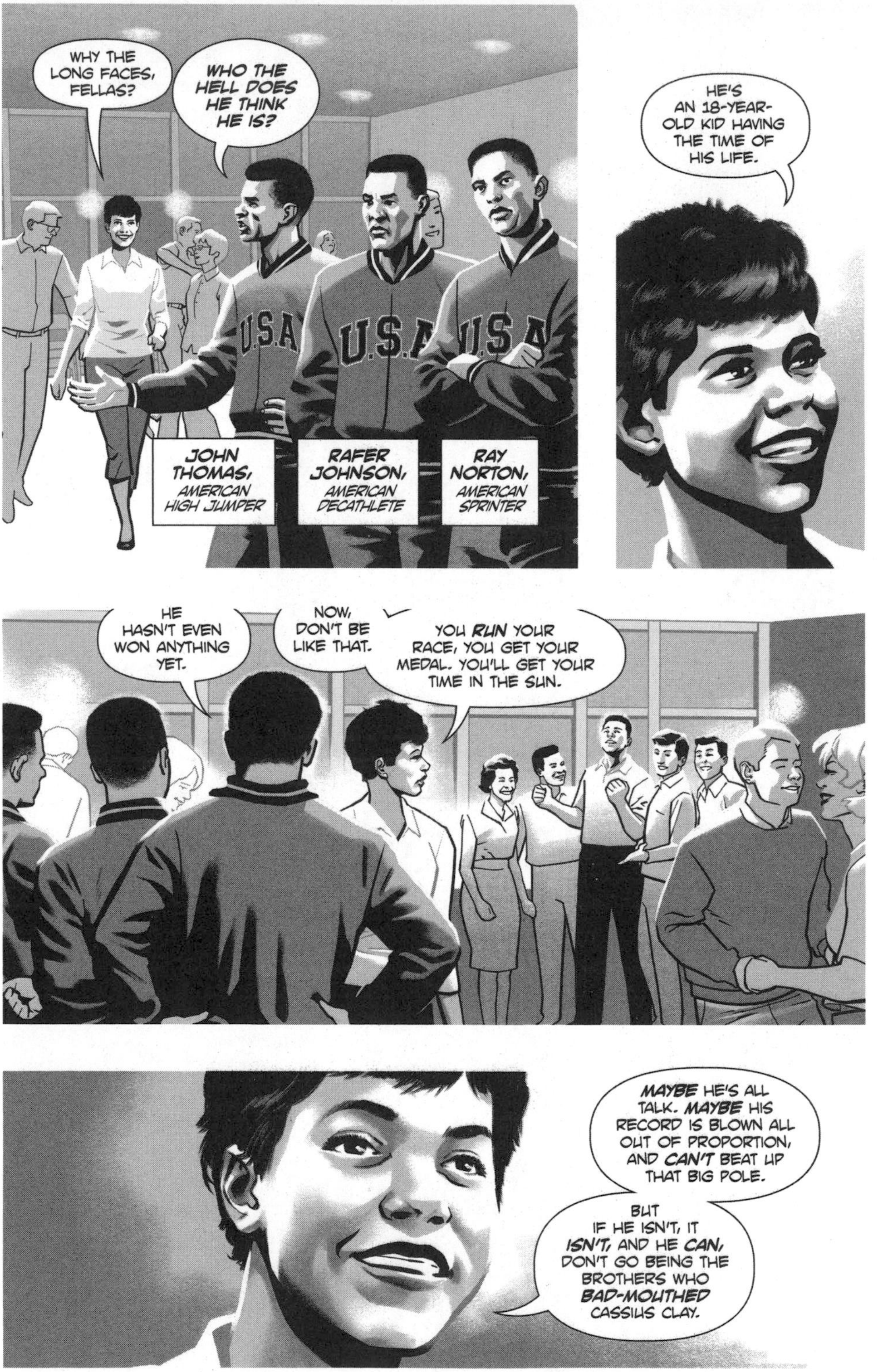
WHY THE LONG FACES, FELLAS?
WHO THE HELL DOES HE THINK HE IS?
JOHN THOMAS, AMERICAN HIGH JUMPER
RAFER JOHNSON, AMERICAN DECATHLETE
RAY NORTON, AMERICAN SPRINTER
HE'S AN 18-YEAR-OLD KID HAVING THE TIME OF HIS LIFE.
HE HASN'T EVEN WON ANYTHING YET.
NOW, DON'T BE LIKE THAT.
YOU RUN YOUR RACE, YOU GET YOUR MEDAL. YOU'LL GET YOUR TIME IN THE SUN.
MAYBE HE'S ALL TALK. MAYBE HIS RECORD IS BLOWN ALL OUT OF PROPORTION, AND CAN'T BEAT UP THAT BIG POLE.
BUT IF HE ISN'T, IT ISN'T, AND HE CAN, DON'T GO BEING THE BROTHERS WHO BAD-MOUTHED CASSIUS CLAY.

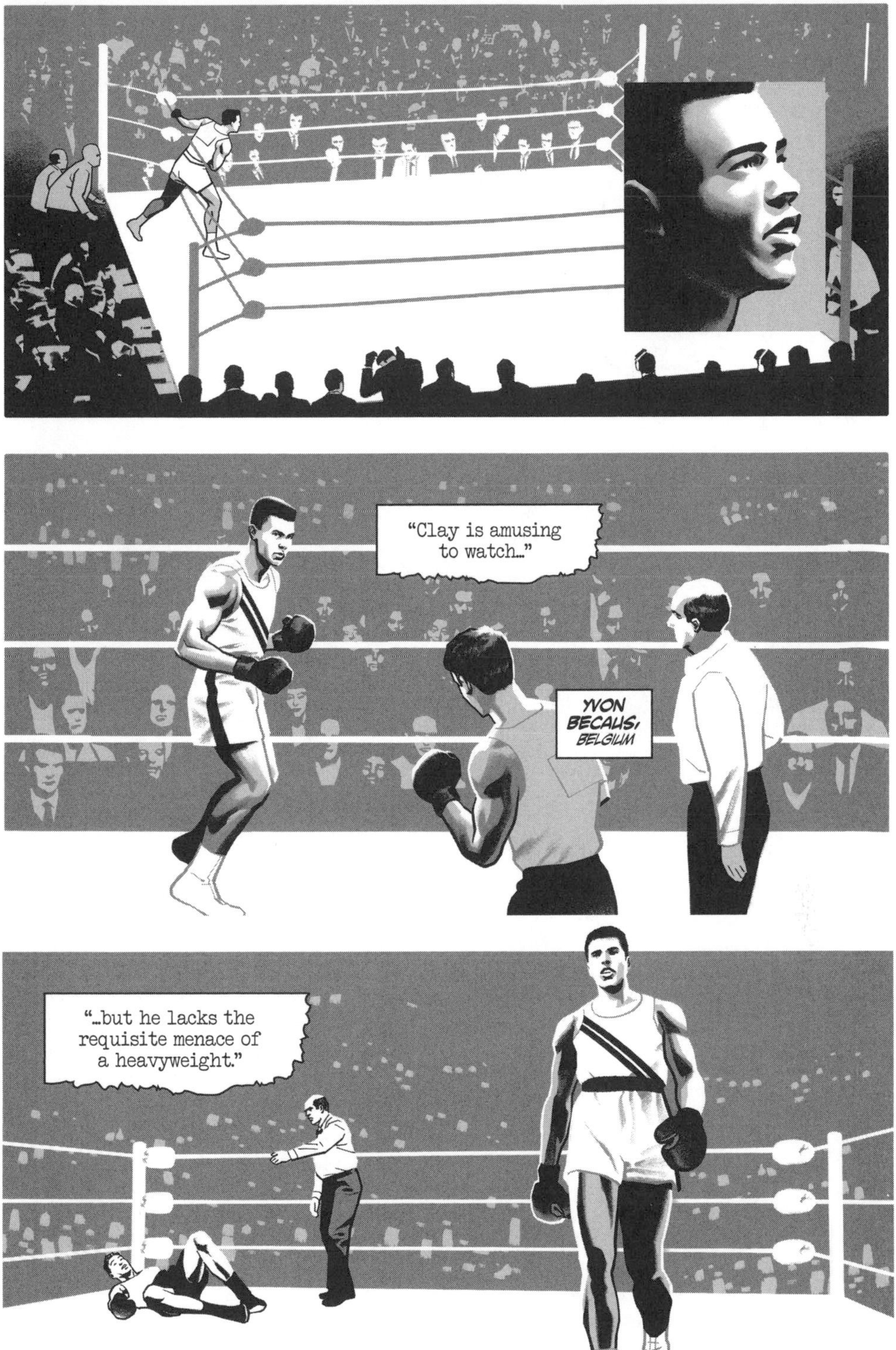

"Clay is amusing to watch…"
YVON BECAUS, BELGIUM
"…but he lacks the requisite menace of a heavyweight."

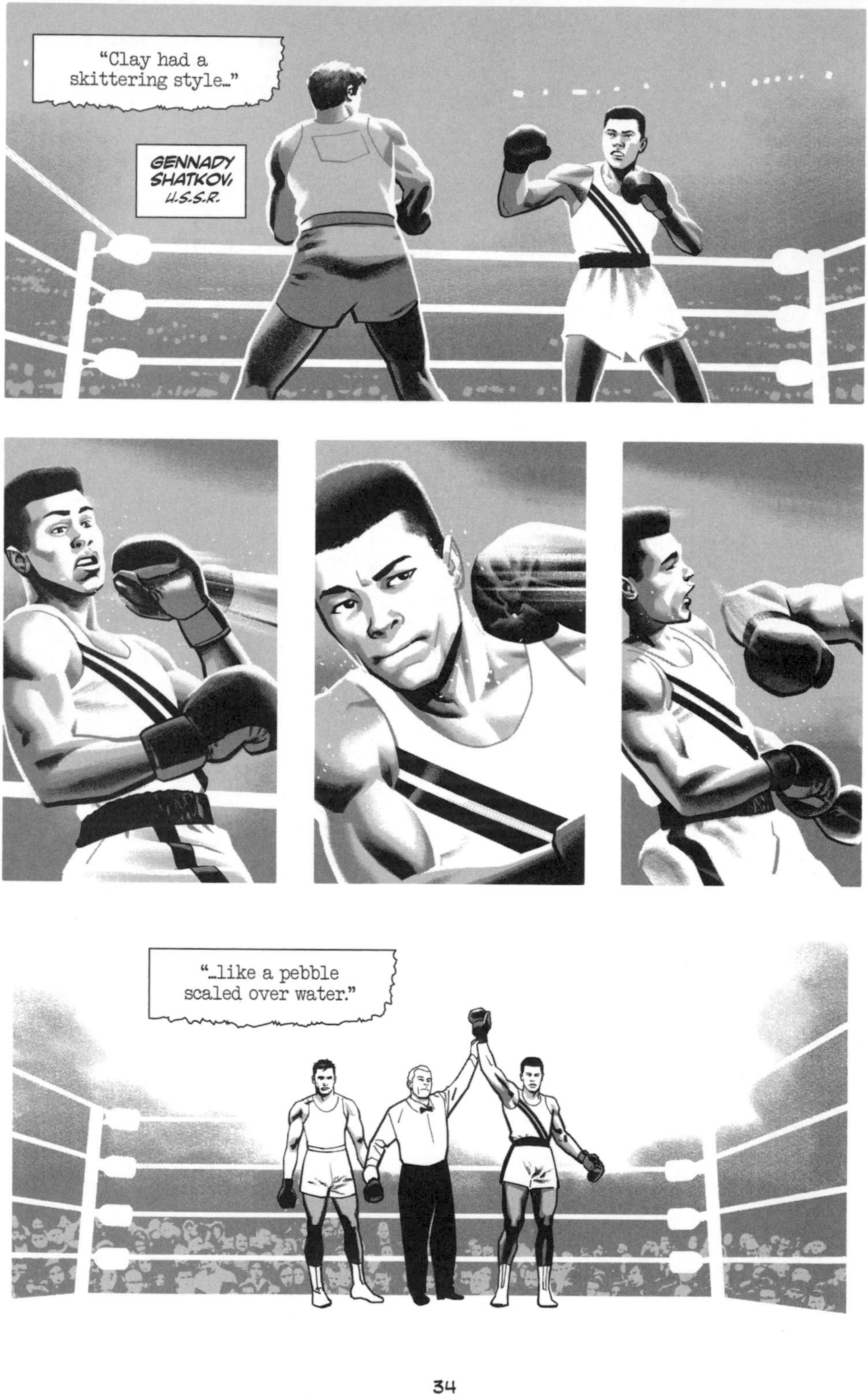
"Clay had a skittering style..."
GENNADY SHATKOV, U.S.S.R.
"...like a pebble scaled over water."

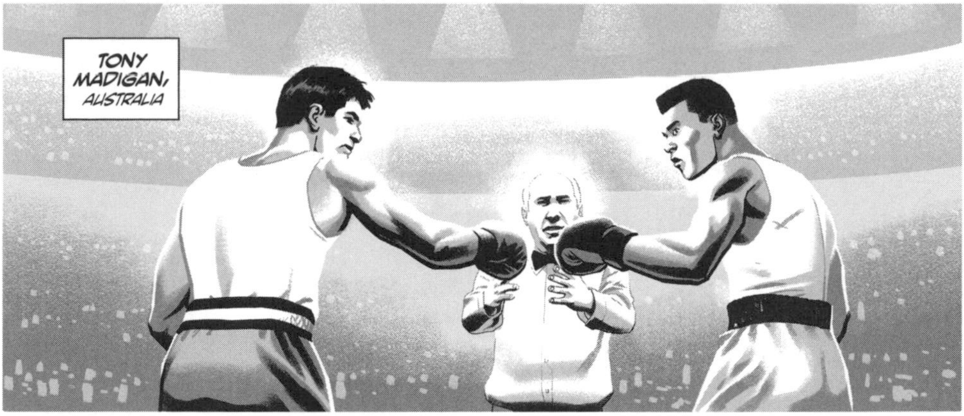
TONY MADIGAN, AUSTRALIA

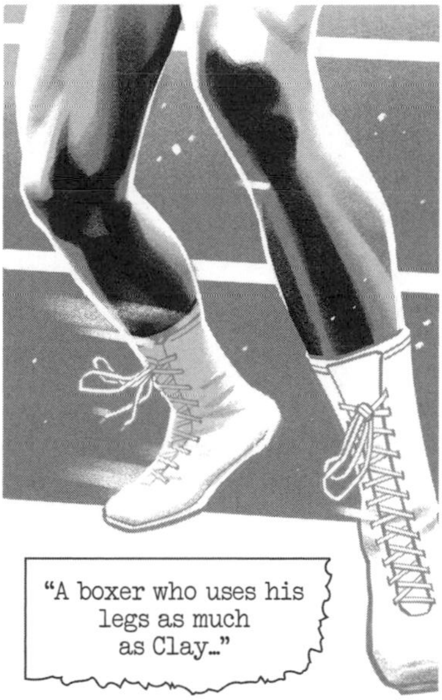
"A boxer who uses his legs as much as Clay..."

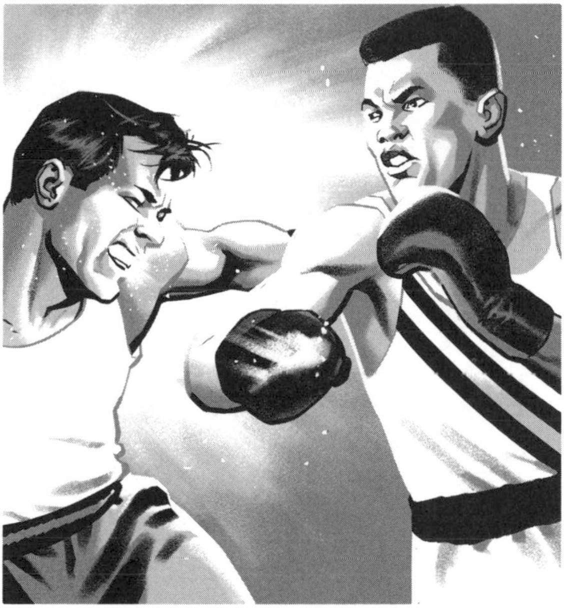

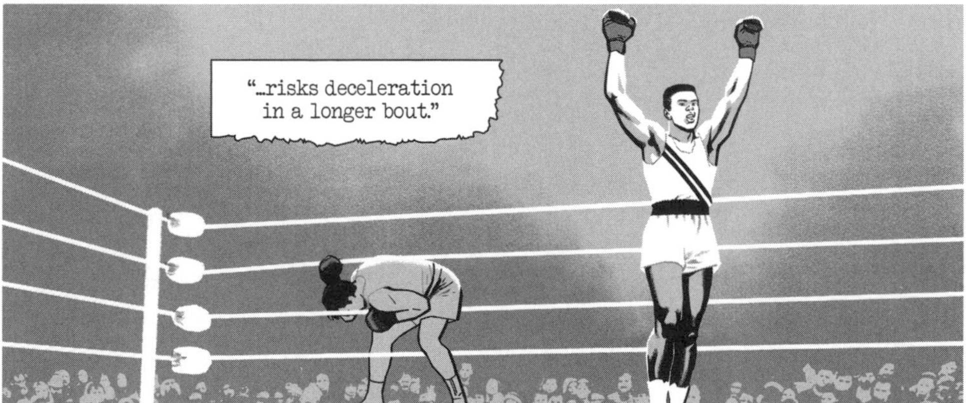
"...risks deceleration in a longer bout."

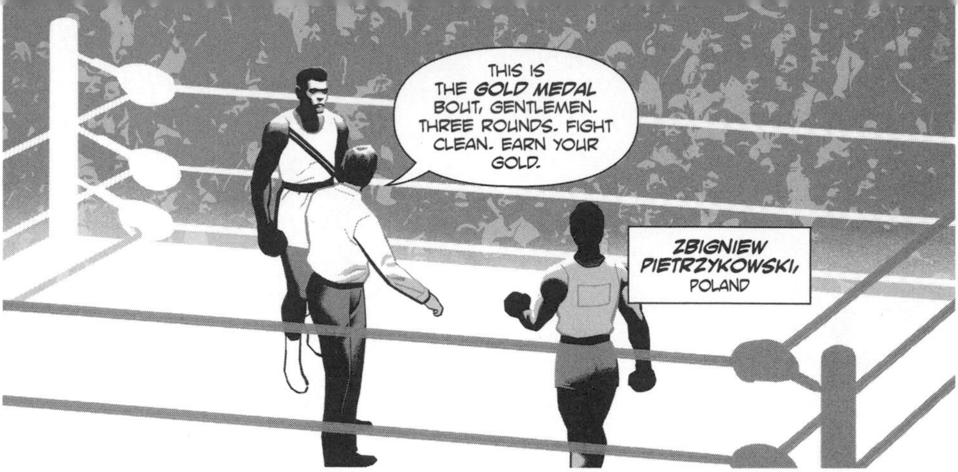
THIS IS THE GOLD MEDAL BOUT, GENTLEMEN. THREE ROUNDS. FIGHT CLEAN. EARN YOUR GOLD.
ZBIGNIEW PIETRZYKOWSKI, POLAND

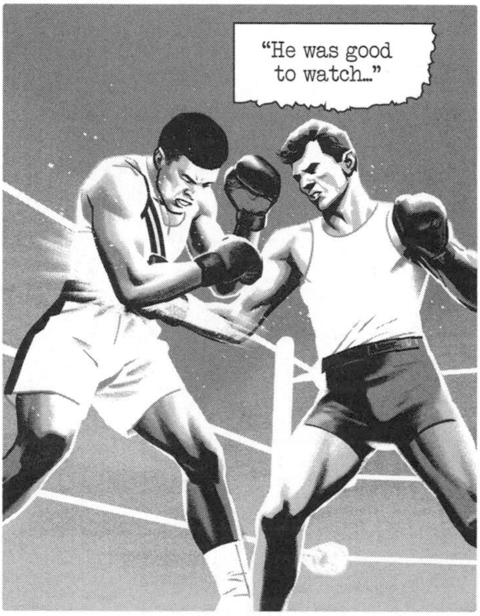
"He was good to watch..."

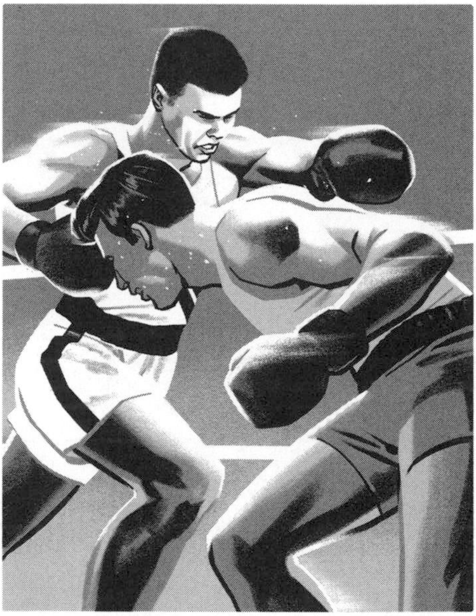

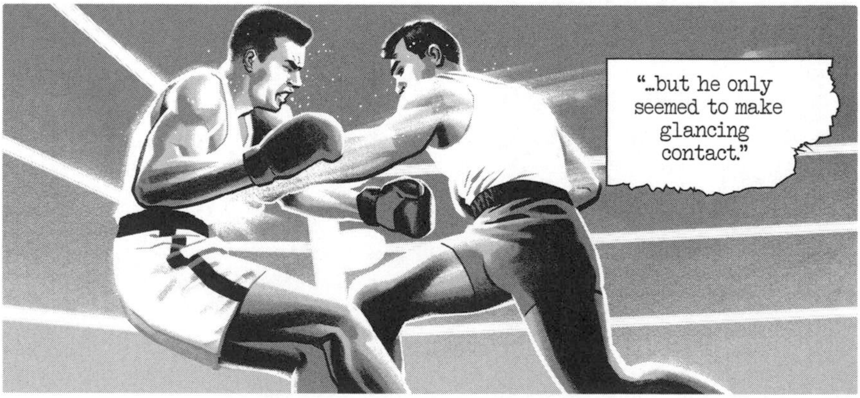
"...but he only seemed to make glancing contact."

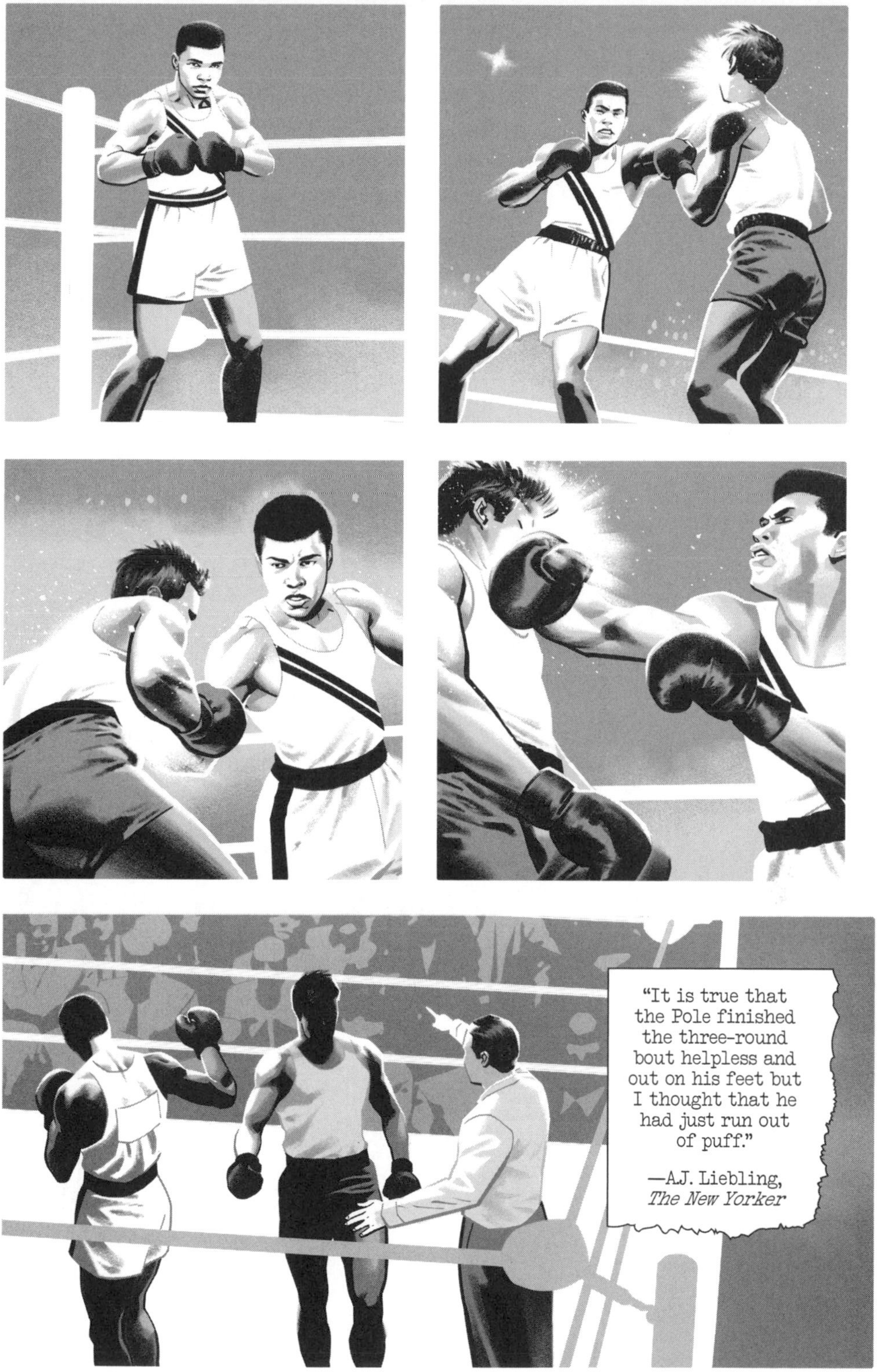
"It is true that the Pole finished the three-round bout helpless and out on his feet but I thought that he had just run out of puff."
—A.J. Liebling, *The New Yorker*

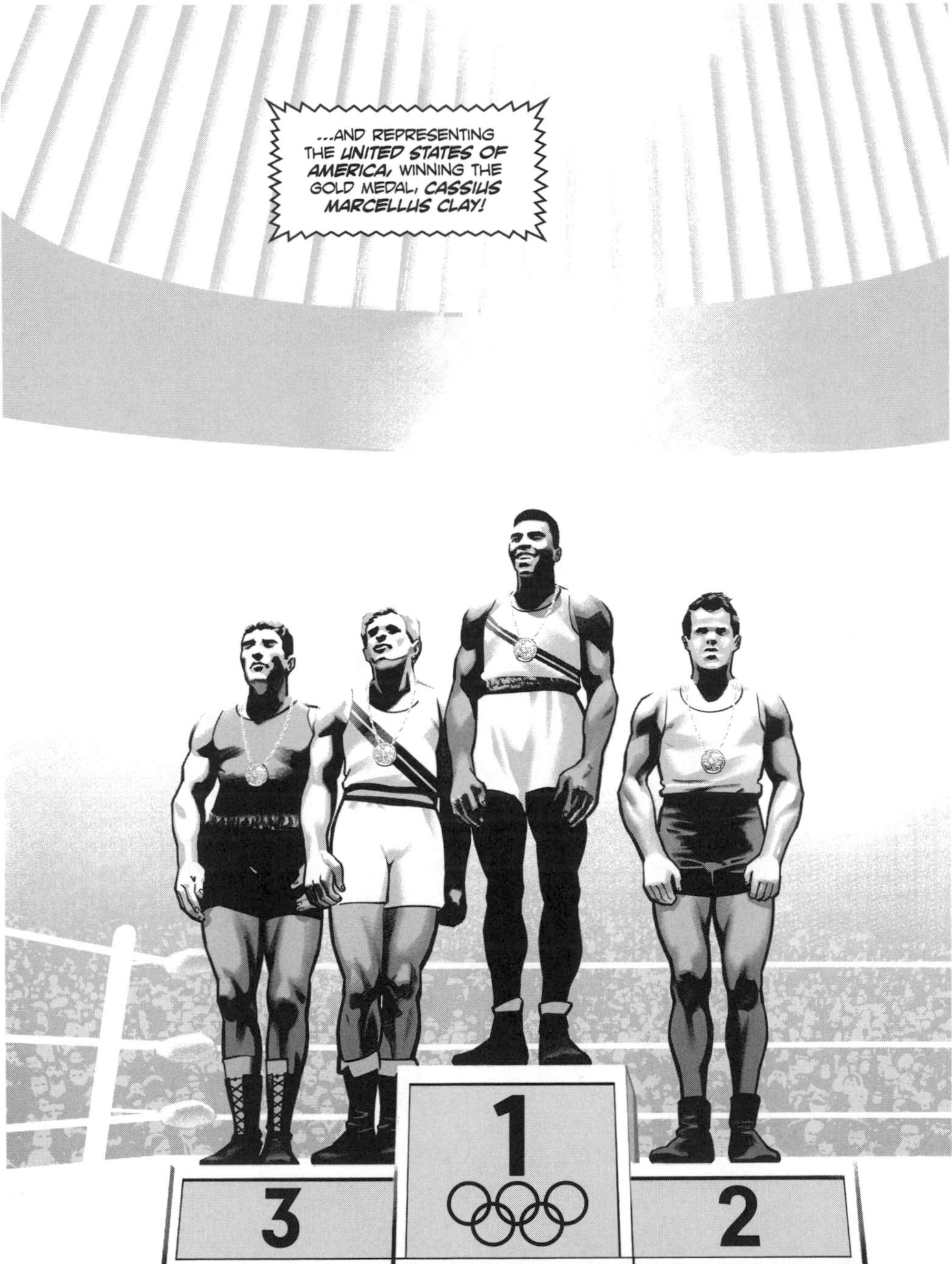
...AND REPRESENTING THE UNITED STATES OF AMERICA, WINNING THE GOLD MEDAL, CASSIUS MARCELLUS CLAY!
1
3
2

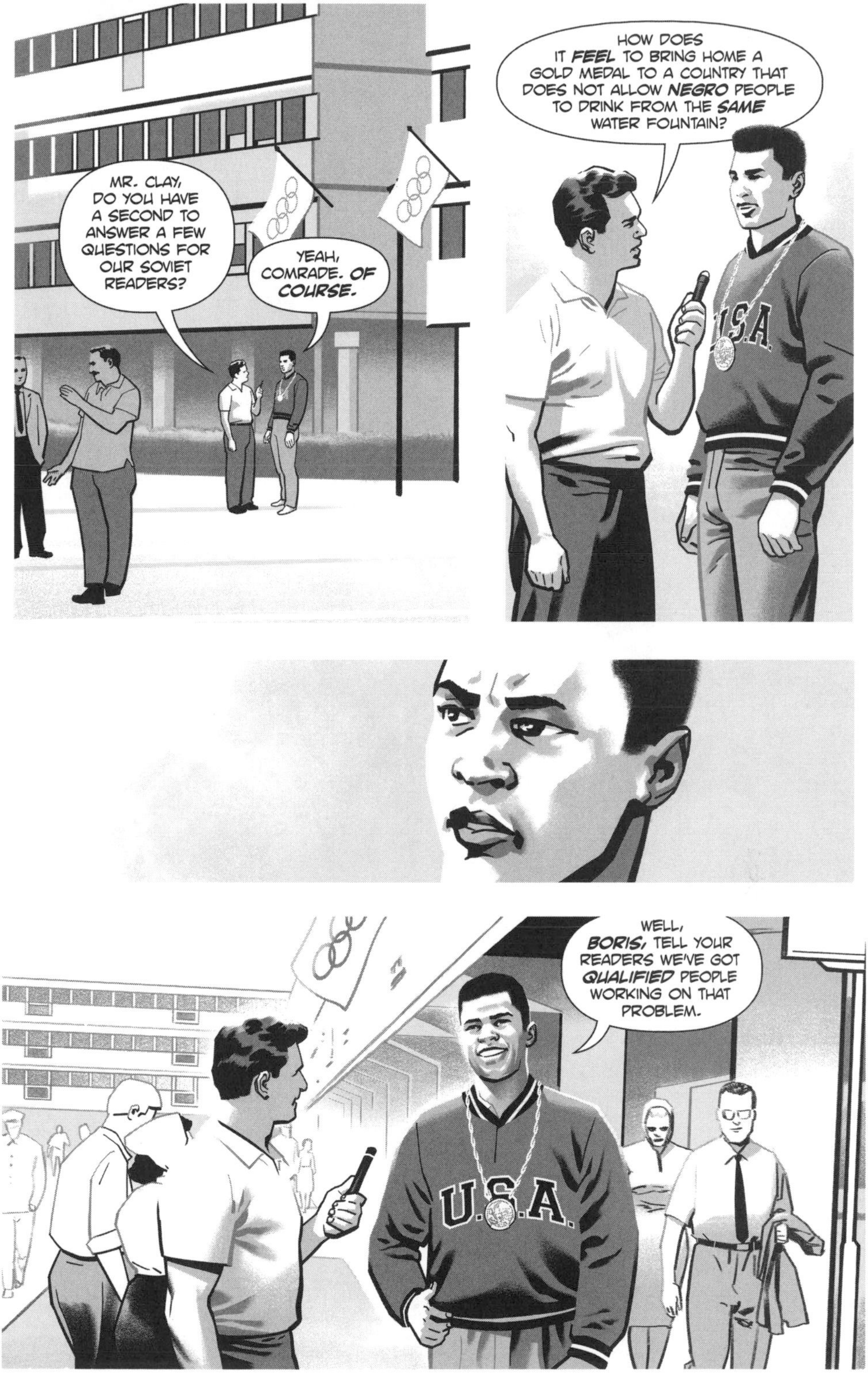
MR. CLAY, DO YOU HAVE A SECOND TO ANSWER A FEW QUESTIONS FOR OUR SOVIET READERS?
YEAH, COMRADE. OF COURSE.
HOW DOES IT FEEL TO BRING HOME A GOLD MEDAL TO A COUNTRY THAT DOES NOT ALLOW NEGRO PEOPLE TO DRINK FROM THE SAME WATER FOUNTAIN?
U.S.A.
WELL, BORIS, TELL YOUR READERS WE'VE GOT QUALIFIED PEOPLE WORKING ON THAT PROBLEM.
U.S.A.

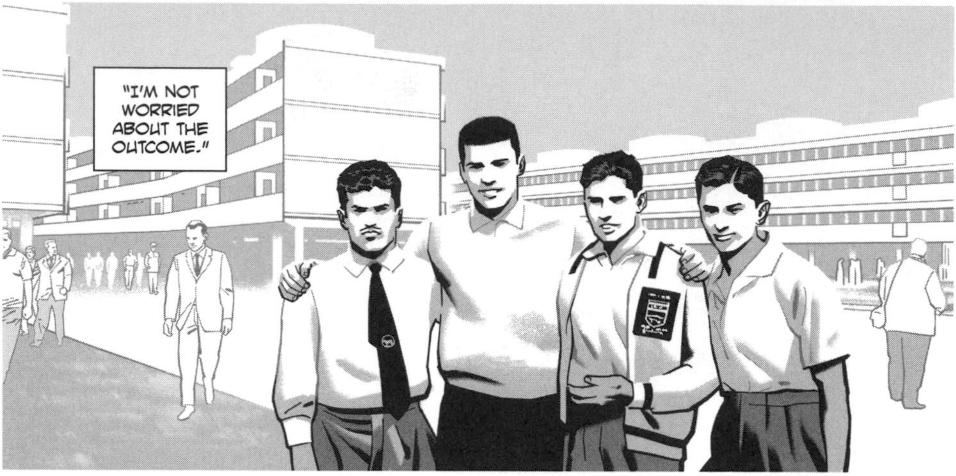
"I'M NOT WORRIED ABOUT THE OUTCOME."

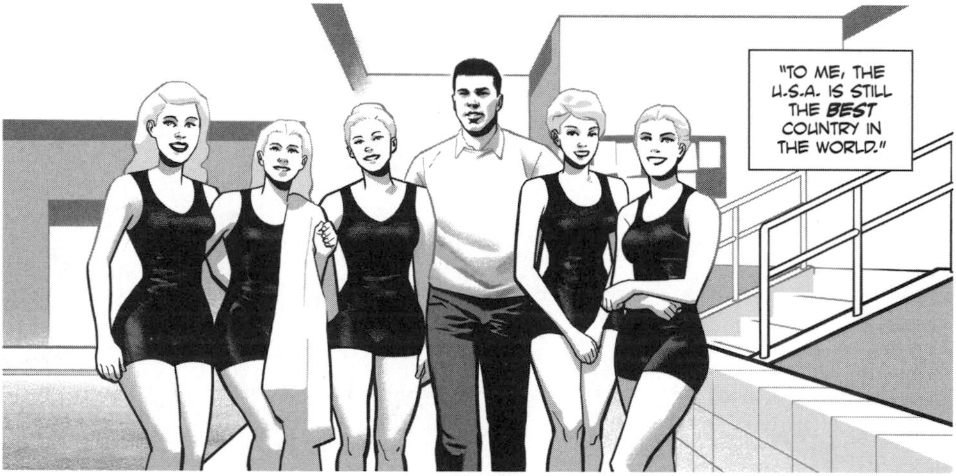
"TO ME, THE U.S.A. IS STILL THE **BEST** COUNTRY IN THE WORLD."

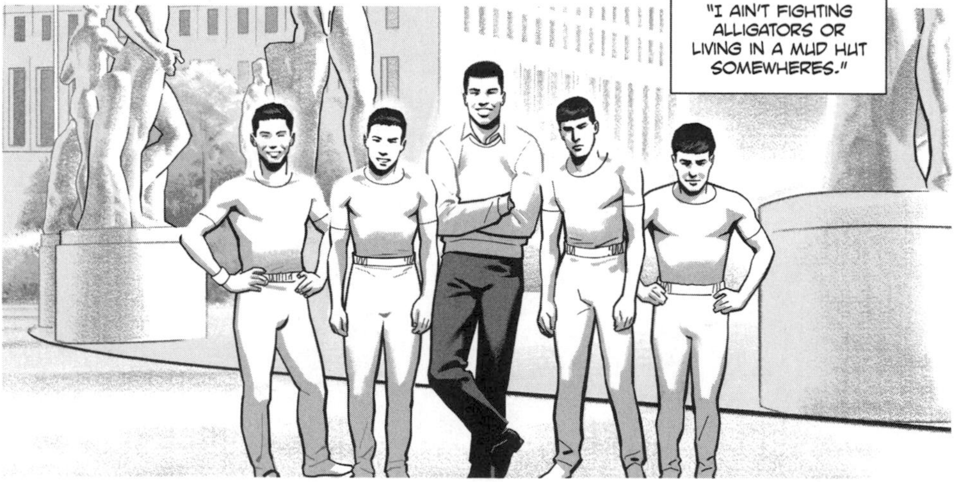
"I AIN'T FIGHTING ALLIGATORS OR LIVING IN A MUD HUT SOMEWHERES."

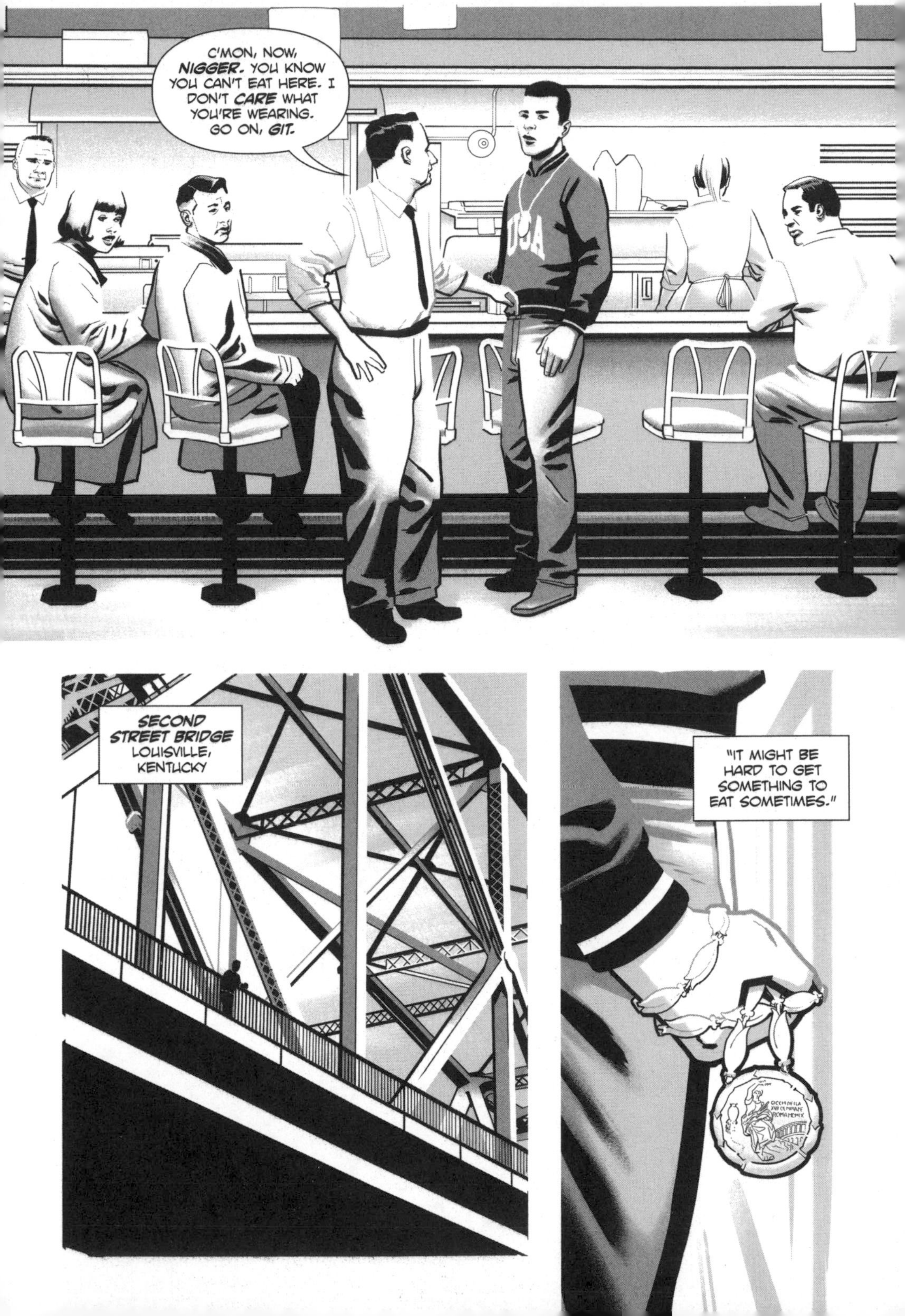
C'MON, NOW, NIGGER. YOU KNOW YOU CAN'T EAT HERE. I DON'T CARE WHAT YOU'RE WEARING. GO ON, GIT.
SECOND STREET BRIDGE LOUISVILLE, KENTUCKY
"IT MIGHT BE HARD TO GET SOMETHING TO EAT SOMETIMES."

ROUND THREE: CHURCH. 1961.

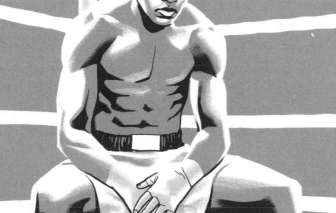

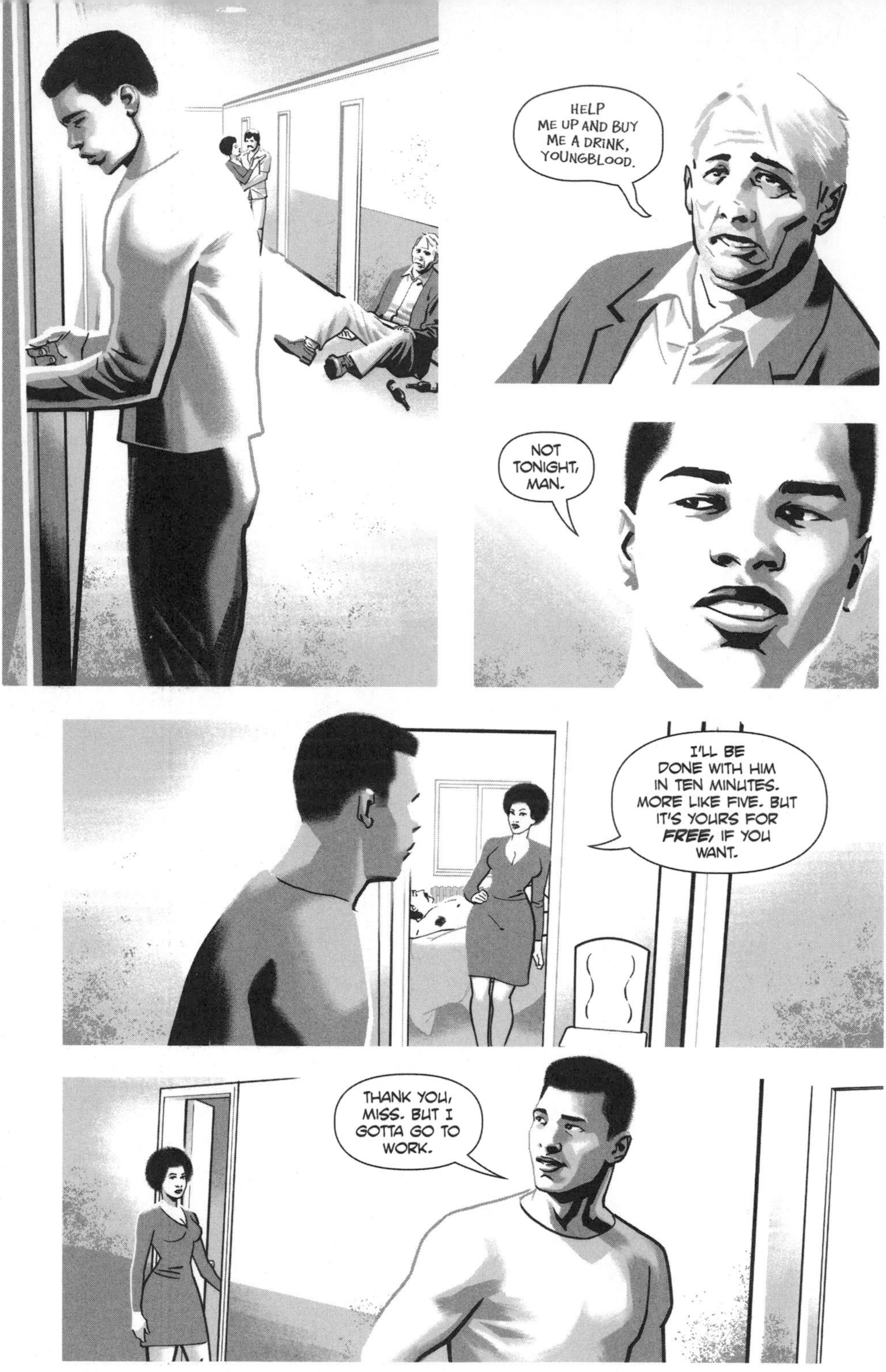
HELP ME UP AND BUY ME A DRINK, YOUNGBLOOD.
NOT TONIGHT, MAN.
I'LL BE DONE WITH HIM IN TEN MINUTES. MORE LIKE FIVE. BUT IT'S YOURS FOR FREE, IF YOU WANT.
THANK YOU, MISS. BUT I GOTTA GO TO WORK.

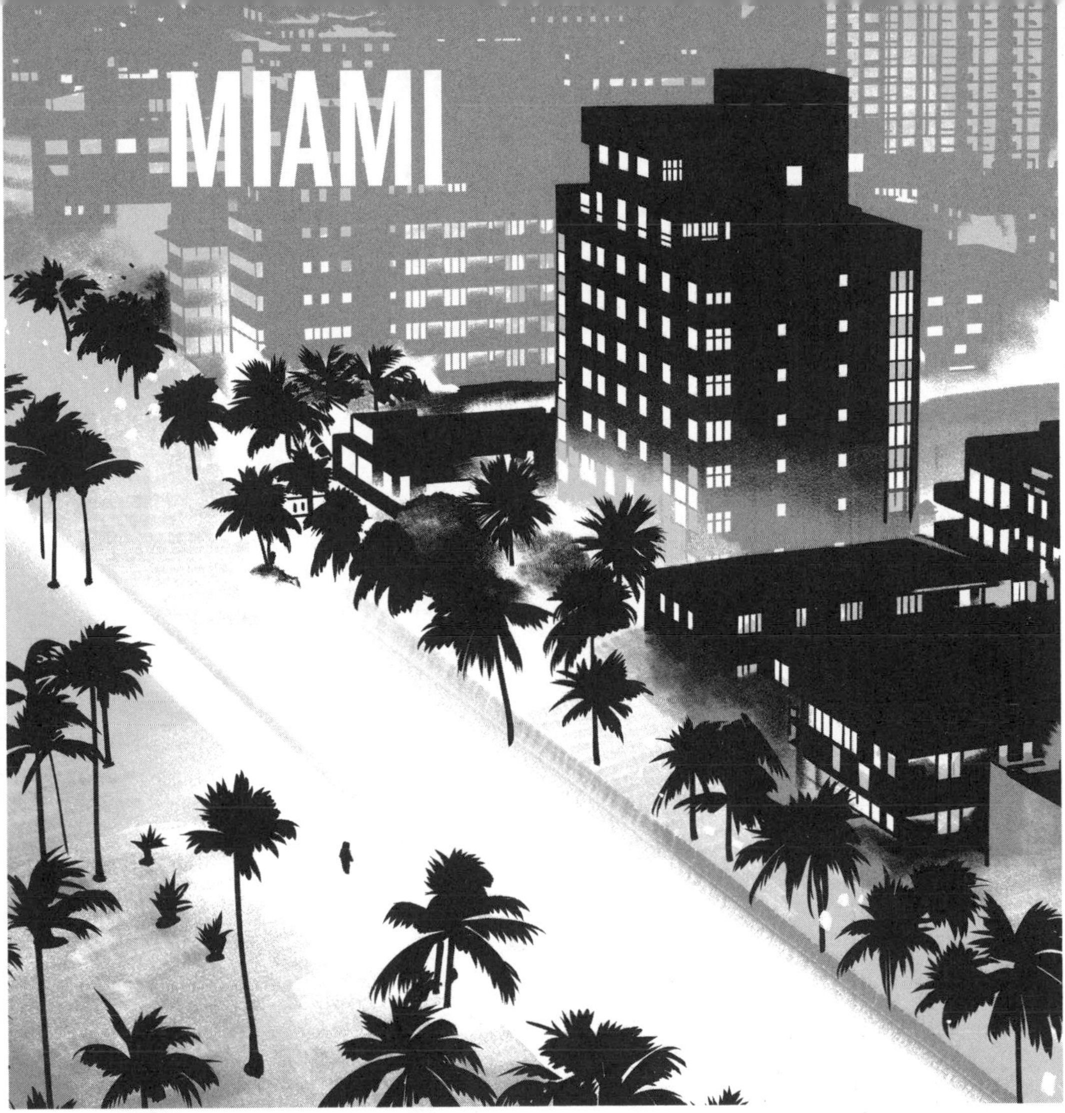
MIAMI

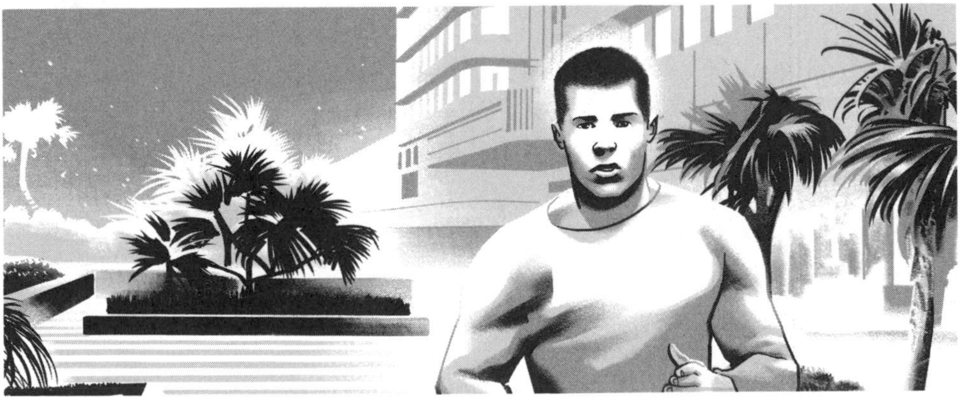

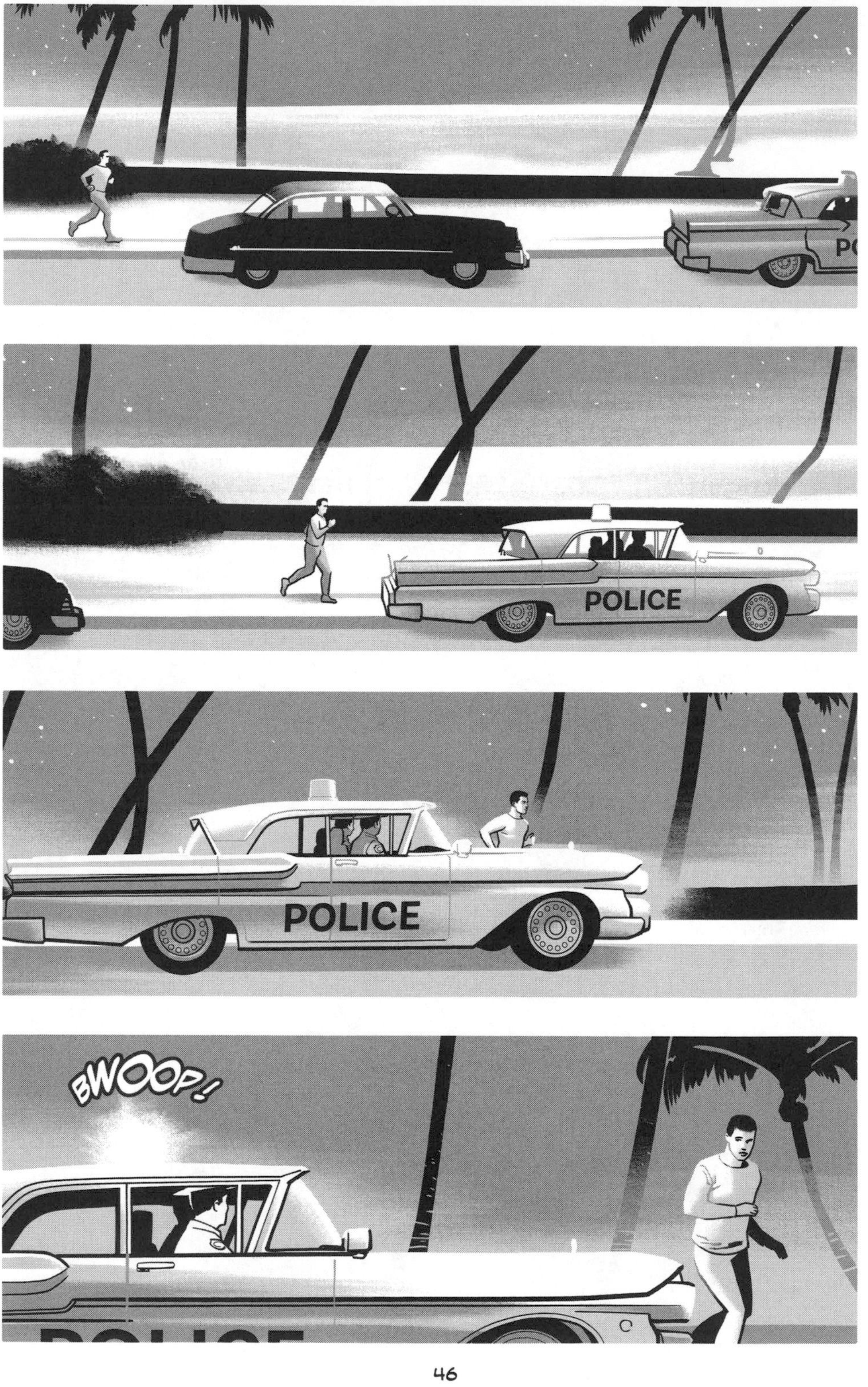
POLICE
POLICE
BWOOP!

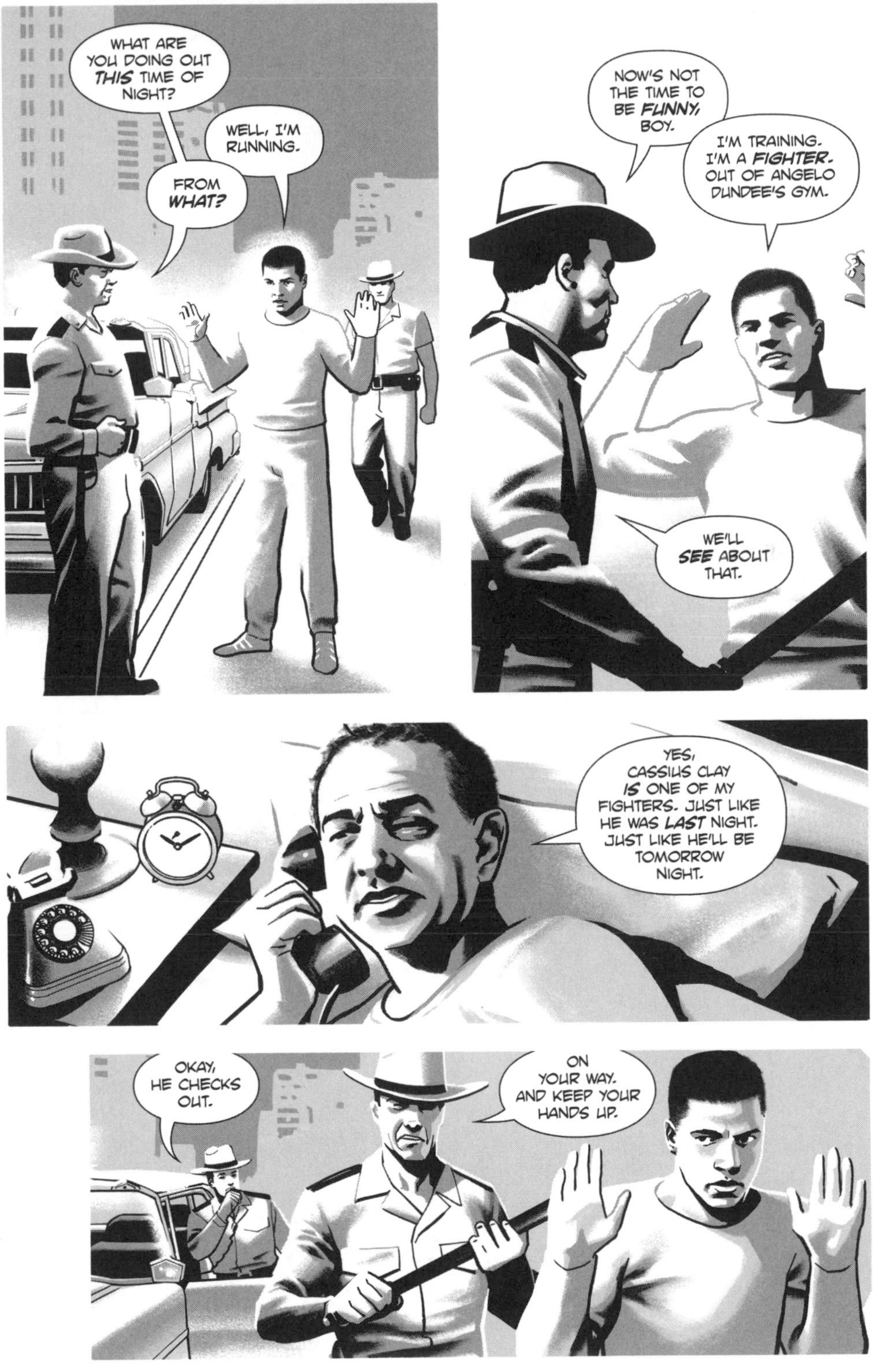
WHAT ARE YOU DOING OUT THIS TIME OF NIGHT?
WELL, I'M RUNNING.
FROM WHAT?
NOW'S NOT THE TIME TO BE FUNNY, BOY.
I'M TRAINING. I'M A FIGHTER. OUT OF ANGELO DUNDEE'S GYM.
WE'LL SEE ABOUT THAT.
YES, CASSIUS CLAY IS ONE OF MY FIGHTERS. JUST LIKE HE WAS LAST NIGHT. JUST LIKE HE'LL BE TOMORROW NIGHT.
OKAY, HE CHECKS OUT.
ON YOUR WAY. AND KEEP YOUR HANDS UP.

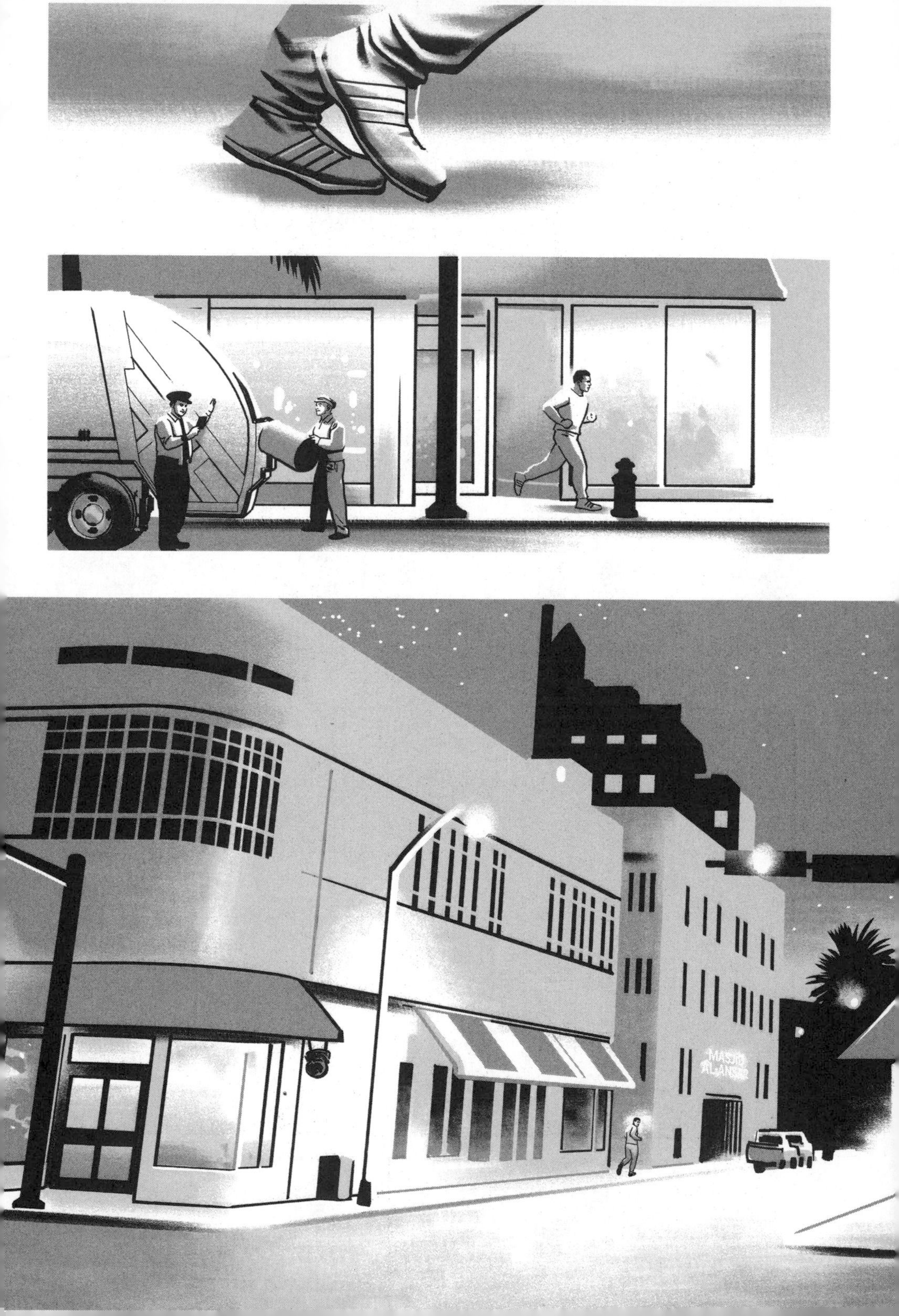
MASJID

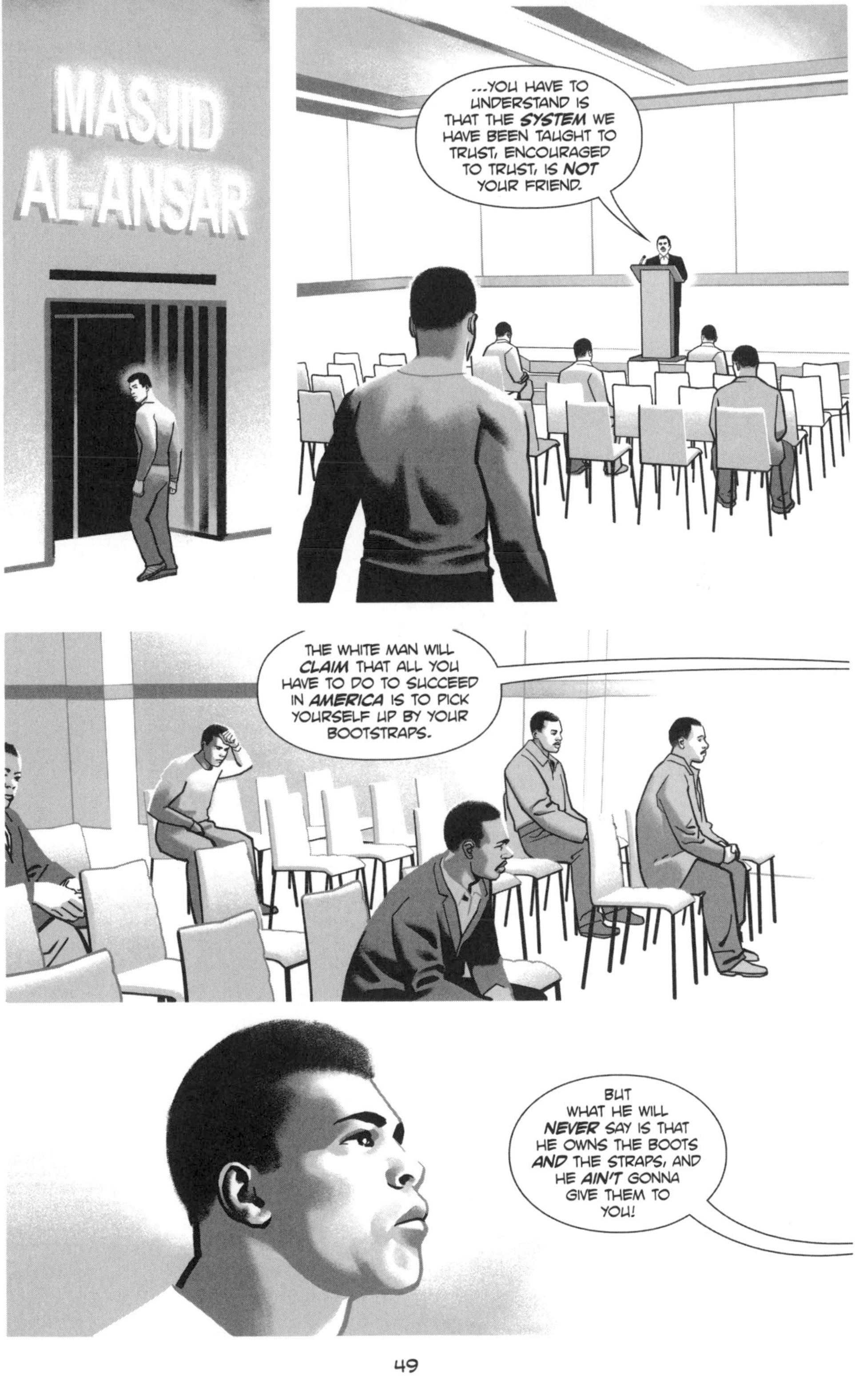
MASJID AL-ANSAR
...YOU HAVE TO UNDERSTAND IS THAT THE **SYSTEM** WE HAVE BEEN TAUGHT TO TRUST, ENCOURAGED TO TRUST, IS **NOT** YOUR FRIEND.
THE WHITE MAN WILL **CLAIM** THAT ALL YOU HAVE TO DO TO SUCCEED IN **AMERICA** IS TO PICK YOURSELF UP BY YOUR BOOTSTRAPS.
BUT WHAT HE WILL **NEVER** SAY IS THAT HE OWNS THE BOOTS **AND** THE STRAPS, AND HE **AIN'T** GONNA GIVE THEM TO YOU!

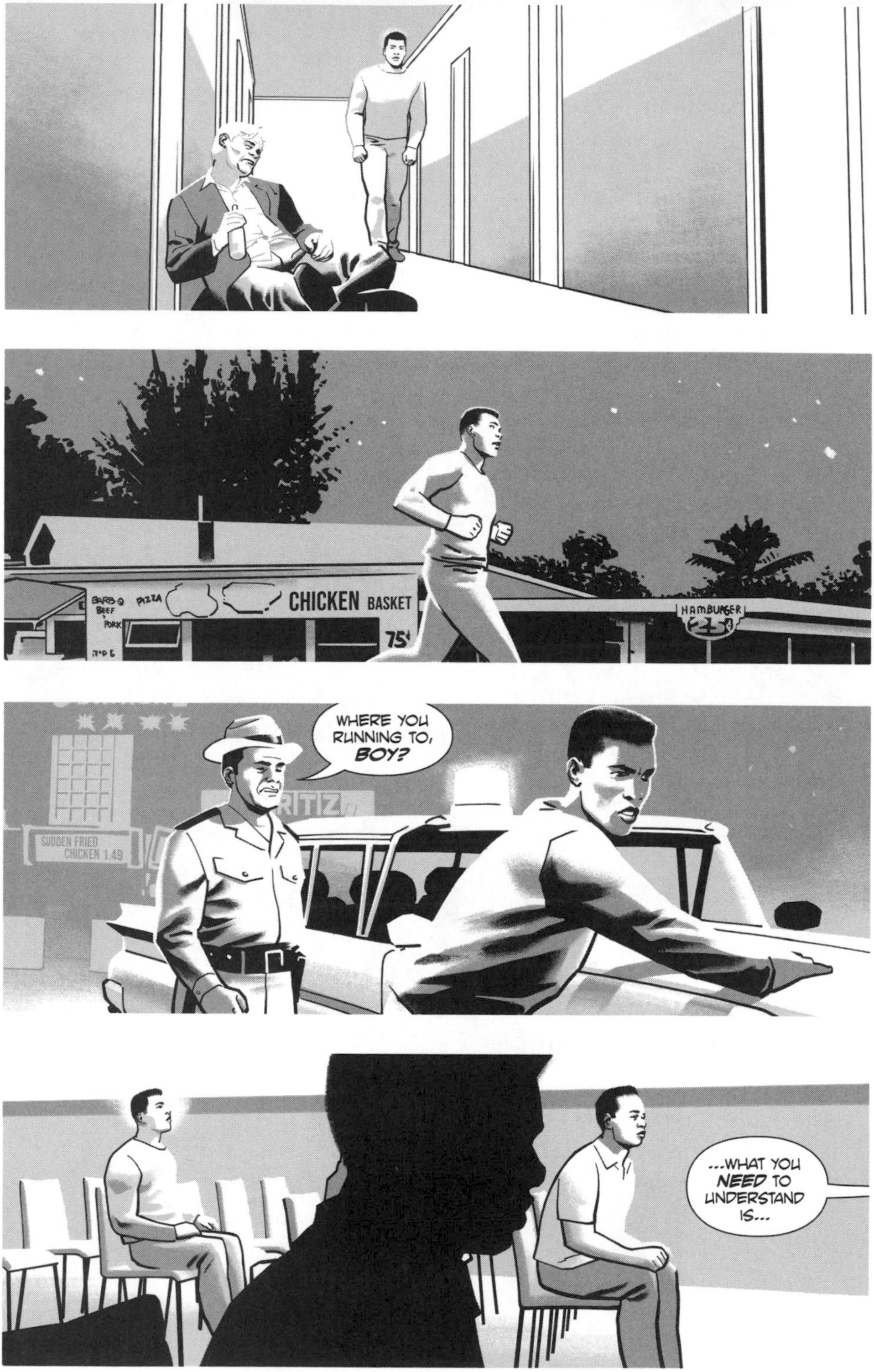
PIZZA
CHICKEN BASKET
75¢
HAMBURGER
WHERE YOU RUNNING TO, **BOY?**
SUDDEN FRIED CHICKEN 1.49
...WHAT YOU **NEED** TO UNDERSTAND IS...

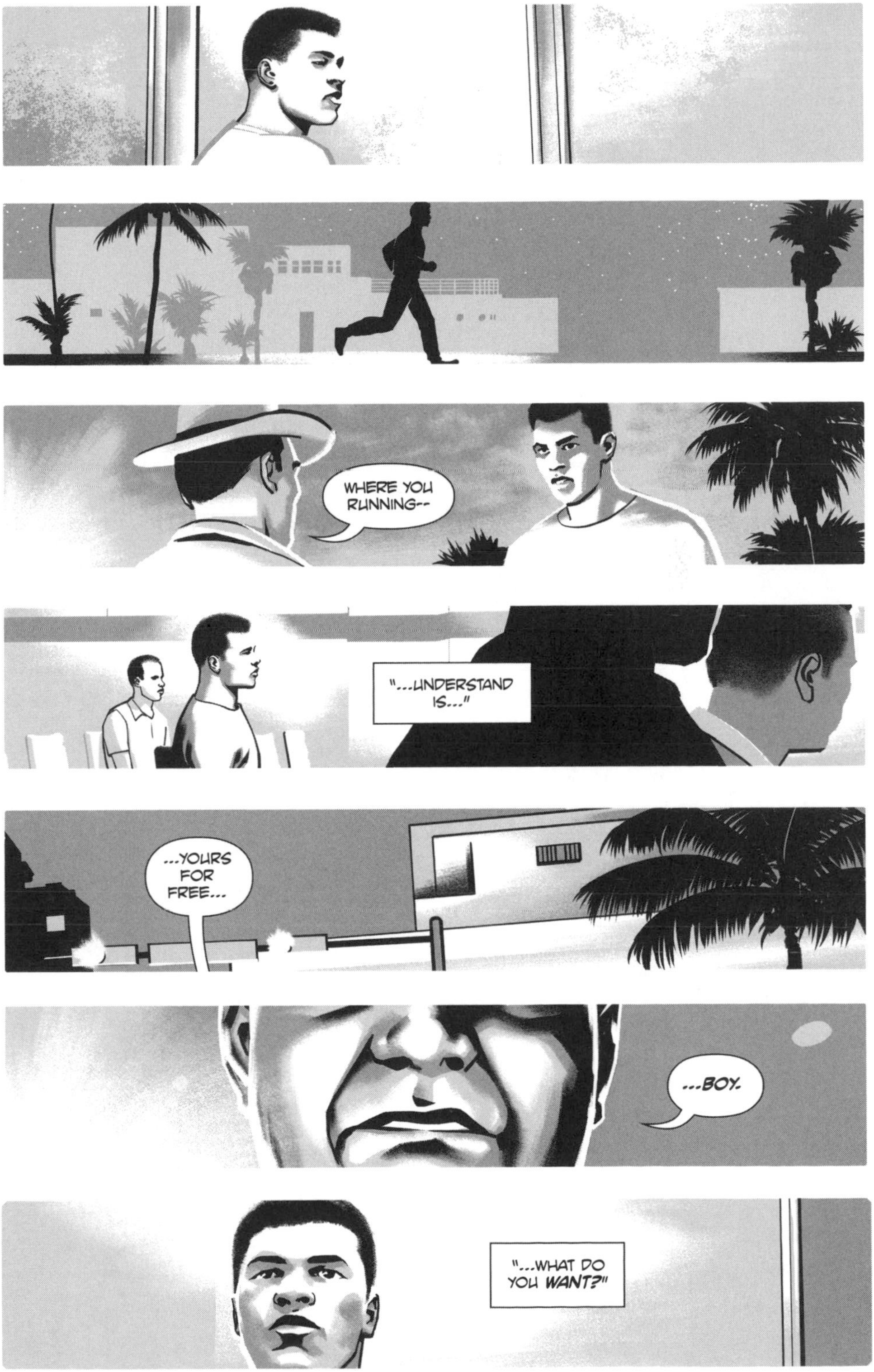
WHERE YOU RUNNING--
"...UNDERSTAND IS..."
...YOURS FOR FREE...
...BOY.
"...WHAT DO YOU *WANT?*"

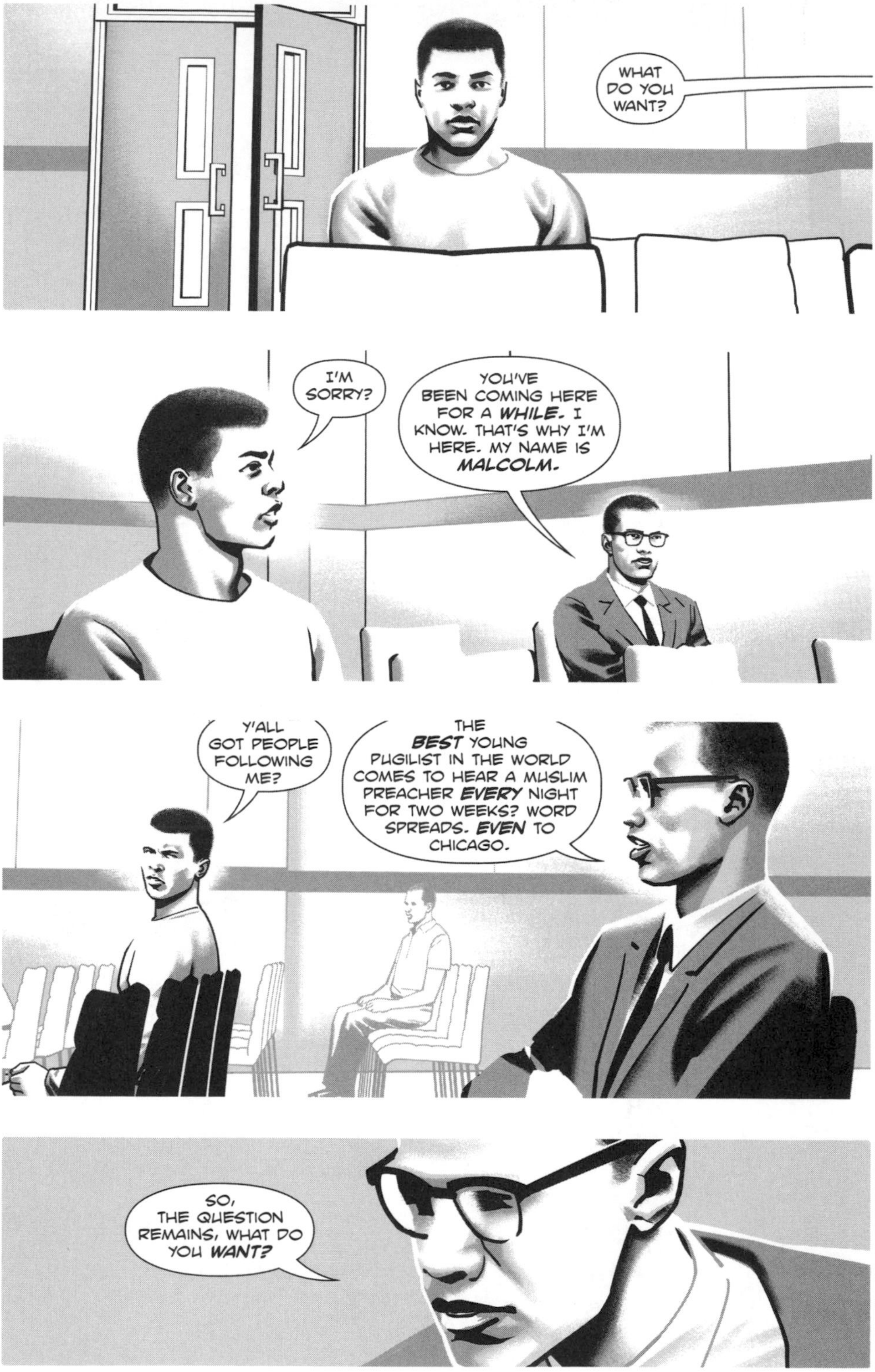
WHAT DO YOU WANT?
I'M SORRY?
YOU'VE BEEN COMING HERE FOR A **WHILE.** I KNOW. THAT'S WHY I'M HERE. MY NAME IS **MALCOLM.**
Y'ALL GOT PEOPLE FOLLOWING ME?
THE **BEST** YOUNG PUGILIST IN THE WORLD COMES TO HEAR A MUSLIM PREACHER **EVERY** NIGHT FOR TWO WEEKS? WORD SPREADS. **EVEN** TO CHICAGO.
SO, THE QUESTION REMAINS, WHAT DO YOU **WANT?**

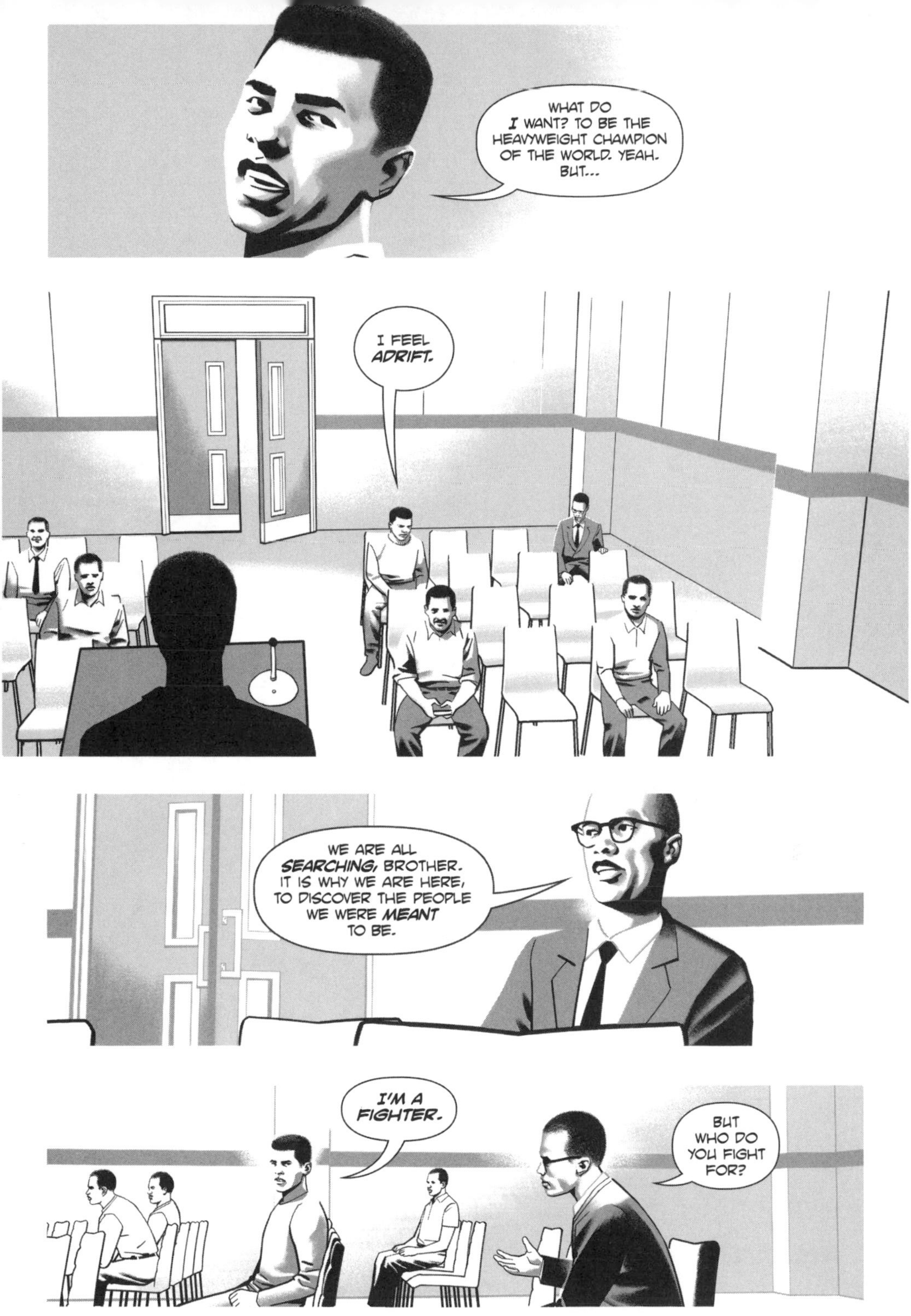
WHAT DO *I* WANT? TO BE THE HEAVYWEIGHT CHAMPION OF THE WORLD. YEAH. BUT...
I FEEL *ADRIFT*.
WE ARE ALL *SEARCHING*, BROTHER. IT IS WHY WE ARE HERE, TO DISCOVER THE PEOPLE WE WERE *MEANT* TO BE.
I'M A FIGHTER.
BUT WHO DO YOU FIGHT FOR?

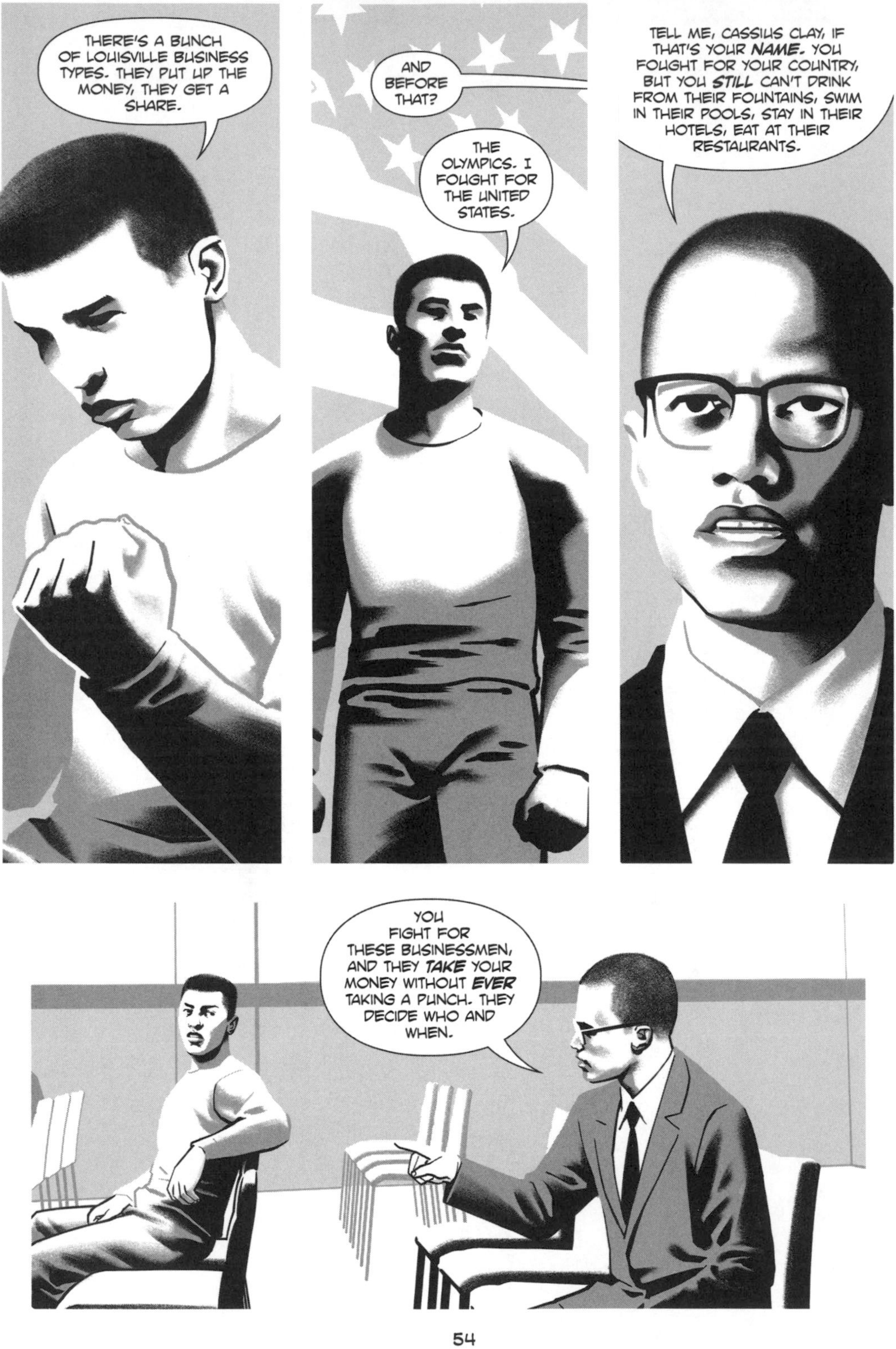
THERE'S A BUNCH OF LOUISVILLE BUSINESS TYPES. THEY PUT UP THE MONEY, THEY GET A SHARE.
AND BEFORE THAT?
THE OLYMPICS. I FOUGHT FOR THE UNITED STATES.
TELL ME, CASSIUS CLAY, IF THAT'S YOUR NAME. YOU FOUGHT FOR YOUR COUNTRY, BUT YOU STILL CAN'T DRINK FROM THEIR FOUNTAINS, SWIM IN THEIR POOLS, STAY IN THEIR HOTELS, EAT AT THEIR RESTAURANTS.
YOU FIGHT FOR THESE BUSINESSMEN, AND THEY TAKE YOUR MONEY WITHOUT EVER TAKING A PUNCH. THEY DECIDE WHO AND WHEN.

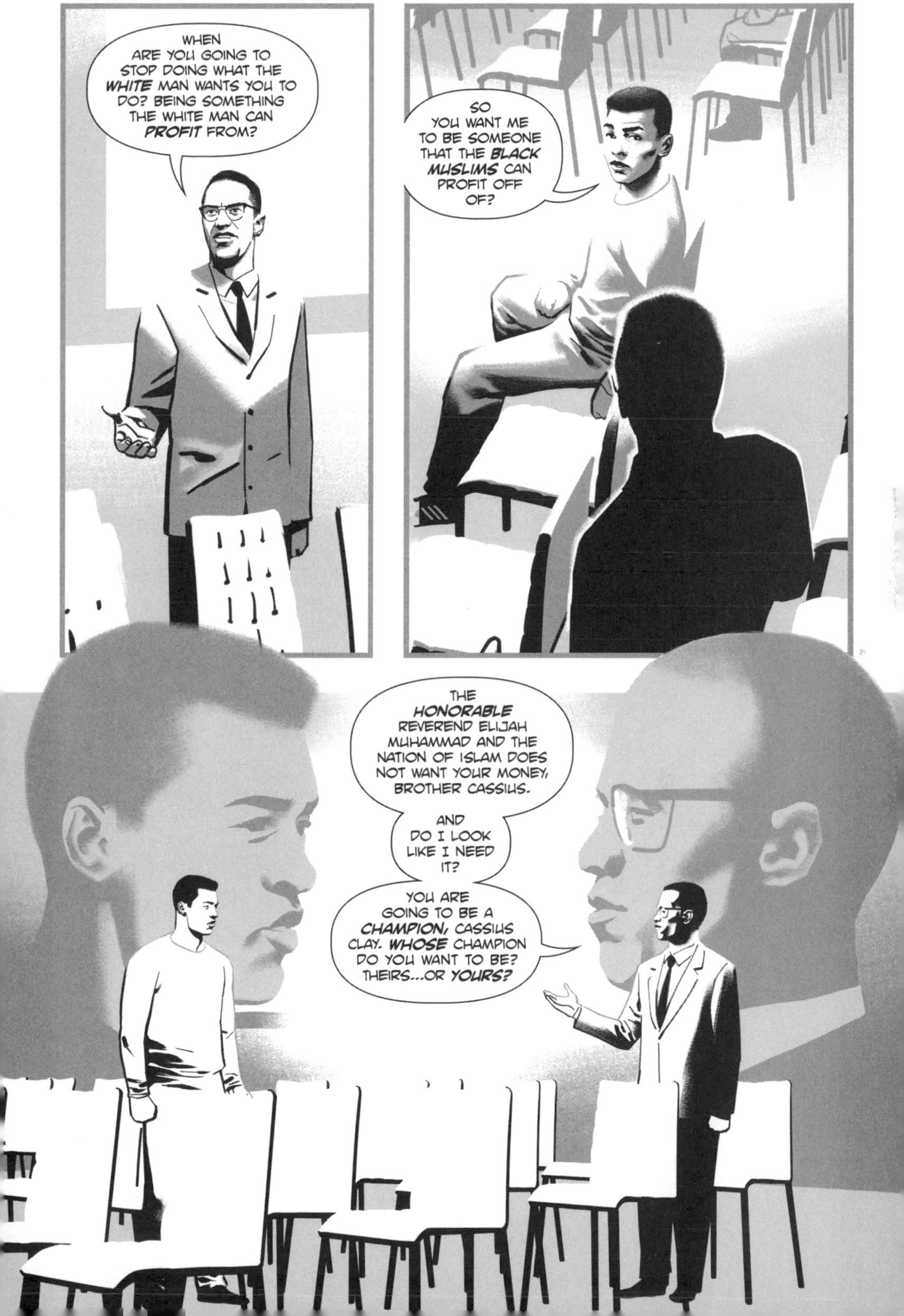
WHEN ARE YOU GOING TO STOP DOING WHAT THE WHITE MAN WANTS YOU TO DO? BEING SOMETHING THE WHITE MAN CAN PROFIT FROM?
SO YOU WANT ME TO BE SOMEONE THAT THE BLACK MUSLIMS CAN PROFIT OFF OF?
THE HONORABLE REVEREND ELIJAH MUHAMMAD AND THE NATION OF ISLAM DOES NOT WANT YOUR MONEY, BROTHER CASSIUS.
AND DO I LOOK LIKE I NEED IT?
YOU ARE GOING TO BE A CHAMPION, CASSIUS CLAY. WHOSE CHAMPION DO YOU WANT TO BE? THEIRS...OR YOURS?

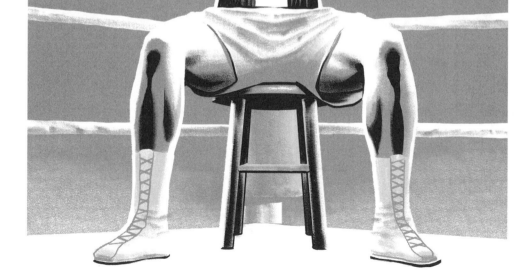

ROUND FOUR:
SONNY LISTON.
1964.

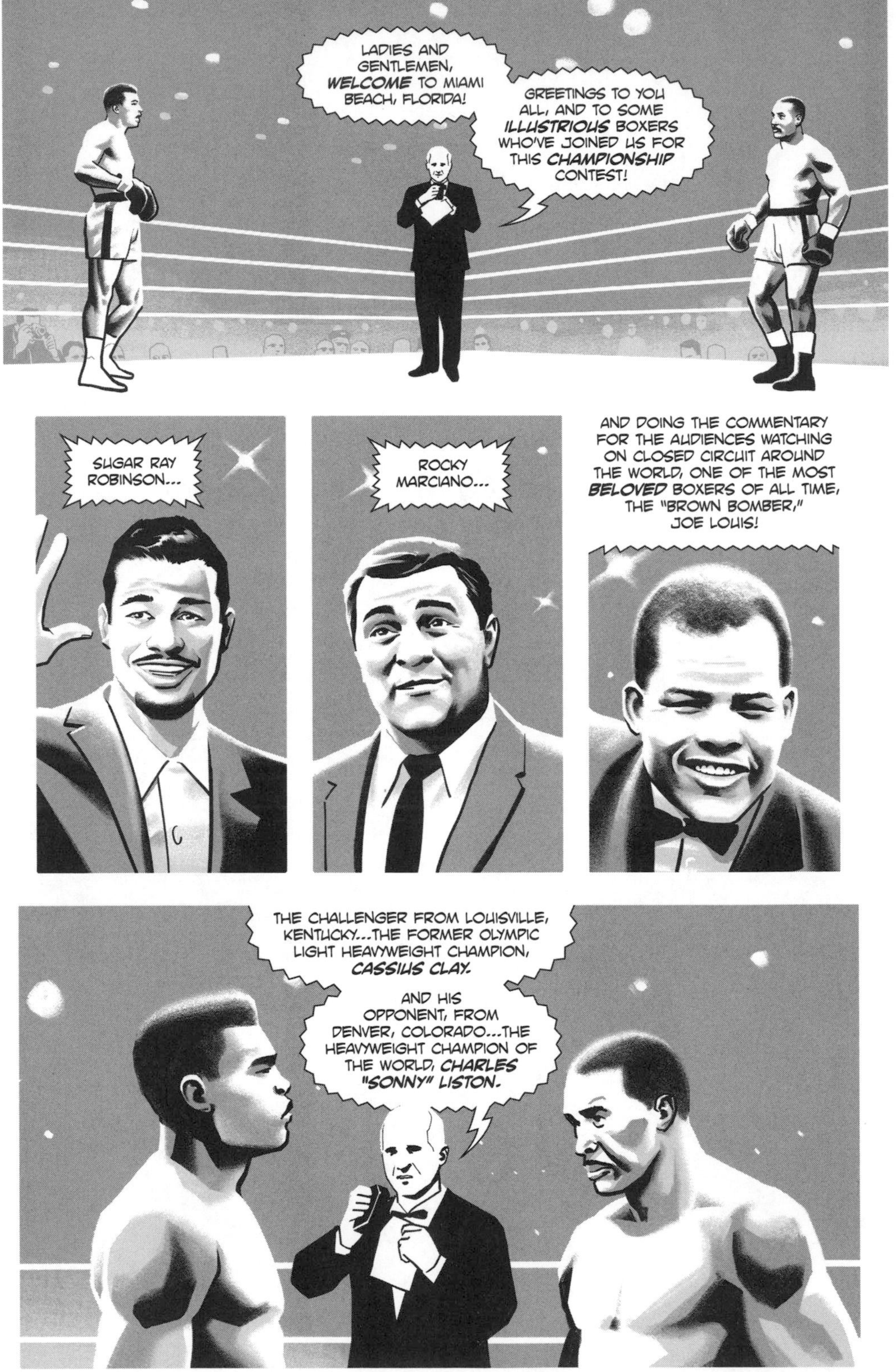
LADIES AND GENTLEMEN, WELCOME TO MIAMI BEACH, FLORIDA!
GREETINGS TO YOU ALL, AND TO SOME ILLUSTRIOUS BOXERS WHO'VE JOINED US FOR THIS CHAMPIONSHIP CONTEST!
SUGAR RAY ROBINSON...
ROCKY MARCIANO...
AND DOING THE COMMENTARY FOR THE AUDIENCES WATCHING ON CLOSED CIRCUIT AROUND THE WORLD, ONE OF THE MOST BELOVED BOXERS OF ALL TIME, THE "BROWN BOMBER," JOE LOUIS!
THE CHALLENGER FROM LOUISVILLE, KENTUCKY...THE FORMER OLYMPIC LIGHT HEAVYWEIGHT CHAMPION, CASSIUS CLAY.
AND HIS OPPONENT, FROM DENVER, COLORADO...THE HEAVYWEIGHT CHAMPION OF THE WORLD, CHARLES "SONNY" LISTON.

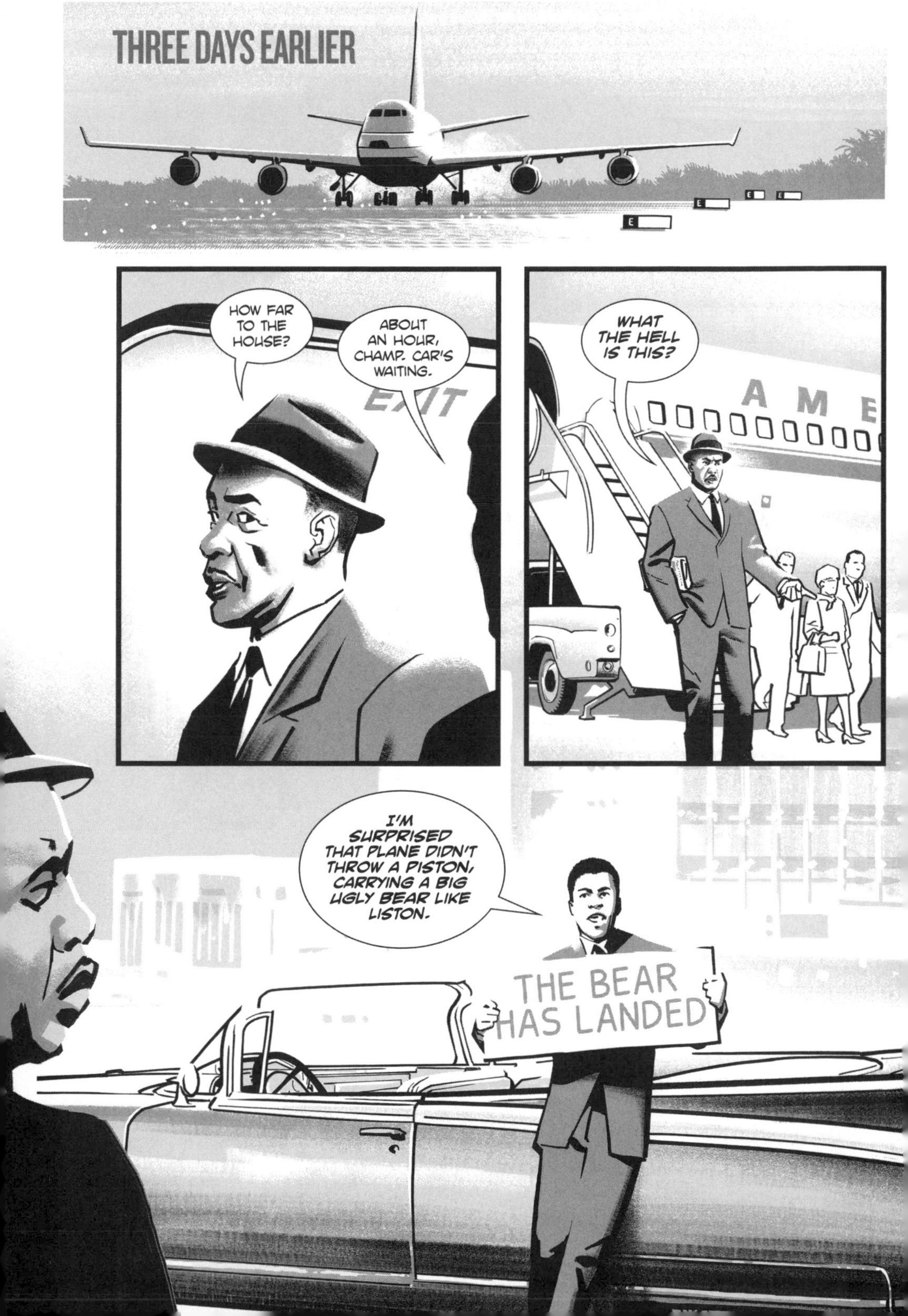
THREE DAYS EARLIER
HOW FAR TO THE HOUSE?
ABOUT AN HOUR, CHAMP. CAR'S WAITING.
EXIT
WHAT THE HELL IS THIS?
A M E
I'M SURPRISED THAT PLANE DIDN'T THROW A PISTON, CARRYING A BIG UGLY BEAR LIKE LISTON.
THE BEAR HAS LANDED

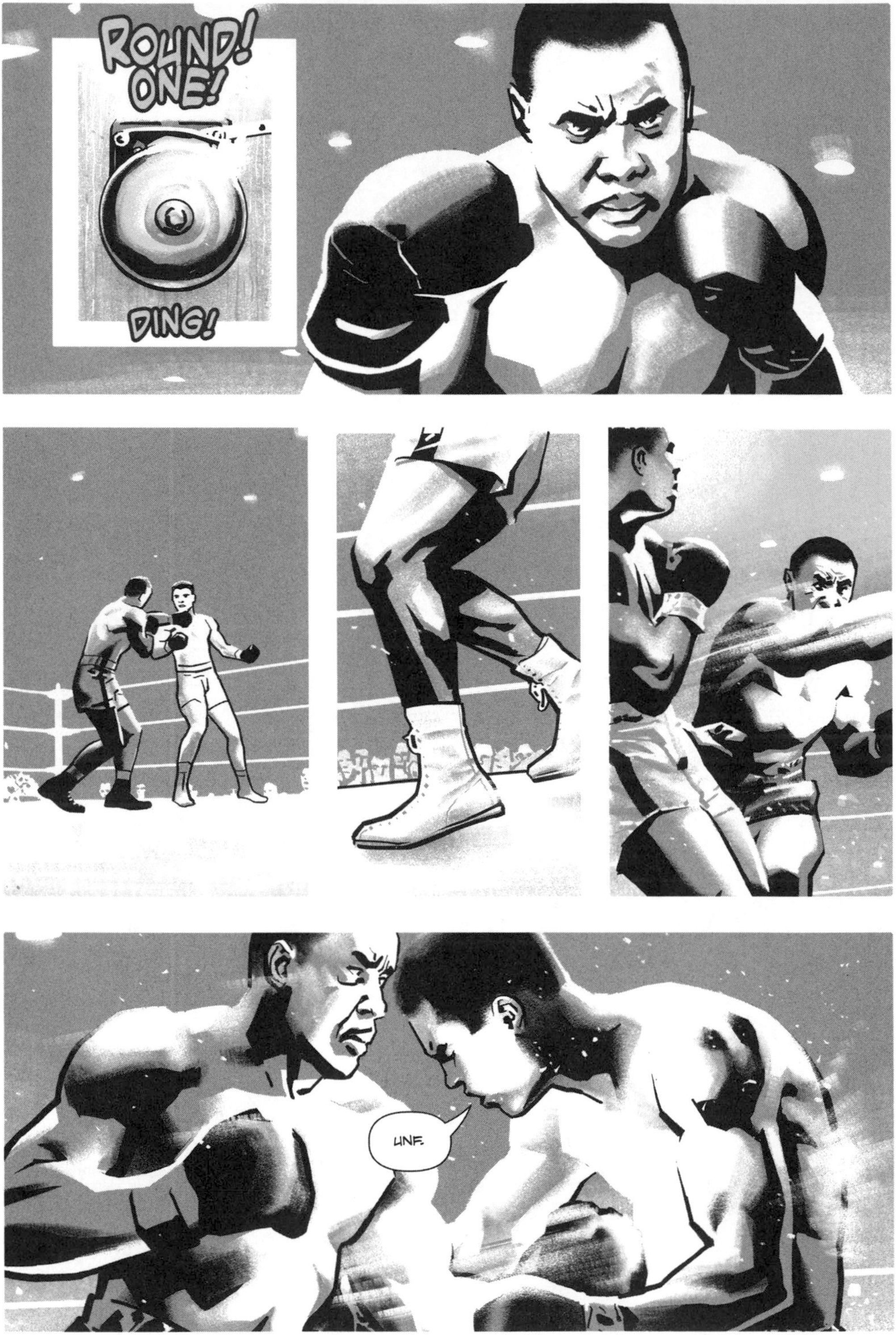
ROUND! ONE!
DING!
UNF.

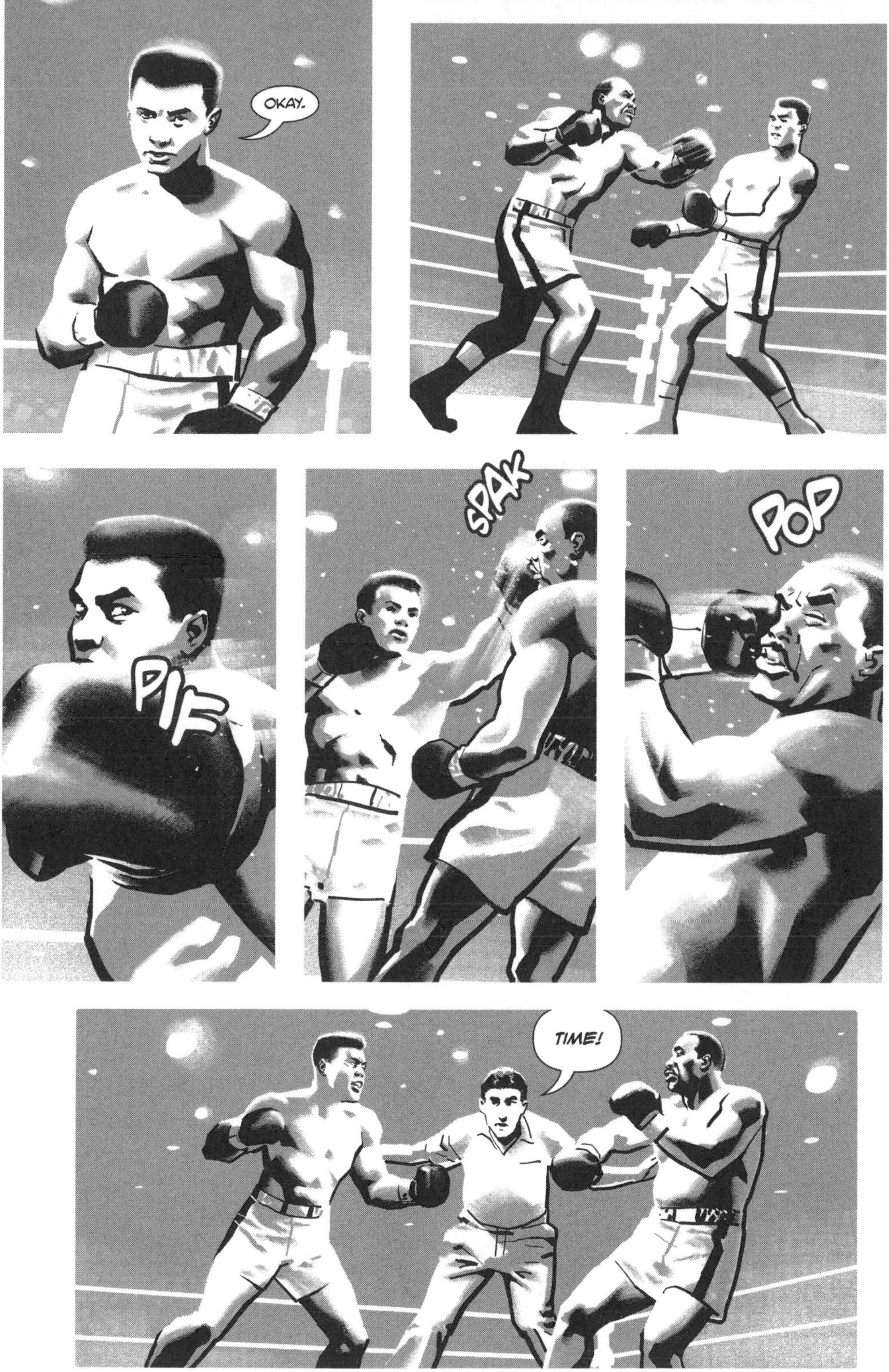
OKAY.
SPAK
POP
PIF
TIME!

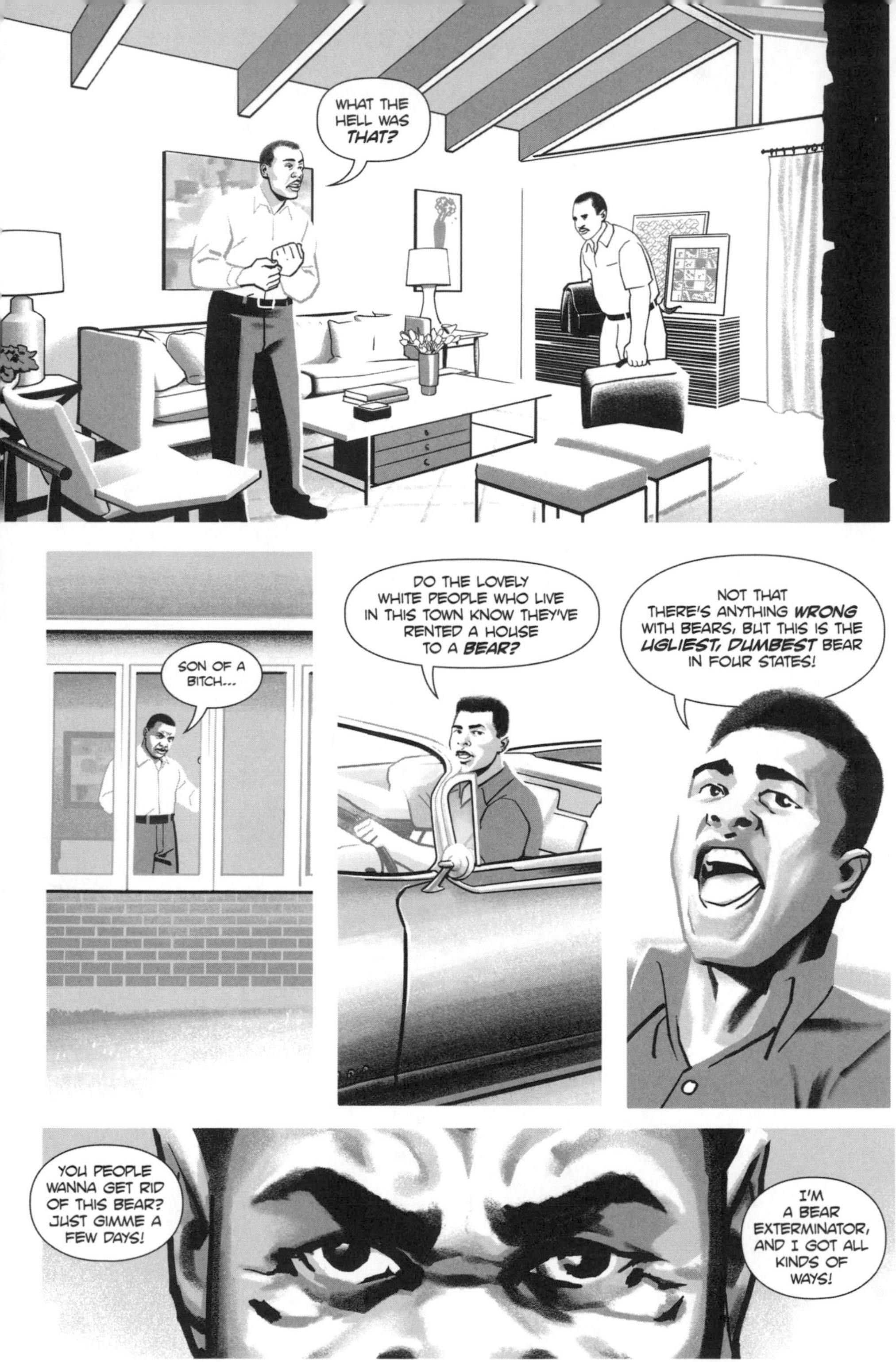
WHAT THE HELL WAS *THAT?*
SON OF A BITCH...
DO THE LOVELY WHITE PEOPLE WHO LIVE IN THIS TOWN KNOW THEY'VE RENTED A HOUSE TO A *BEAR?*
NOT THAT THERE'S ANYTHING *WRONG* WITH BEARS, BUT THIS IS THE *UGLIEST, DUMBEST* BEAR IN FOUR STATES!
YOU PEOPLE WANNA GET RID OF THIS BEAR? JUST GIMME A FEW DAYS!
I'M A BEAR EXTERMINATOR, AND I GOT ALL KINDS OF WAYS!

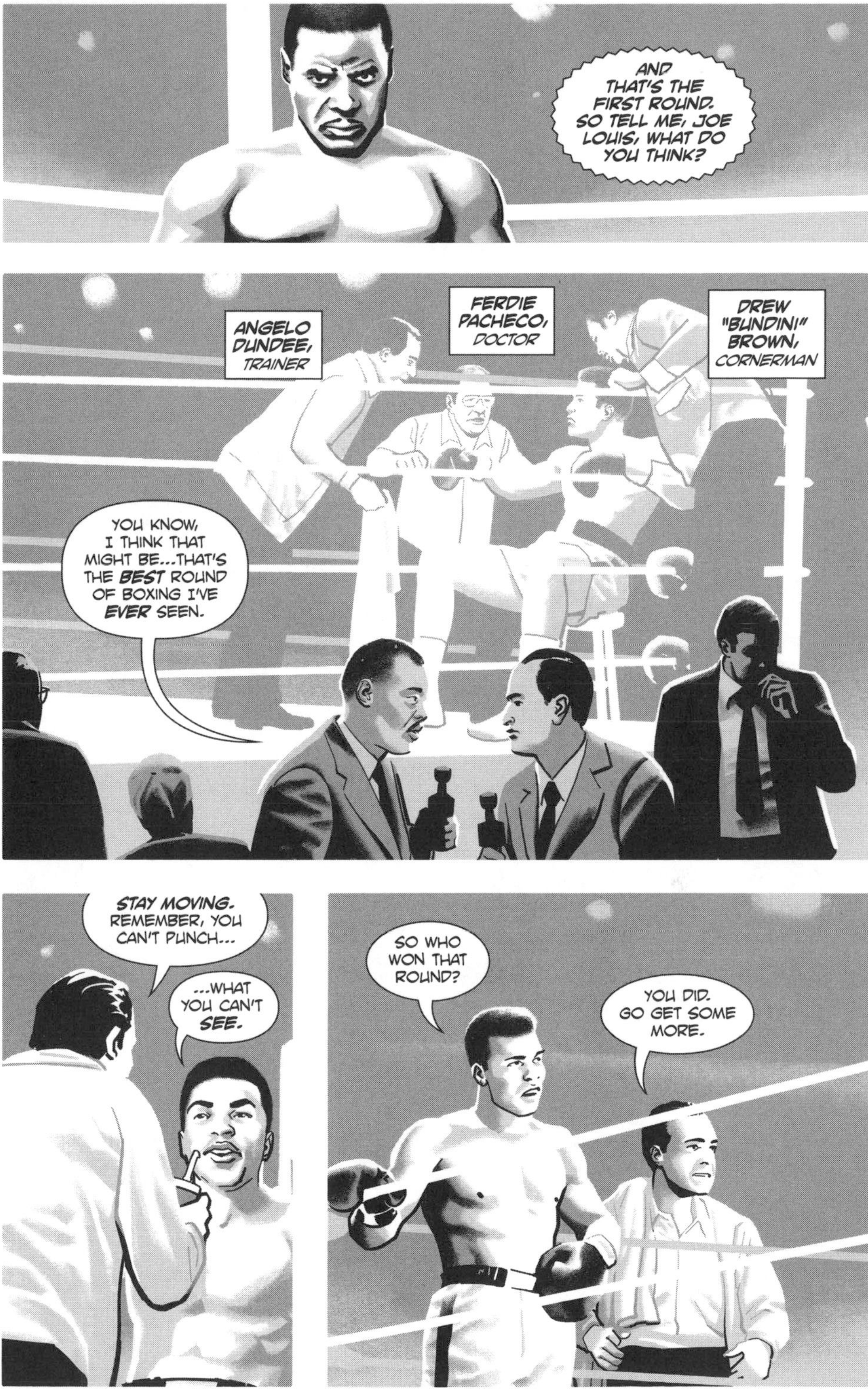
AND THAT'S THE FIRST ROUND. SO TELL ME, JOE LOUIS, WHAT DO YOU THINK?
ANGELO DUNDEE, TRAINER
FERDIE PACHECO, DOCTOR
DREW "BUNDINI" BROWN, CORNERMAN
YOU KNOW, I THINK THAT MIGHT BE...THAT'S THE BEST ROUND OF BOXING I'VE EVER SEEN.
STAY MOVING. REMEMBER, YOU CAN'T PUNCH...
...WHAT YOU CAN'T SEE.
SO WHO WON THAT ROUND?
YOU DID. GO GET SOME MORE.

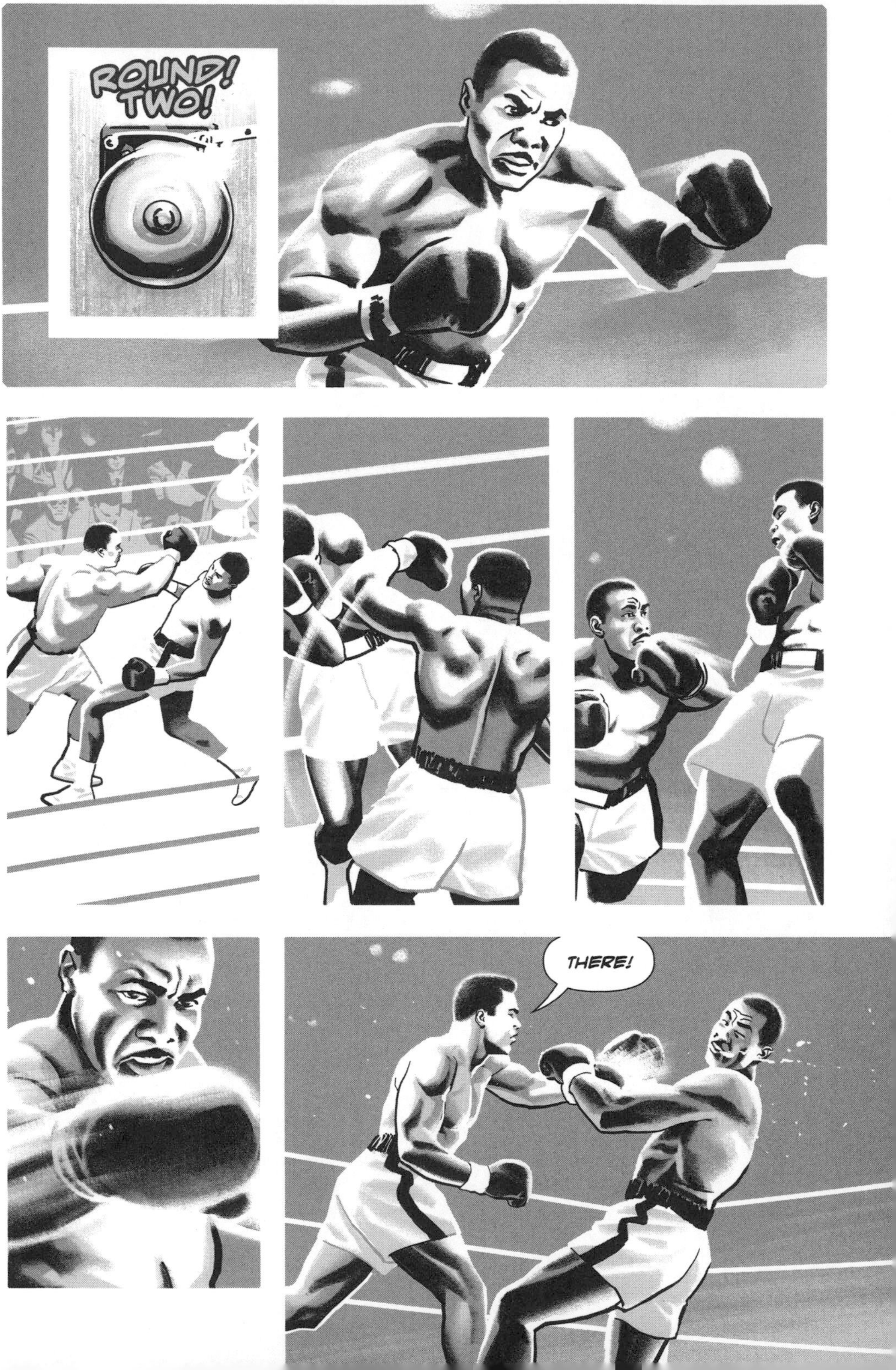
ROUND! TWO!
THERE!

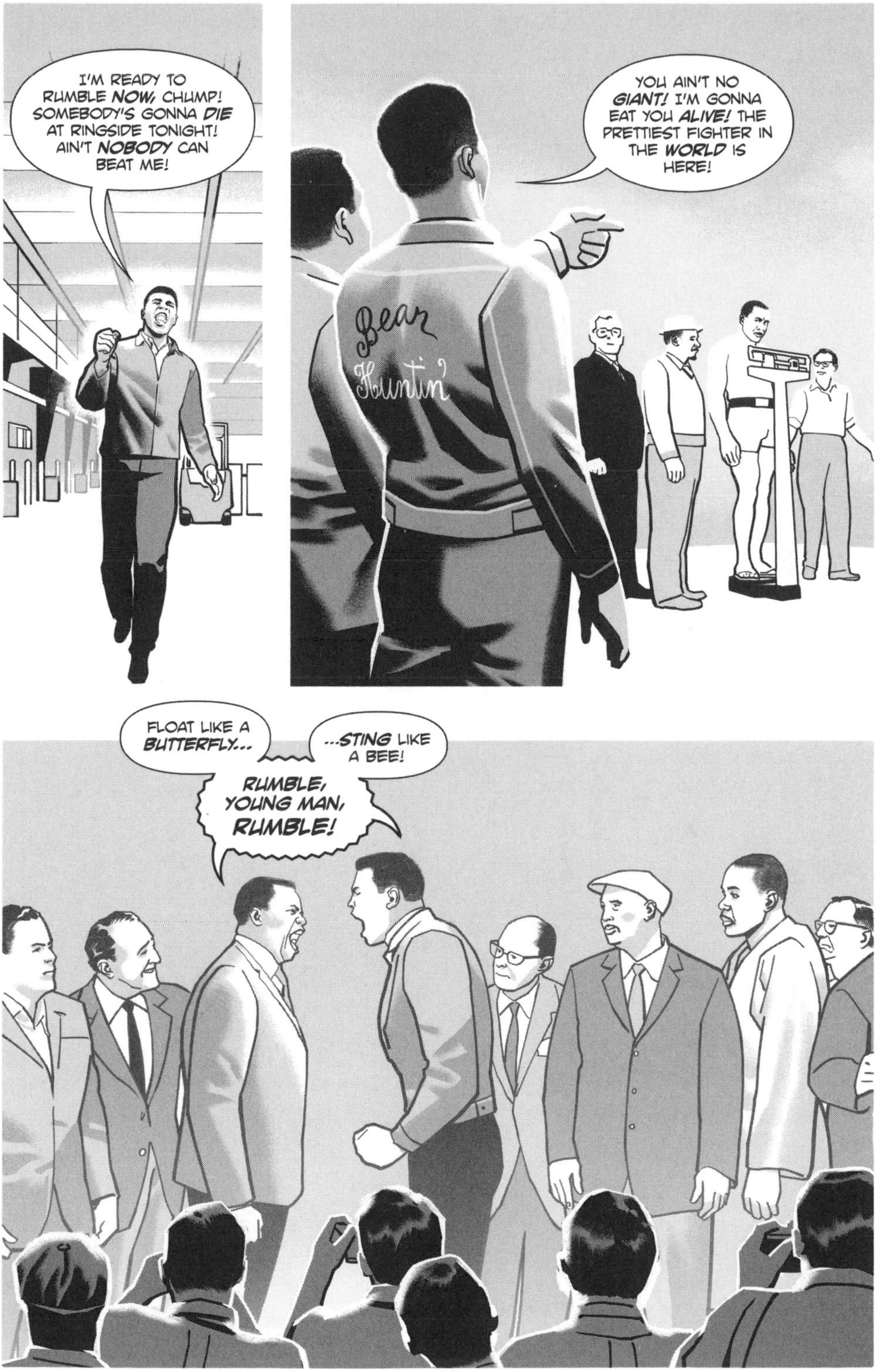
I'M READY TO RUMBLE NOW, CHUMP! SOMEBODY'S GONNA DIE AT RINGSIDE TONIGHT! AIN'T NOBODY CAN BEAT ME!
YOU AIN'T NO GIANT! I'M GONNA EAT YOU ALIVE! THE PRETTIEST FIGHTER IN THE WORLD IS HERE!
Bear Huntin'
FLOAT LIKE A BUTTERFLY...
...STING LIKE A BEE!
RUMBLE, YOUNG MAN, RUMBLE!

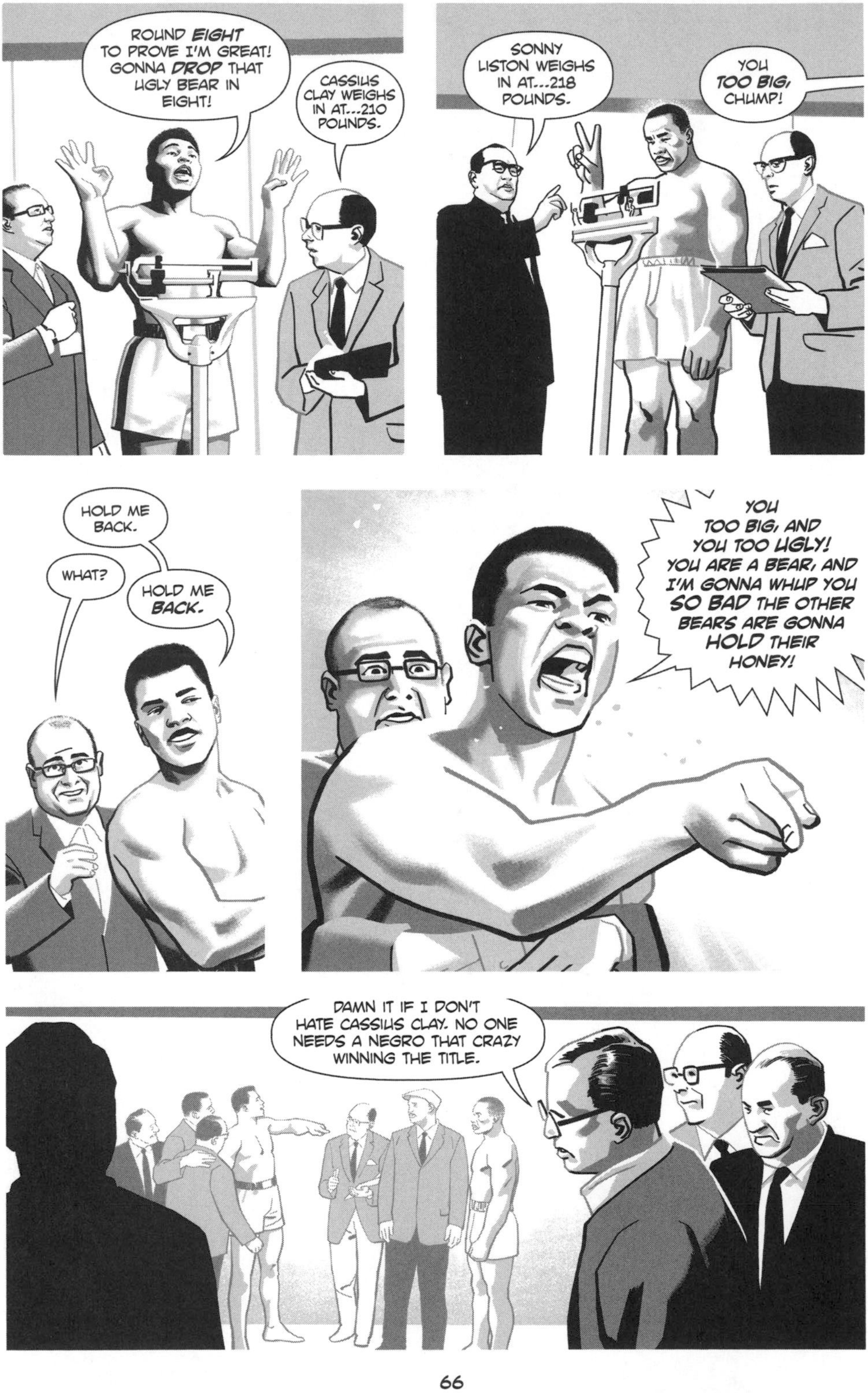
ROUND EIGHT TO PROVE I'M GREAT! GONNA DROP THAT UGLY BEAR IN EIGHT!
CASSIUS CLAY WEIGHS IN AT...210 POUNDS.
SONNY LISTON WEIGHS IN AT...218 POUNDS.
YOU TOO BIG, CHUMP!
HOLD ME BACK.
WHAT?
HOLD ME BACK.
YOU TOO BIG, AND YOU TOO UGLY! YOU ARE A BEAR, AND I'M GONNA WHUP YOU SO BAD THE OTHER BEARS ARE GONNA HOLD THEIR HONEY!
DAMN IT IF I DON'T HATE CASSIUS CLAY. NO ONE NEEDS A NEGRO THAT CRAZY WINNING THE TITLE.

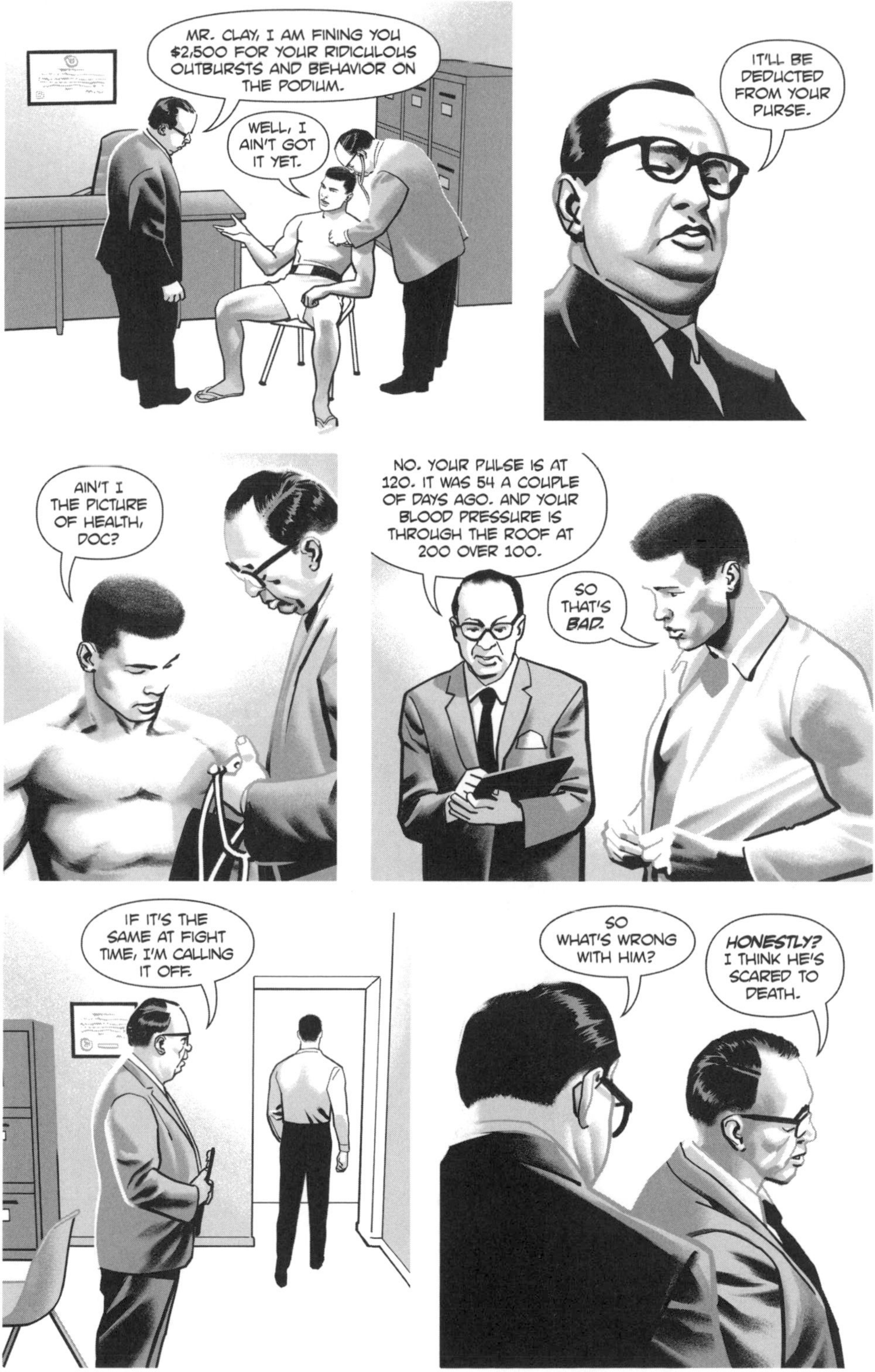
MR. CLAY, I AM FINING YOU $2,500 FOR YOUR RIDICULOUS OUTBURSTS AND BEHAVIOR ON THE PODIUM.
WELL, I AIN'T GOT IT YET.
IT'LL BE DEDUCTED FROM YOUR PURSE.
AIN'T I THE PICTURE OF HEALTH, DOC?
NO. YOUR PULSE IS AT 120. IT WAS 54 A COUPLE OF DAYS AGO. AND YOUR BLOOD PRESSURE IS THROUGH THE ROOF AT 200 OVER 100.
SO THAT'S *BAD.*
IF IT'S THE SAME AT FIGHT TIME, I'M CALLING IT OFF.
SO WHAT'S WRONG WITH HIM?
HONESTLY? I THINK HE'S SCARED TO DEATH.

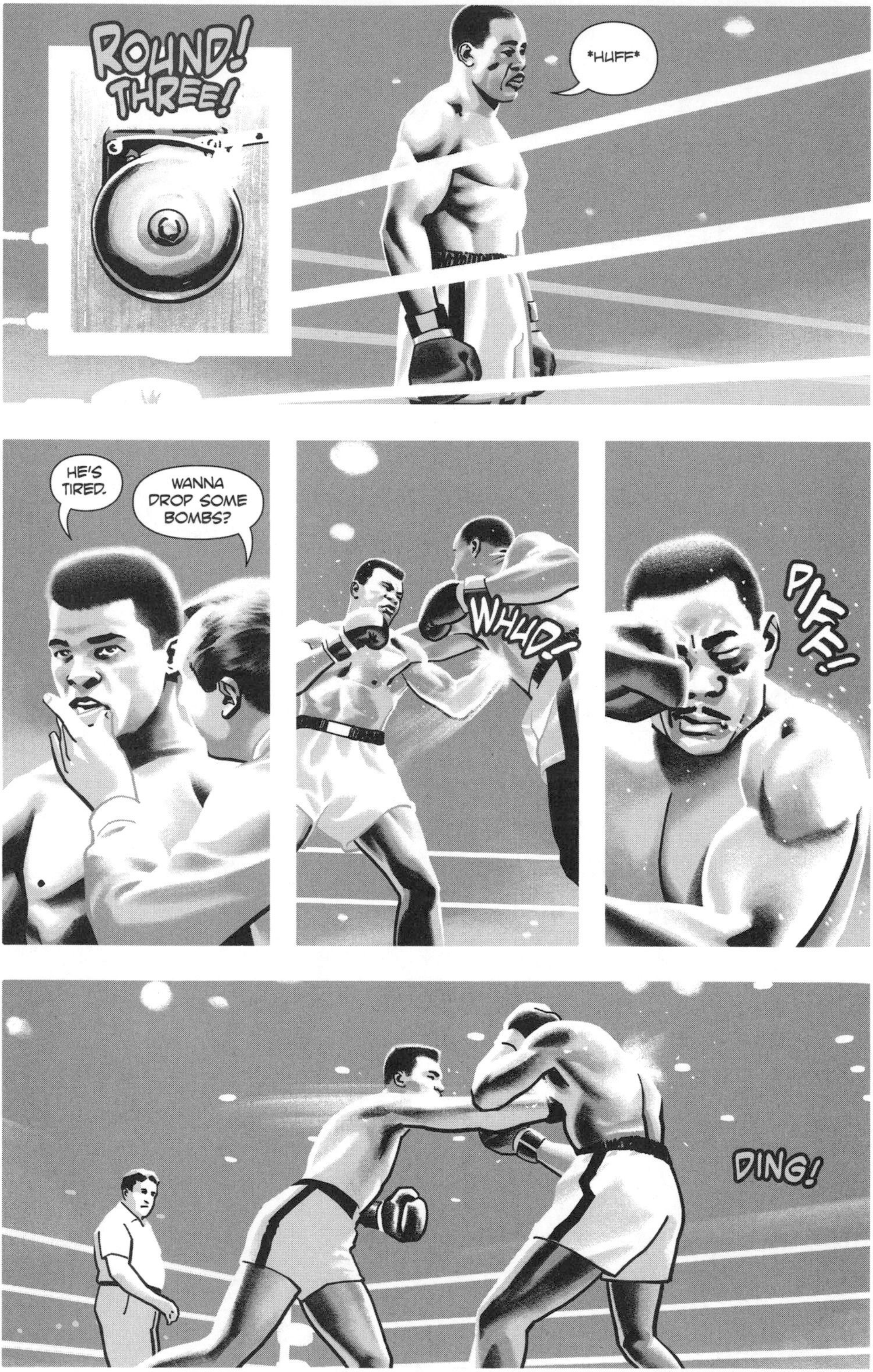
ROUND! THREE!
HUFF
HE'S TIRED.
WANNA DROP SOME BOMBS?
WHUD!
PIFF!
DING!

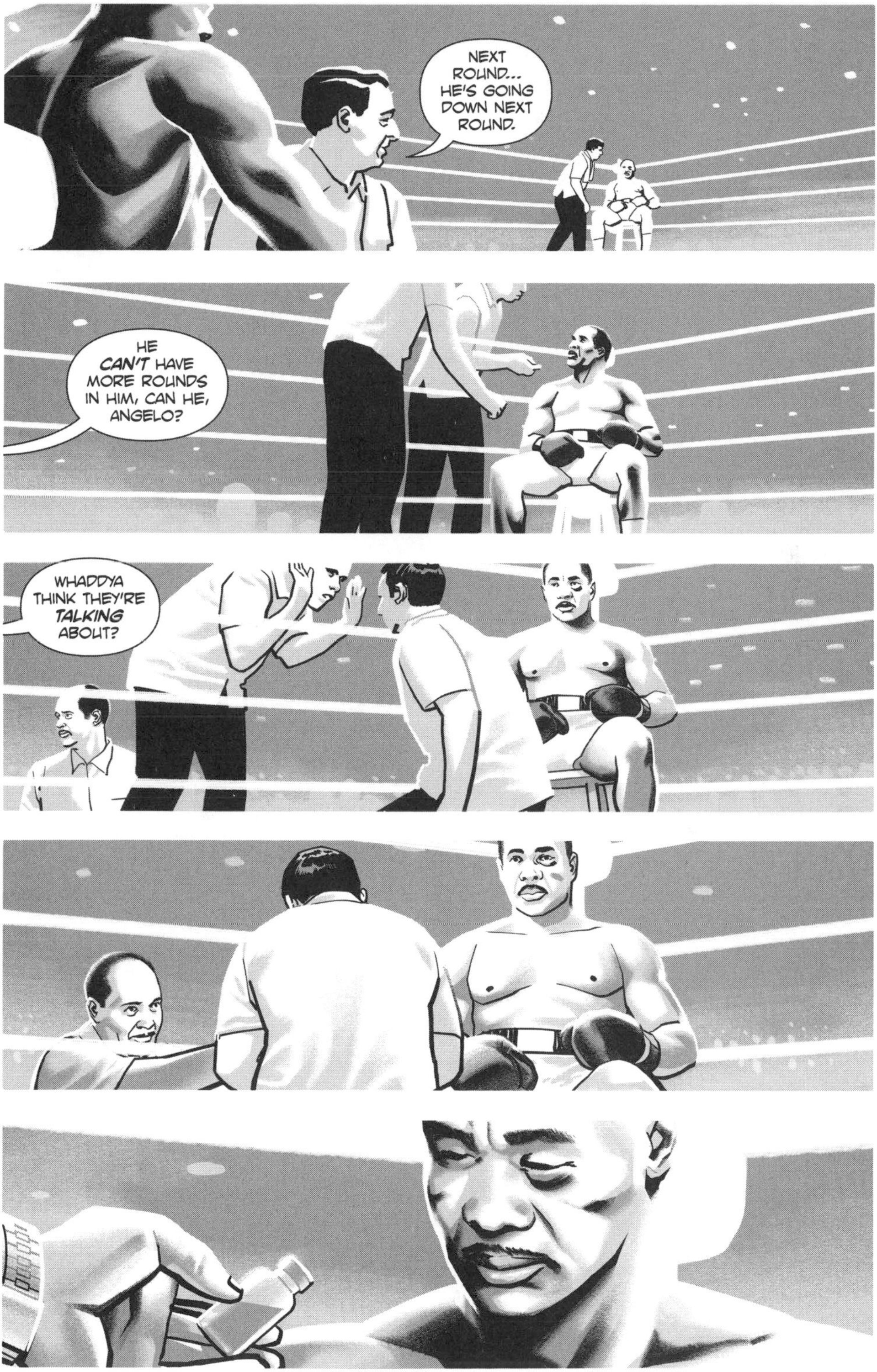
NEXT ROUND... HE'S GOING DOWN NEXT ROUND.
HE CAN'T HAVE MORE ROUNDS IN HIM, CAN HE, ANGELO?
WHADDYA THINK THEY'RE TALKING ABOUT?

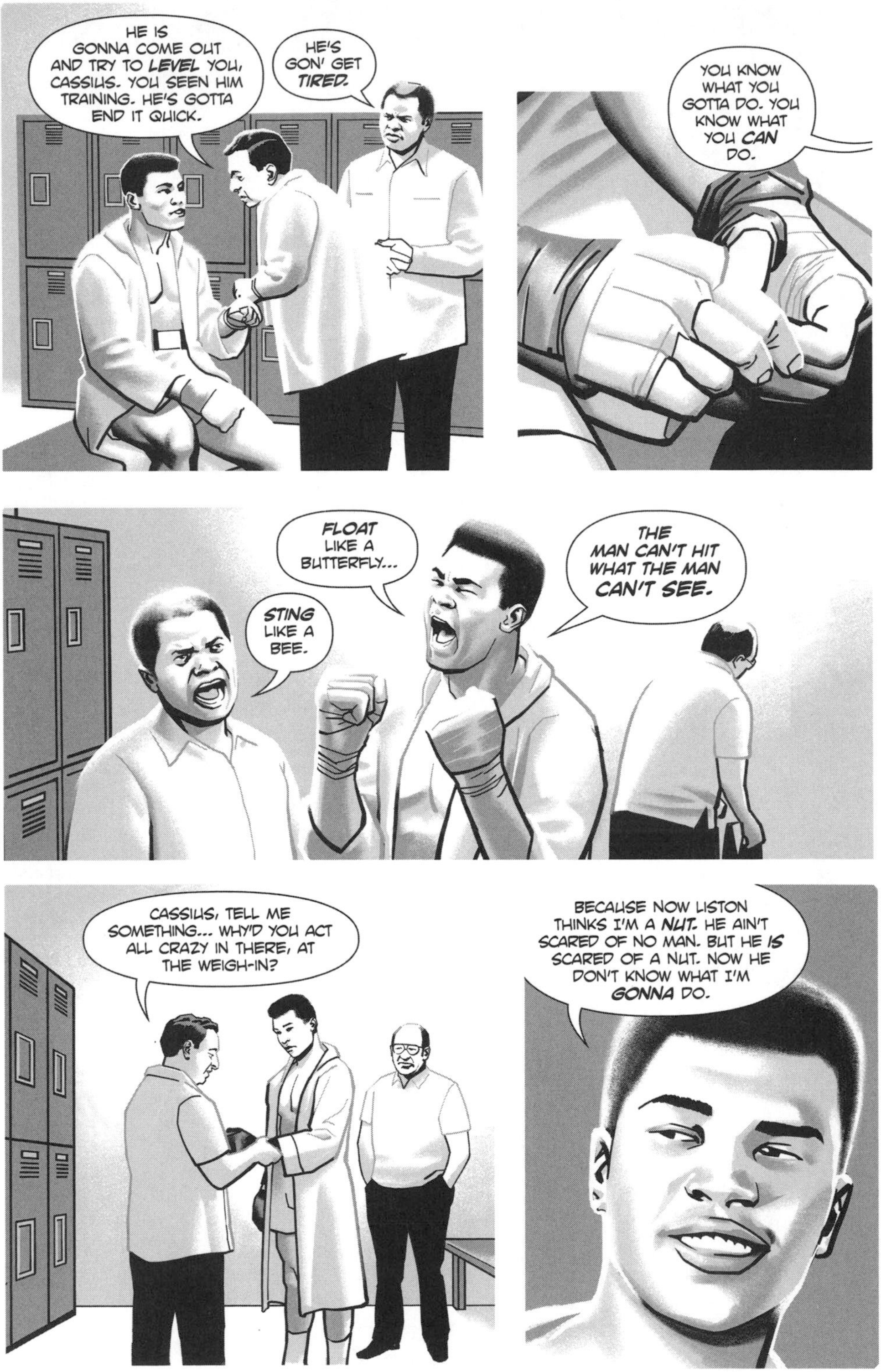
HE IS GONNA COME OUT AND TRY TO LEVEL YOU, CASSIUS. YOU SEEN HIM TRAINING. HE'S GOTTA END IT QUICK.
HE'S GON' GET TIRED.
YOU KNOW WHAT YOU GOTTA DO. YOU KNOW WHAT YOU CAN DO.
FLOAT LIKE A BUTTERFLY...
STING LIKE A BEE.
THE MAN CAN'T HIT WHAT THE MAN CAN'T SEE.
CASSIUS, TELL ME SOMETHING... WHY'D YOU ACT ALL CRAZY IN THERE, AT THE WEIGH-IN?
BECAUSE NOW LISTON THINKS I'M A NUT. HE AIN'T SCARED OF NO MAN. BUT HE IS SCARED OF A NUT. NOW HE DON'T KNOW WHAT I'M GONNA DO.

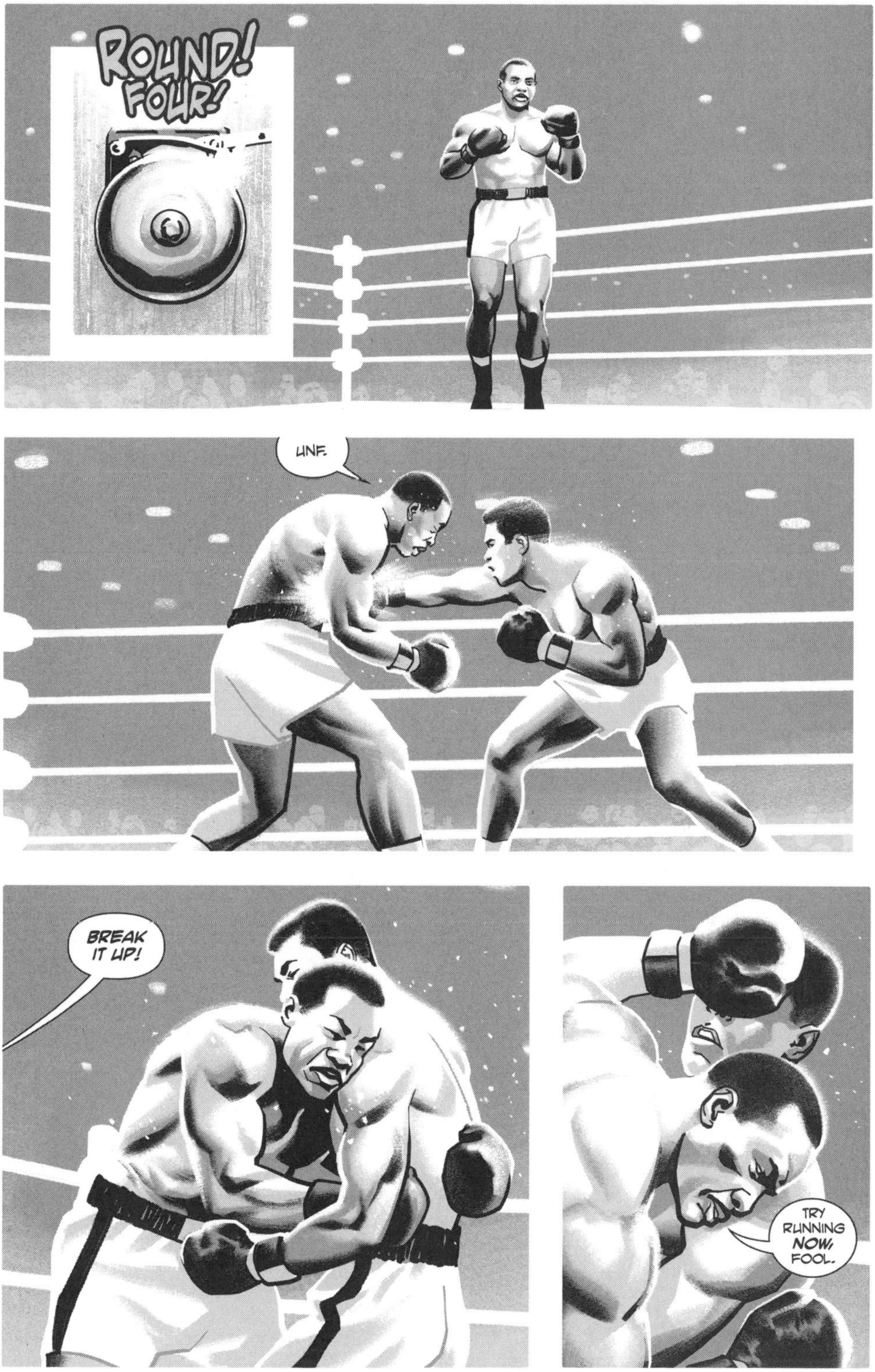
ROUND! FOUR!
UNF.
BREAK IT UP!
TRY RUNNING NOW, FOOL.

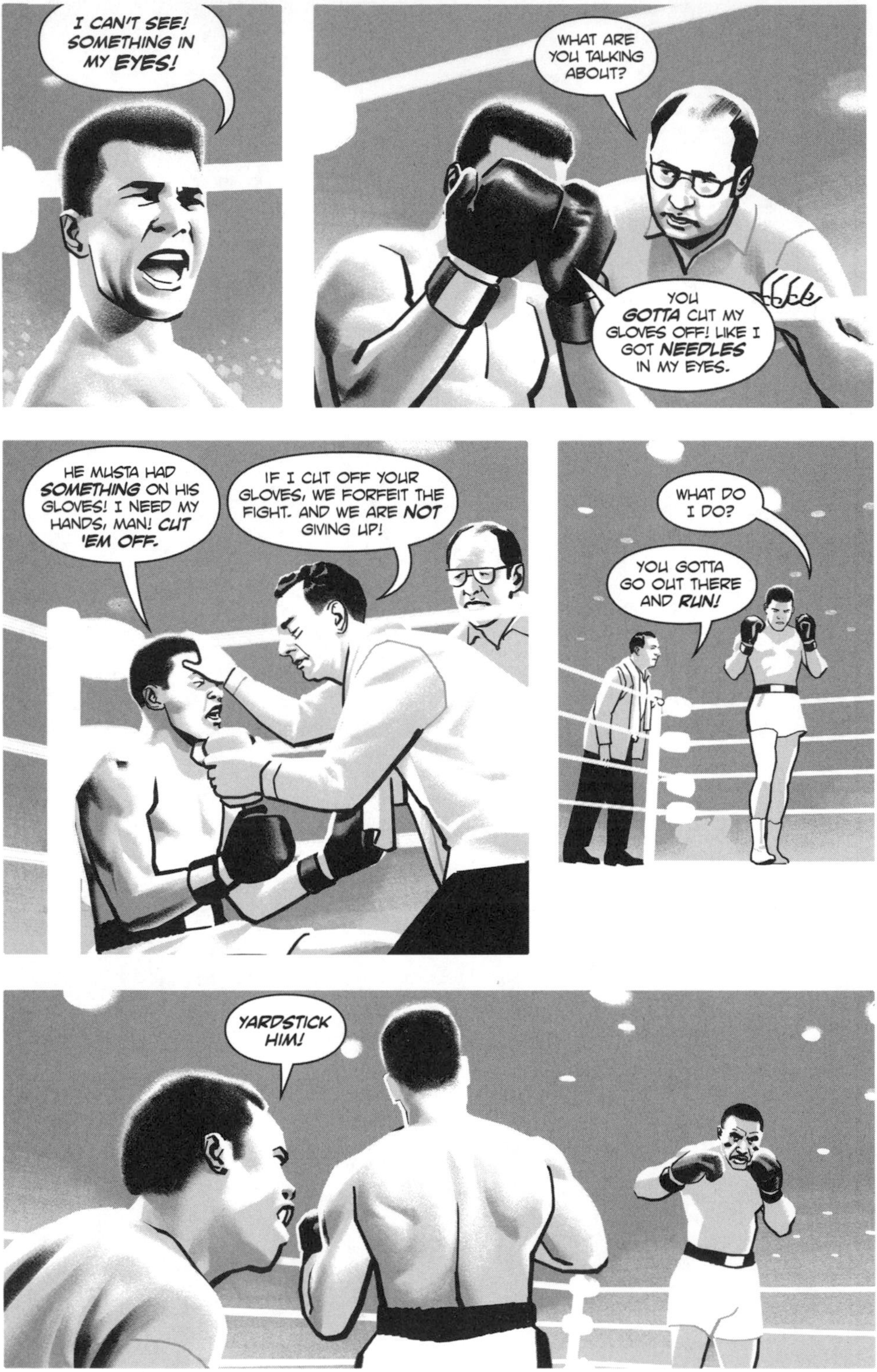
I CAN'T SEE! SOMETHING IN MY EYES!
WHAT ARE YOU TALKING ABOUT?
YOU GOTTA CUT MY GLOVES OFF! LIKE I GOT NEEDLES IN MY EYES.
HE MUSTA HAD SOMETHING ON HIS GLOVES! I NEED MY HANDS, MAN! CUT 'EM OFF.
IF I CUT OFF YOUR GLOVES, WE FORFEIT THE FIGHT. AND WE ARE NOT GIVING UP!
WHAT DO I DO?
YOU GOTTA GO OUT THERE AND RUN!
YARDSTICK HIM!

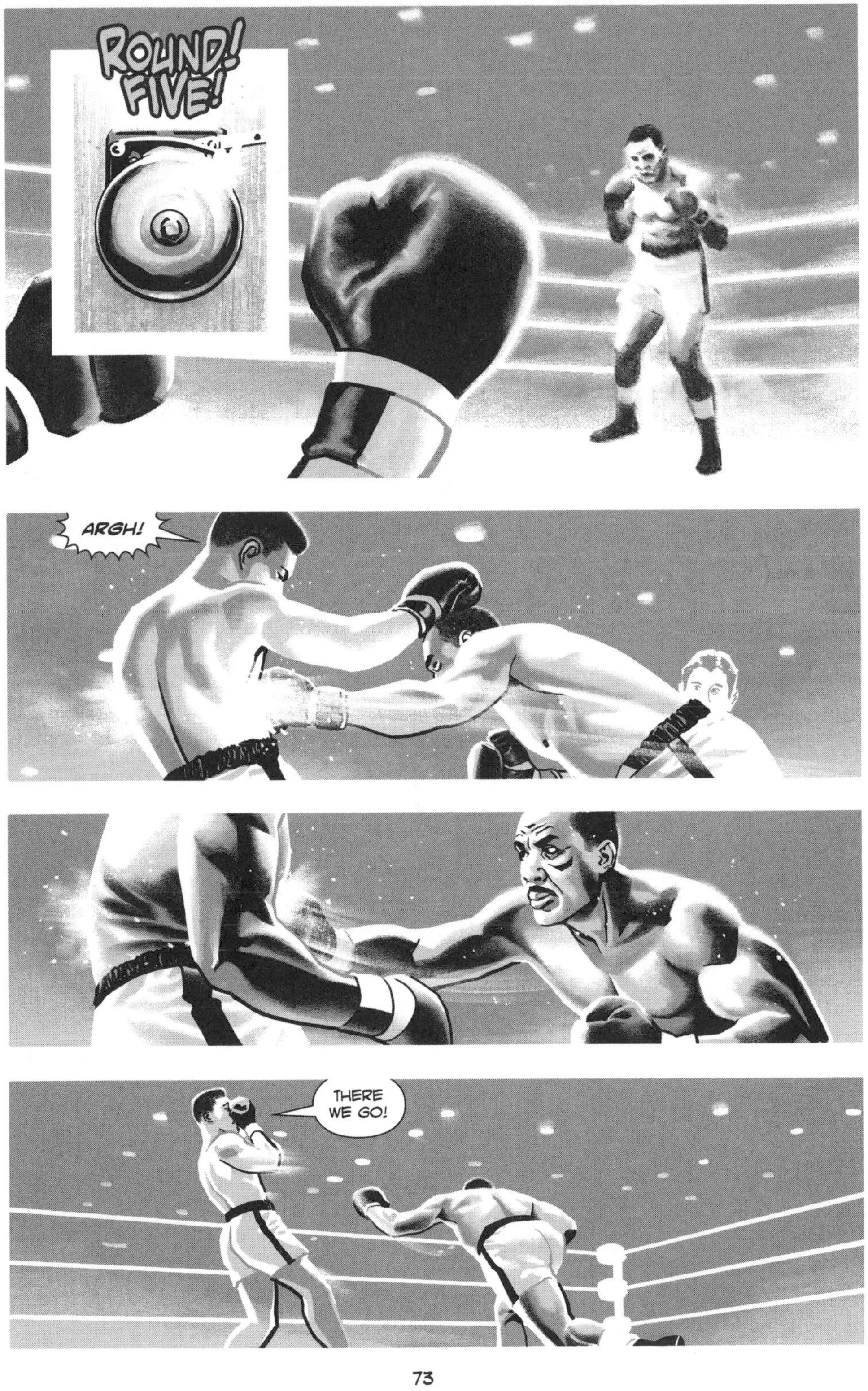
ROUND! FIVE!
ARGH!
THERE WE GO!

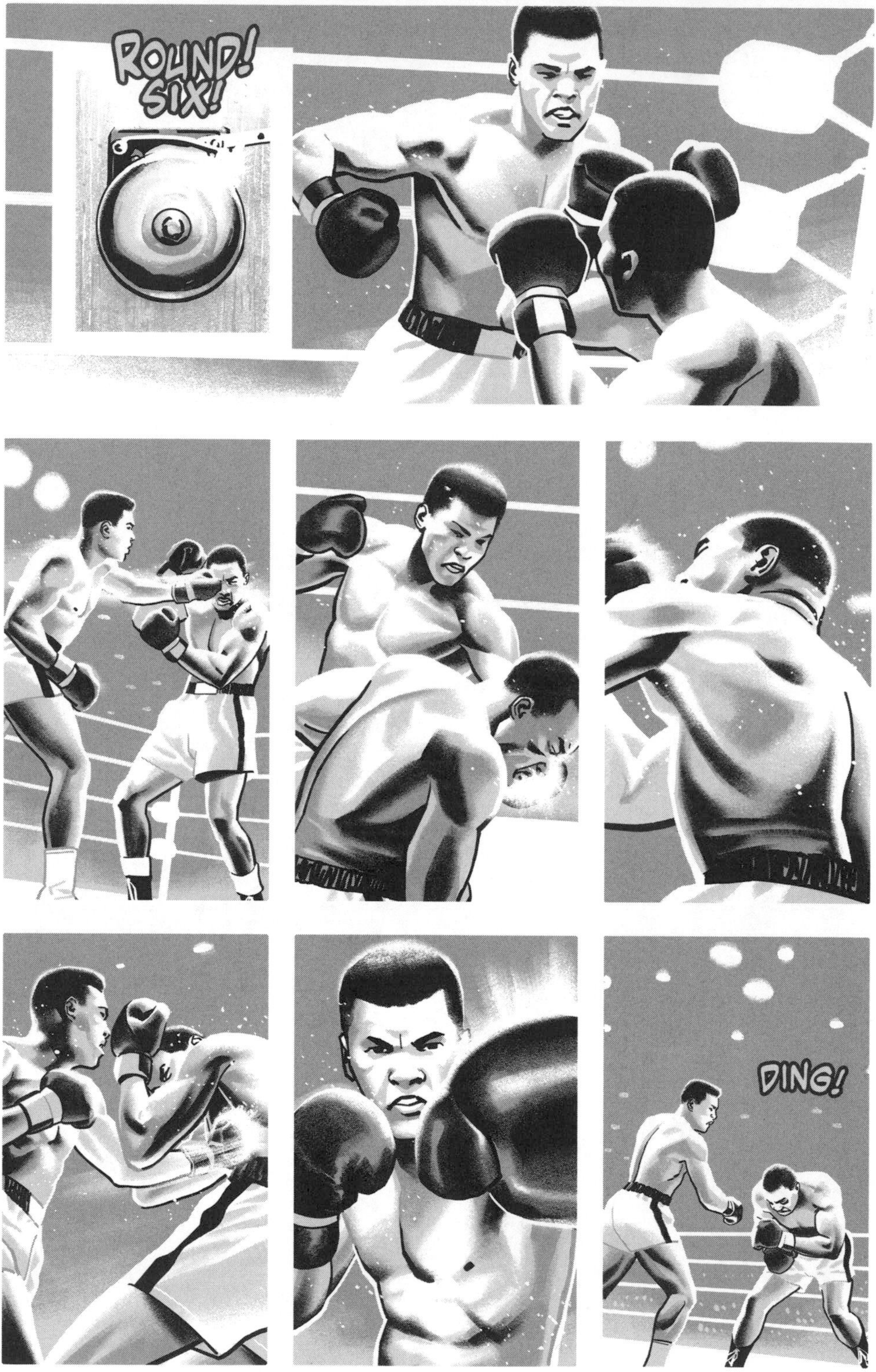
ROUND! SIX!
DING!

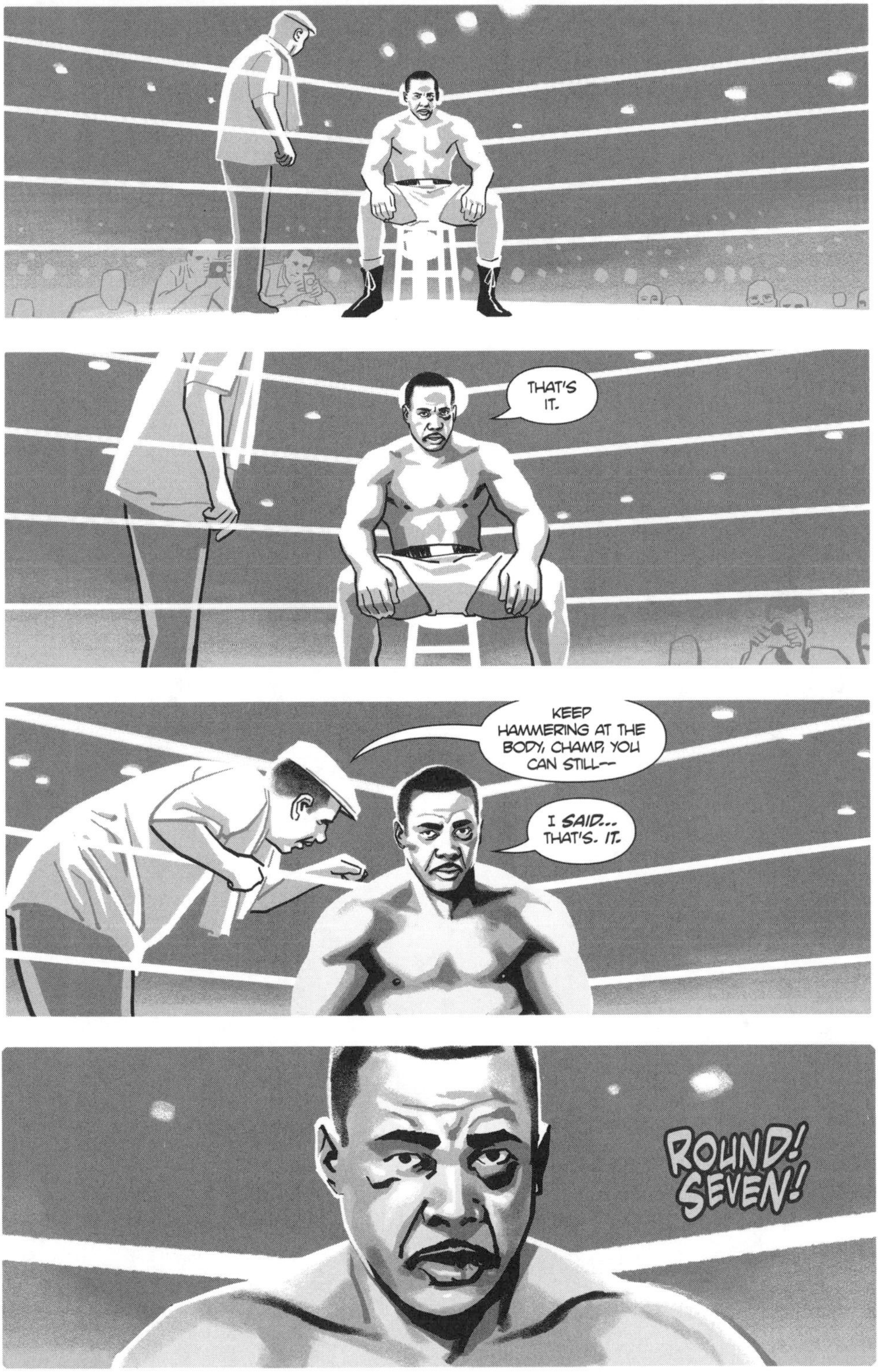
THAT'S IT.
KEEP HAMMERING AT THE BODY, CHAMP, YOU CAN STILL--
I SAID... THAT'S. IT.
ROUND! SEVEN!

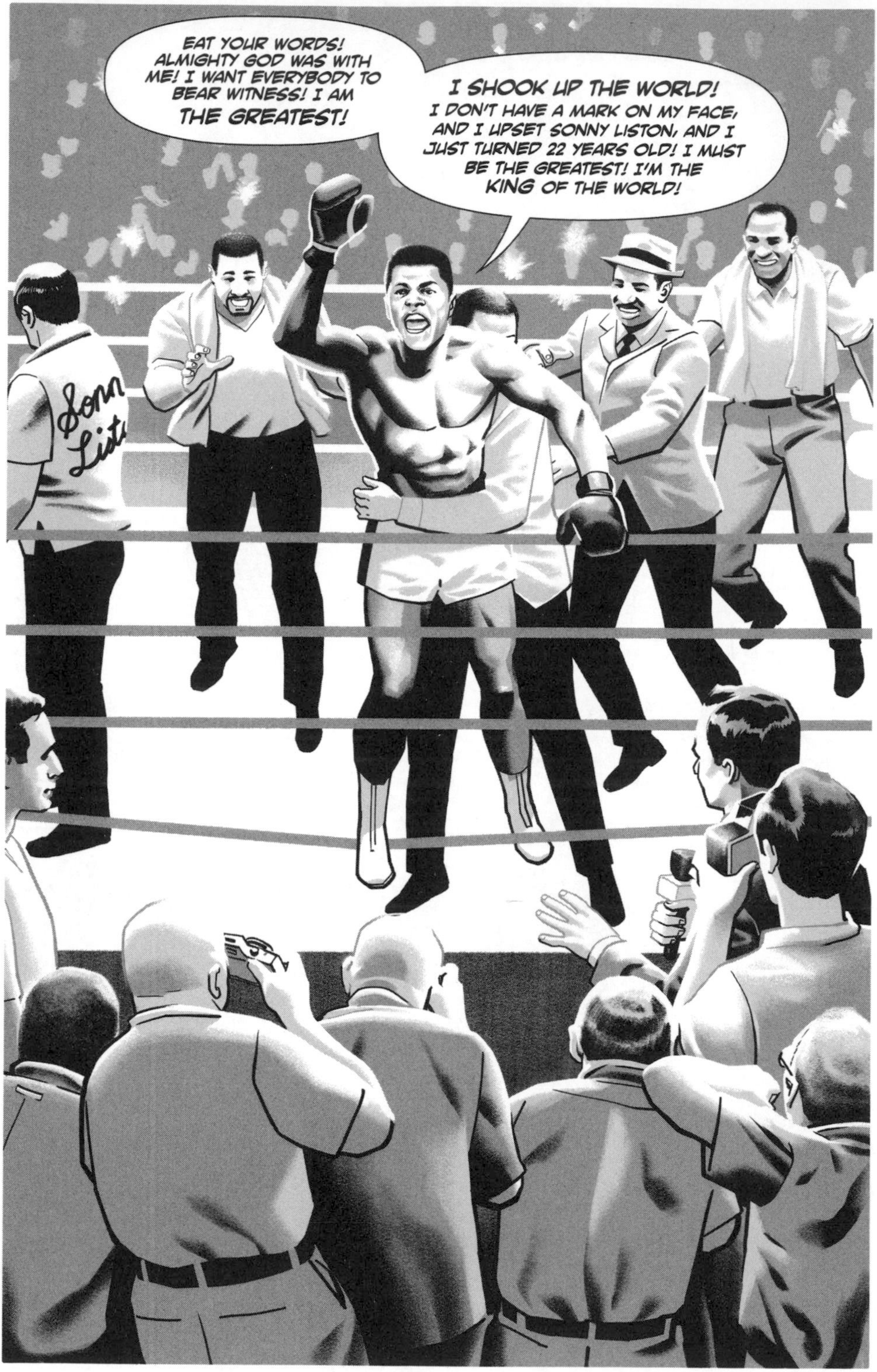
EAT YOUR WORDS! ALMIGHTY GOD WAS WITH ME! I WANT EVERYBODY TO BEAR WITNESS! I AM THE GREATEST!
I SHOOK UP THE WORLD! I DON'T HAVE A MARK ON MY FACE, AND I UPSET SONNY LISTON, AND I JUST TURNED 22 YEARS OLD! I MUST BE THE GREATEST! I'M THE KING OF THE WORLD!
Sonny Liston

ROUND FIVE:
MEDIA. 1967.

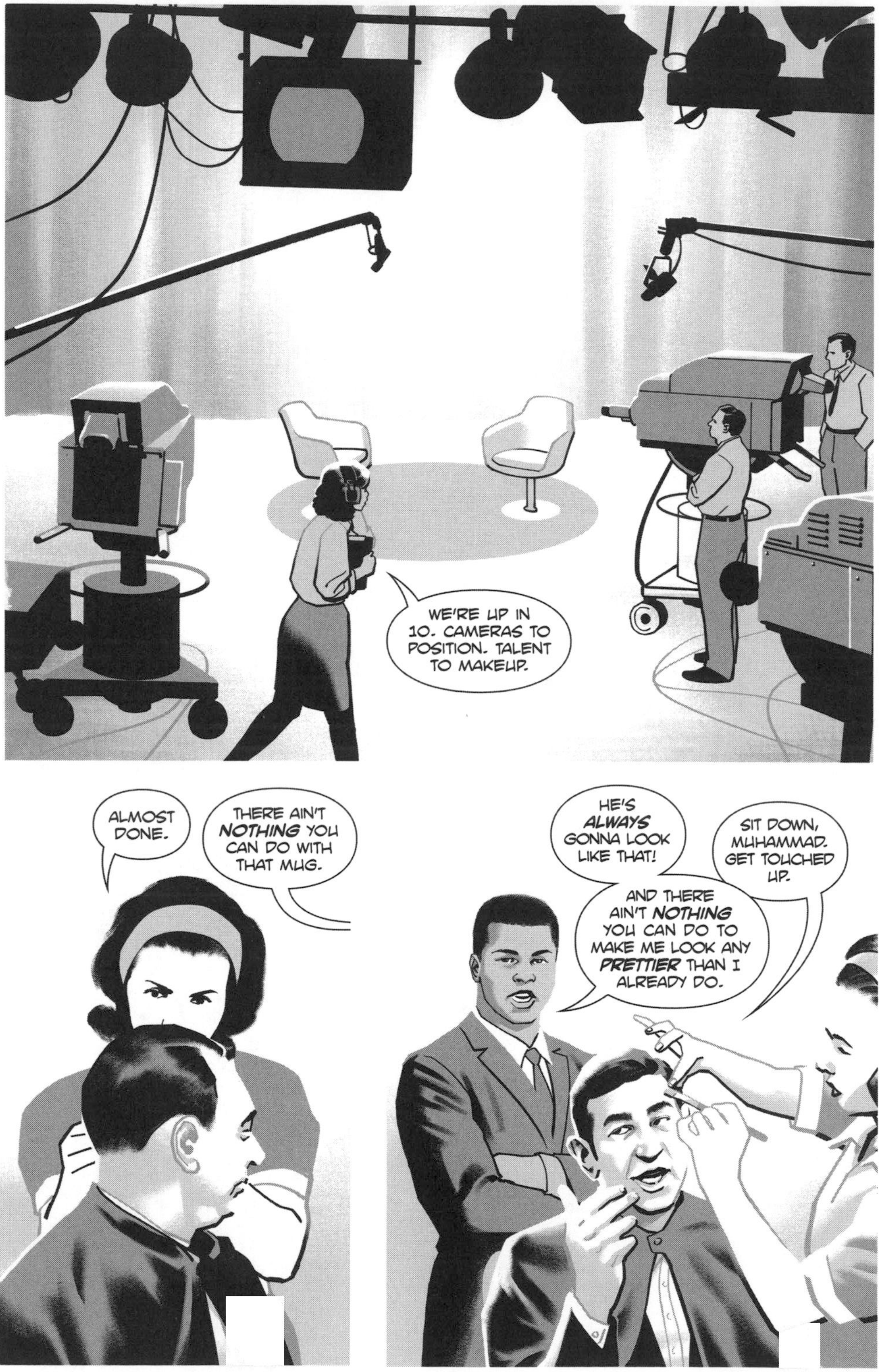

WE'RE UP IN 10. CAMERAS TO POSITION. TALENT TO MAKEUP.
ALMOST DONE.
THERE AIN'T ***NOTHING*** YOU CAN DO WITH THAT MUG.
HE'S ***ALWAYS*** GONNA LOOK LIKE THAT!
AND THERE AIN'T ***NOTHING*** YOU CAN DO TO MAKE ME LOOK ANY ***PRETTIER*** THAN I ALREADY DO.
SIT DOWN, MUHAMMAD. GET TOUCHED UP.

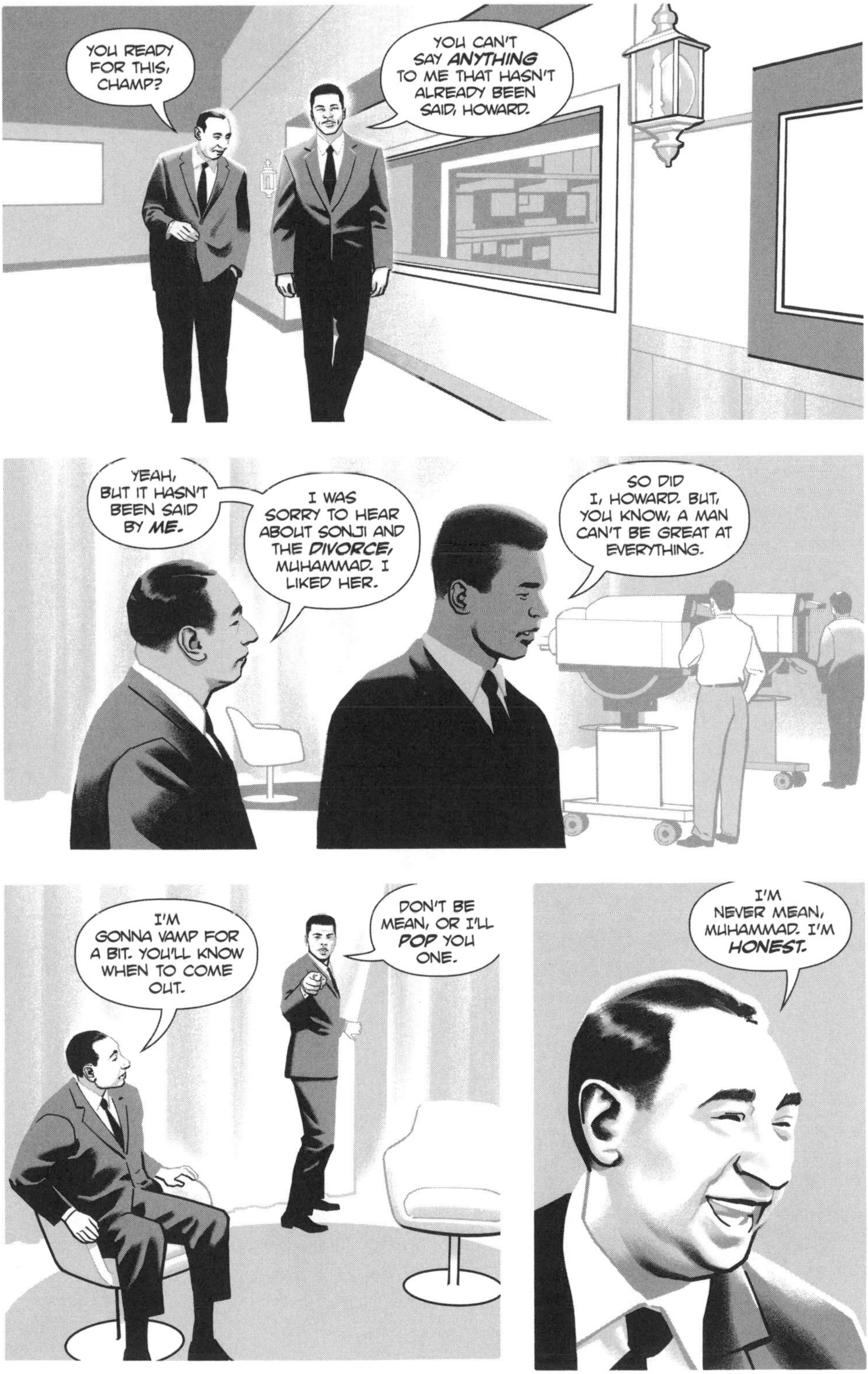
YOU READY FOR THIS, CHAMP?
YOU CAN'T SAY ANYTHING TO ME THAT HASN'T ALREADY BEEN SAID, HOWARD.
YEAH, BUT IT HASN'T BEEN SAID BY ME.
I WAS SORRY TO HEAR ABOUT SONJI AND THE DIVORCE, MUHAMMAD. I LIKED HER.
SO DID I, HOWARD. BUT, YOU KNOW, A MAN CAN'T BE GREAT AT EVERYTHING.
I'M GONNA VAMP FOR A BIT. YOU'LL KNOW WHEN TO COME OUT.
DON'T BE MEAN, OR I'LL POP YOU ONE.
I'M NEVER MEAN, MUHAMMAD. I'M HONEST.

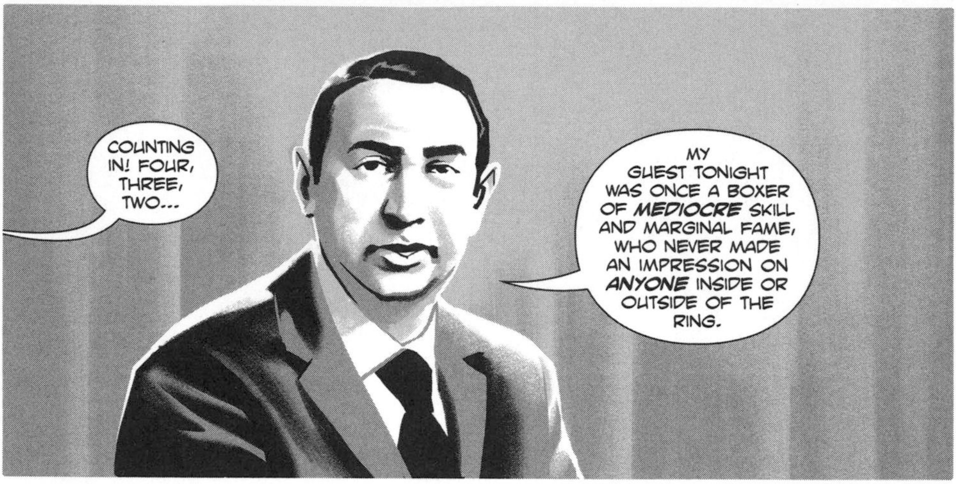
COUNTING IN! FOUR, THREE, TWO...
MY GUEST TONIGHT WAS ONCE A BOXER OF MEDIOCRE SKILL AND MARGINAL FAME, WHO NEVER MADE AN IMPRESSION ON ANYONE INSIDE OR OUTSIDE OF THE RING.

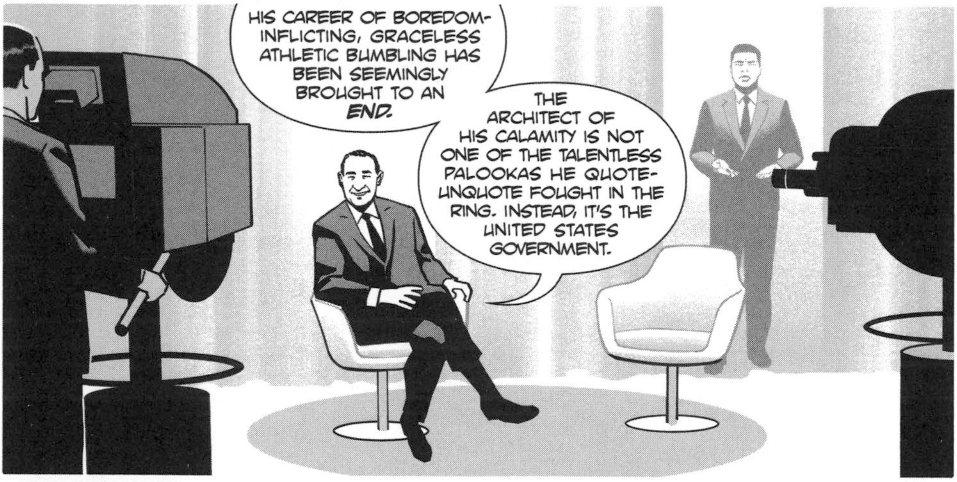
HIS CAREER OF BOREDOM-INFLICTING, GRACELESS ATHLETIC BUMBLING HAS BEEN SEEMINGLY BROUGHT TO AN END.
THE ARCHITECT OF HIS CALAMITY IS NOT ONE OF THE TALENTLESS PALOOKAS HE QUOTE-UNQUOTE FOUGHT IN THE RING. INSTEAD, IT'S THE UNITED STATES GOVERNMENT.

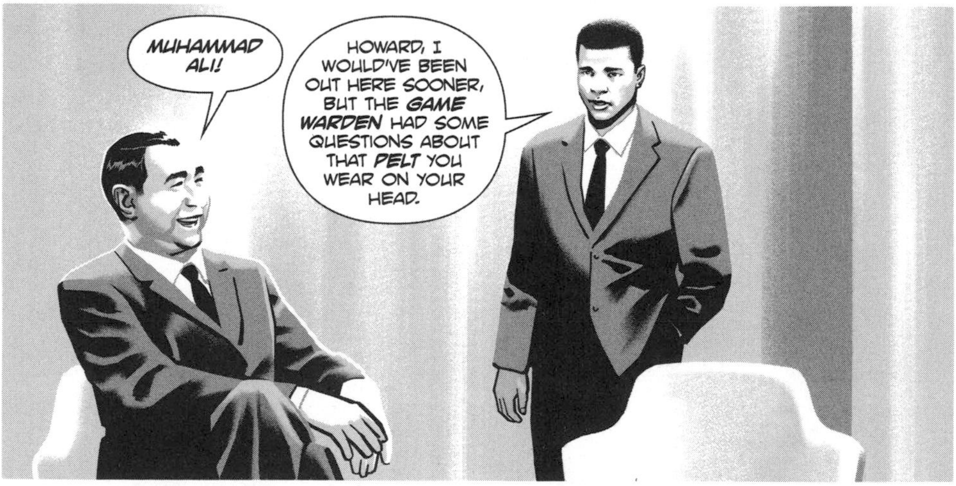
MUHAMMAD ALI!
HOWARD, I WOULD'VE BEEN OUT HERE SOONER, BUT THE GAME WARDEN HAD SOME QUESTIONS ABOUT THAT PELT YOU WEAR ON YOUR HEAD.

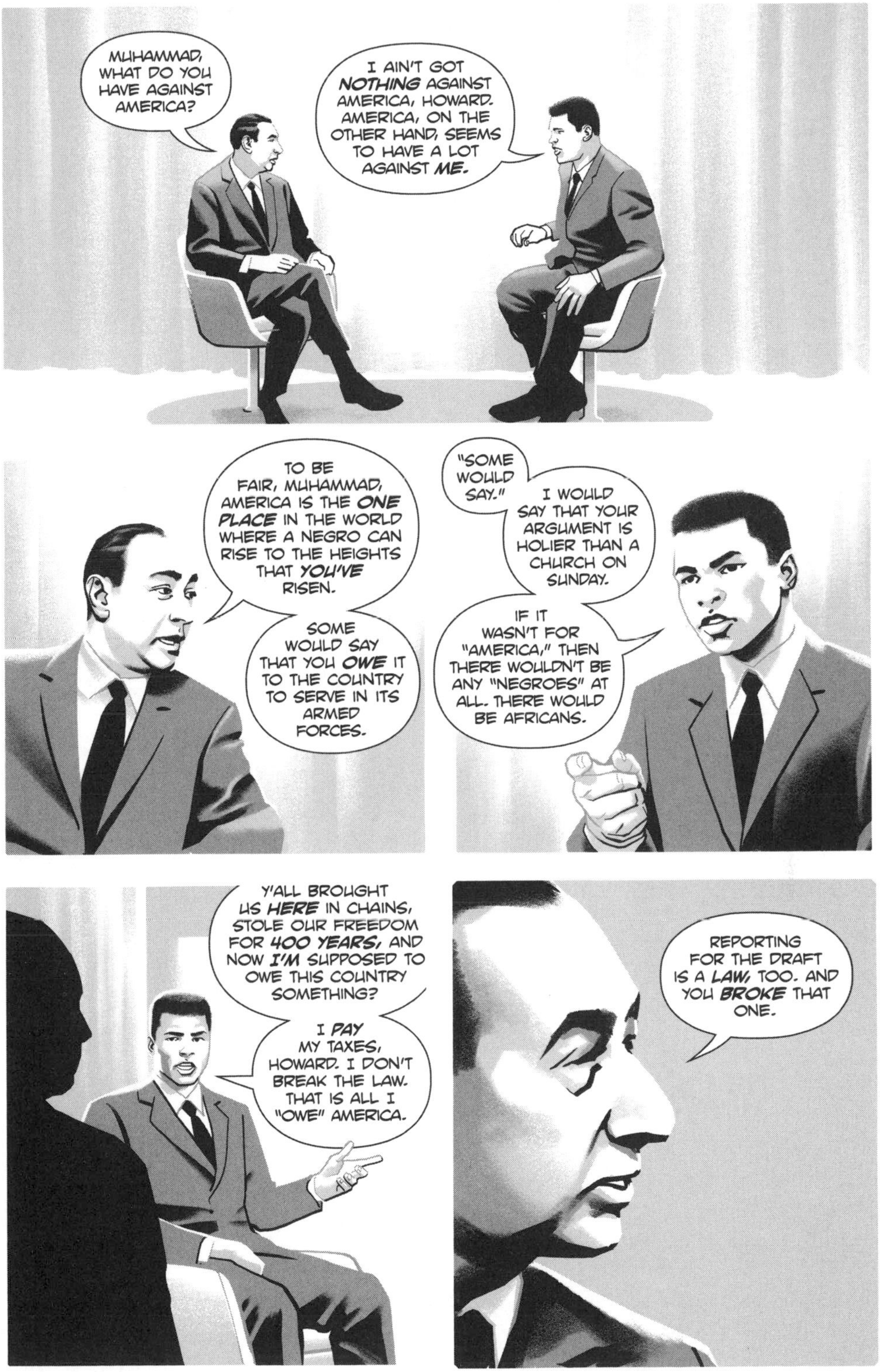
MUHAMMAD, WHAT DO YOU HAVE AGAINST AMERICA?
I AIN'T GOT NOTHING AGAINST AMERICA, HOWARD. AMERICA, ON THE OTHER HAND, SEEMS TO HAVE A LOT AGAINST ME.
TO BE FAIR, MUHAMMAD, AMERICA IS THE ONE PLACE IN THE WORLD WHERE A NEGRO CAN RISE TO THE HEIGHTS THAT YOU'VE RISEN.
SOME WOULD SAY THAT YOU OWE IT TO THE COUNTRY TO SERVE IN ITS ARMED FORCES.
"SOME WOULD SAY."
I WOULD SAY THAT YOUR ARGUMENT IS HOLIER THAN A CHURCH ON SUNDAY.
IF IT WASN'T FOR "AMERICA," THEN THERE WOULDN'T BE ANY "NEGROES" AT ALL. THERE WOULD BE AFRICANS.
Y'ALL BROUGHT US HERE IN CHAINS, STOLE OUR FREEDOM FOR 400 YEARS, AND NOW I'M SUPPOSED TO OWE THIS COUNTRY SOMETHING?
I PAY MY TAXES, HOWARD. I DON'T BREAK THE LAW. THAT IS ALL I "OWE" AMERICA.
REPORTING FOR THE DRAFT IS A LAW, TOO. AND YOU BROKE THAT ONE.

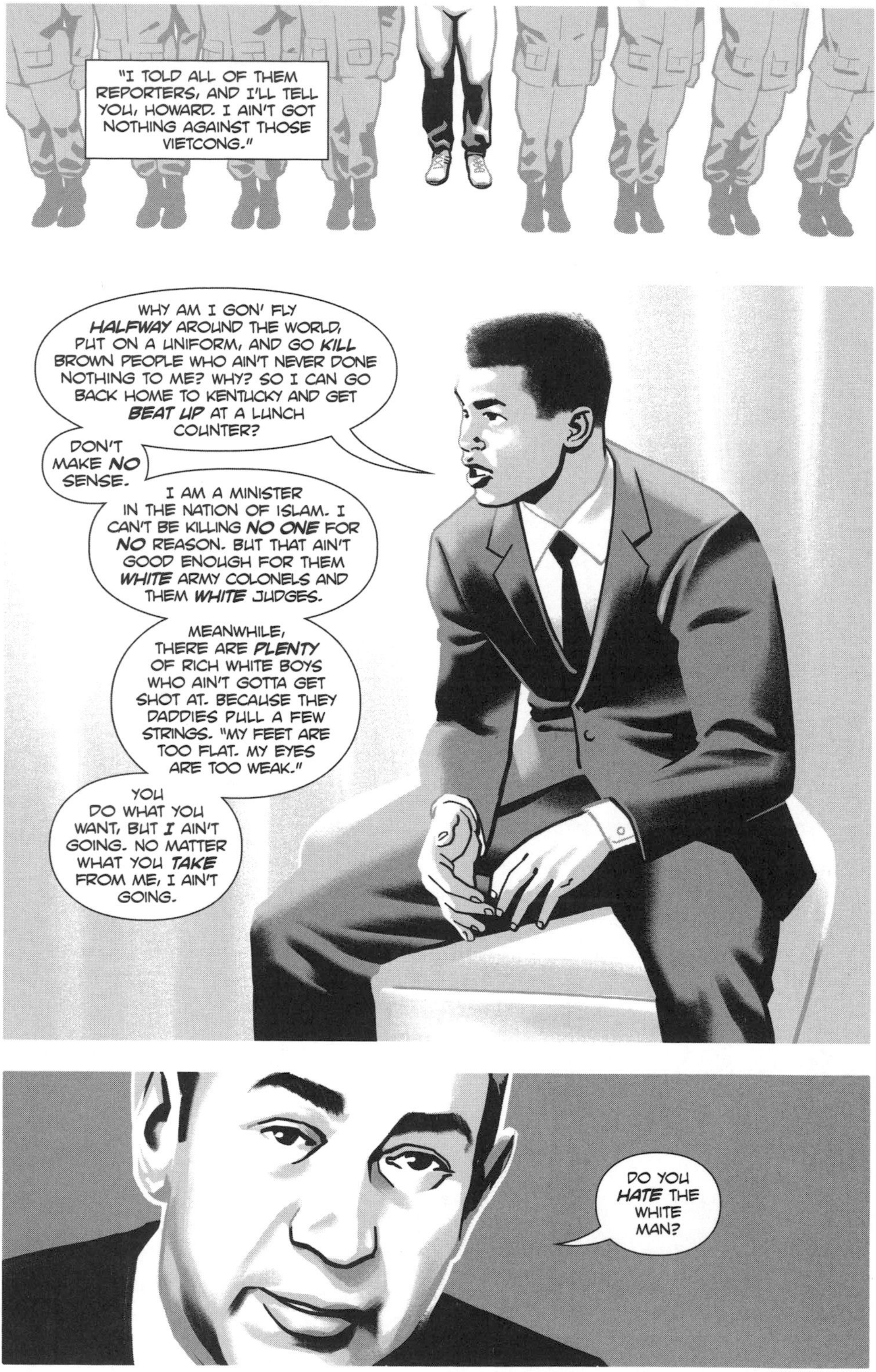
"I TOLD ALL OF THEM REPORTERS, AND I'LL TELL YOU, HOWARD. I AIN'T GOT NOTHING AGAINST THOSE VIETCONG."
WHY AM I GON' FLY HALFWAY AROUND THE WORLD, PUT ON A UNIFORM, AND GO KILL BROWN PEOPLE WHO AIN'T NEVER DONE NOTHING TO ME? WHY? SO I CAN GO BACK HOME TO KENTUCKY AND GET BEAT UP AT A LUNCH COUNTER?
DON'T MAKE NO SENSE.
I AM A MINISTER IN THE NATION OF ISLAM. I CAN'T BE KILLING NO ONE FOR NO REASON. BUT THAT AIN'T GOOD ENOUGH FOR THEM WHITE ARMY COLONELS AND THEM WHITE JUDGES.
MEANWHILE, THERE ARE PLENTY OF RICH WHITE BOYS WHO AIN'T GOTTA GET SHOT AT. BECAUSE THEY DADDIES PULL A FEW STRINGS. "MY FEET ARE TOO FLAT. MY EYES ARE TOO WEAK."
YOU DO WHAT YOU WANT, BUT I AIN'T GOING. NO MATTER WHAT YOU TAKE FROM ME, I AIN'T GOING.
DO YOU HATE THE WHITE MAN?

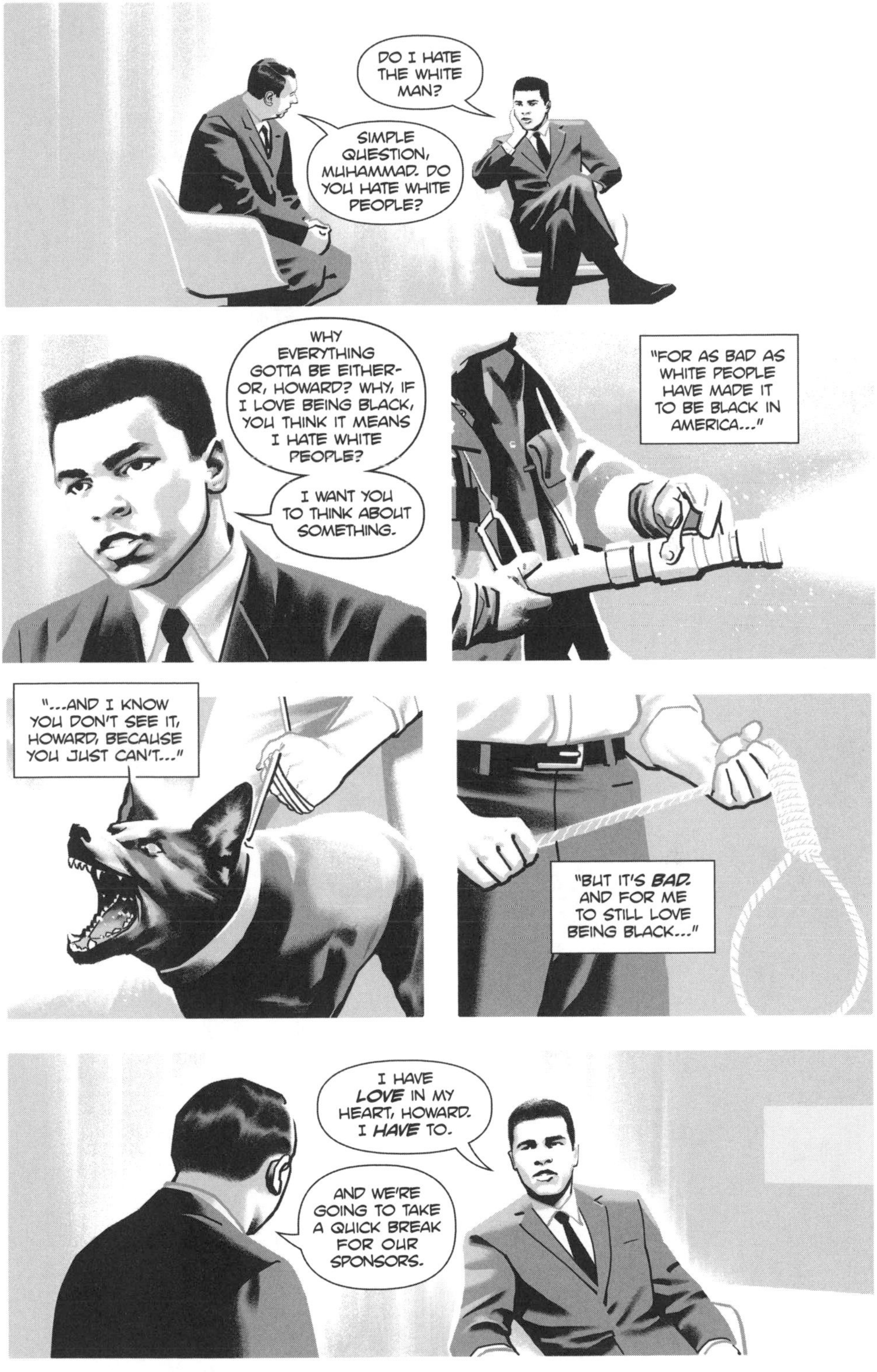
DO I HATE THE WHITE MAN?
SIMPLE QUESTION, MUHAMMAD. DO YOU HATE WHITE PEOPLE?
WHY EVERYTHING GOTTA BE EITHER-OR, HOWARD? WHY, IF I LOVE BEING BLACK, YOU THINK IT MEANS I HATE WHITE PEOPLE?
I WANT YOU TO THINK ABOUT SOMETHING.
"FOR AS BAD AS WHITE PEOPLE HAVE MADE IT TO BE BLACK IN AMERICA..."
"...AND I KNOW YOU DON'T SEE IT, HOWARD, BECAUSE YOU JUST CAN'T..."
"BUT IT'S *BAD.* AND FOR ME TO STILL LOVE BEING BLACK..."
I HAVE ***LOVE*** IN MY HEART, HOWARD. I ***HAVE*** TO.
AND WE'RE GOING TO TAKE A QUICK BREAK FOR OUR SPONSORS.

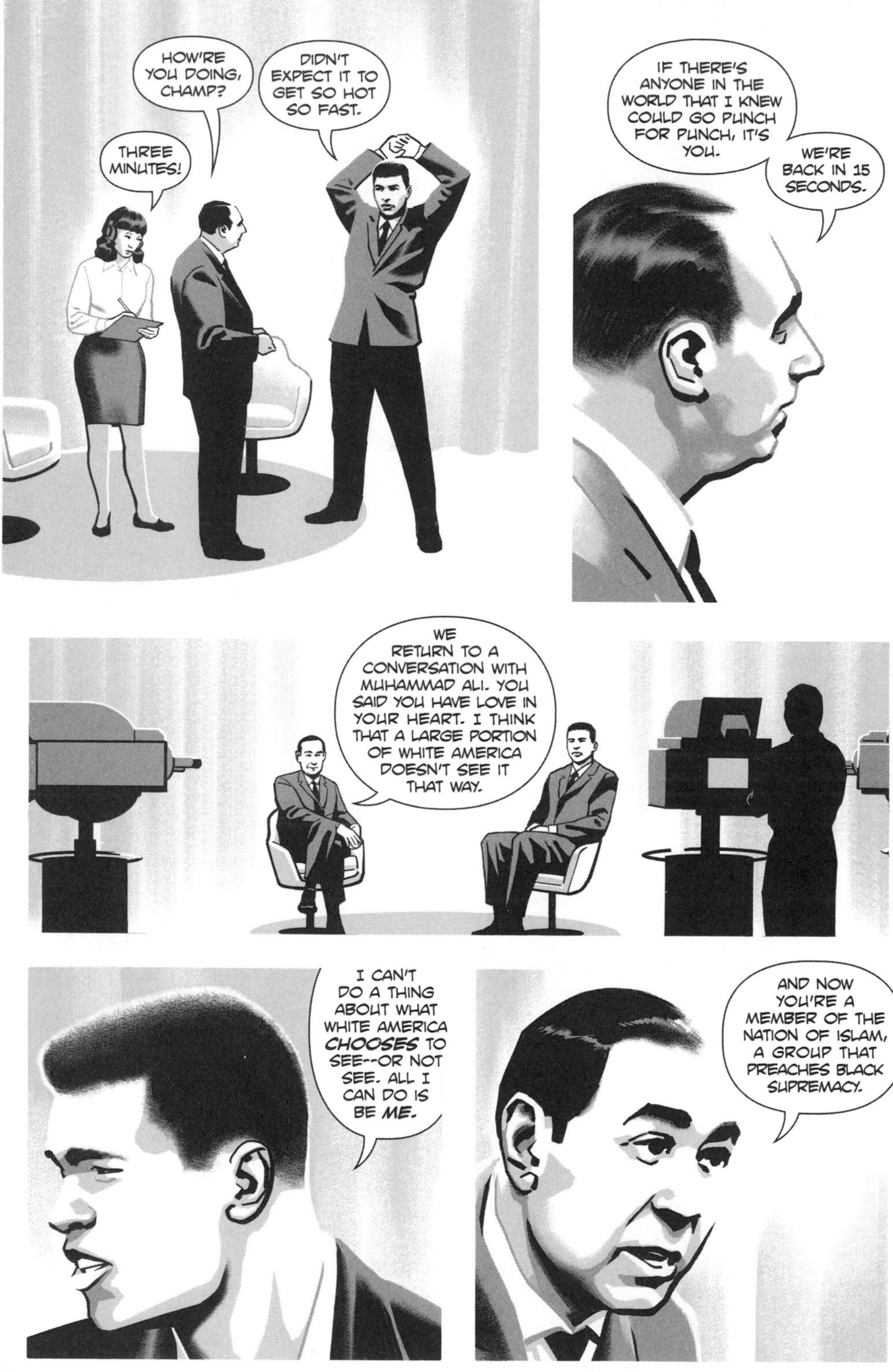
HOW'RE YOU DOING, CHAMP?
THREE MINUTES!
DIDN'T EXPECT IT TO GET SO HOT SO FAST.
IF THERE'S ANYONE IN THE WORLD THAT I KNEW COULD GO PUNCH FOR PUNCH, IT'S YOU.
WE'RE BACK IN 15 SECONDS.
WE RETURN TO A CONVERSATION WITH MUHAMMAD ALI. YOU SAID YOU HAVE LOVE IN YOUR HEART. I THINK THAT A LARGE PORTION OF WHITE AMERICA DOESN'T SEE IT THAT WAY.
I CAN'T DO A THING ABOUT WHAT WHITE AMERICA *CHOOSES* TO SEE--OR NOT SEE. ALL I CAN DO IS BE *ME.*
AND NOW YOU'RE A MEMBER OF THE NATION OF ISLAM, A GROUP THAT PREACHES BLACK SUPREMACY.

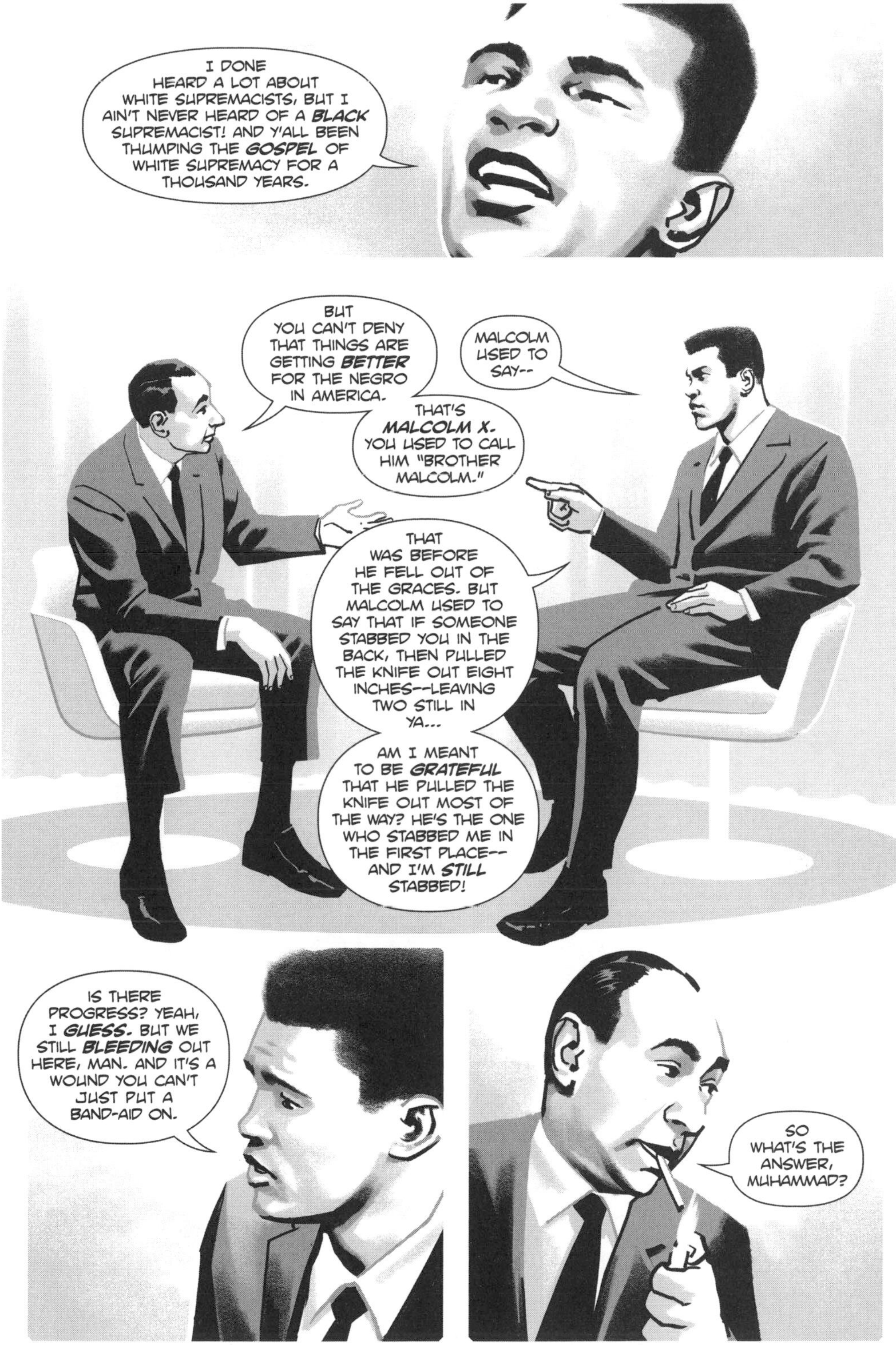
I DONE HEARD A LOT ABOUT WHITE SUPREMACISTS, BUT I AIN'T NEVER HEARD OF A BLACK SUPREMACIST! AND Y'ALL BEEN THUMPING THE GOSPEL OF WHITE SUPREMACY FOR A THOUSAND YEARS.
BUT YOU CAN'T DENY THAT THINGS ARE GETTING BETTER FOR THE NEGRO IN AMERICA.
MALCOLM USED TO SAY--
THAT'S MALCOLM X. YOU USED TO CALL HIM "BROTHER MALCOLM."
THAT WAS BEFORE HE FELL OUT OF THE GRACES. BUT MALCOLM USED TO SAY THAT IF SOMEONE STABBED YOU IN THE BACK, THEN PULLED THE KNIFE OUT EIGHT INCHES--LEAVING TWO STILL IN YA...
AM I MEANT TO BE GRATEFUL THAT HE PULLED THE KNIFE OUT MOST OF THE WAY? HE'S THE ONE WHO STABBED ME IN THE FIRST PLACE-- AND I'M STILL STABBED!
IS THERE PROGRESS? YEAH, I GUESS. BUT WE STILL BLEEDING OUT HERE, MAN. AND IT'S A WOUND YOU CAN'T JUST PUT A BAND-AID ON.
SO WHAT'S THE ANSWER, MUHAMMAD?

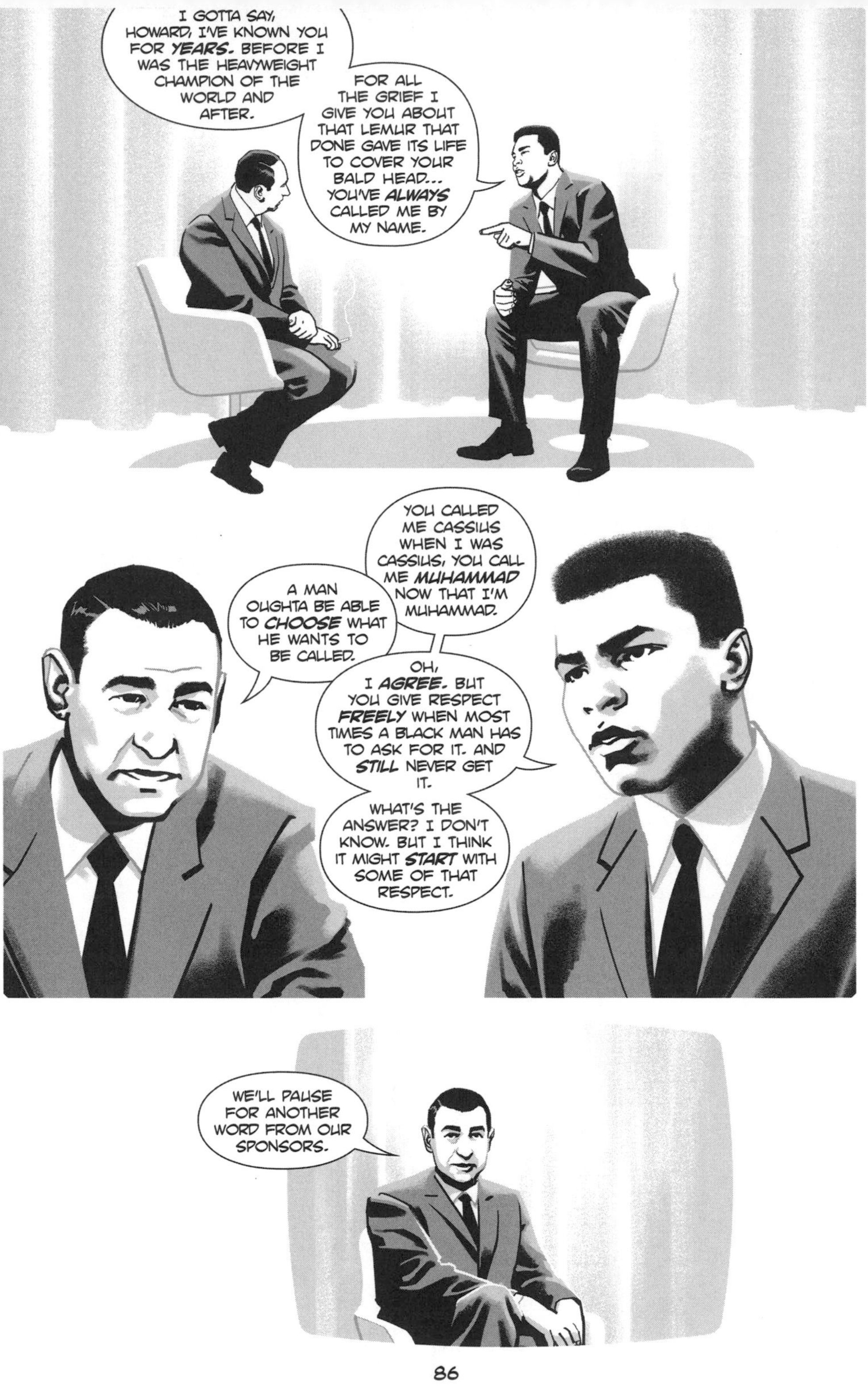
I GOTTA SAY, HOWARD, I'VE KNOWN YOU FOR YEARS. BEFORE I WAS THE HEAVYWEIGHT CHAMPION OF THE WORLD AND AFTER.
FOR ALL THE GRIEF I GIVE YOU ABOUT THAT LEMUR THAT DONE GAVE ITS LIFE TO COVER YOUR BALD HEAD... YOU'VE ALWAYS CALLED ME BY MY NAME.
A MAN OUGHTA BE ABLE TO CHOOSE WHAT HE WANTS TO BE CALLED.
YOU CALLED ME CASSIUS WHEN I WAS CASSIUS, YOU CALL ME MUHAMMAD NOW THAT I'M MUHAMMAD.
OH, I AGREE. BUT YOU GIVE RESPECT FREELY WHEN MOST TIMES A BLACK MAN HAS TO ASK FOR IT. AND STILL NEVER GET IT.
WHAT'S THE ANSWER? I DON'T KNOW. BUT I THINK IT MIGHT START WITH SOME OF THAT RESPECT.
WE'LL PAUSE FOR ANOTHER WORD FROM OUR SPONSORS.

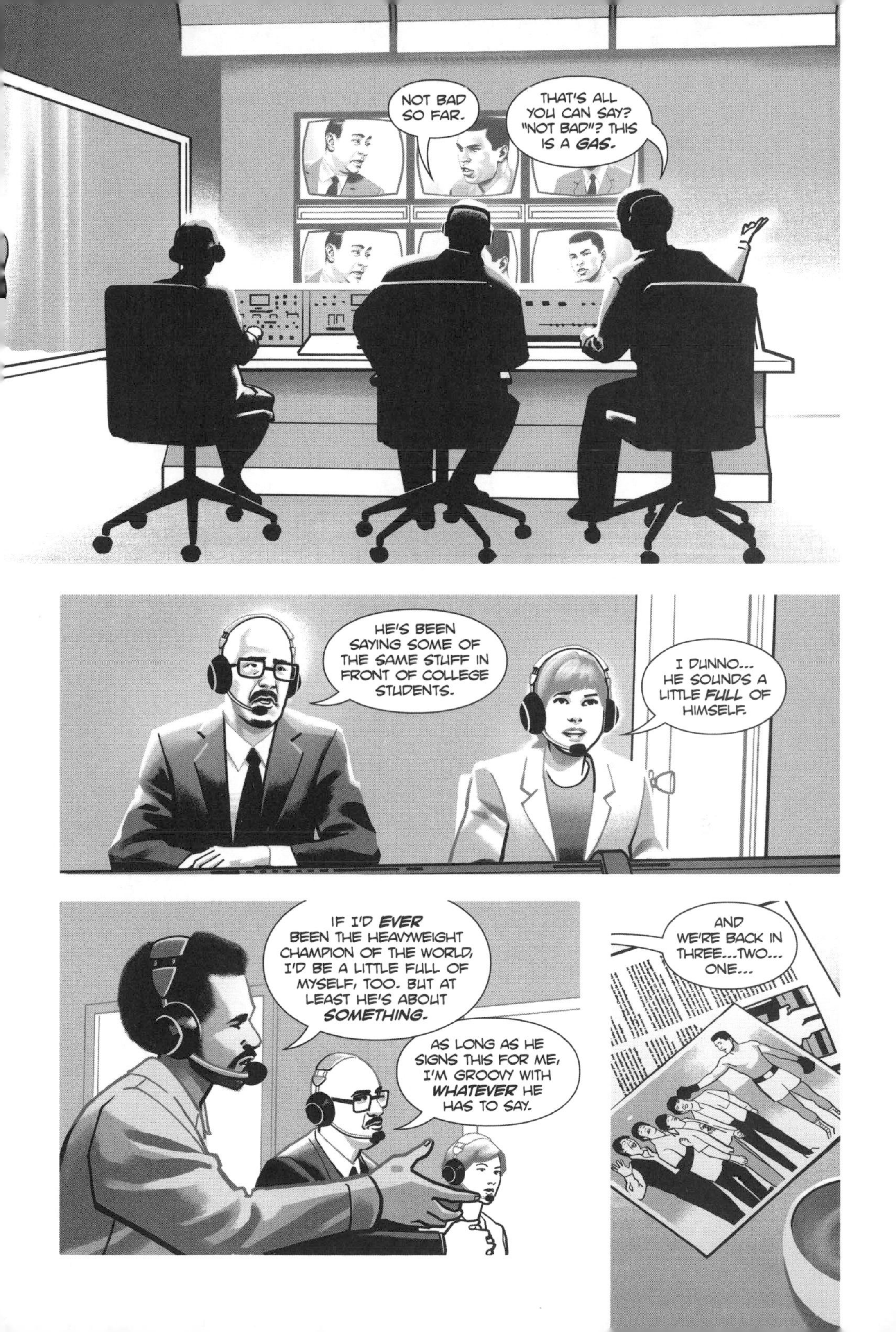
NOT BAD SO FAR.
THAT'S ALL YOU CAN SAY? "NOT BAD"? THIS IS A GAS.
HE'S BEEN SAYING SOME OF THE SAME STUFF IN FRONT OF COLLEGE STUDENTS.
I DUNNO... HE SOUNDS A LITTLE FULL OF HIMSELF.
IF I'D EVER BEEN THE HEAVYWEIGHT CHAMPION OF THE WORLD, I'D BE A LITTLE FULL OF MYSELF, TOO. BUT AT LEAST HE'S ABOUT SOMETHING.
AS LONG AS HE SIGNS THIS FOR ME, I'M GROOVY WITH WHATEVER HE HAS TO SAY.
AND WE'RE BACK IN THREE...TWO... ONE...

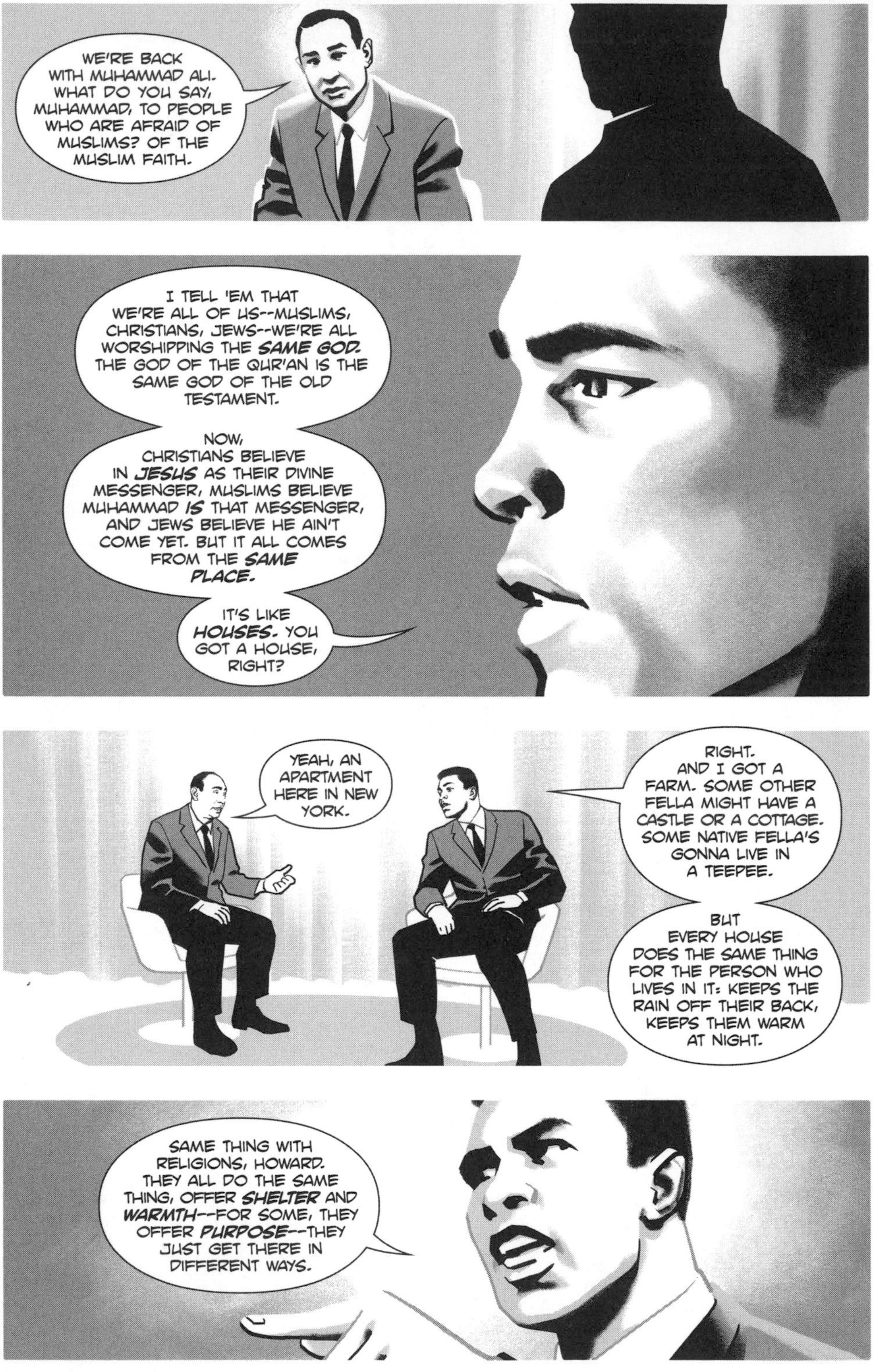
WE'RE BACK WITH MUHAMMAD ALI. WHAT DO YOU SAY, MUHAMMAD, TO PEOPLE WHO ARE AFRAID OF MUSLIMS? OF THE MUSLIM FAITH.
I TELL 'EM THAT WE'RE ALL OF US--MUSLIMS, CHRISTIANS, JEWS--WE'RE ALL WORSHIPPING THE *SAME GOD.* THE GOD OF THE QUR'AN IS THE SAME GOD OF THE OLD TESTAMENT.
NOW, CHRISTIANS BELIEVE IN *JESUS* AS THEIR DIVINE MESSENGER, MUSLIMS BELIEVE MUHAMMAD *IS* THAT MESSENGER, AND JEWS BELIEVE HE AIN'T COME YET. BUT IT ALL COMES FROM THE *SAME PLACE.*
IT'S LIKE *HOUSES.* YOU GOT A HOUSE, RIGHT?
YEAH, AN APARTMENT HERE IN NEW YORK.
RIGHT. AND I GOT A FARM. SOME OTHER FELLA MIGHT HAVE A CASTLE OR A COTTAGE. SOME NATIVE FELLA'S GONNA LIVE IN A TEEPEE.
BUT EVERY HOUSE DOES THE SAME THING FOR THE PERSON WHO LIVES IN IT: KEEPS THE RAIN OFF THEIR BACK, KEEPS THEM WARM AT NIGHT.
SAME THING WITH RELIGIONS, HOWARD. THEY ALL DO THE SAME THING, OFFER *SHELTER* AND *WARMTH*--FOR SOME, THEY OFFER *PURPOSE*--THEY JUST GET THERE IN DIFFERENT WAYS.

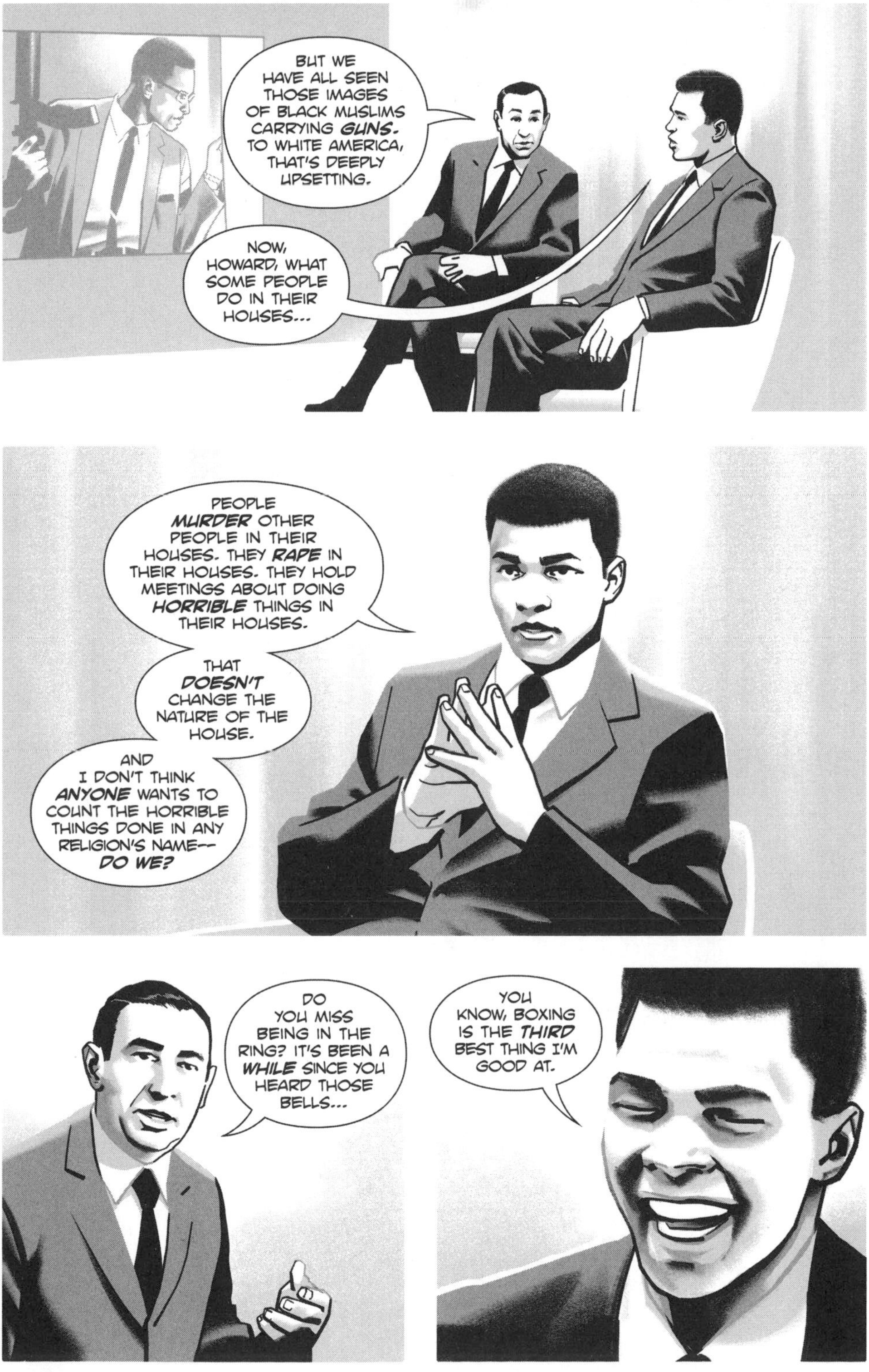

BUT WE HAVE ALL SEEN THOSE IMAGES OF BLACK MUSLIMS CARRYING GUNS. TO WHITE AMERICA, THAT'S DEEPLY UPSETTING.
NOW, HOWARD, WHAT SOME PEOPLE DO IN THEIR HOUSES...
PEOPLE MURDER OTHER PEOPLE IN THEIR HOUSES. THEY RAPE IN THEIR HOUSES. THEY HOLD MEETINGS ABOUT DOING HORRIBLE THINGS IN THEIR HOUSES.
THAT DOESN'T CHANGE THE NATURE OF THE HOUSE.
AND I DON'T THINK ANYONE WANTS TO COUNT THE HORRIBLE THINGS DONE IN ANY RELIGION'S NAME-- DO WE?
DO YOU MISS BEING IN THE RING? IT'S BEEN A WHILE SINCE YOU HEARD THOSE BELLS...
YOU KNOW, BOXING IS THE THIRD BEST THING I'M GOOD AT.

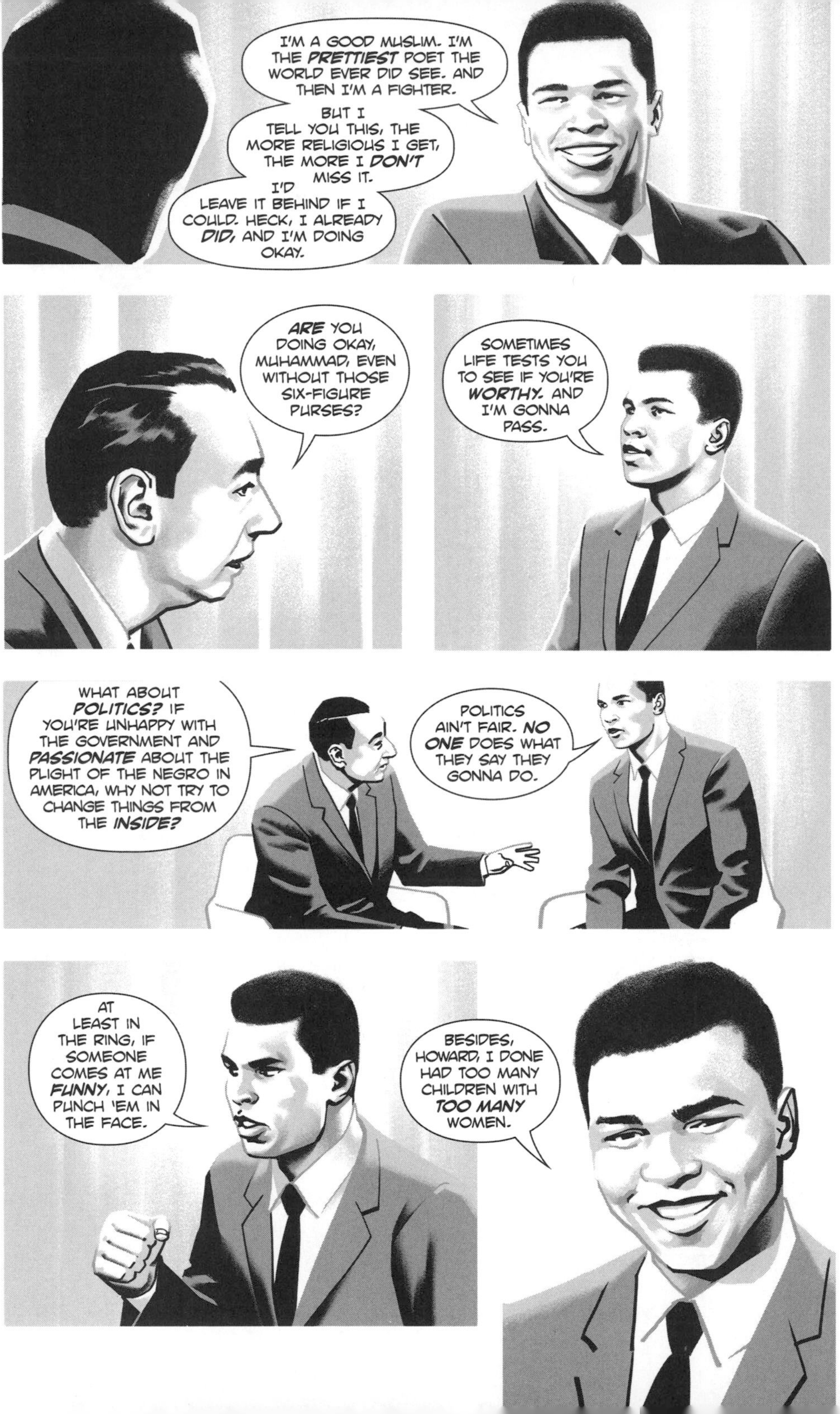
I'M A GOOD MUSLIM. I'M THE PRETTIEST POET THE WORLD EVER DID SEE. AND THEN I'M A FIGHTER.
BUT I TELL YOU THIS, THE MORE RELIGIOUS I GET, THE MORE I DON'T MISS IT.
I'D LEAVE IT BEHIND IF I COULD. HECK, I ALREADY DID, AND I'M DOING OKAY.
ARE YOU DOING OKAY, MUHAMMAD, EVEN WITHOUT THOSE SIX-FIGURE PURSES?
SOMETIMES LIFE TESTS YOU TO SEE IF YOU'RE WORTHY. AND I'M GONNA PASS.
WHAT ABOUT POLITICS? IF YOU'RE UNHAPPY WITH THE GOVERNMENT AND PASSIONATE ABOUT THE PLIGHT OF THE NEGRO IN AMERICA, WHY NOT TRY TO CHANGE THINGS FROM THE INSIDE?
POLITICS AIN'T FAIR. NO ONE DOES WHAT THEY SAY THEY GONNA DO.
AT LEAST IN THE RING, IF SOMEONE COMES AT ME FUNNY, I CAN PUNCH 'EM IN THE FACE.
BESIDES, HOWARD, I DONE HAD TOO MANY CHILDREN WITH TOO MANY WOMEN.

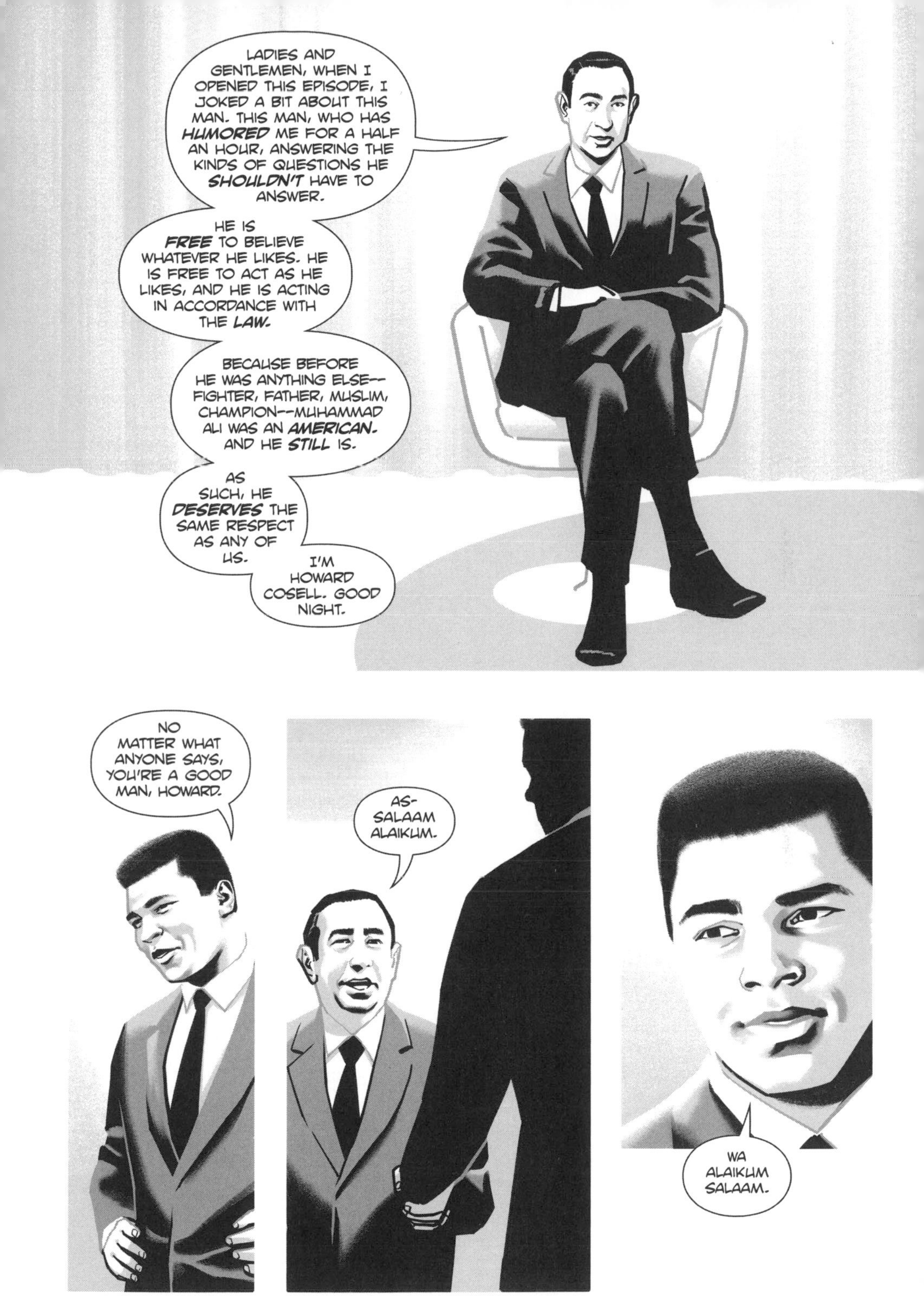
LADIES AND GENTLEMEN, WHEN I OPENED THIS EPISODE, I JOKED A BIT ABOUT THIS MAN. THIS MAN, WHO HAS **HUMORED** ME FOR A HALF AN HOUR, ANSWERING THE KINDS OF QUESTIONS HE **SHOULDN'T** HAVE TO ANSWER.
HE IS **FREE** TO BELIEVE WHATEVER HE LIKES. HE IS FREE TO ACT AS HE LIKES, AND HE IS ACTING IN ACCORDANCE WITH THE **LAW.**
BECAUSE BEFORE HE WAS ANYTHING ELSE-- FIGHTER, FATHER, MUSLIM, CHAMPION--MUHAMMAD ALI WAS AN **AMERICAN.** AND HE **STILL** IS.
AS SUCH, HE **DESERVES** THE SAME RESPECT AS ANY OF US.
I'M HOWARD COSELL. GOOD NIGHT.
NO MATTER WHAT ANYONE SAYS, YOU'RE A GOOD MAN, HOWARD.
AS-SALAAM ALAIKUM.
WA ALAIKUM SALAAM.

ROUND SIX: MARTYR. 1968.

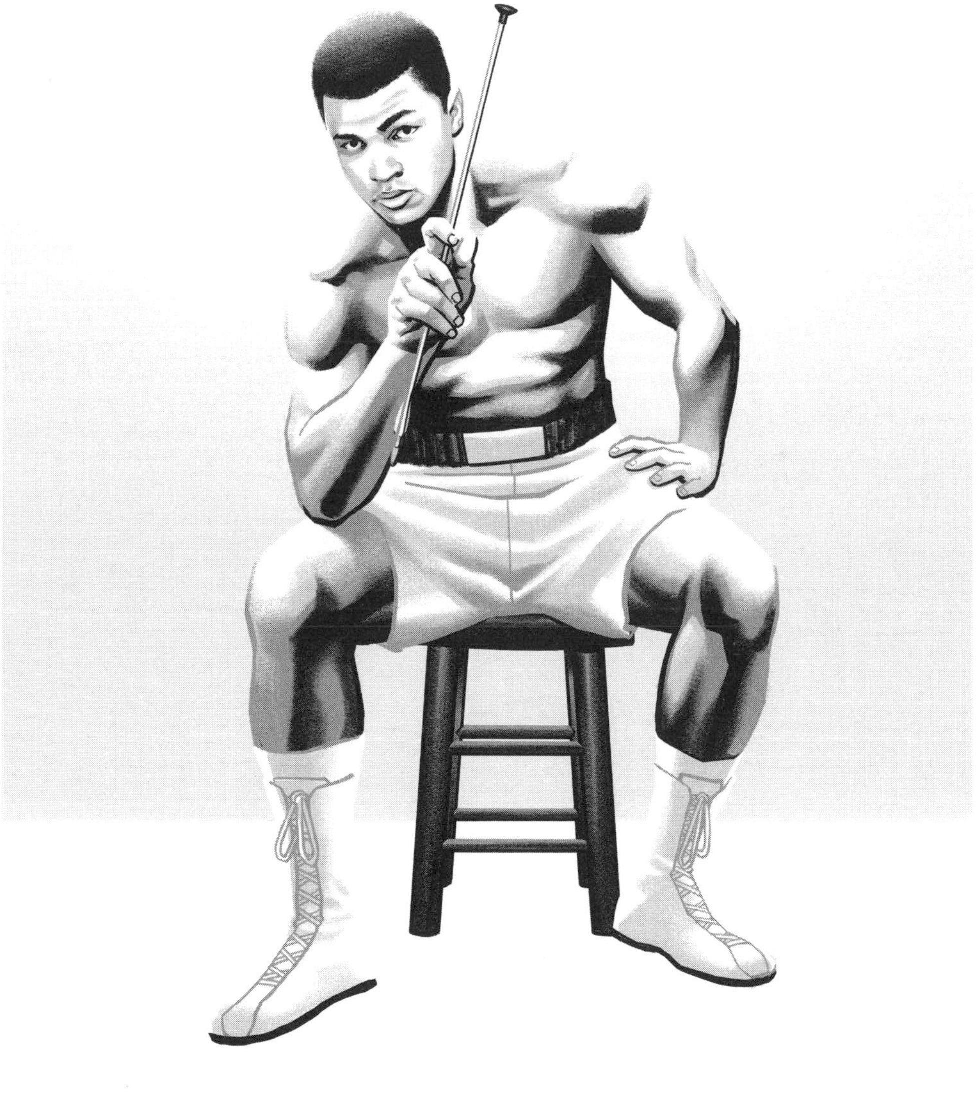

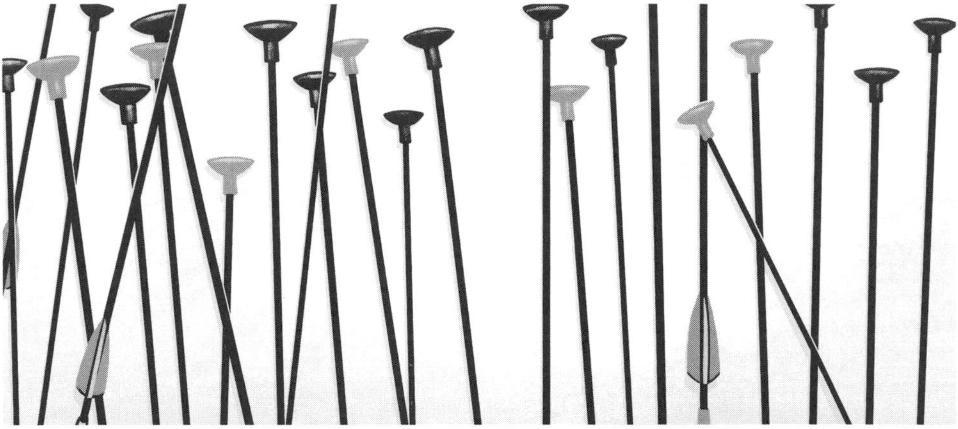

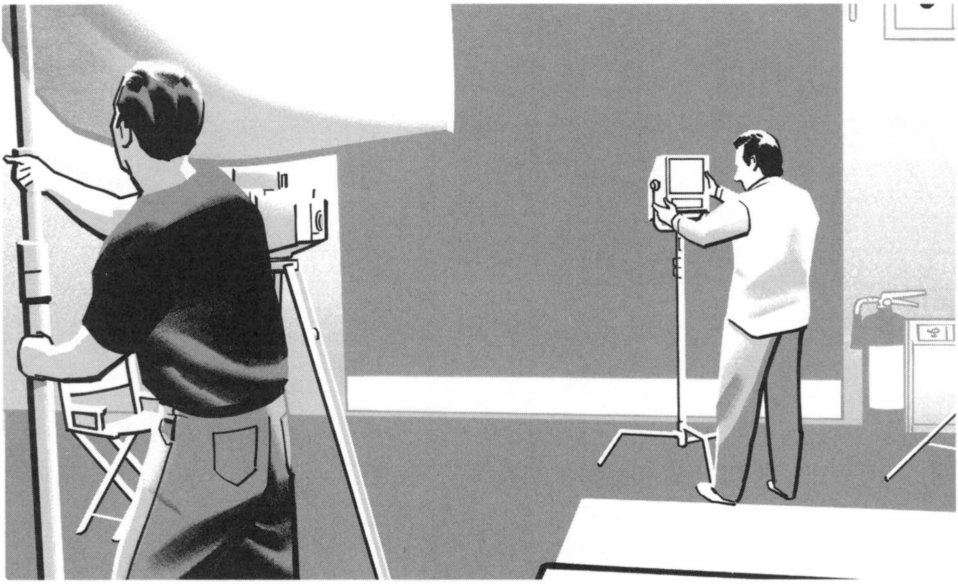

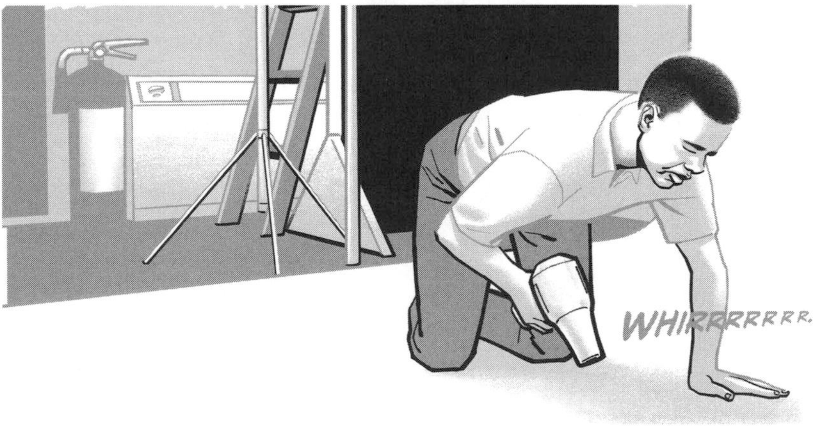
WHIRRRRRRR.

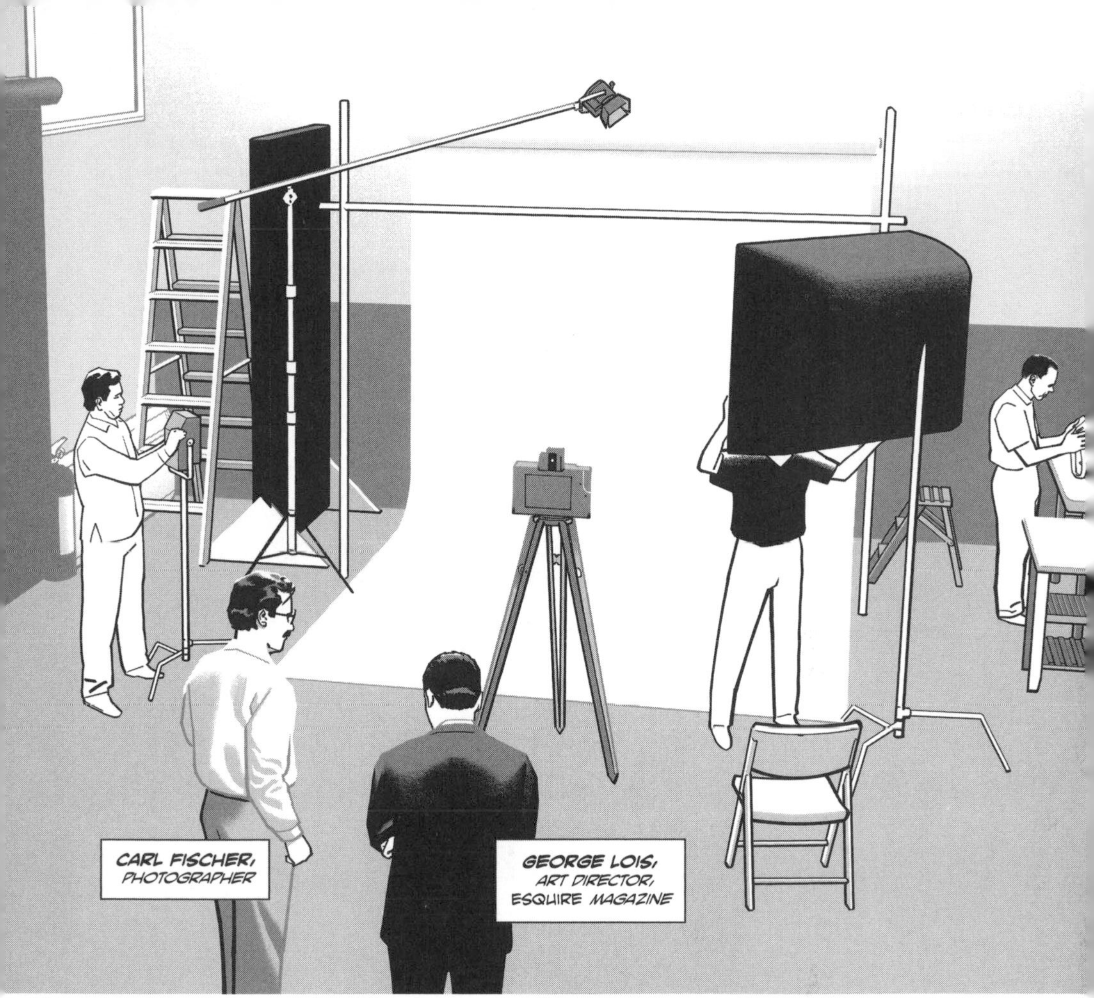
CARL FISCHER,
PHOTOGRAPHER
GEORGE LOIS,
ART DIRECTOR,
ESQUIRE MAGAZINE

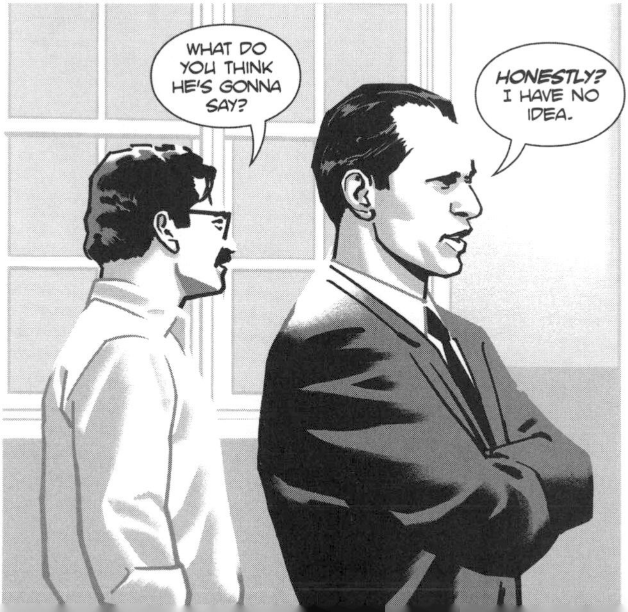
WHAT DO YOU THINK HE'S GONNA SAY?
HONESTLY? I HAVE NO IDEA.

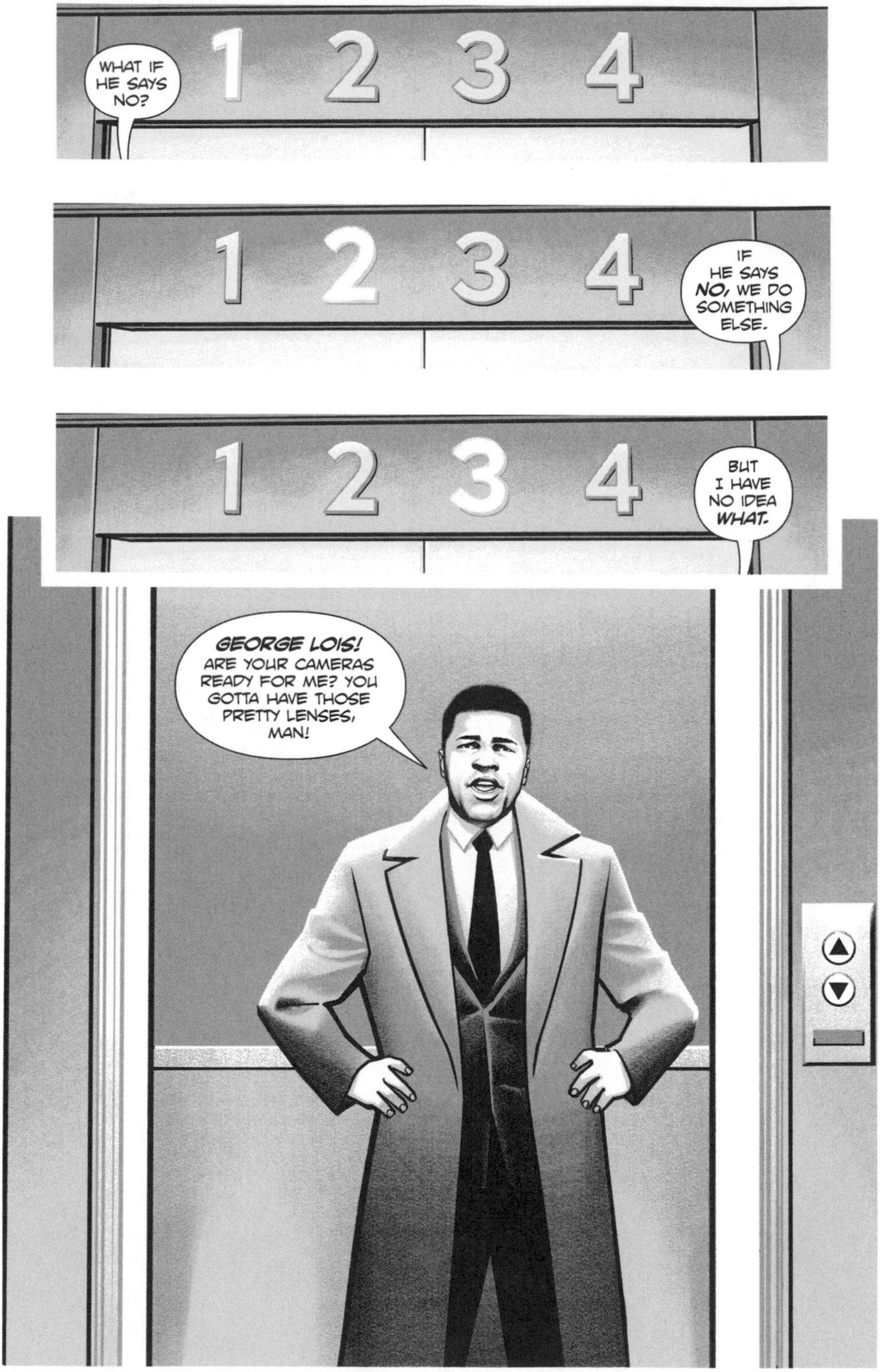
WHAT IF HE SAYS NO?
IF HE SAYS NO, WE DO SOMETHING ELSE.
BUT I HAVE NO IDEA WHAT.
GEORGE LOIS! ARE YOUR CAMERAS READY FOR ME? YOU GOTTA HAVE THOSE PRETTY LENSES, MAN!

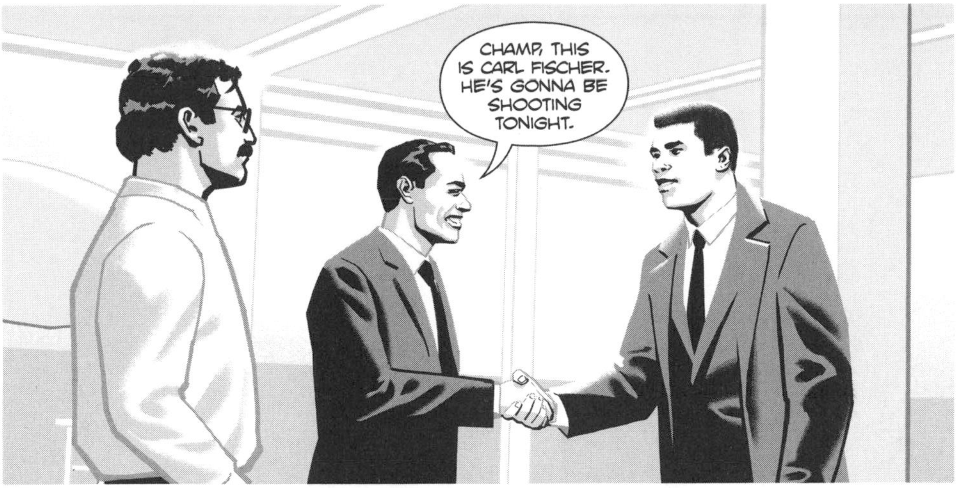
CHAMP, THIS IS CARL FISCHER. HE'S GONNA BE SHOOTING TONIGHT.

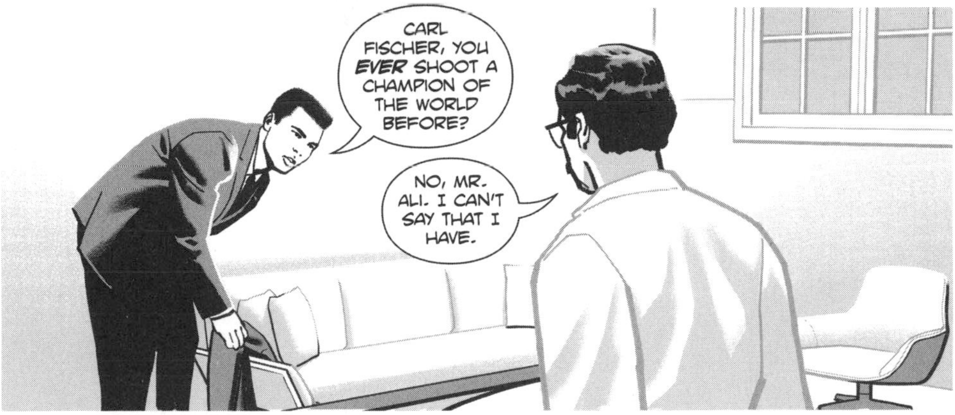
CARL FISCHER, YOU EVER SHOOT A CHAMPION OF THE WORLD BEFORE?
NO, MR. ALI. I CAN'T SAY THAT I HAVE.

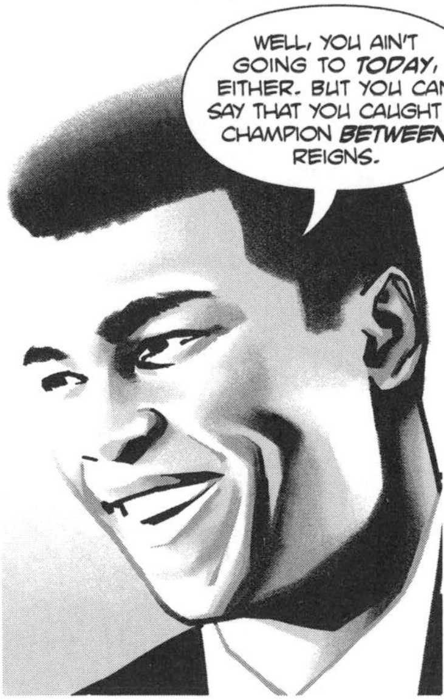
WELL, YOU AIN'T GOING TO TODAY, EITHER. BUT YOU CAN SAY THAT YOU CAUGHT A CHAMPION BETWEEN REIGNS.

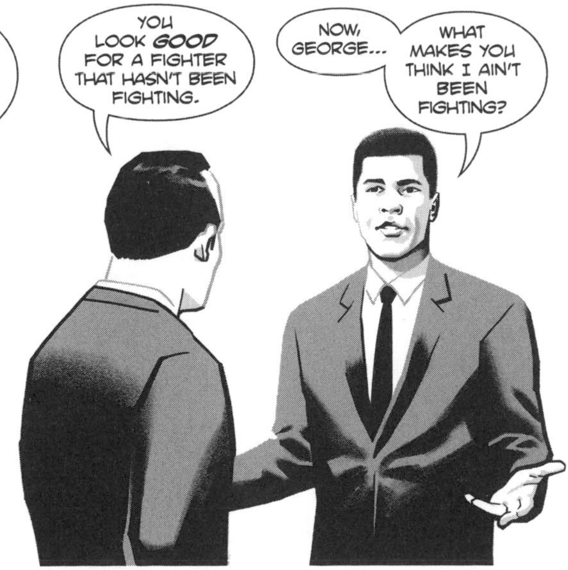
YOU LOOK GOOD FOR A FIGHTER THAT HASN'T BEEN FIGHTING.
NOW, GEORGE...
WHAT MAKES YOU THINK I AIN'T BEEN FIGHTING?

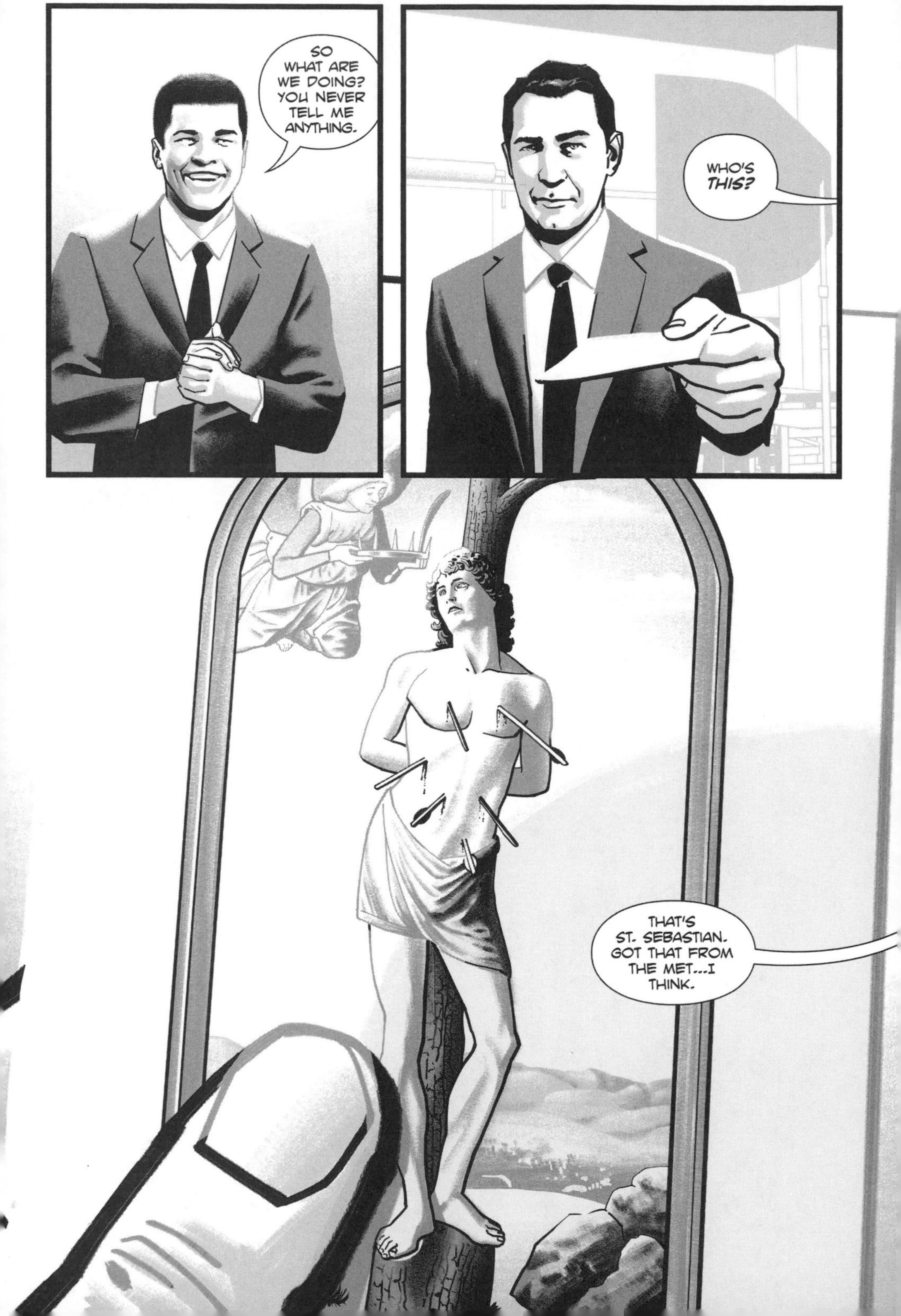

SO WHAT ARE WE DOING? YOU NEVER TELL ME ANYTHING.
WHO'S *THIS?*
THAT'S ST. SEBASTIAN. GOT THAT FROM THE MET...I THINK.

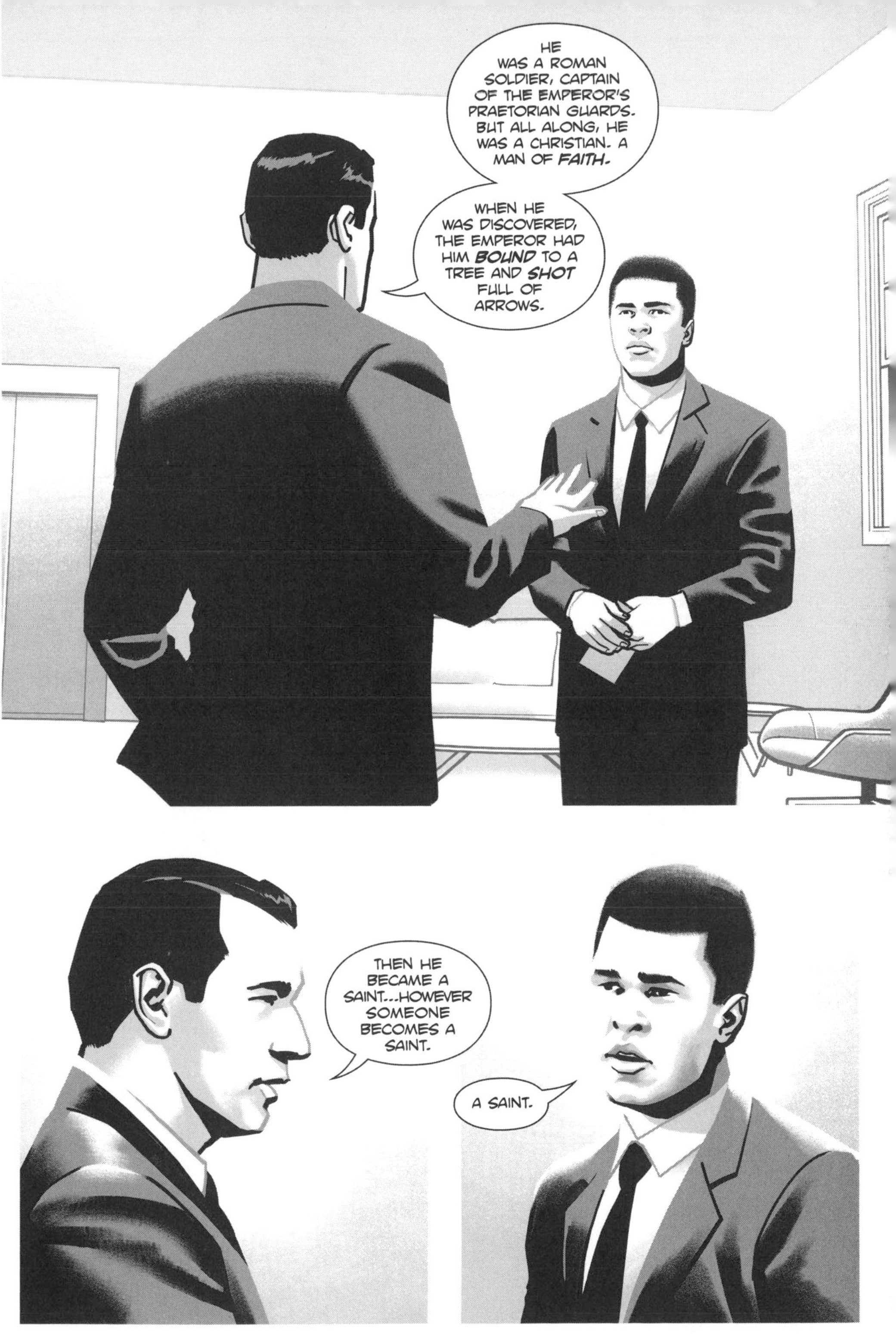
HE WAS A ROMAN SOLDIER, CAPTAIN OF THE EMPEROR'S PRAETORIAN GUARDS. BUT ALL ALONG, HE WAS A CHRISTIAN. A MAN OF *FAITH*.
WHEN HE WAS DISCOVERED, THE EMPEROR HAD HIM *BOUND* TO A TREE AND *SHOT* FULL OF ARROWS.
THEN HE BECAME A SAINT...HOWEVER SOMEONE BECOMES A SAINT.
A SAINT.

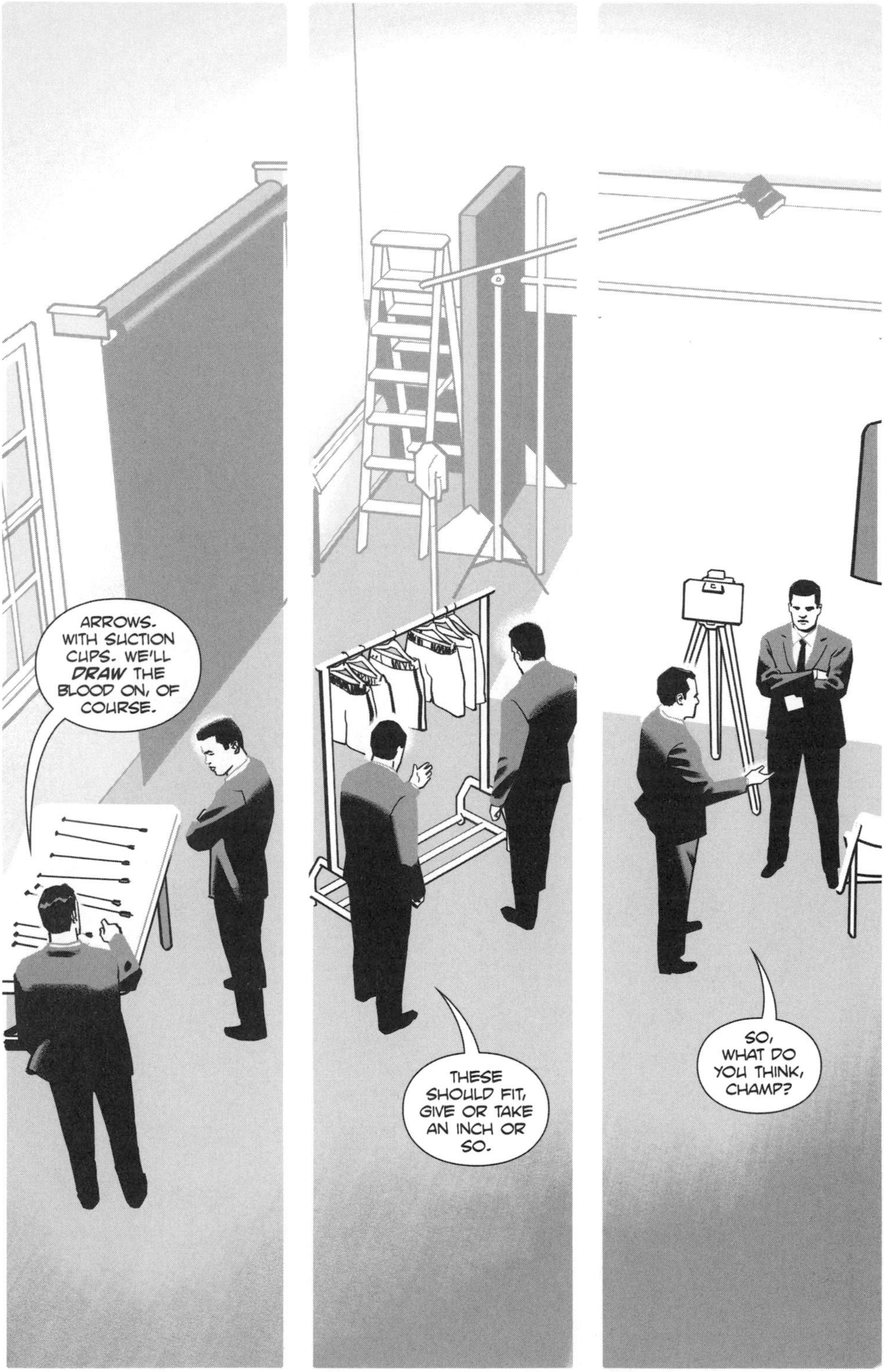
ARROWS. WITH SUCTION CUPS. WE'LL DRAW THE BLOOD ON, OF COURSE.
THESE SHOULD FIT, GIVE OR TAKE AN INCH OR SO.
SO, WHAT DO YOU THINK, CHAMP?

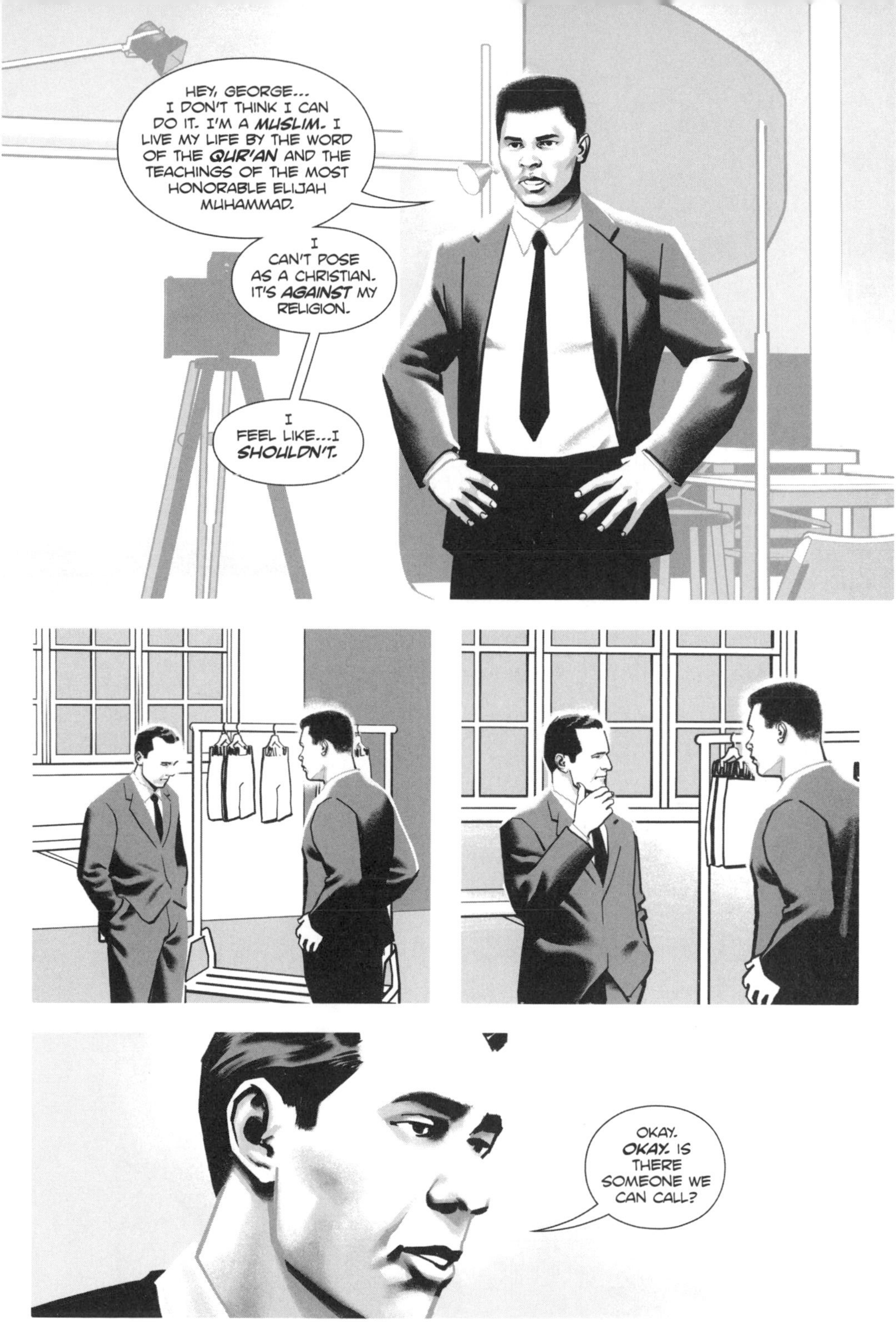
HEY, GEORGE... I DON'T THINK I CAN DO IT. I'M A MUSLIM. I LIVE MY LIFE BY THE WORD OF THE QUR'AN AND THE TEACHINGS OF THE MOST HONORABLE ELIJAH MUHAMMAD.
I CAN'T POSE AS A CHRISTIAN. IT'S AGAINST MY RELIGION.
I FEEL LIKE...I SHOULDN'T.
OKAY. OKAY. IS THERE SOMEONE WE CAN CALL?

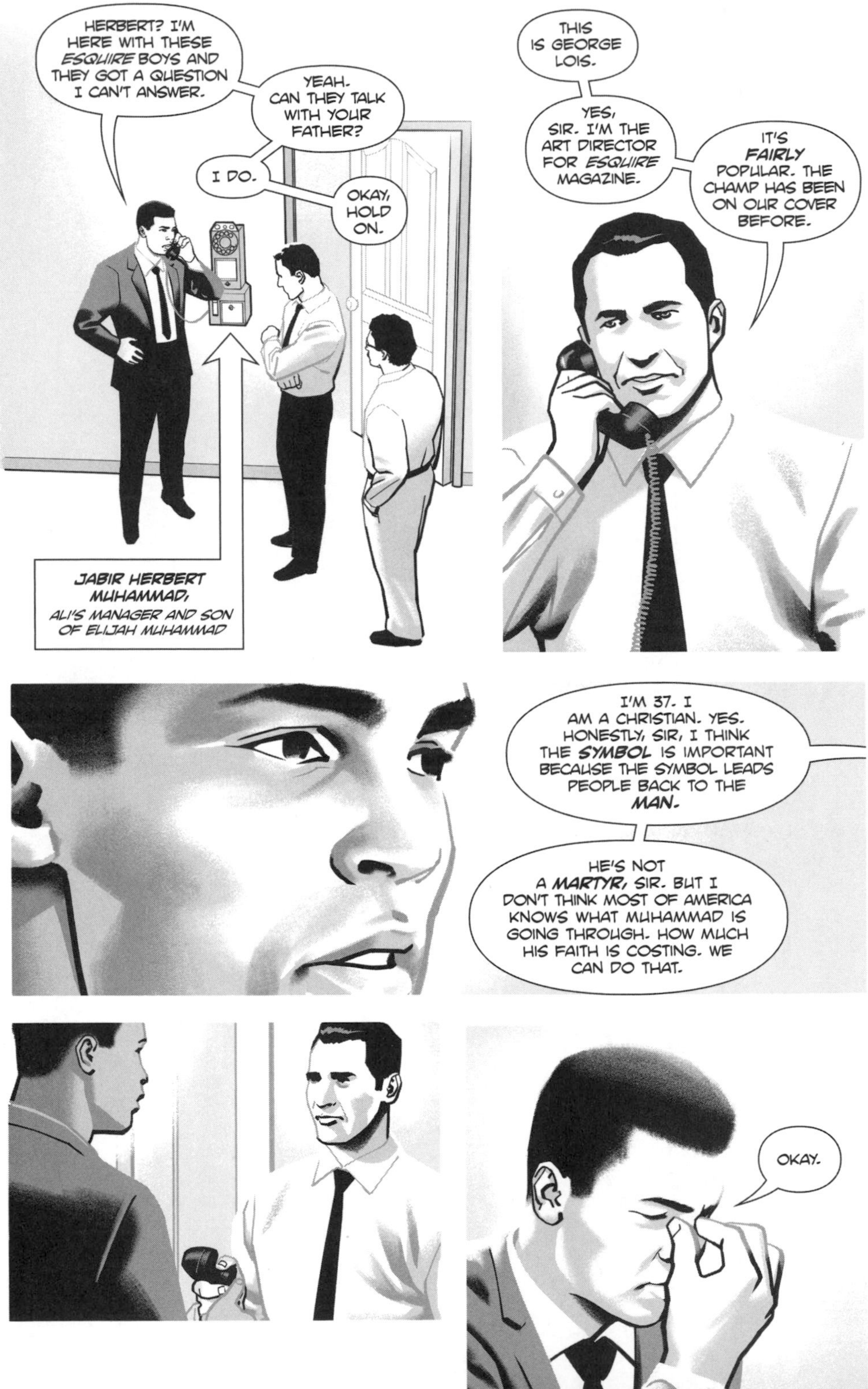
HERBERT? I'M HERE WITH THESE ESQUIRE BOYS AND THEY GOT A QUESTION I CAN'T ANSWER.
YEAH. CAN THEY TALK WITH YOUR FATHER?
I DO.
OKAY, HOLD ON.
JABIR HERBERT MUHAMMAD, ALI'S MANAGER AND SON OF ELIJAH MUHAMMAD
THIS IS GEORGE LOIS.
YES, SIR. I'M THE ART DIRECTOR FOR ESQUIRE MAGAZINE.
IT'S FAIRLY POPULAR. THE CHAMP HAS BEEN ON OUR COVER BEFORE.
I'M 37. I AM A CHRISTIAN. YES. HONESTLY, SIR, I THINK THE SYMBOL IS IMPORTANT BECAUSE THE SYMBOL LEADS PEOPLE BACK TO THE MAN.
HE'S NOT A MARTYR, SIR. BUT I DON'T THINK MOST OF AMERICA KNOWS WHAT MUHAMMAD IS GOING THROUGH. HOW MUCH HIS FAITH IS COSTING. WE CAN DO THAT.
OKAY.

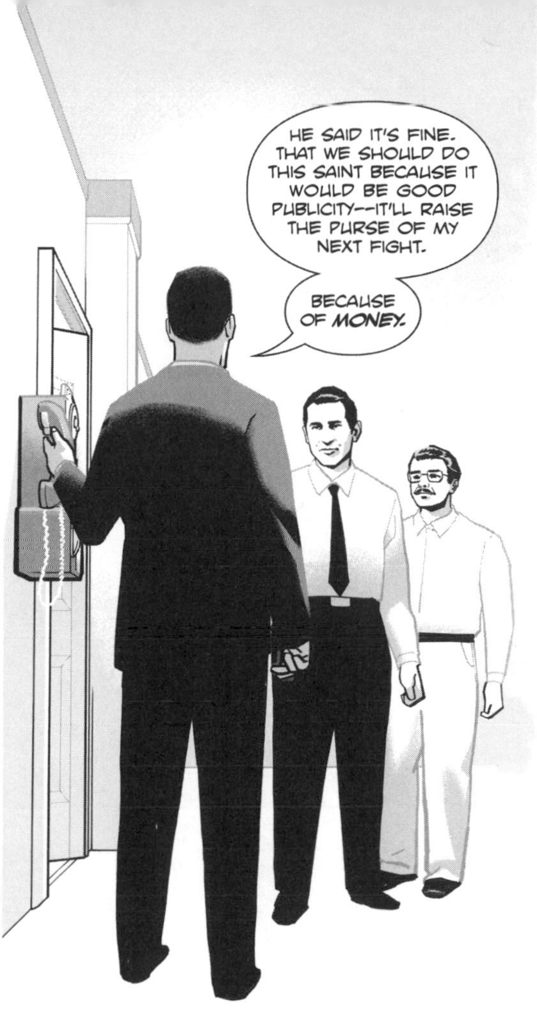
HE SAID IT'S FINE. THAT WE SHOULD DO THIS SAINT BECAUSE IT WOULD BE GOOD PUBLICITY--IT'LL RAISE THE PURSE OF MY NEXT FIGHT.
BECAUSE OF **MONEY.**

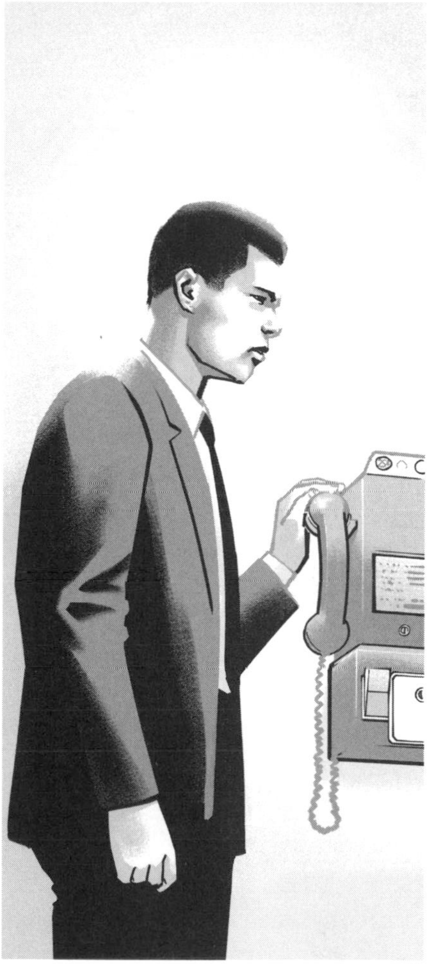

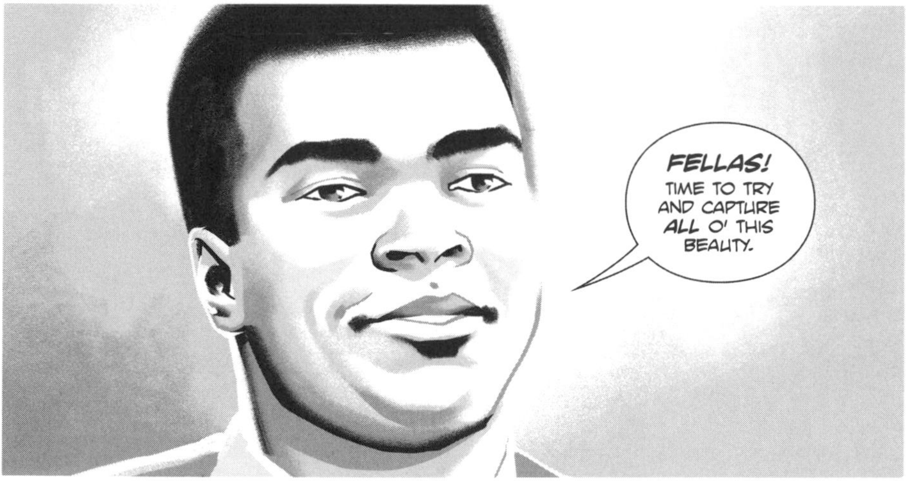
FELLAS! TIME TO TRY AND CAPTURE **ALL** O' THIS BEAUTY.

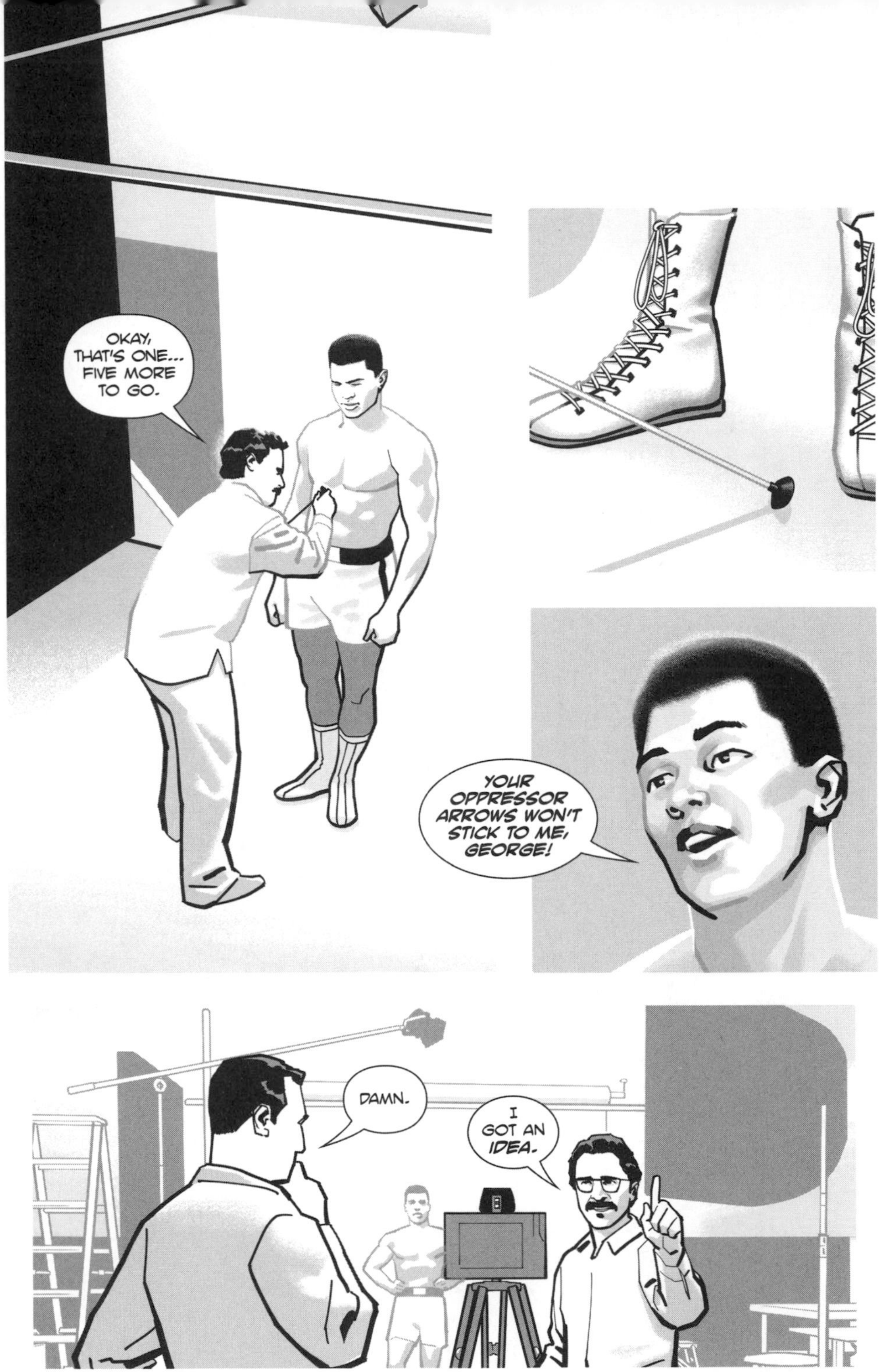
OKAY, THAT'S ONE... FIVE MORE TO GO.
YOUR OPPRESSOR ARROWS WON'T STICK TO ME, GEORGE!
DAMN.
I GOT AN IDEA.

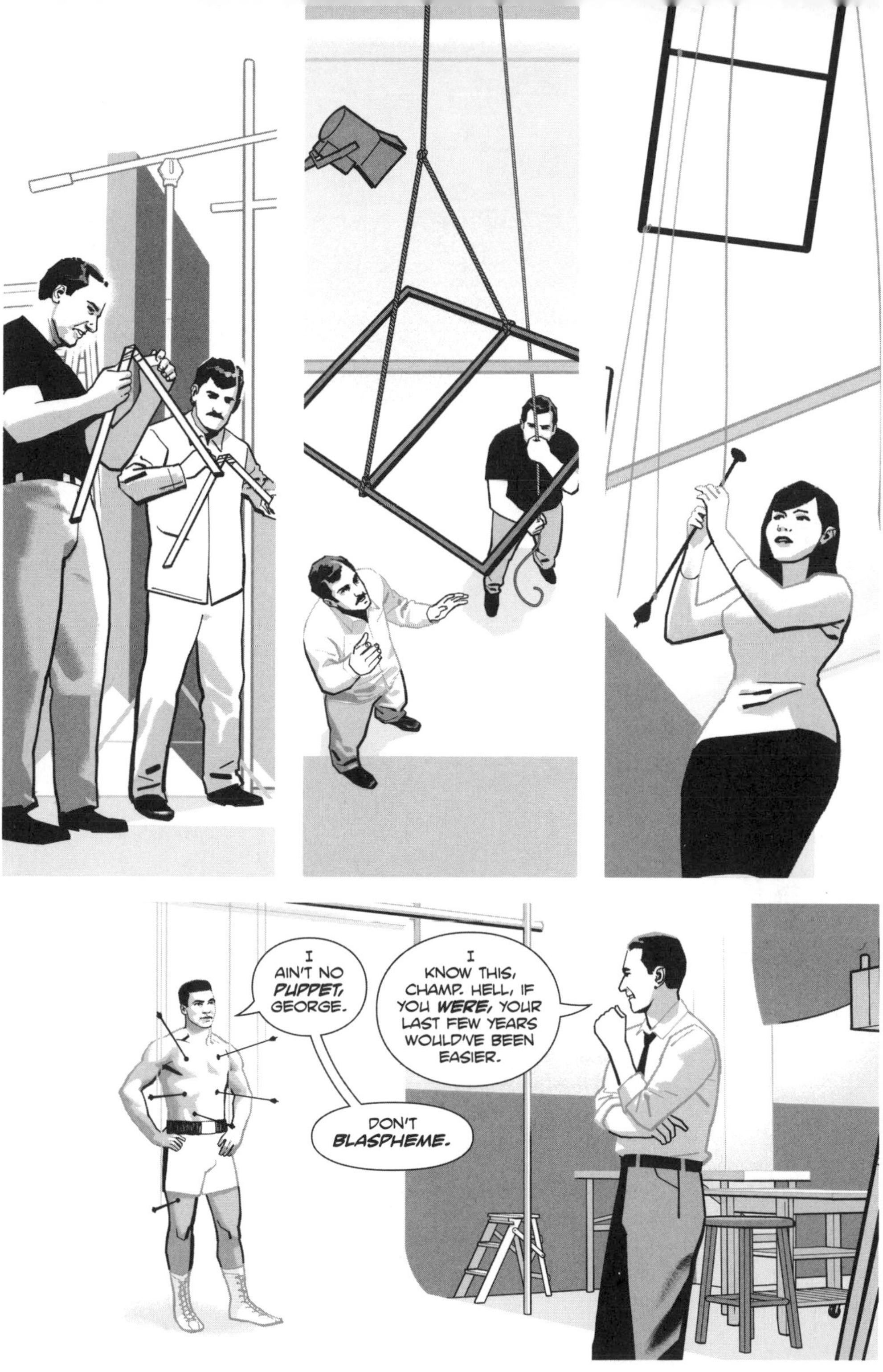
I AIN'T NO *PUPPET,* GEORGE.
I KNOW THIS, CHAMP. HELL, IF YOU *WERE,* YOUR LAST FEW YEARS WOULD'VE BEEN EASIER.
DON'T *BLASPHEME.*

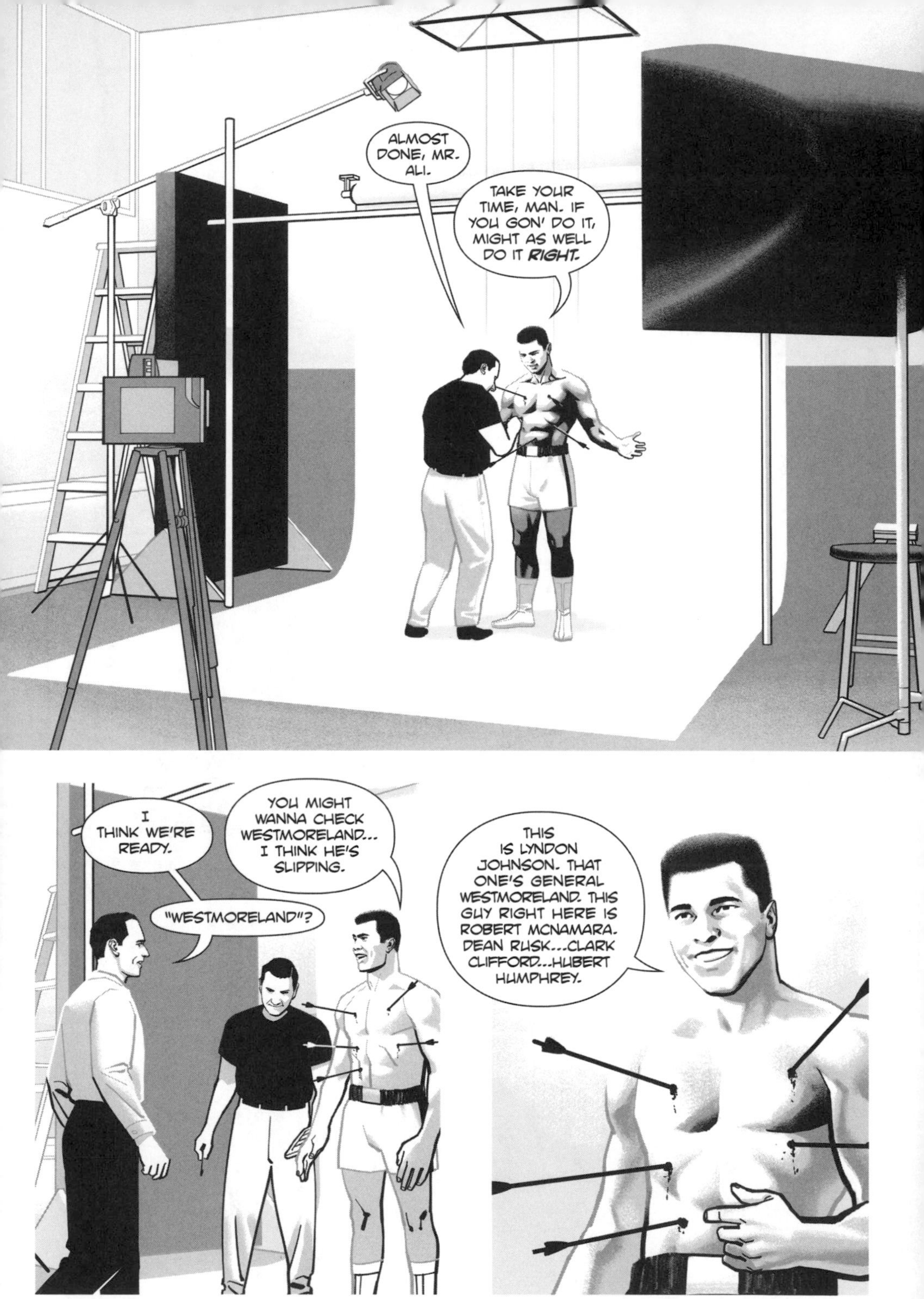
ALMOST DONE, MR. ALI.
TAKE YOUR TIME, MAN. IF YOU GON' DO IT, MIGHT AS WELL DO IT ***RIGHT.***
I THINK WE'RE READY.
YOU MIGHT WANNA CHECK WESTMORELAND... I THINK HE'S SLIPPING.
"WESTMORELAND"?
THIS IS LYNDON JOHNSON. THAT ONE'S GENERAL WESTMORELAND. THIS GUY RIGHT HERE IS ROBERT MCNAMARA. DEAN RUSK...CLARK CLIFFORD...HUBERT HUMPHREY.

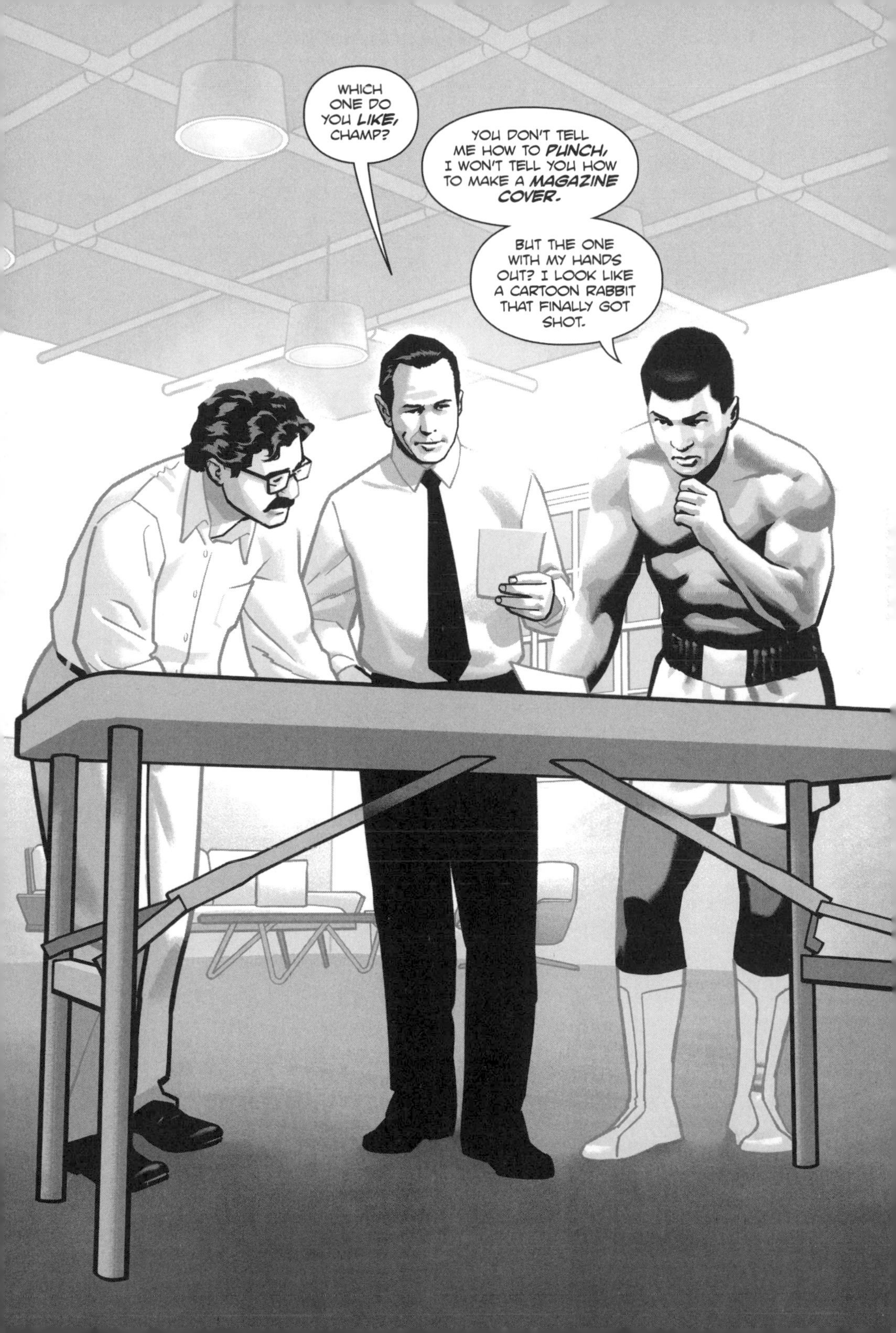
WHICH ONE DO YOU LIKE, CHAMP?
YOU DON'T TELL ME HOW TO PUNCH, I WON'T TELL YOU HOW TO MAKE A MAGAZINE COVER.
BUT THE ONE WITH MY HANDS OUT? I LOOK LIKE A CARTOON RABBIT THAT FINALLY GOT SHOT.

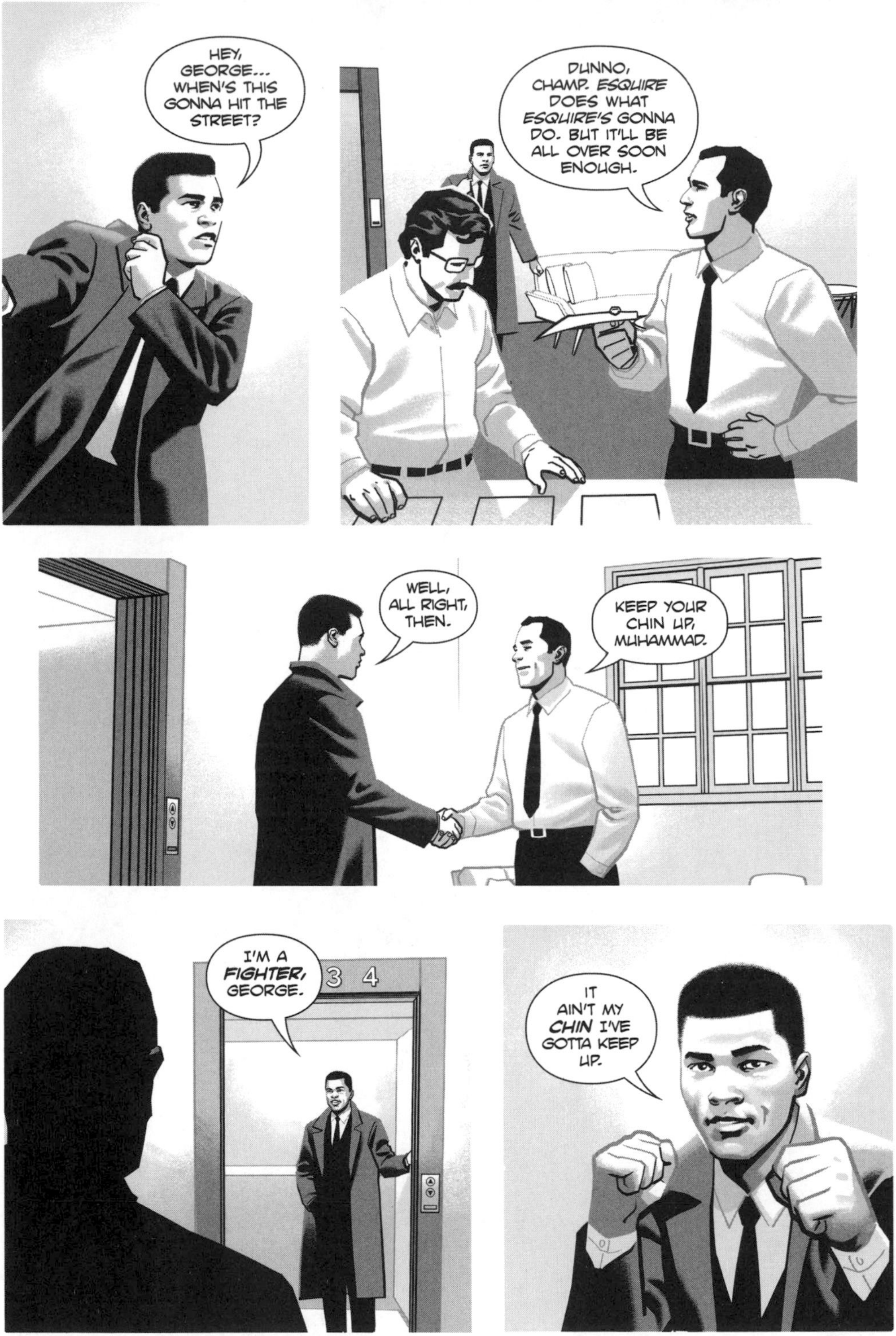
HEY, GEORGE... WHEN'S THIS GONNA HIT THE STREET?
DUNNO, CHAMP. ESQUIRE DOES WHAT ESQUIRE'S GONNA DO. BUT IT'LL BE ALL OVER SOON ENOUGH.
WELL, ALL RIGHT, THEN.
KEEP YOUR CHIN UP, MUHAMMAD.
3 4
I'M A FIGHTER, GEORGE.
IT AIN'T MY CHIN I'VE GOTTA KEEP UP.

ROUND SEVEN: DEFENDANT. 1971.

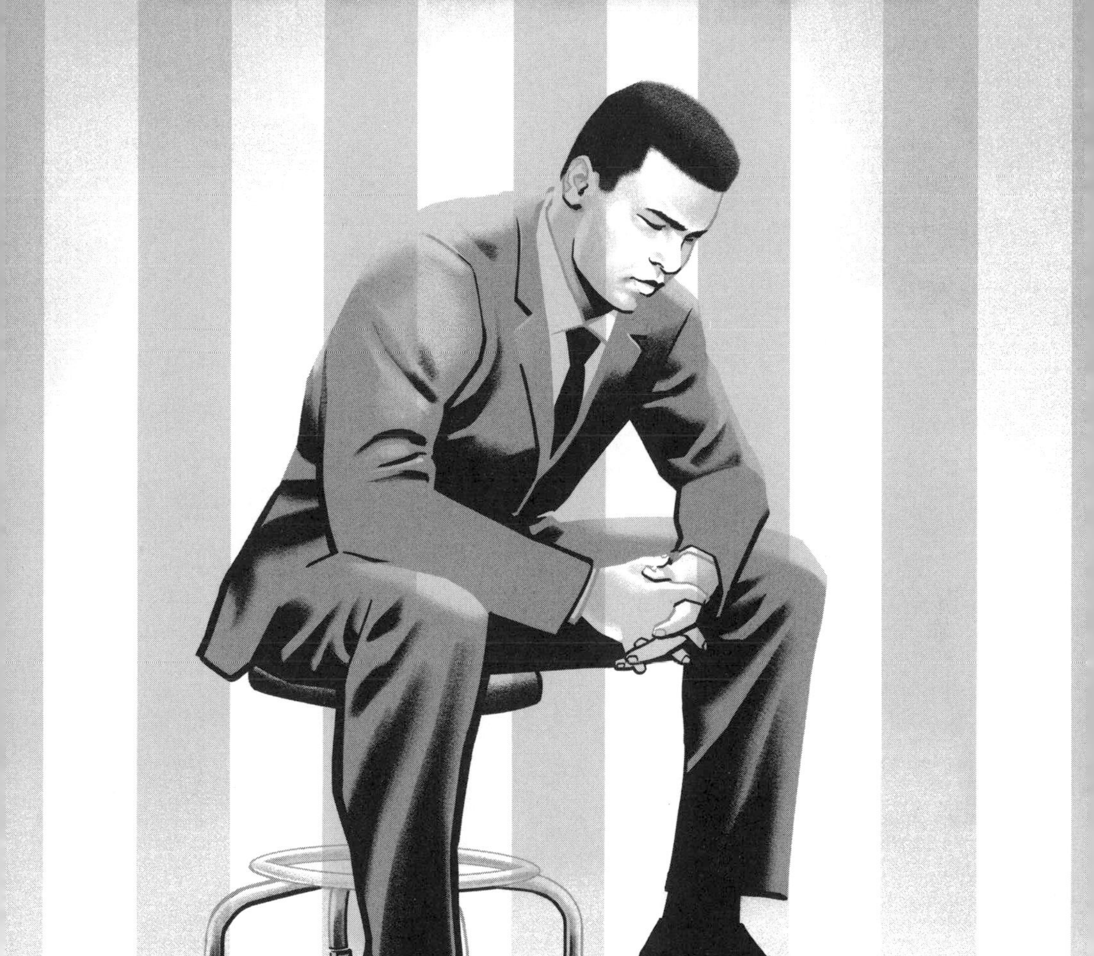

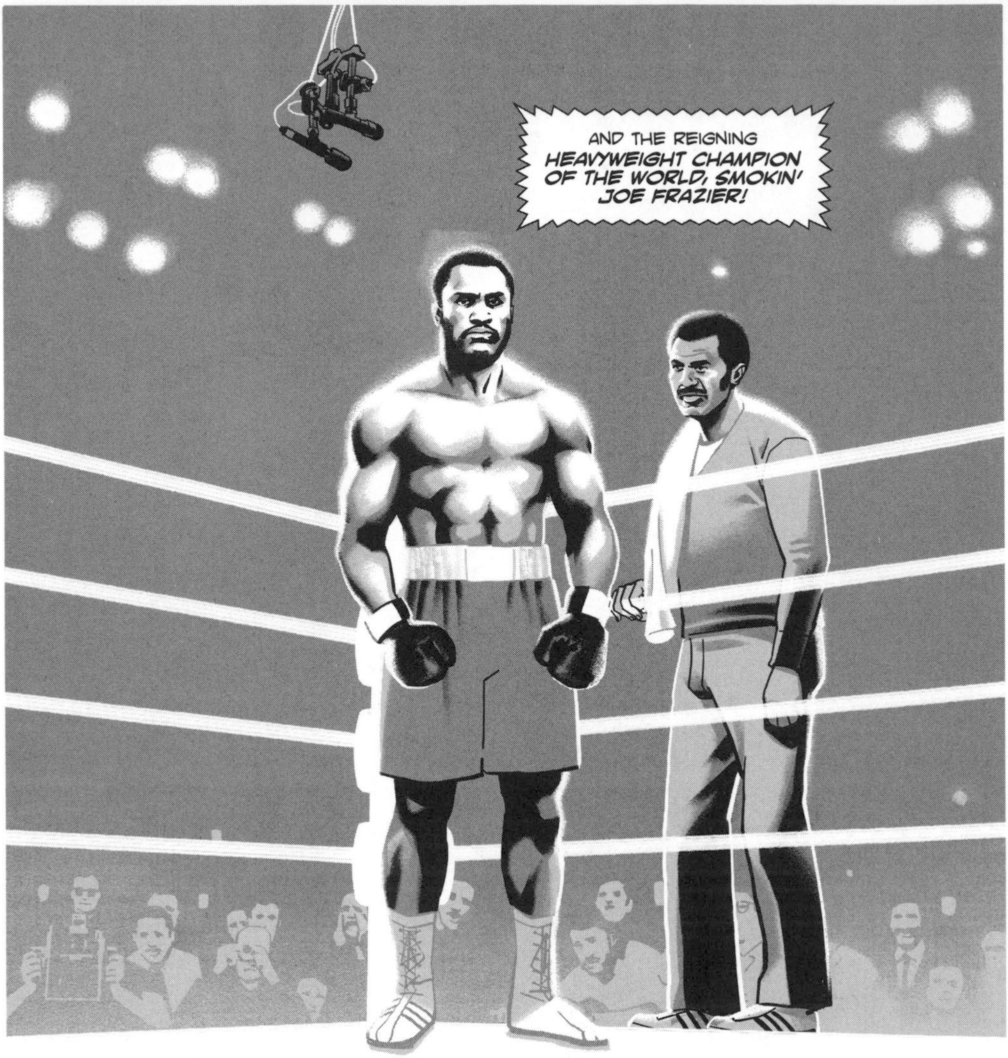
AND THE REIGNING HEAVYWEIGHT CHAMPION OF THE WORLD, SMOKIN' JOE FRAZIER!

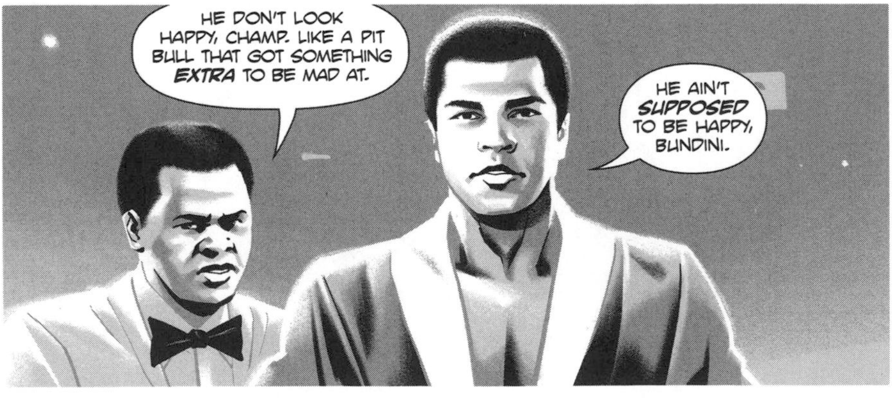
HE DON'T LOOK HAPPY, CHAMP. LIKE A PIT BULL THAT GOT SOMETHING EXTRA TO BE MAD AT.
HE AIN'T SUPPOSED TO BE HAPPY, BUNDINI.

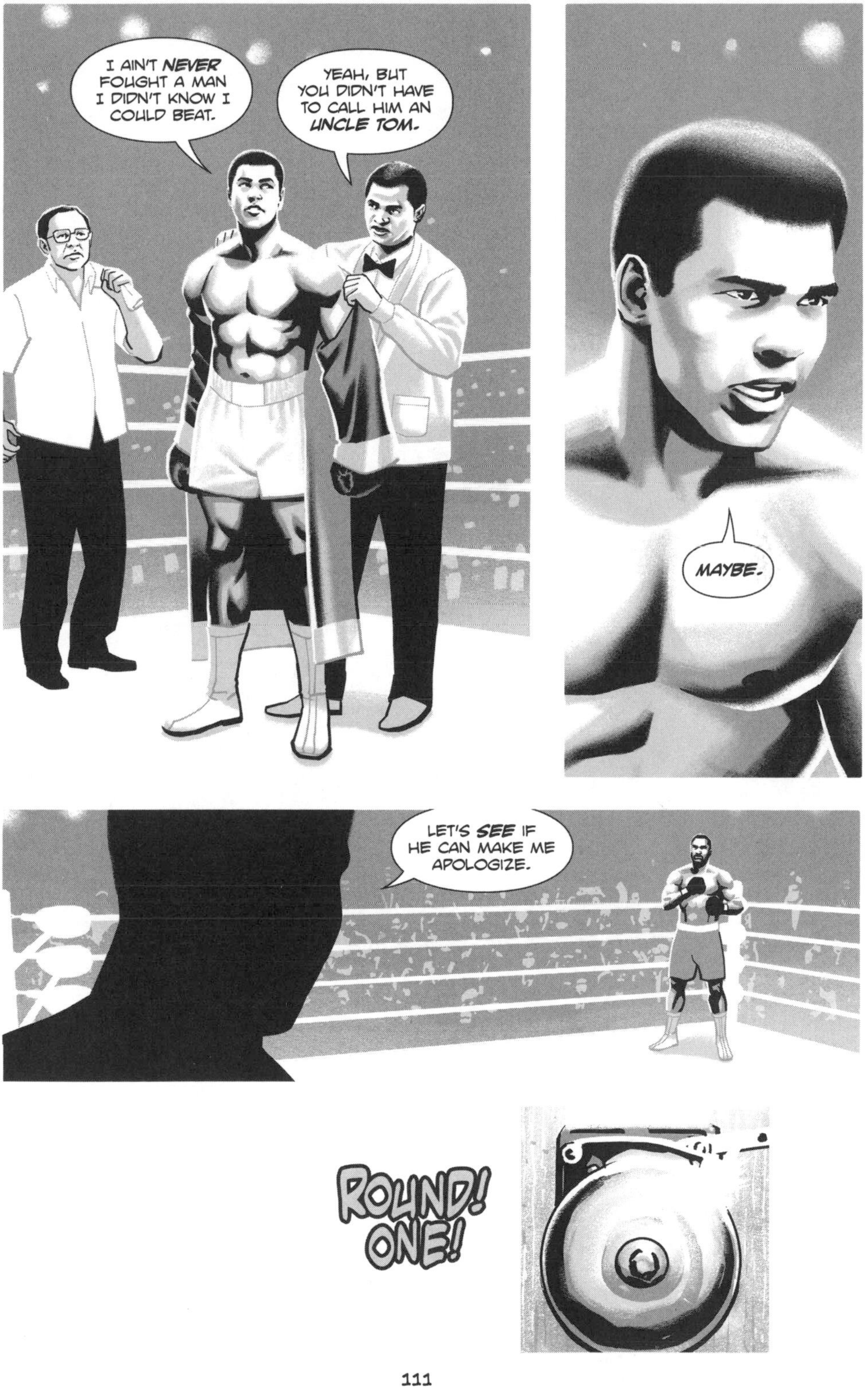
I AIN'T NEVER FOUGHT A MAN I DIDN'T KNOW I COULD BEAT.
YEAH, BUT YOU DIDN'T HAVE TO CALL HIM AN UNCLE TOM.
MAYBE.
LET'S SEE IF HE CAN MAKE ME APOLOGIZE.
ROUND! ONE!

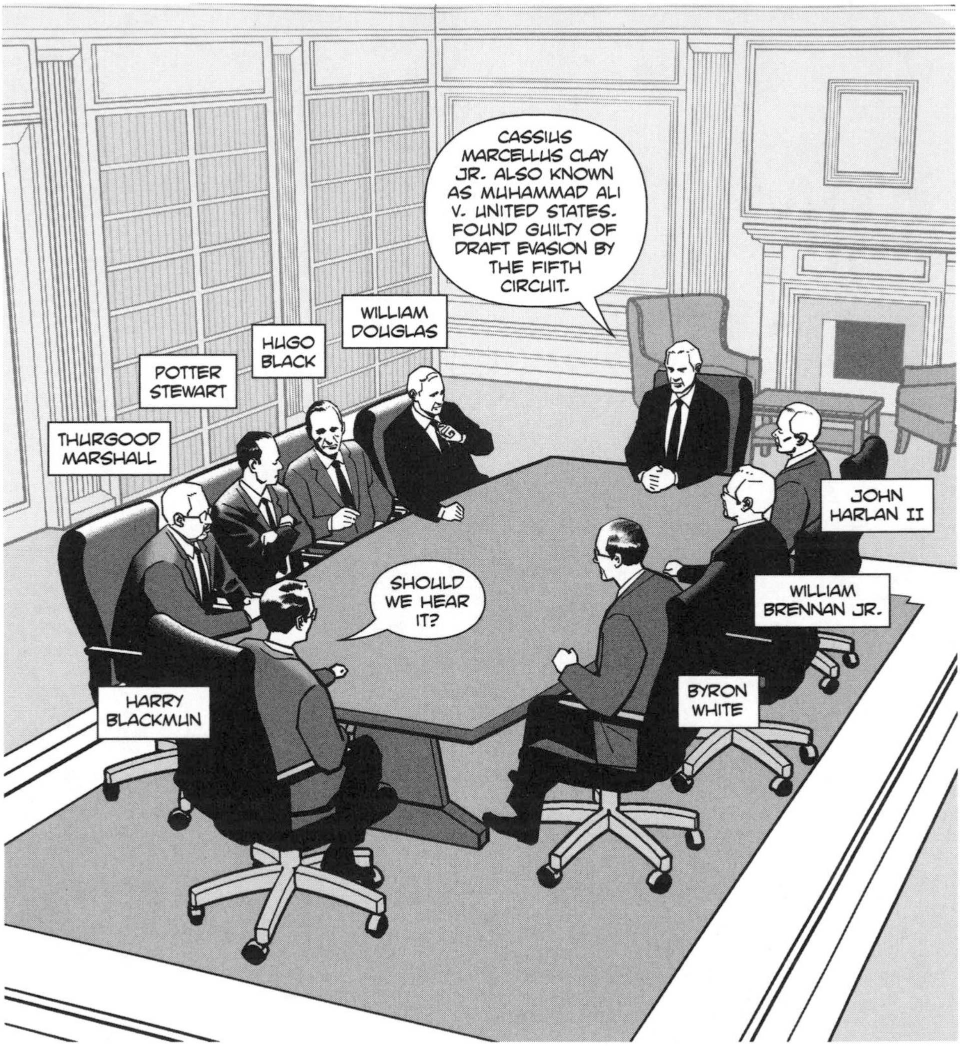
CASSIUS MARCELLUS CLAY JR. ALSO KNOWN AS MUHAMMAD ALI V. UNITED STATES. FOUND GUILTY OF DRAFT EVASION BY THE FIFTH CIRCUIT.
WILLIAM DOUGLAS
HUGO BLACK
POTTER STEWART
THURGOOD MARSHALL
JOHN HARLAN II
WILLIAM BRENNAN JR.
SHOULD WE HEAR IT?
BYRON WHITE
HARRY BLACKMUN

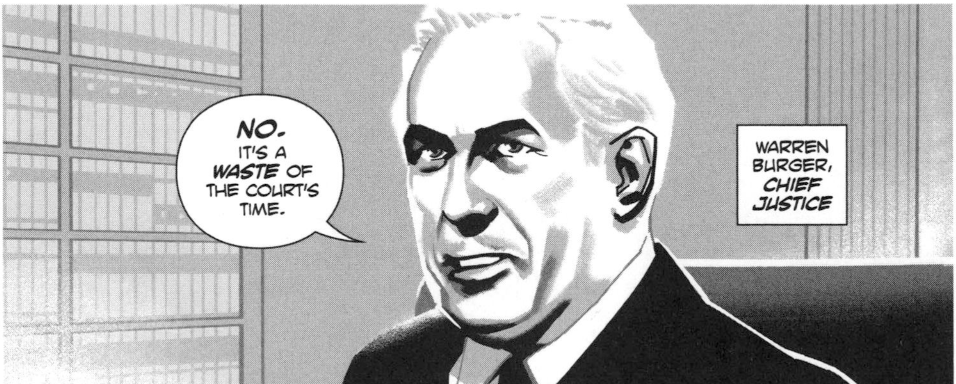
NO. IT'S A WASTE OF THE COURT'S TIME.
WARREN BURGER, CHIEF JUSTICE

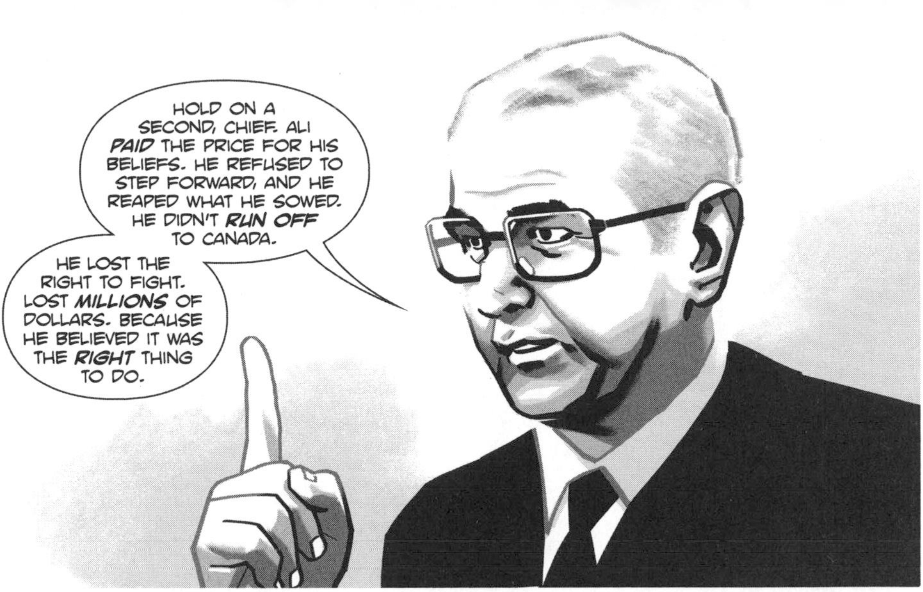
HOLD ON A SECOND, CHIEF. ALI *PAID* THE PRICE FOR HIS BELIEFS. HE REFUSED TO STEP FORWARD, AND HE REAPED WHAT HE SOWED. HE DIDN'T *RUN OFF* TO CANADA.
HE LOST THE RIGHT TO FIGHT. LOST *MILLIONS* OF DOLLARS. BECAUSE HE BELIEVED IT WAS THE *RIGHT* THING TO DO.

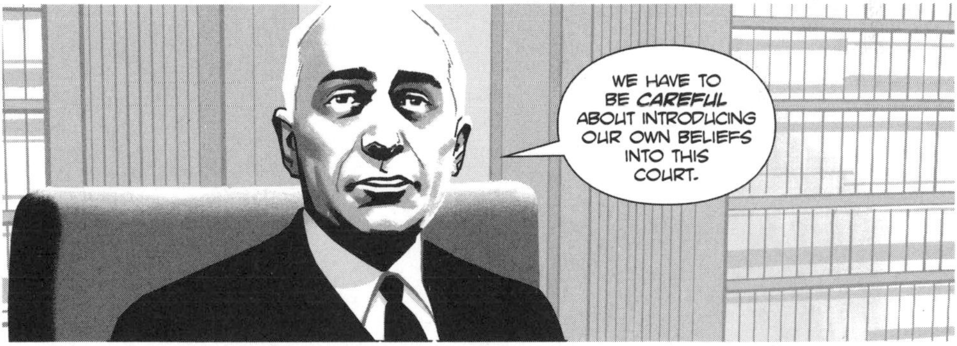
WE HAVE TO BE *CAREFUL* ABOUT INTRODUCING OUR OWN BELIEFS INTO THIS COURT.

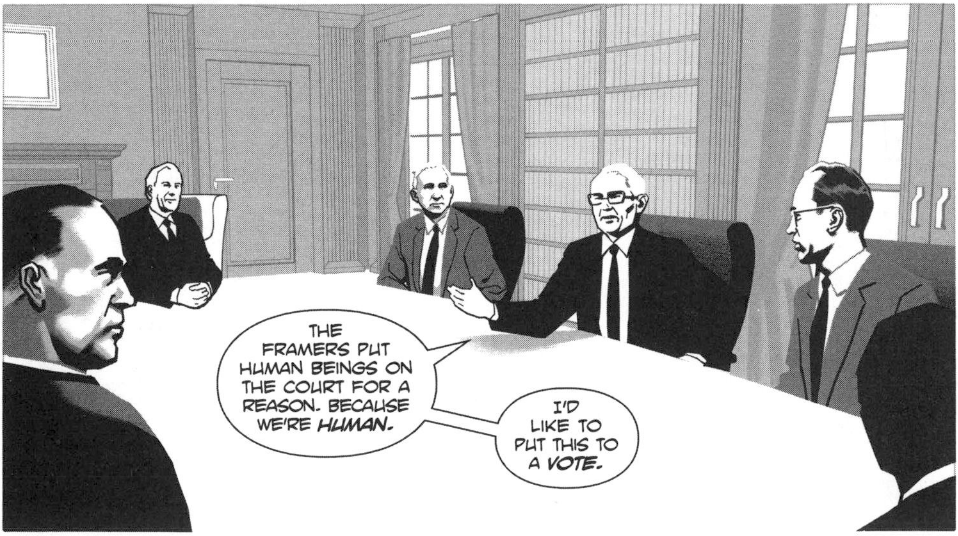
THE FRAMERS PUT HUMAN BEINGS ON THE COURT FOR A REASON. BECAUSE WE'RE *HUMAN.*
I'D LIKE TO PUT THIS TO A *VOTE.*

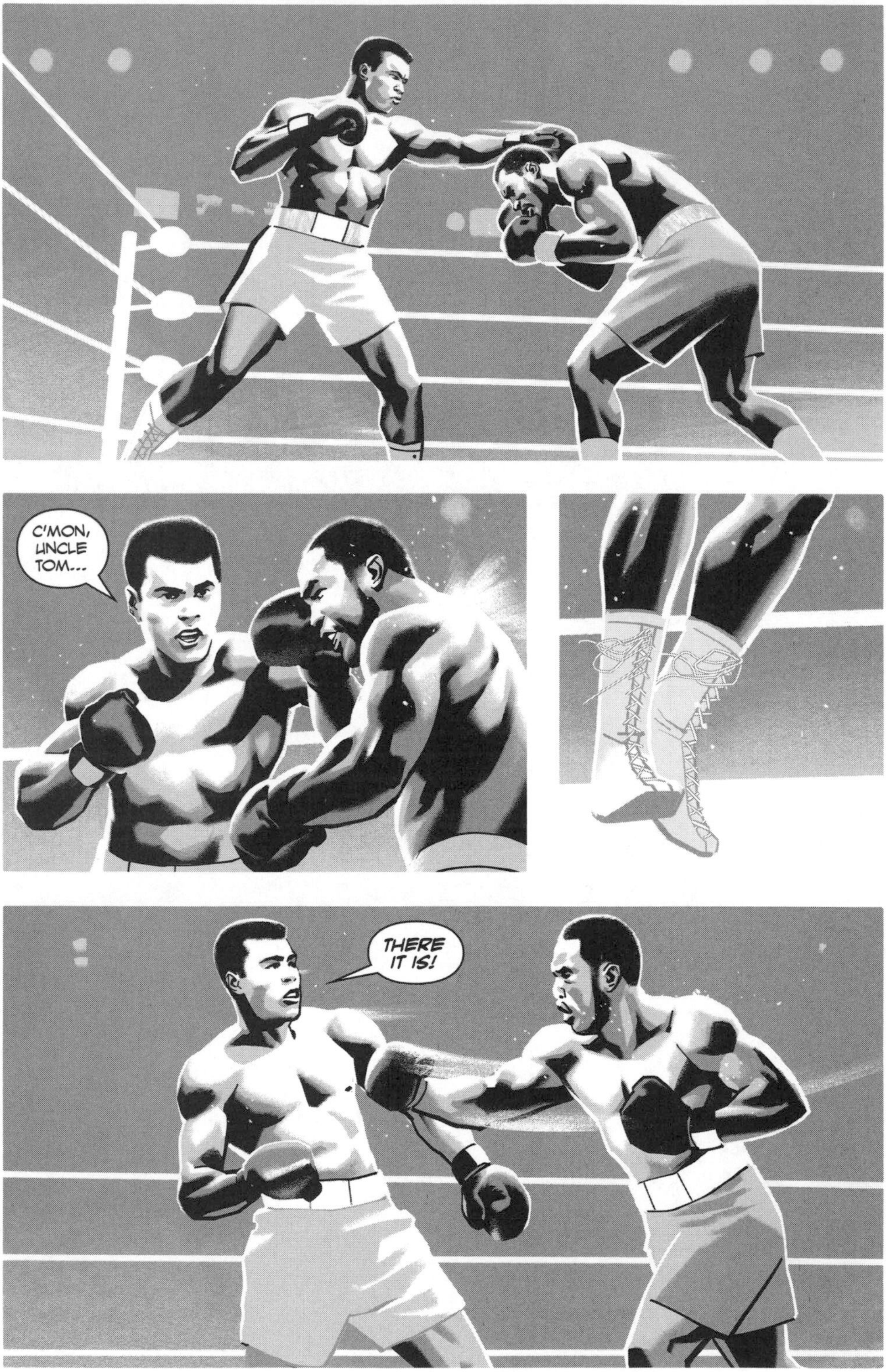
C'MON, UNCLE TOM...
THERE IT IS!

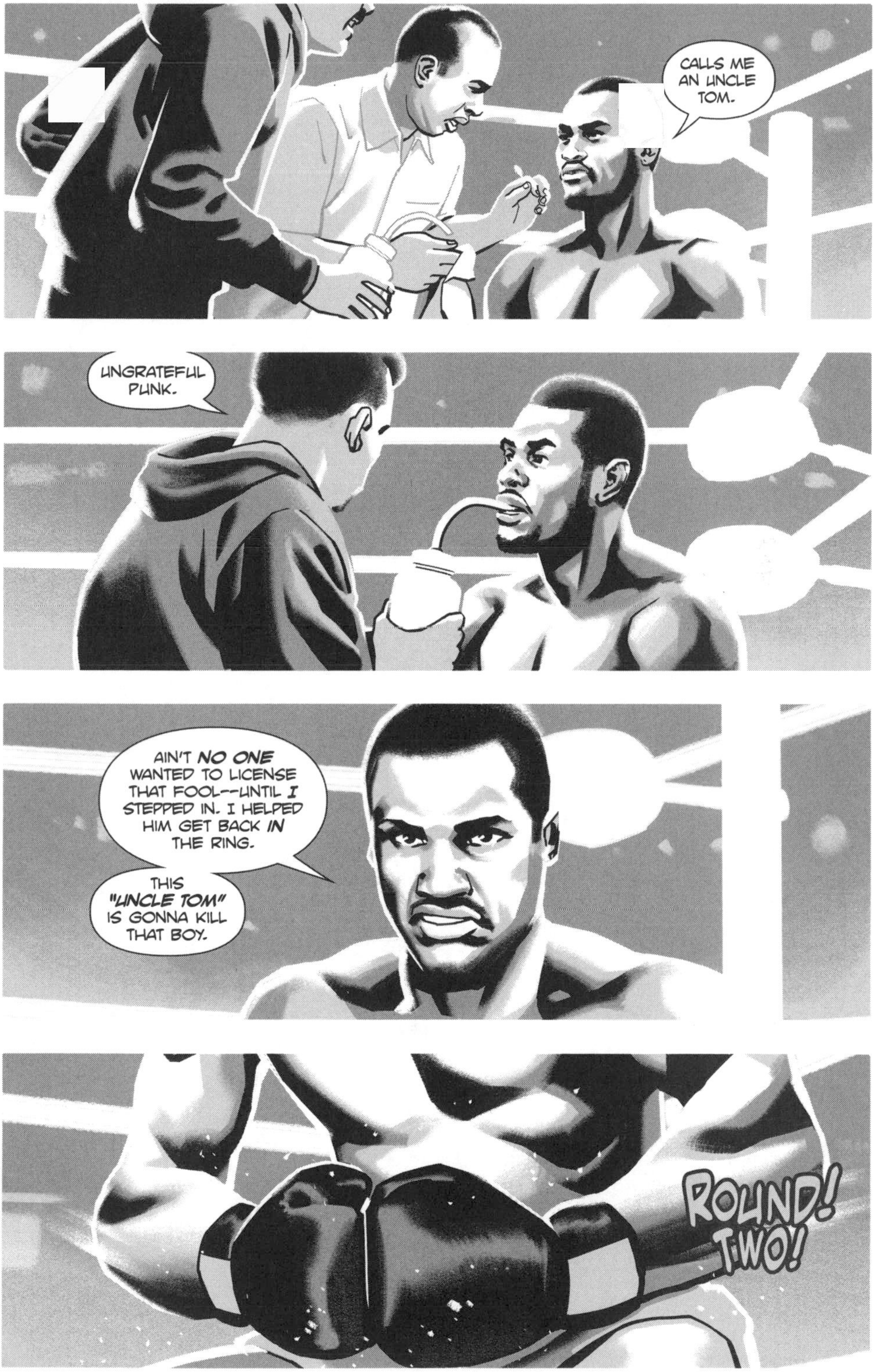
CALLS ME AN UNCLE TOM.
UNGRATEFUL PUNK.
AIN'T **NO ONE** WANTED TO LICENSE THAT FOOL--UNTIL *I* STEPPED IN. I HELPED HIM GET BACK *IN* THE RING.
THIS ***"UNCLE TOM"*** IS GONNA KILL THAT BOY.
ROUND! TWO!

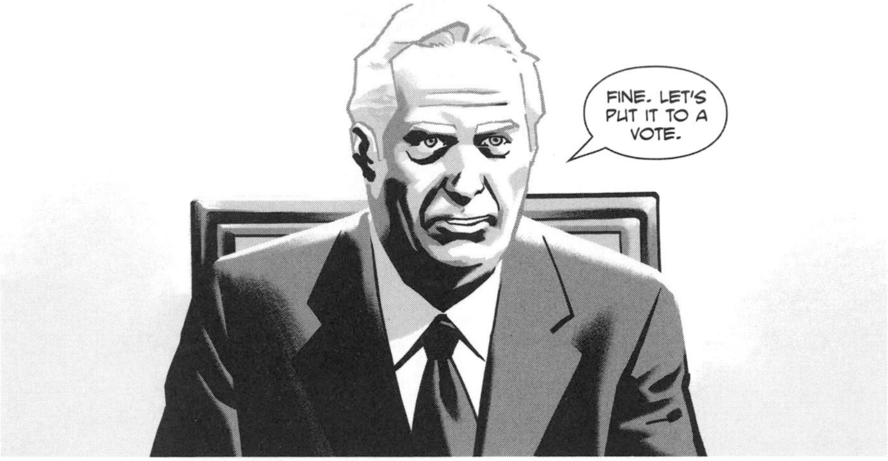
FINE. LET'S PUT IT TO A VOTE.

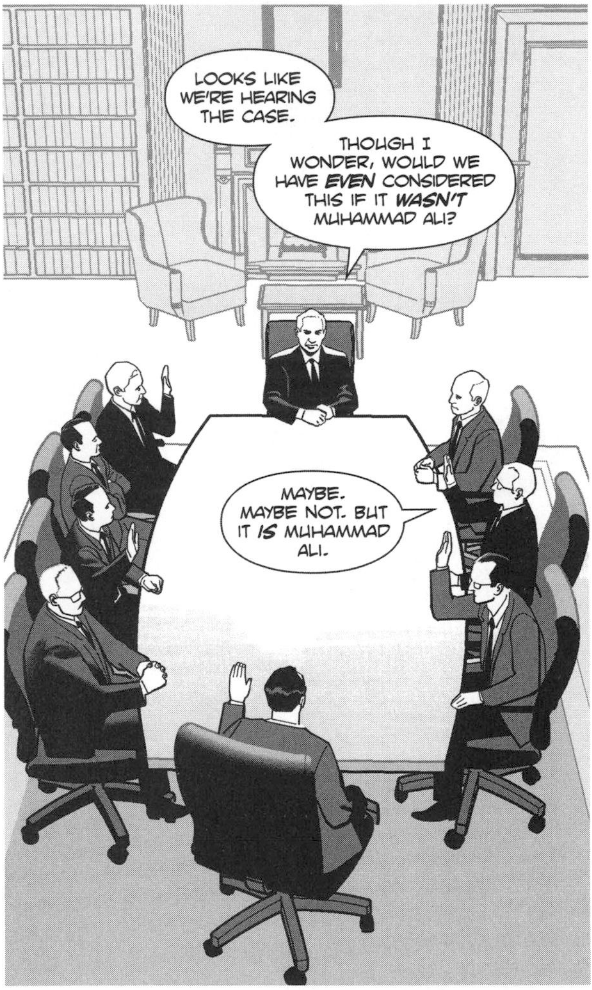
LOOKS LIKE WE'RE HEARING THE CASE.
THOUGH I WONDER, WOULD WE HAVE *EVEN* CONSIDERED THIS IF IT *WASN'T* MUHAMMAD ALI?
MAYBE. MAYBE NOT. BUT IT *IS* MUHAMMAD ALI.

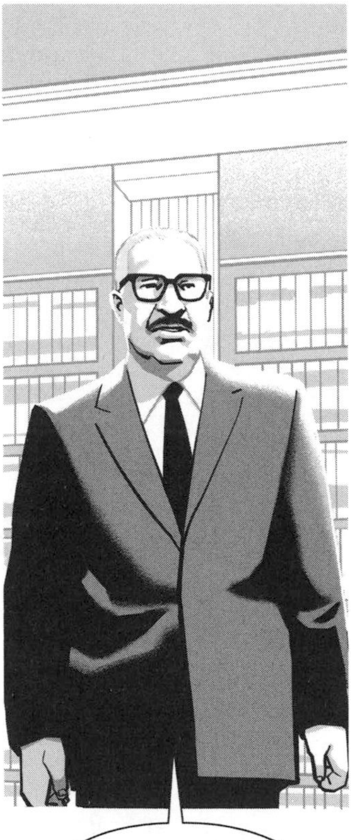
I WAS THE SOLICITOR GENERAL AT THE START OF THE CASE. I'VE GOT TO RECUSE MYSELF FROM THIS ONE.
GOOD LUCK.

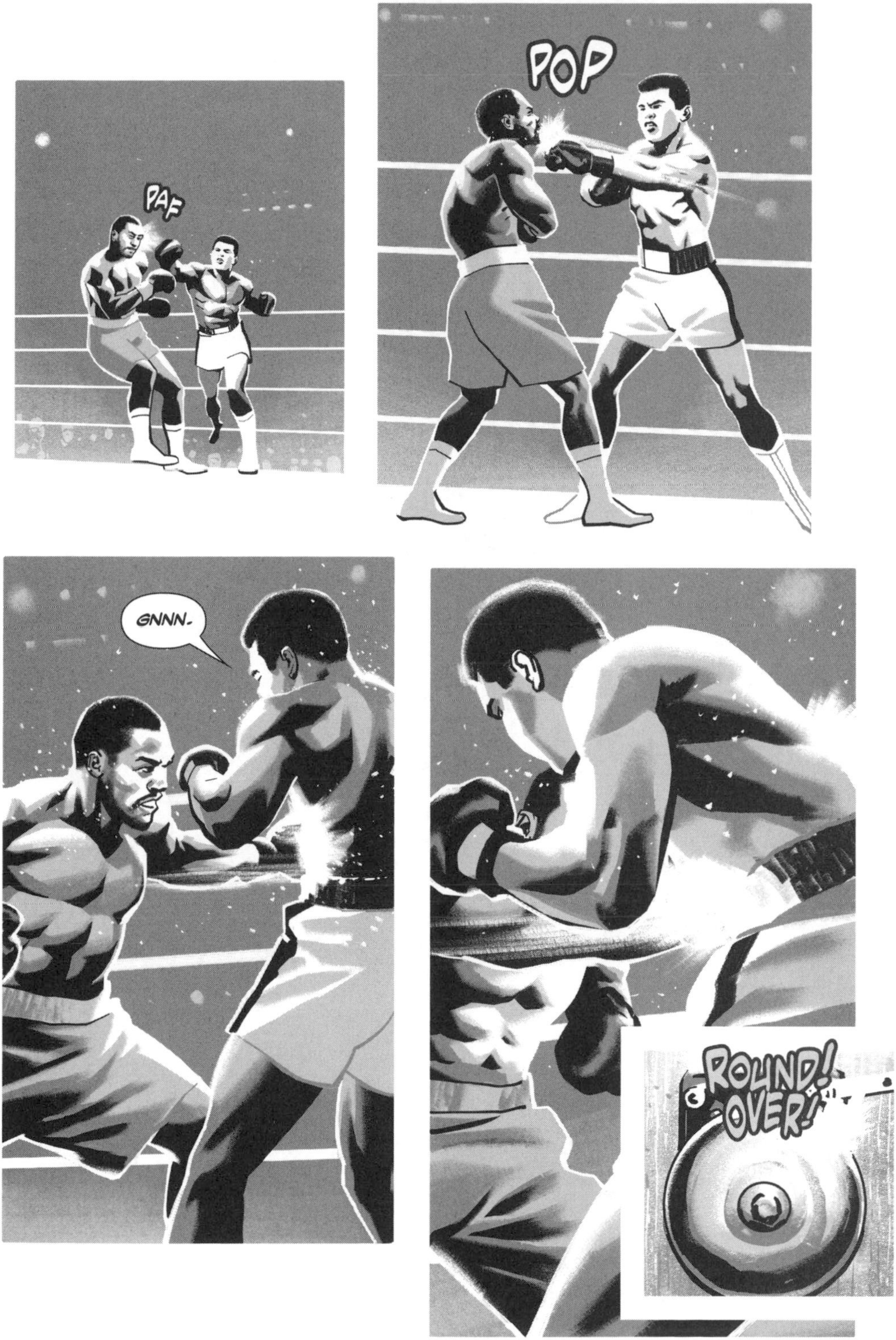
PAF
POP
GNNN-
ROUND! OVER!

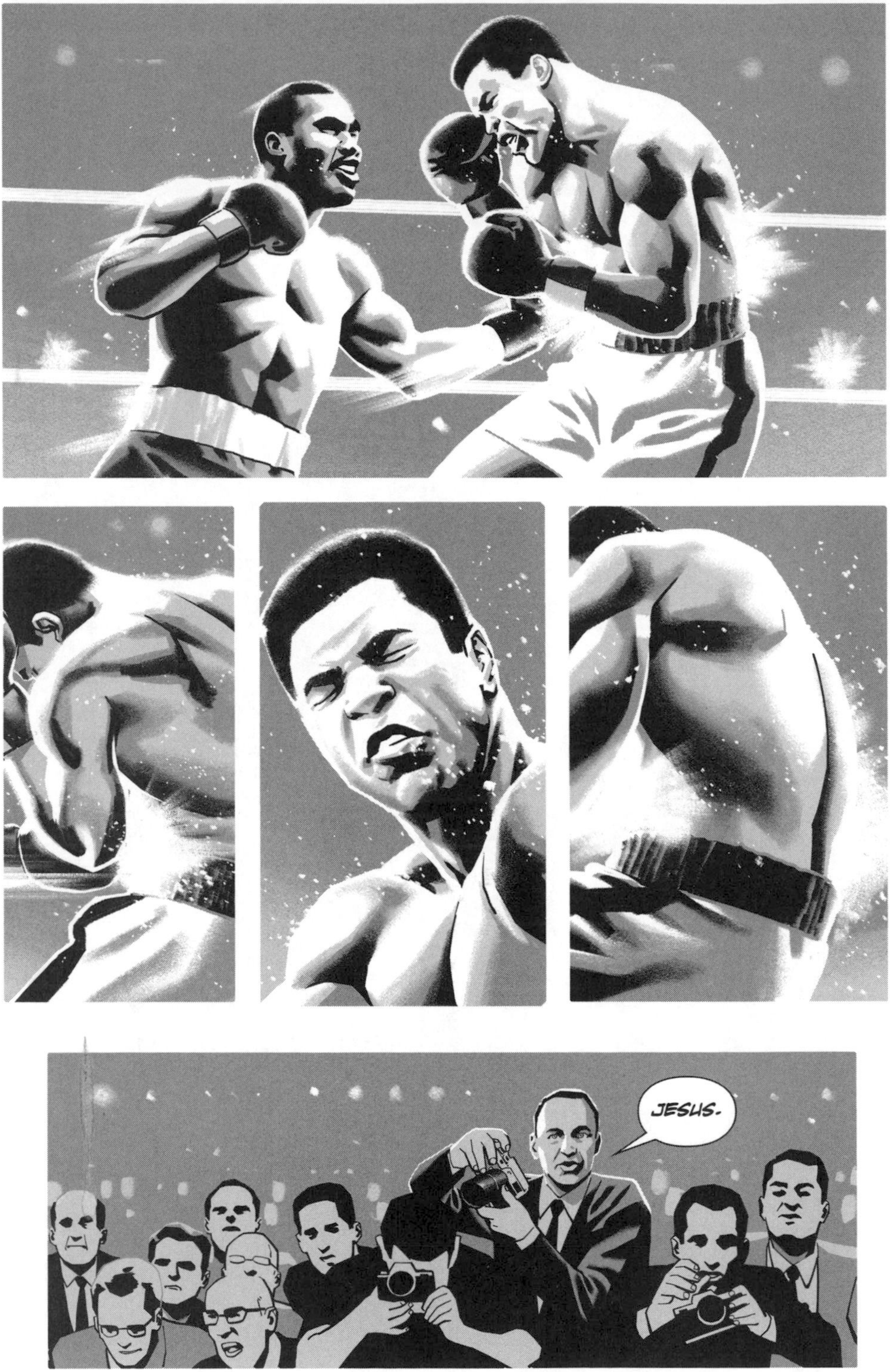
JESUS.

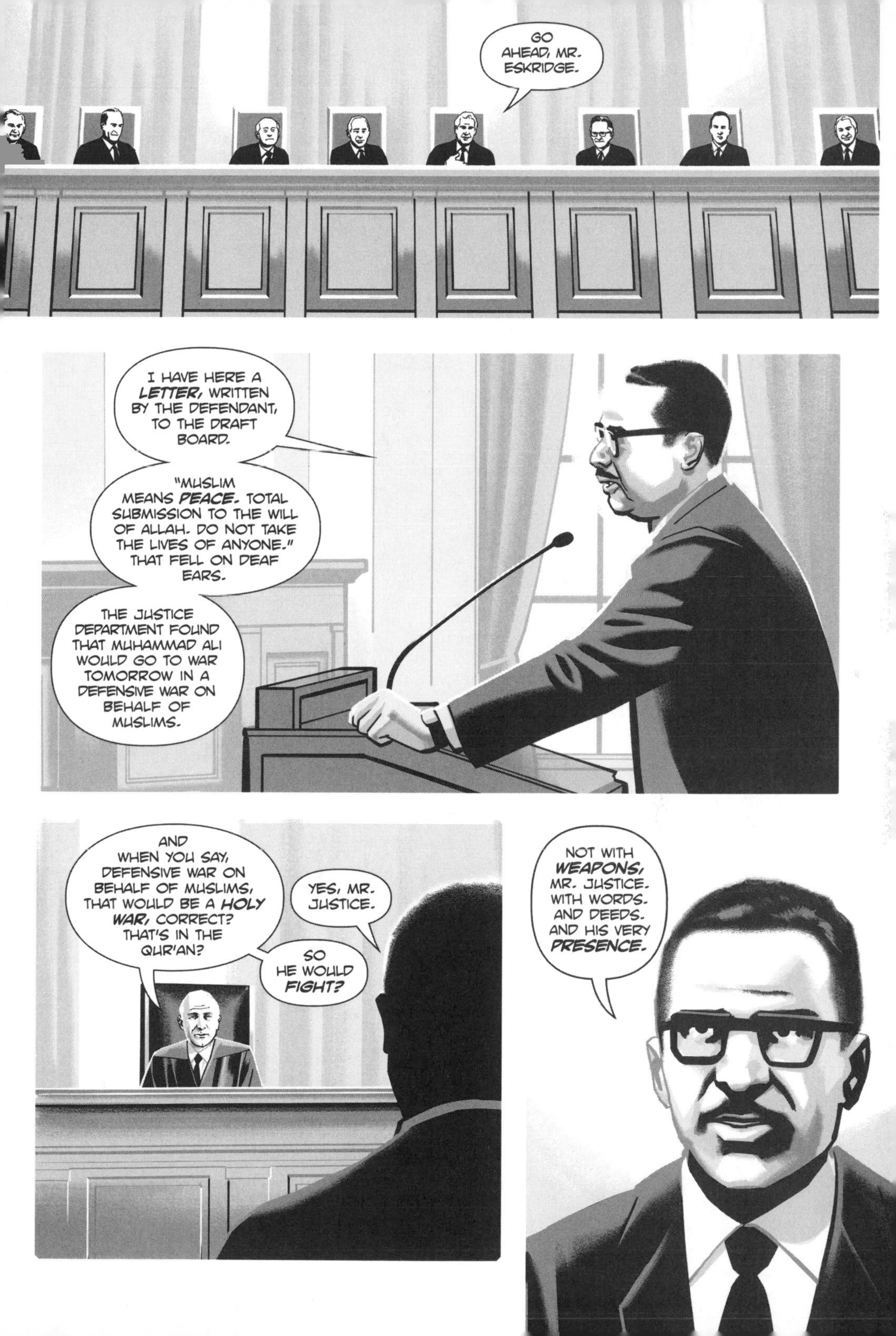
GO AHEAD, MR. ESKRIDGE.
I HAVE HERE A LETTER, WRITTEN BY THE DEFENDANT, TO THE DRAFT BOARD.
"MUSLIM MEANS PEACE. TOTAL SUBMISSION TO THE WILL OF ALLAH. DO NOT TAKE THE LIVES OF ANYONE." THAT FELL ON DEAF EARS.
THE JUSTICE DEPARTMENT FOUND THAT MUHAMMAD ALI WOULD GO TO WAR TOMORROW IN A DEFENSIVE WAR ON BEHALF OF MUSLIMS.
AND WHEN YOU SAY, DEFENSIVE WAR ON BEHALF OF MUSLIMS, THAT WOULD BE A HOLY WAR, CORRECT? THAT'S IN THE QUR'AN?
YES, MR. JUSTICE.
SO HE WOULD FIGHT?
NOT WITH WEAPONS, MR. JUSTICE. WITH WORDS. AND DEEDS. AND HIS VERY PRESENCE.

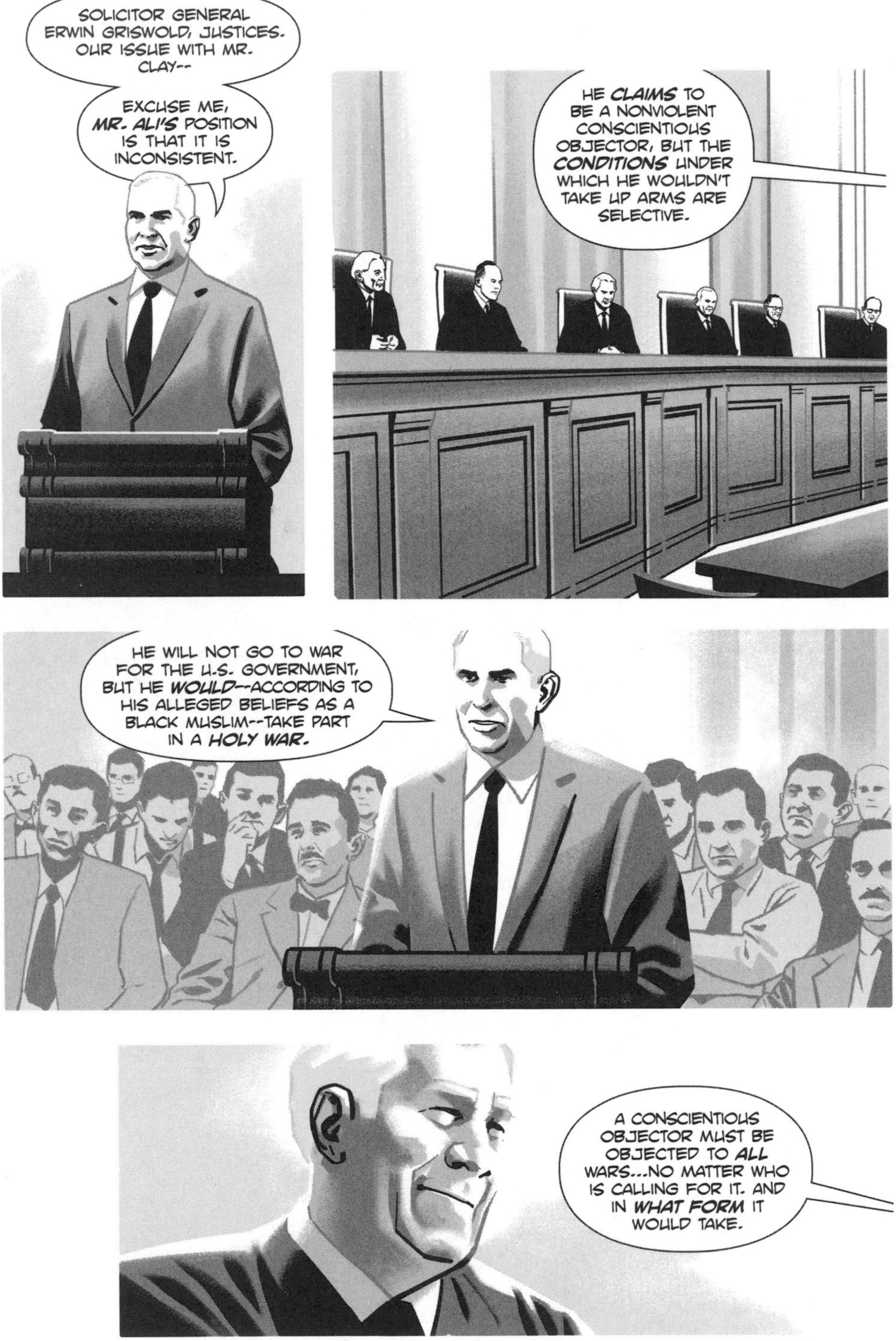
SOLICITOR GENERAL ERWIN GRISWOLD, JUSTICES. OUR ISSUE WITH MR. CLAY--
EXCUSE ME, MR. ALI'S POSITION IS THAT IT IS INCONSISTENT.
HE CLAIMS TO BE A NONVIOLENT CONSCIENTIOUS OBJECTOR, BUT THE CONDITIONS UNDER WHICH HE WOULDN'T TAKE UP ARMS ARE SELECTIVE.
HE WILL NOT GO TO WAR FOR THE U.S. GOVERNMENT, BUT HE WOULD--ACCORDING TO HIS ALLEGED BELIEFS AS A BLACK MUSLIM--TAKE PART IN A HOLY WAR.
A CONSCIENTIOUS OBJECTOR MUST BE OBJECTED TO ALL WARS...NO MATTER WHO IS CALLING FOR IT. AND IN WHAT FORM IT WOULD TAKE.

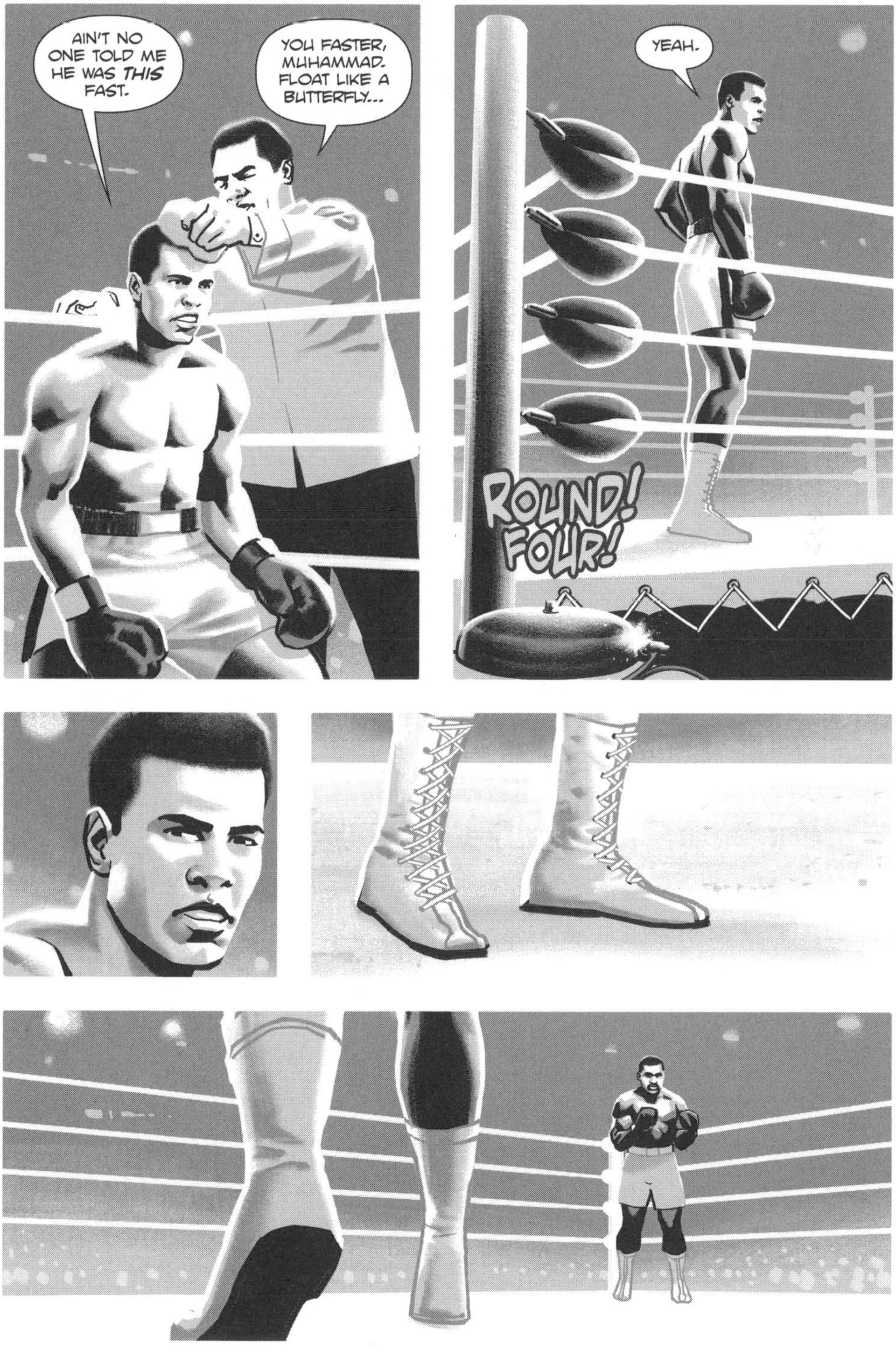
AIN'T NO ONE TOLD ME HE WAS *THIS* FAST.
YOU FASTER, MUHAMMAD. FLOAT LIKE A BUTTERFLY...
YEAH.
ROUND! FOUR!

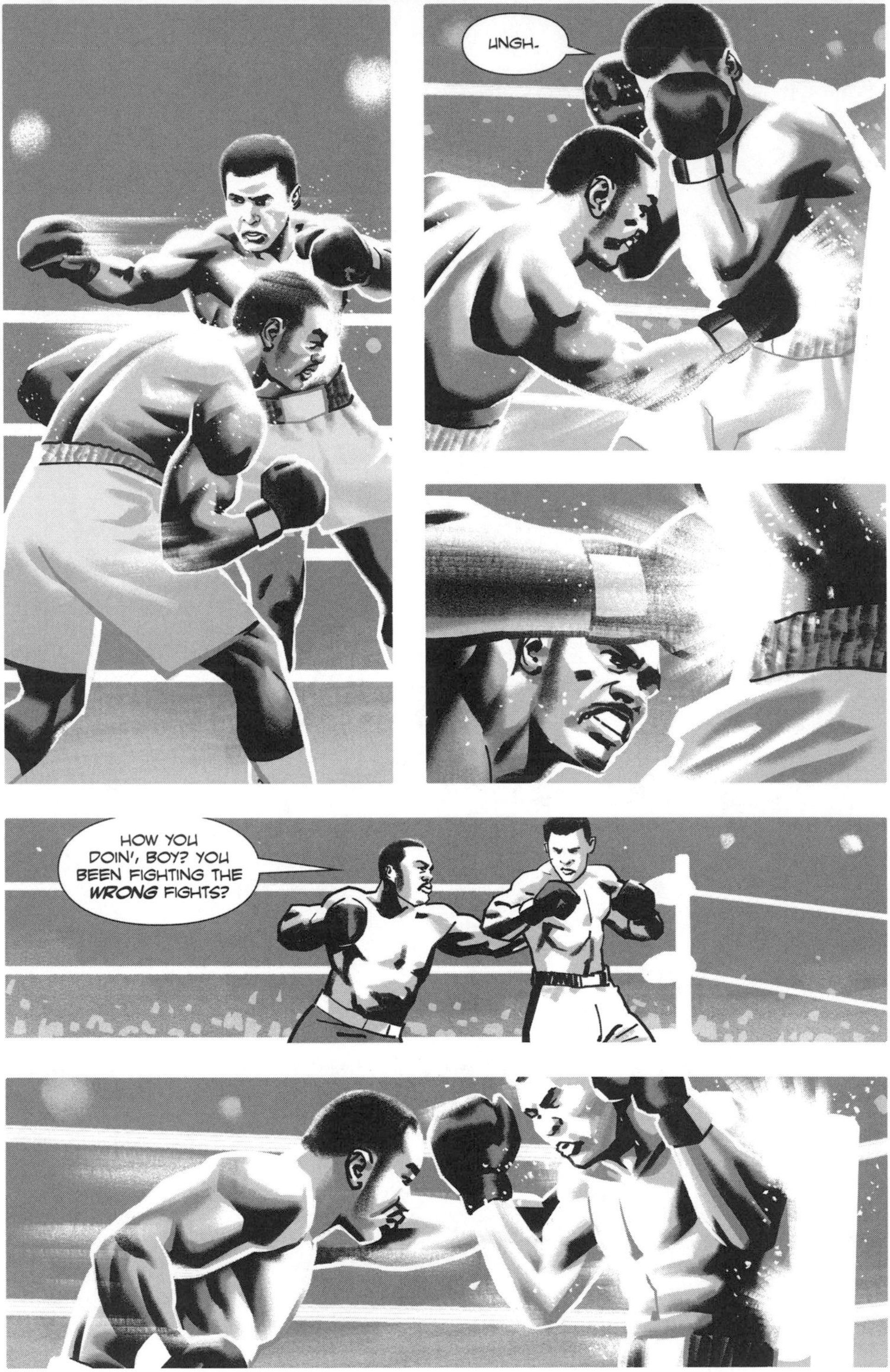
UNGH.
HOW YOU DOIN', BOY? YOU BEEN FIGHTING THE ***WRONG*** FIGHTS?

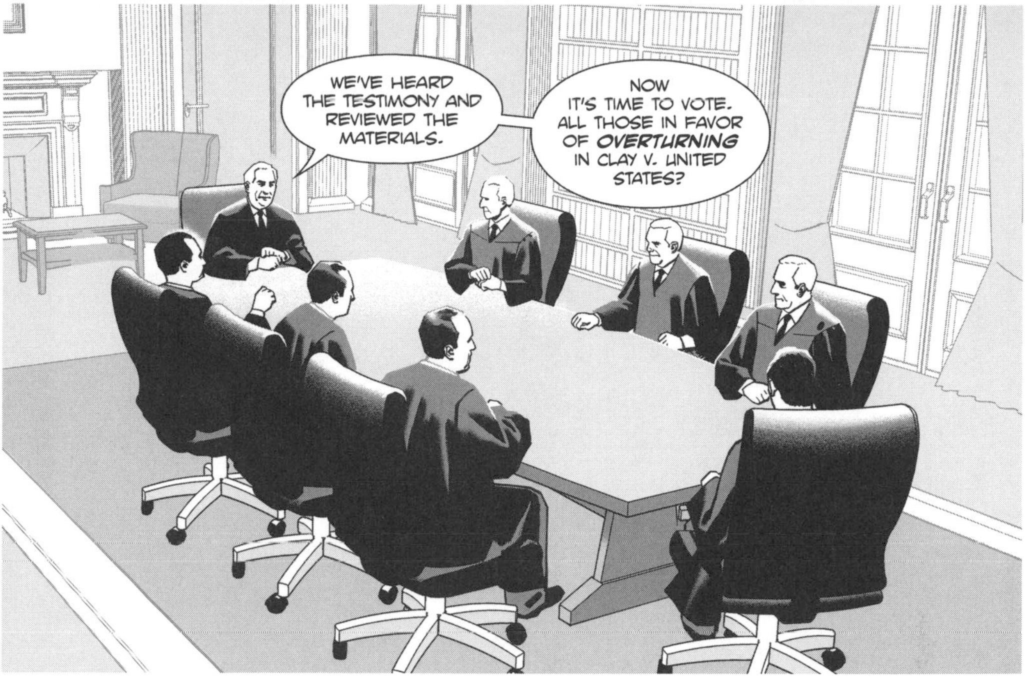
WE'VE HEARD THE TESTIMONY AND REVIEWED THE MATERIALS.
NOW IT'S TIME TO VOTE. ALL THOSE IN FAVOR OF OVERTURNING IN CLAY V. UNITED STATES?

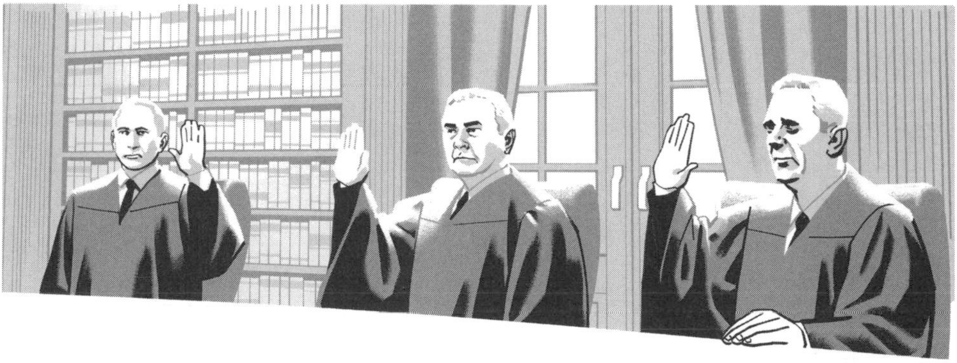

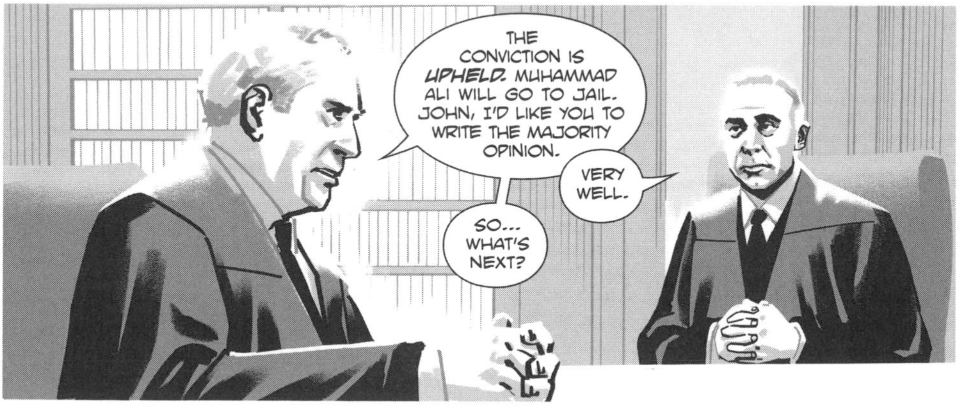
THE CONVICTION IS UPHELD. MUHAMMAD ALI WILL GO TO JAIL. JOHN, I'D LIKE YOU TO WRITE THE MAJORITY OPINION.
VERY WELL.
SO... WHAT'S NEXT?

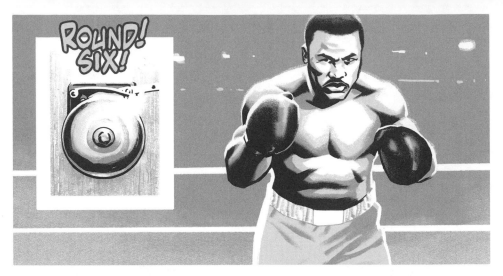

ROUND! SIX!

POP

PAF

PIFF

P-TOOO!

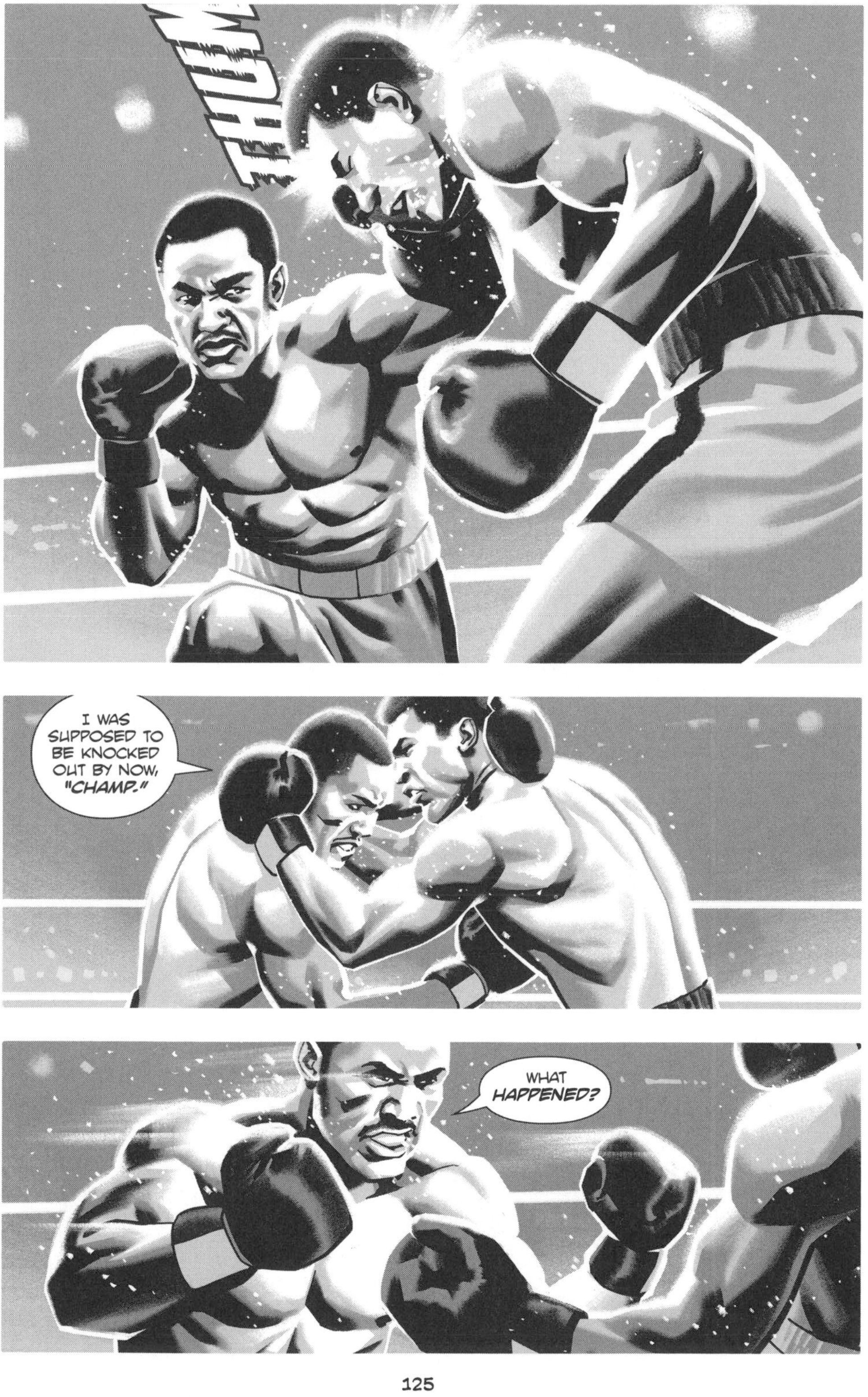
I WAS SUPPOSED TO BE KNOCKED OUT BY NOW, "CHAMP."
WHAT HAPPENED?

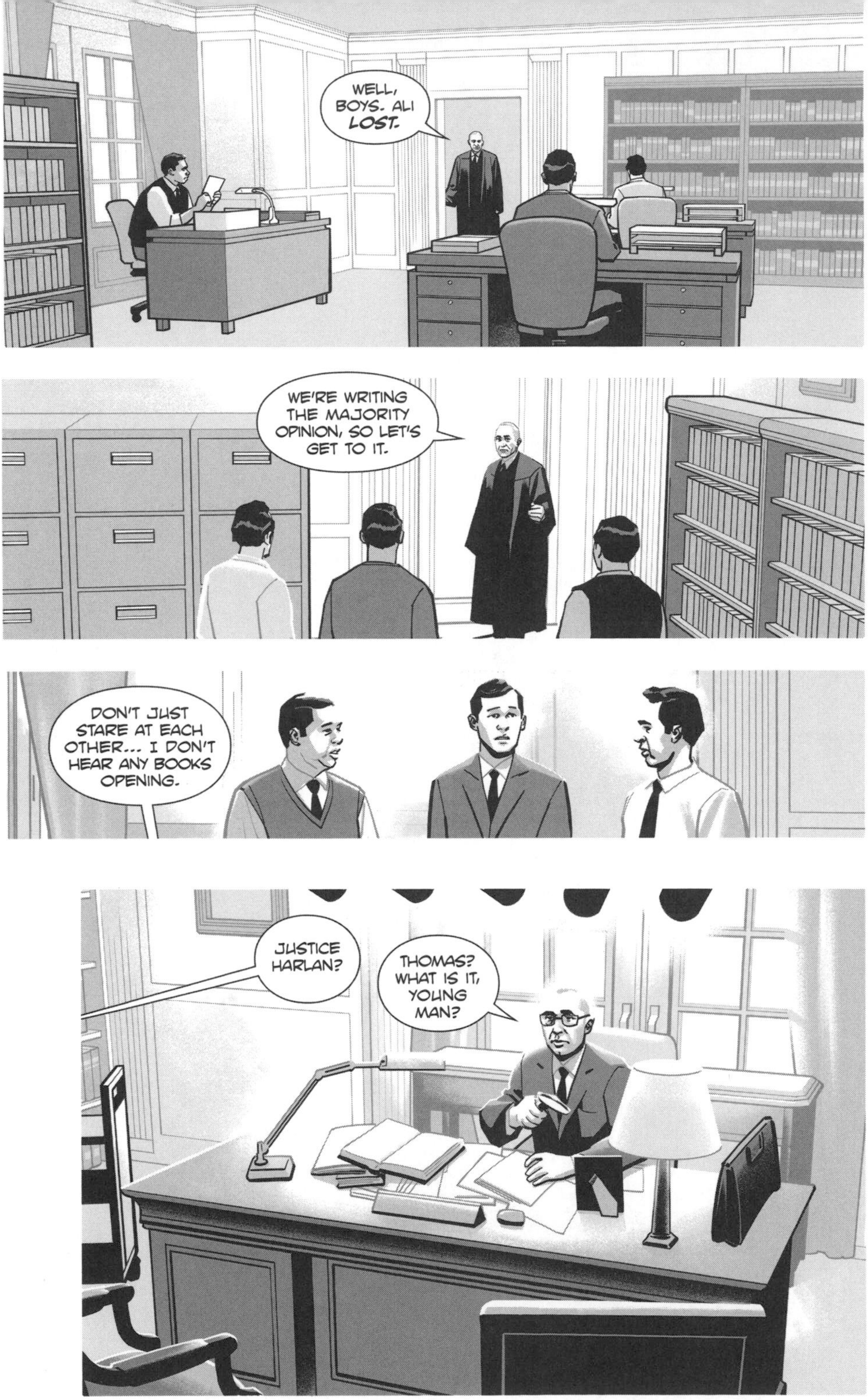
WELL, BOYS. ALI LOST.
WE'RE WRITING THE MAJORITY OPINION, SO LET'S GET TO IT.
DON'T JUST STARE AT EACH OTHER... I DON'T HEAR ANY BOOKS OPENING.
JUSTICE HARLAN?
THOMAS? WHAT IS IT, YOUNG MAN?

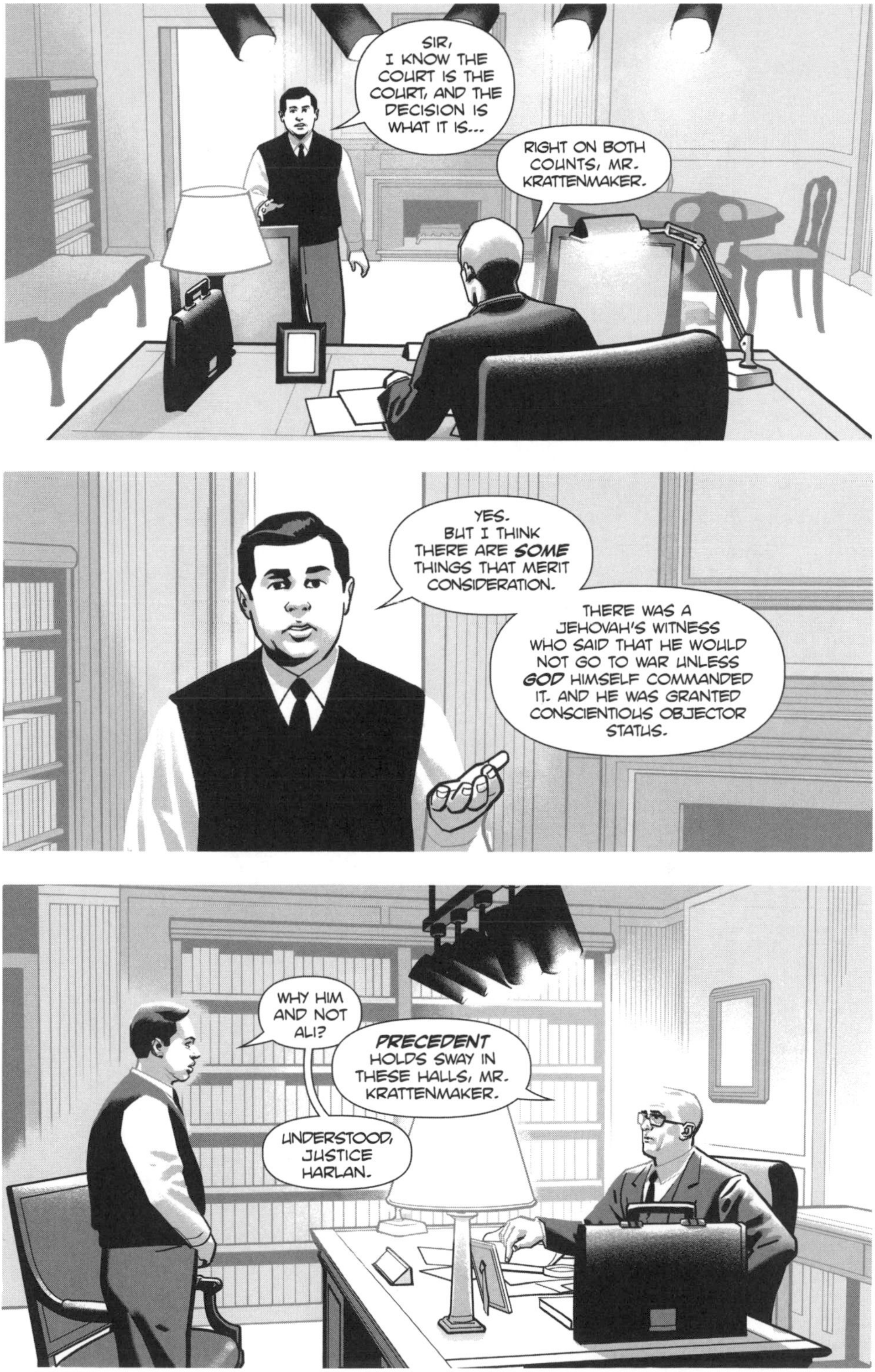
SIR, I KNOW THE COURT IS THE COURT, AND THE DECISION IS WHAT IT IS...
RIGHT ON BOTH COUNTS, MR. KRATTENMAKER.
YES. BUT I THINK THERE ARE SOME THINGS THAT MERIT CONSIDERATION.
THERE WAS A JEHOVAH'S WITNESS WHO SAID THAT HE WOULD NOT GO TO WAR UNLESS GOD HIMSELF COMMANDED IT. AND HE WAS GRANTED CONSCIENTIOUS OBJECTOR STATUS.
WHY HIM AND NOT ALI?
PRECEDENT HOLDS SWAY IN THESE HALLS, MR. KRATTENMAKER.
UNDERSTOOD, JUSTICE HARLAN.

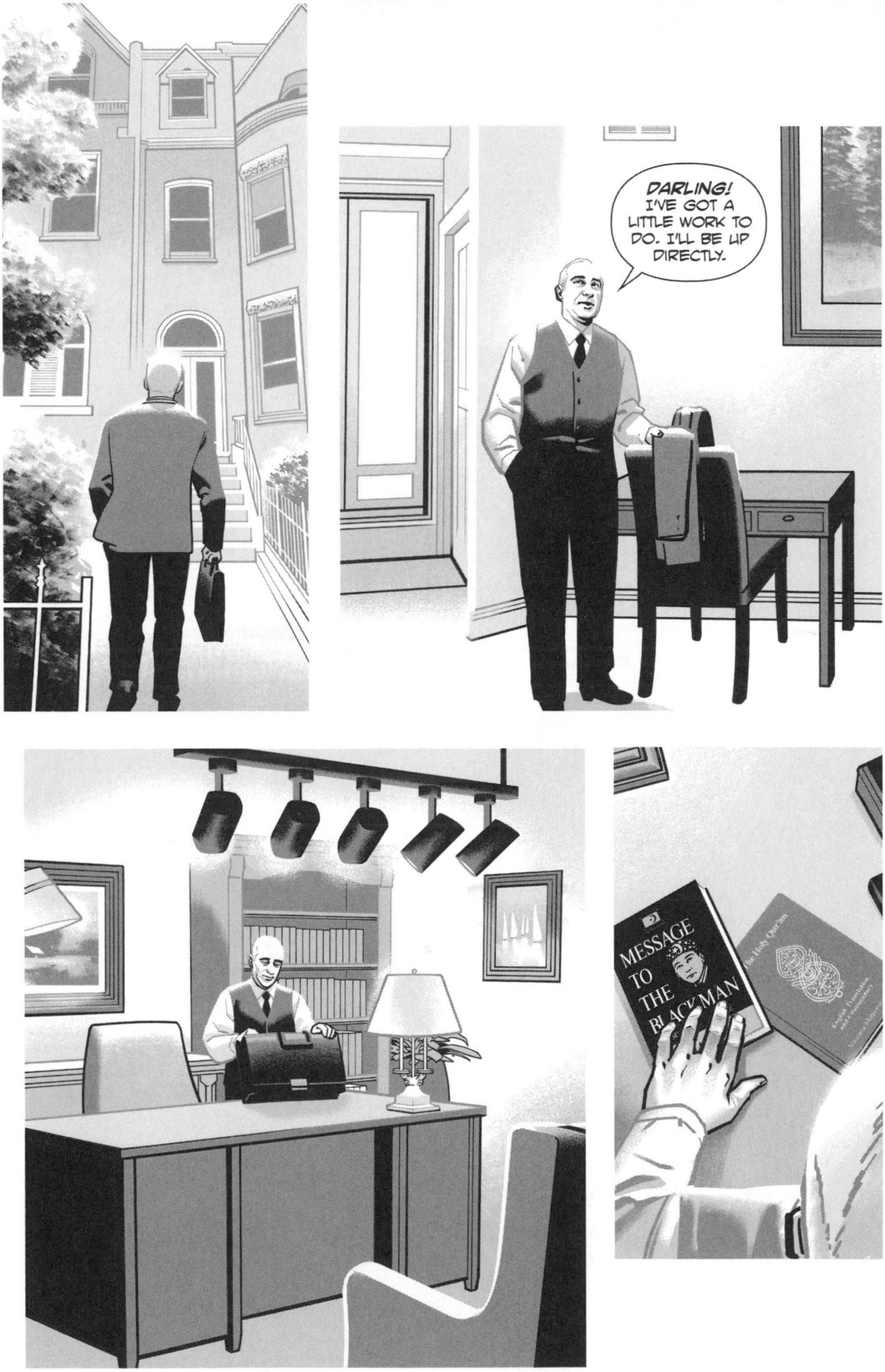
DARLING! I'VE GOT A LITTLE WORK TO DO. I'LL BE UP DIRECTLY.
MESSAGE TO THE BLACKMAN
The Holy Qur'an

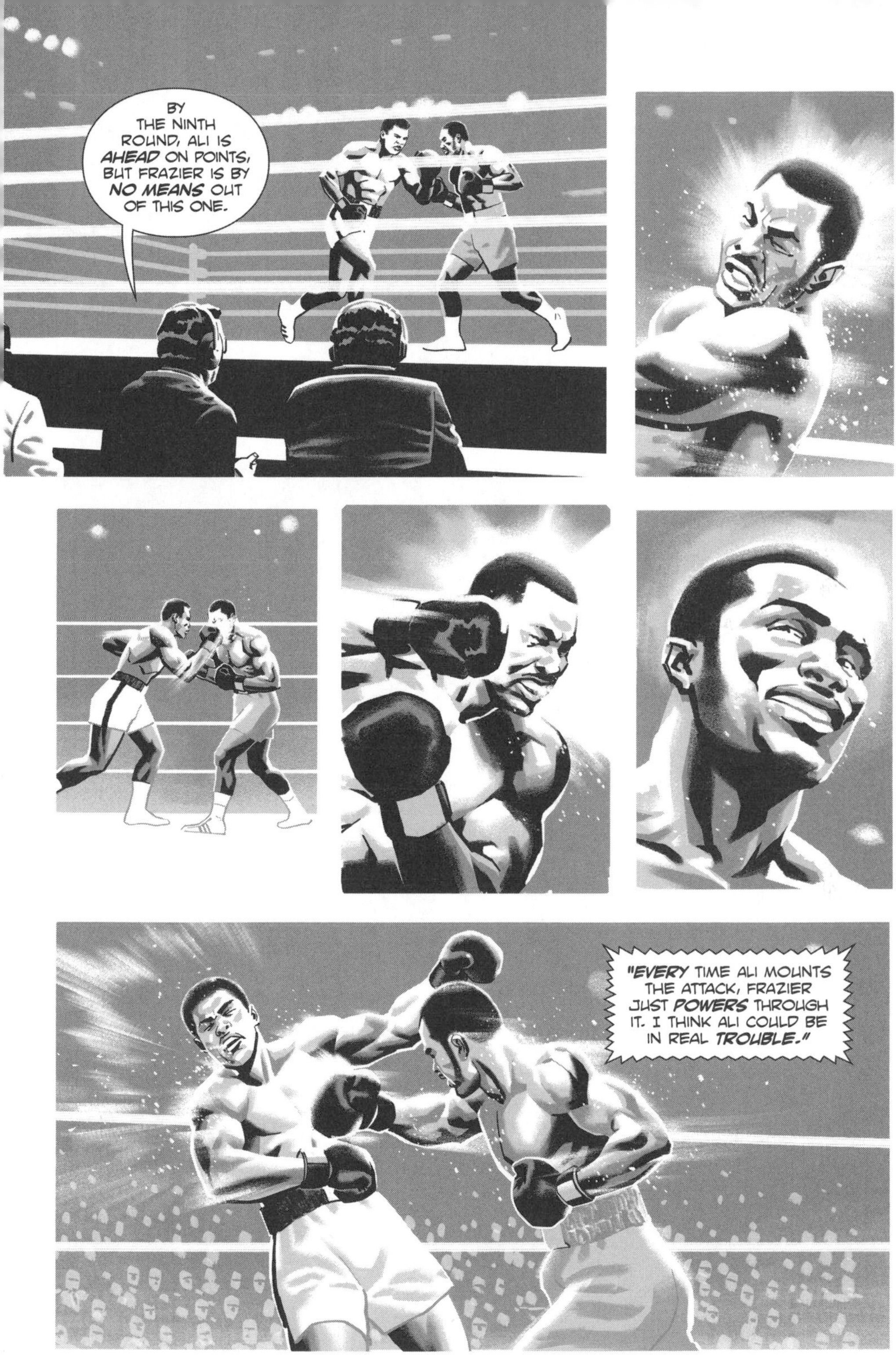
BY THE NINTH ROUND, ALI IS AHEAD ON POINTS, BUT FRAZIER IS BY NO MEANS OUT OF THIS ONE.
"EVERY TIME ALI MOUNTS THE ATTACK, FRAZIER JUST POWERS THROUGH IT. I THINK ALI COULD BE IN REAL TROUBLE."

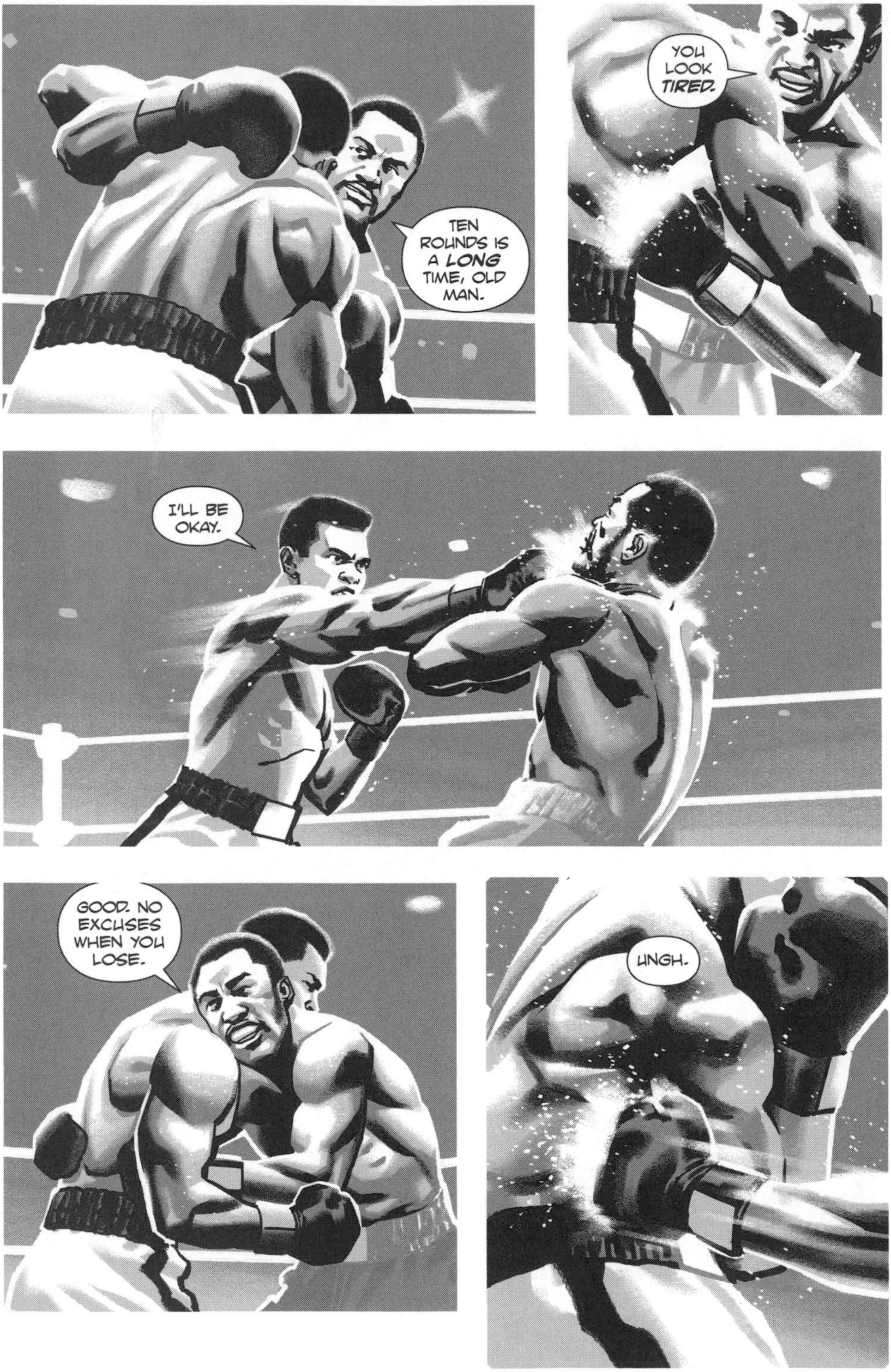
TEN ROUNDS IS A LONG TIME, OLD MAN.
YOU LOOK TIRED.
I'LL BE OKAY.
GOOD. NO EXCUSES WHEN YOU LOSE.
UNGH.

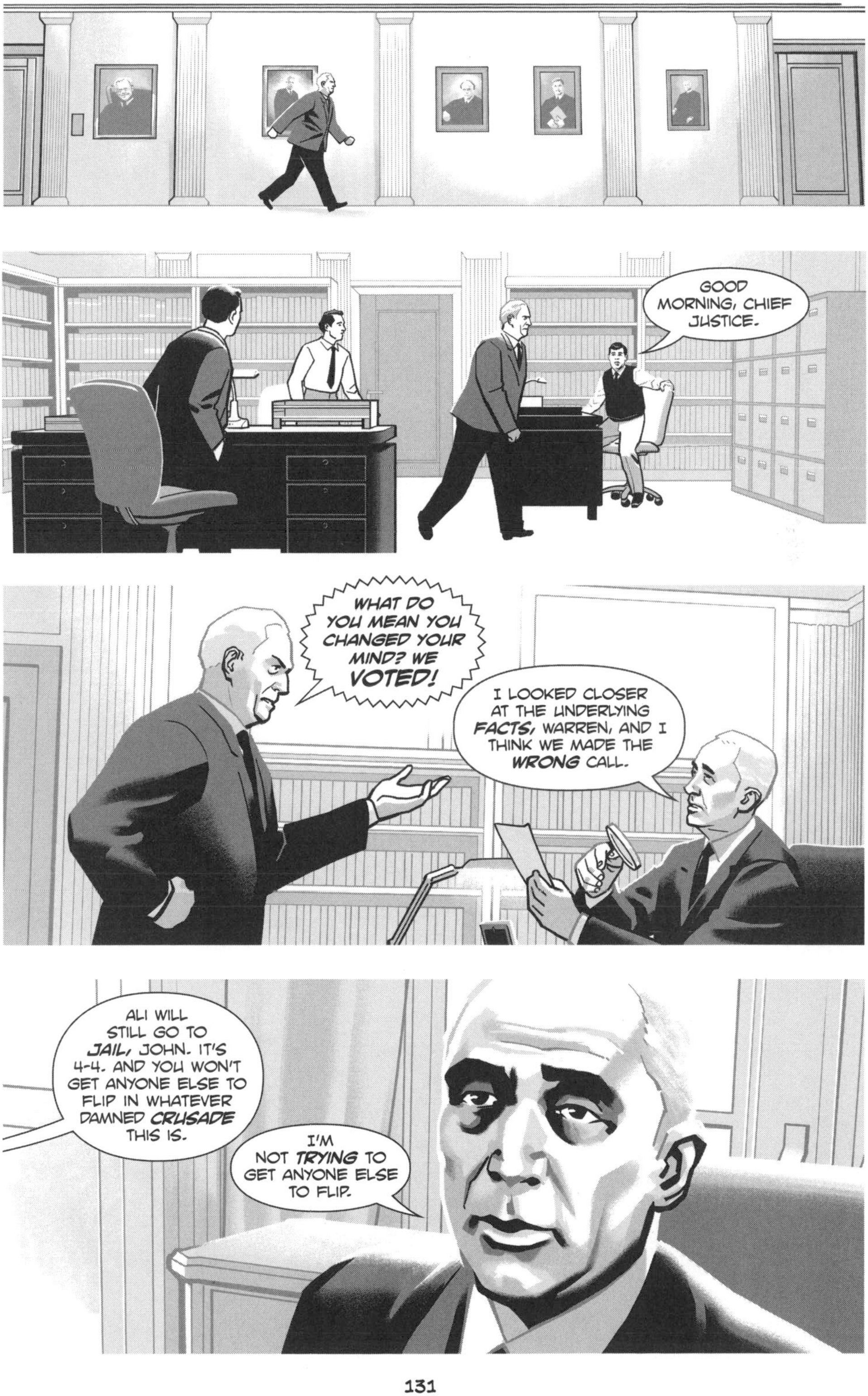
GOOD MORNING, CHIEF JUSTICE.
WHAT DO YOU MEAN YOU CHANGED YOUR MIND? WE VOTED!
I LOOKED CLOSER AT THE UNDERLYING FACTS, WARREN, AND I THINK WE MADE THE WRONG CALL.
ALI WILL STILL GO TO JAIL, JOHN. IT'S 4-4. AND YOU WON'T GET ANYONE ELSE TO FLIP IN WHATEVER DAMNED CRUSADE THIS IS.
I'M NOT TRYING TO GET ANYONE ELSE TO FLIP.

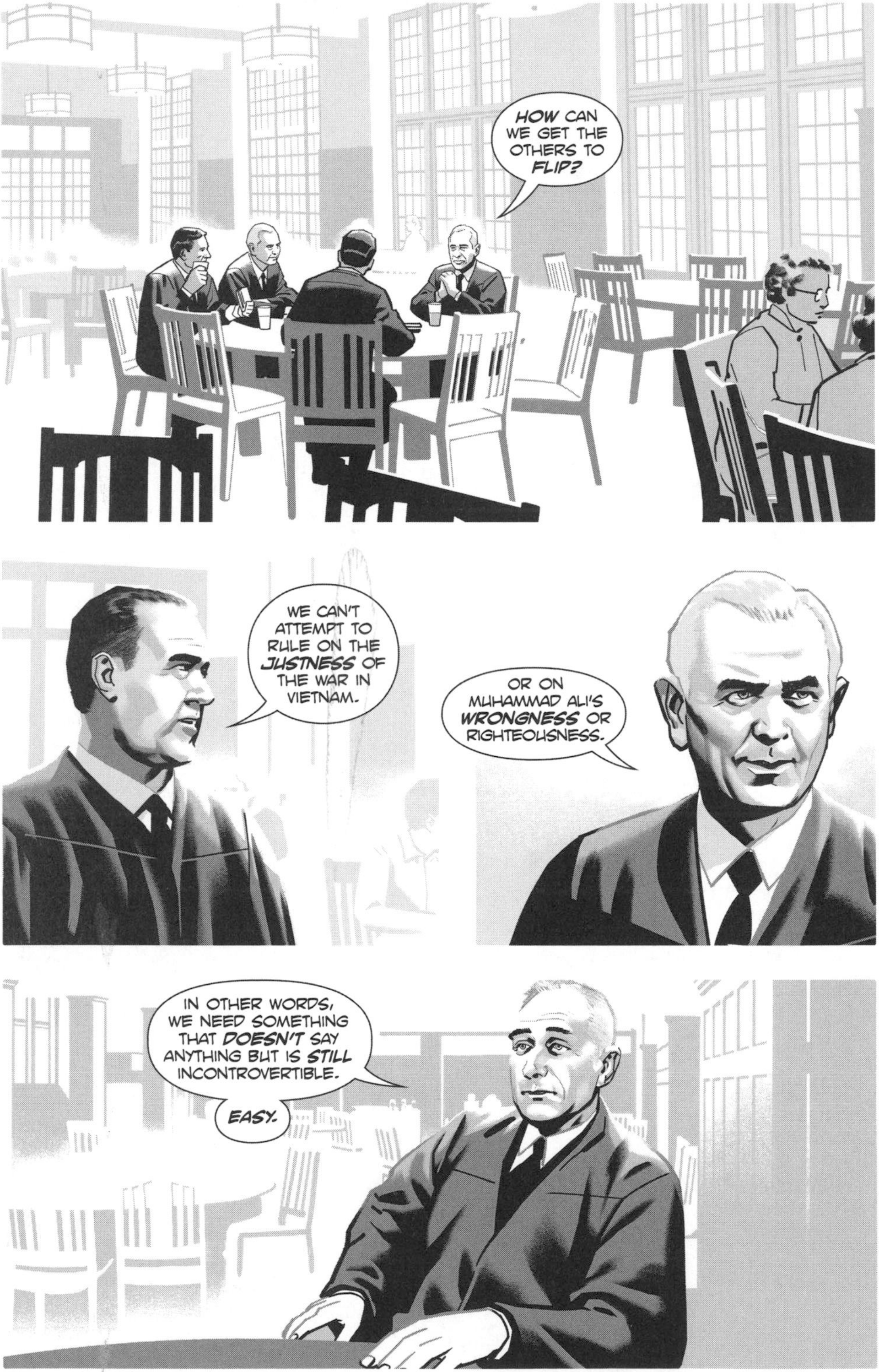
HOW CAN WE GET THE OTHERS TO FLIP?
WE CAN'T ATTEMPT TO RULE ON THE JUSTNESS OF THE WAR IN VIETNAM.
OR ON MUHAMMAD ALI'S WRONGNESS OR RIGHTEOUSNESS.
IN OTHER WORDS, WE NEED SOMETHING THAT DOESN'T SAY ANYTHING BUT IS STILL INCONTROVERTIBLE.
EASY.

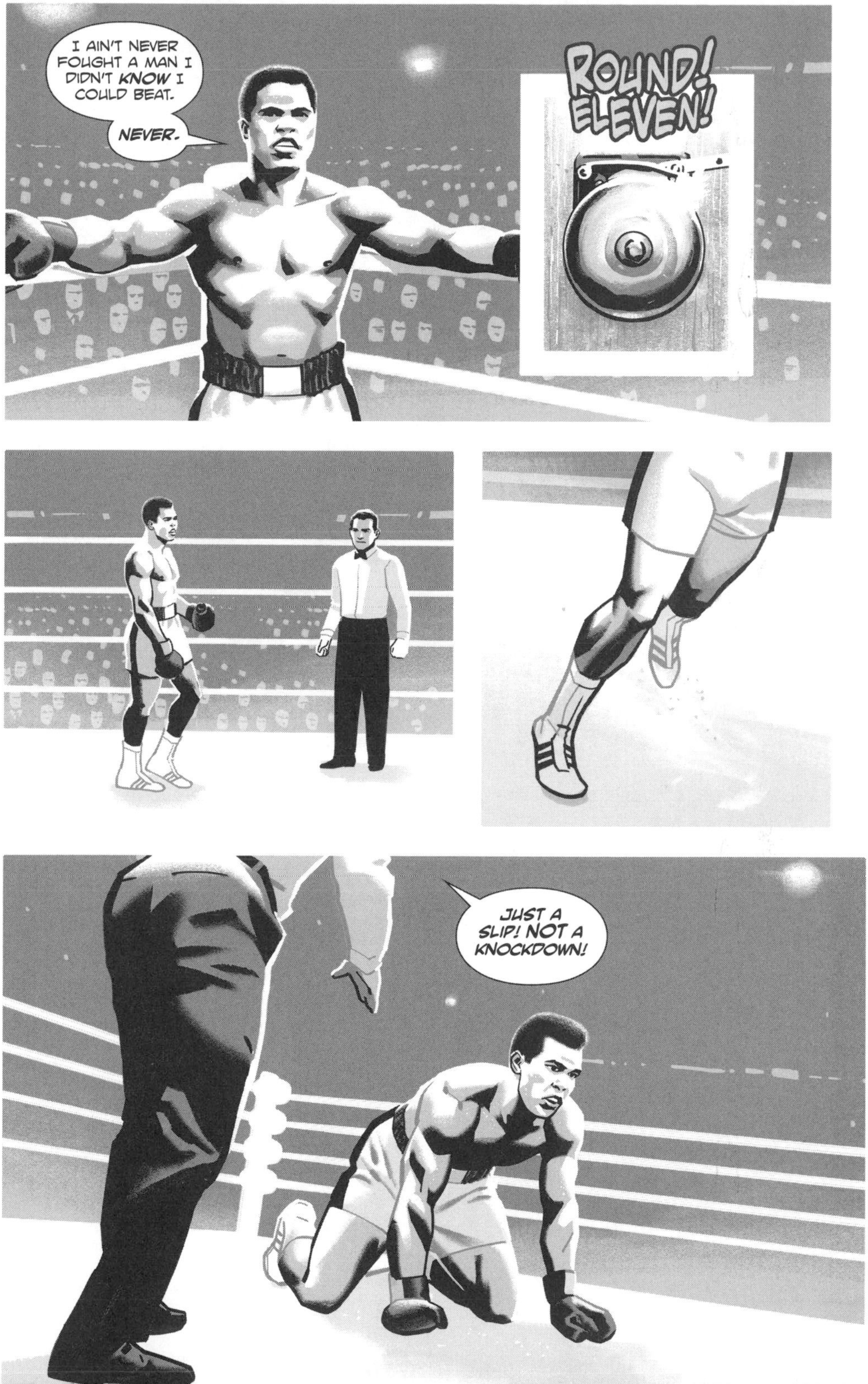
I AIN'T NEVER FOUGHT A MAN I DIDN'T KNOW I COULD BEAT.
NEVER.
ROUND! ELEVEN!
JUST A SLIP! NOT A KNOCKDOWN!

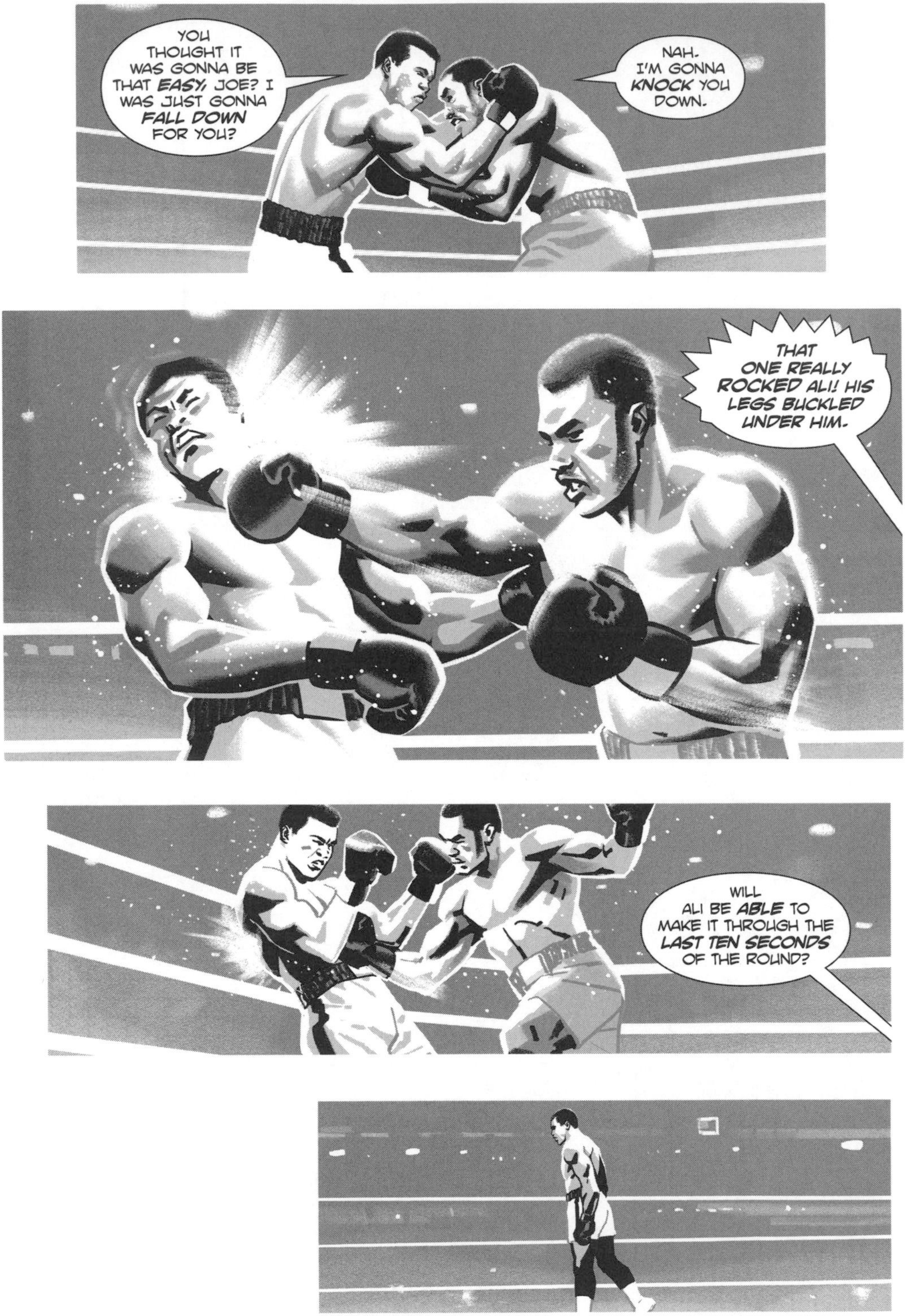
YOU THOUGHT IT WAS GONNA BE THAT **EASY**, JOE? I WAS JUST GONNA **FALL DOWN** FOR YOU?
NAH. I'M GONNA **KNOCK** YOU DOWN.
THAT ONE REALLY ROCKED ALI! HIS LEGS BUCKLED UNDER HIM.
WILL ALI BE ***ABLE*** TO MAKE IT THROUGH THE ***LAST TEN SECONDS*** OF THE ROUND?

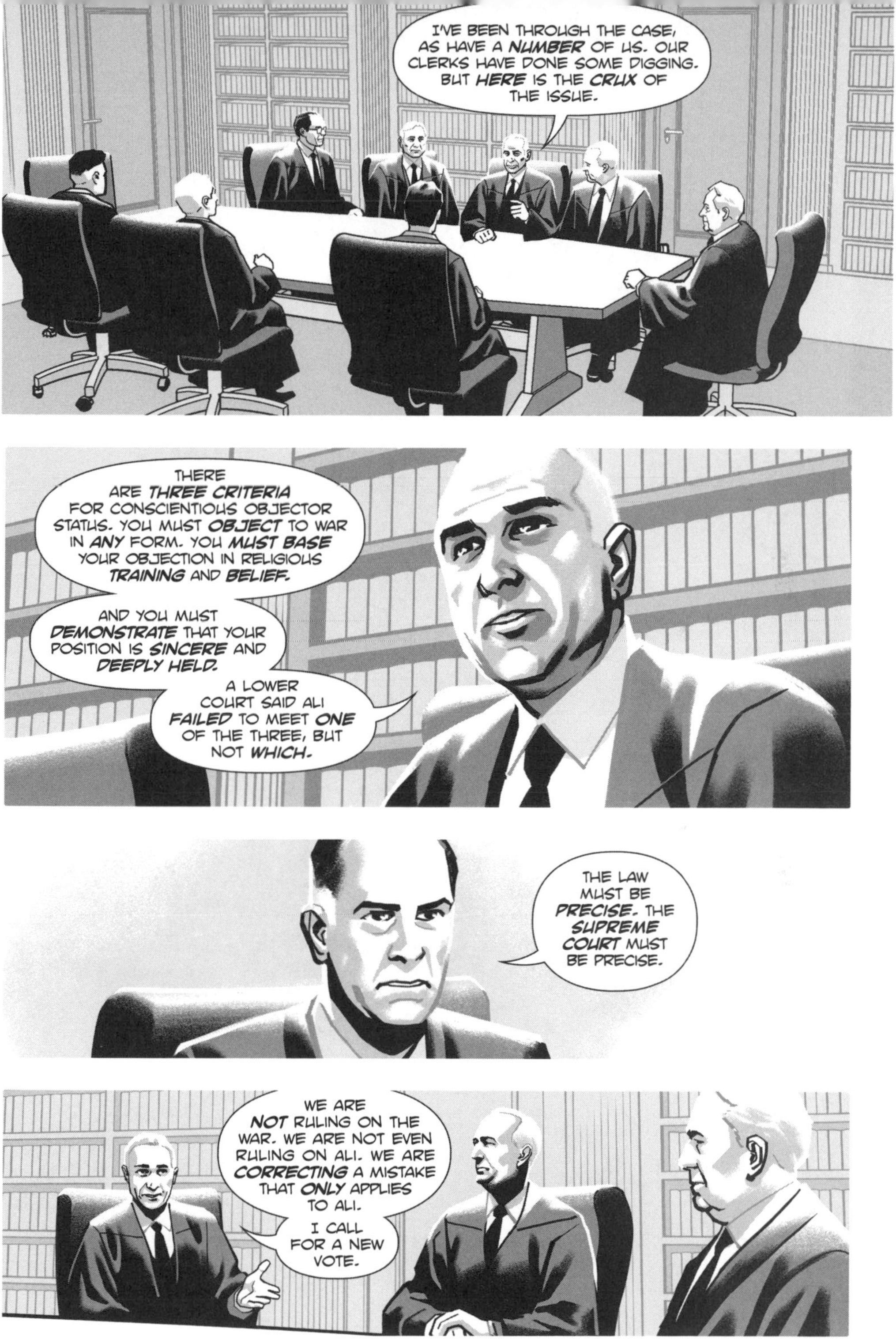
I'VE BEEN THROUGH THE CASE, AS HAVE A NUMBER OF US. OUR CLERKS HAVE DONE SOME DIGGING. BUT HERE IS THE CRUX OF THE ISSUE.
THERE ARE THREE CRITERIA FOR CONSCIENTIOUS OBJECTOR STATUS. YOU MUST OBJECT TO WAR IN ANY FORM. YOU MUST BASE YOUR OBJECTION IN RELIGIOUS TRAINING AND BELIEF.
AND YOU MUST DEMONSTRATE THAT YOUR POSITION IS SINCERE AND DEEPLY HELD.
A LOWER COURT SAID ALI FAILED TO MEET ONE OF THE THREE, BUT NOT WHICH.
THE LAW MUST BE PRECISE. THE SUPREME COURT MUST BE PRECISE.
WE ARE NOT RULING ON THE WAR. WE ARE NOT EVEN RULING ON ALI. WE ARE CORRECTING A MISTAKE THAT ONLY APPLIES TO ALI.
I CALL FOR A NEW VOTE.

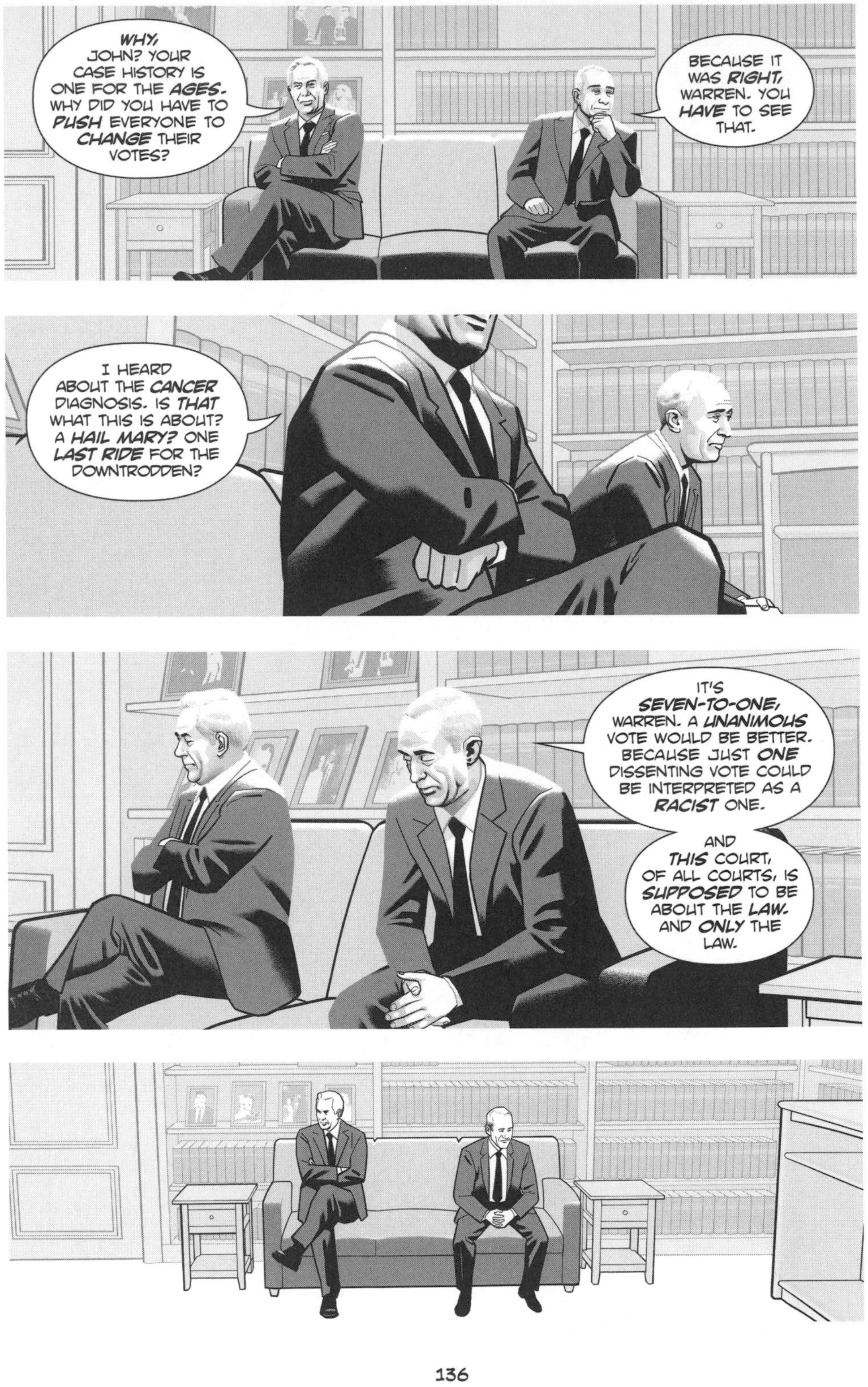
WHY, JOHN? YOUR CASE HISTORY IS ONE FOR THE AGES. WHY DID YOU HAVE TO PUSH EVERYONE TO CHANGE THEIR VOTES?
BECAUSE IT WAS RIGHT, WARREN. YOU HAVE TO SEE THAT.
I HEARD ABOUT THE CANCER DIAGNOSIS. IS THAT WHAT THIS IS ABOUT? A HAIL MARY? ONE LAST RIDE FOR THE DOWNTRODDEN?
IT'S SEVEN-TO-ONE, WARREN. A UNANIMOUS VOTE WOULD BE BETTER. BECAUSE JUST ONE DISSENTING VOTE COULD BE INTERPRETED AS A RACIST ONE.
AND THIS COURT, OF ALL COURTS, IS SUPPOSED TO BE ABOUT THE LAW. AND ONLY THE LAW.

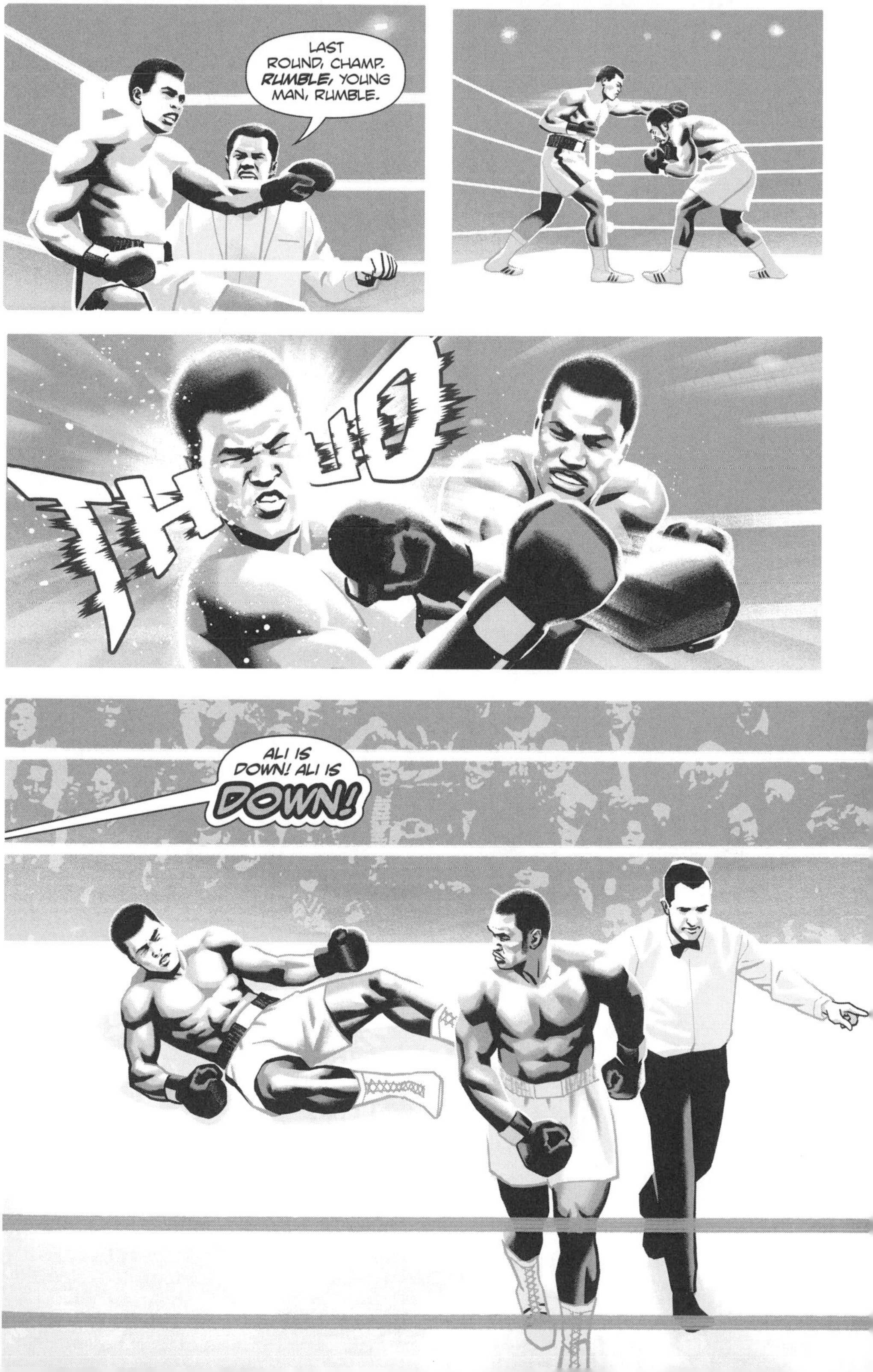
LAST ROUND, CHAMP. **RUMBLE,** YOUNG MAN, RUMBLE.
THUD
ALI IS DOWN! ALI IS DOWN!

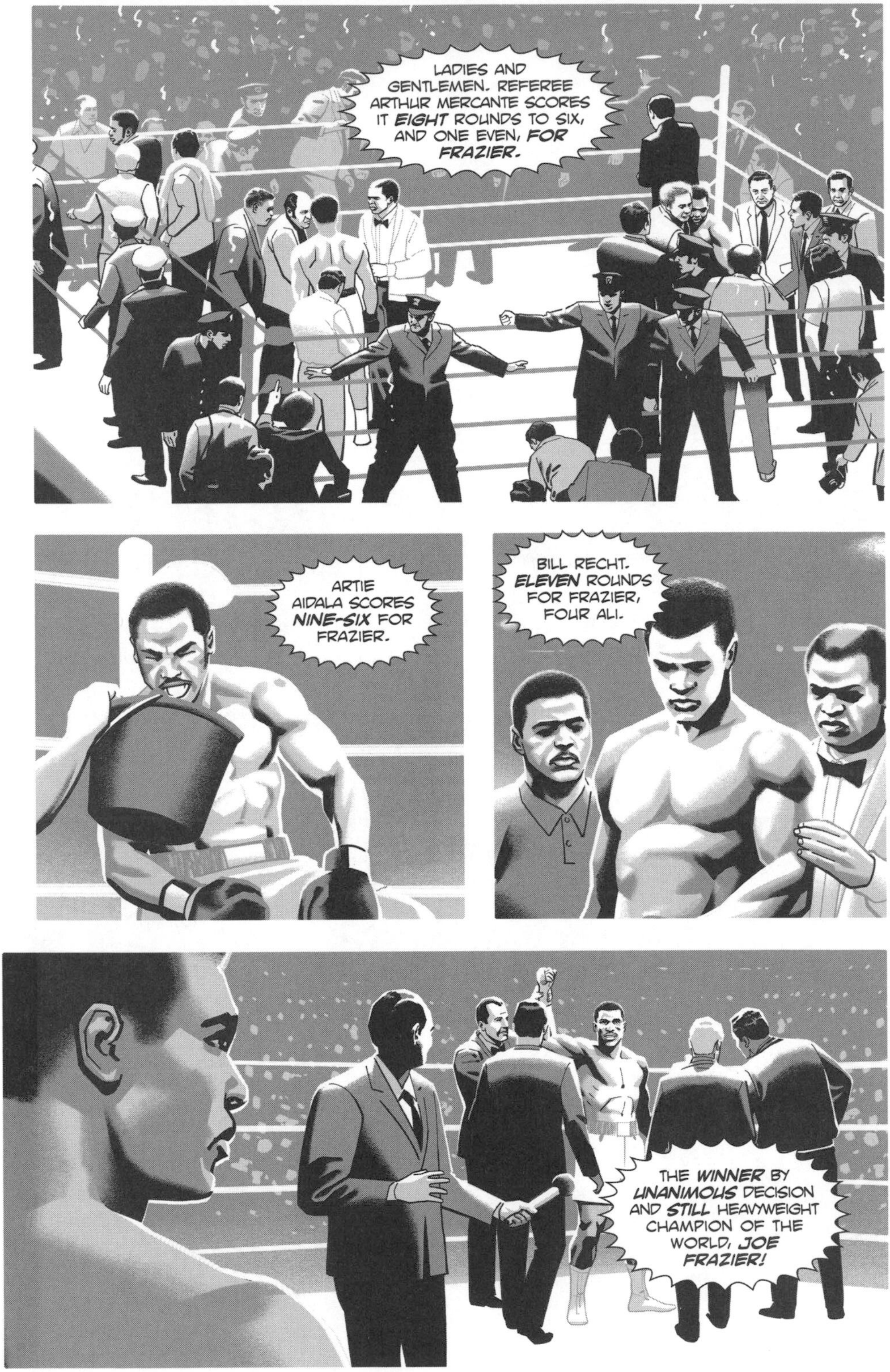
LADIES AND GENTLEMEN. REFEREE ARTHUR MERCANTE SCORES IT EIGHT ROUNDS TO SIX, AND ONE EVEN, FOR FRAZIER.
ARTIE AIDALA SCORES NINE-SIX FOR FRAZIER.
BILL RECHT. ELEVEN ROUNDS FOR FRAZIER, FOUR ALI.
THE WINNER BY UNANIMOUS DECISION AND STILL HEAVYWEIGHT CHAMPION OF THE WORLD, JOE FRAZIER!

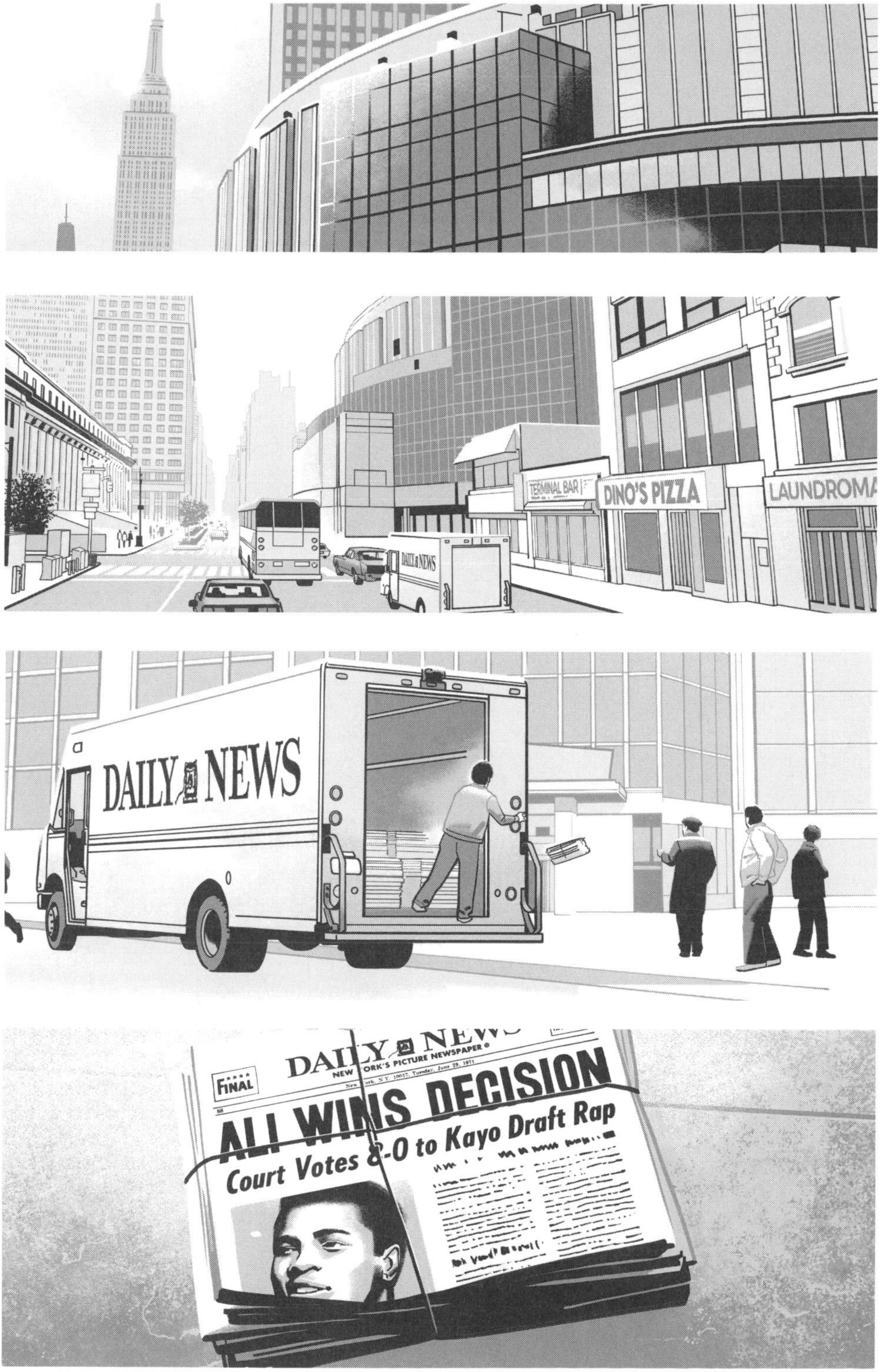
TERMINAL BAR
DINO'S PIZZA
LAUNDROMA
DAILY NEWS
DAILY NEWS
DAILY NEWS
NEW YORK'S PICTURE NEWSPAPER ®
FINAL
ALI WINS DECISION
Court Votes 8-0 to Kayo Draft Rap

ROUND EIGHT: CANDLE. 1974.

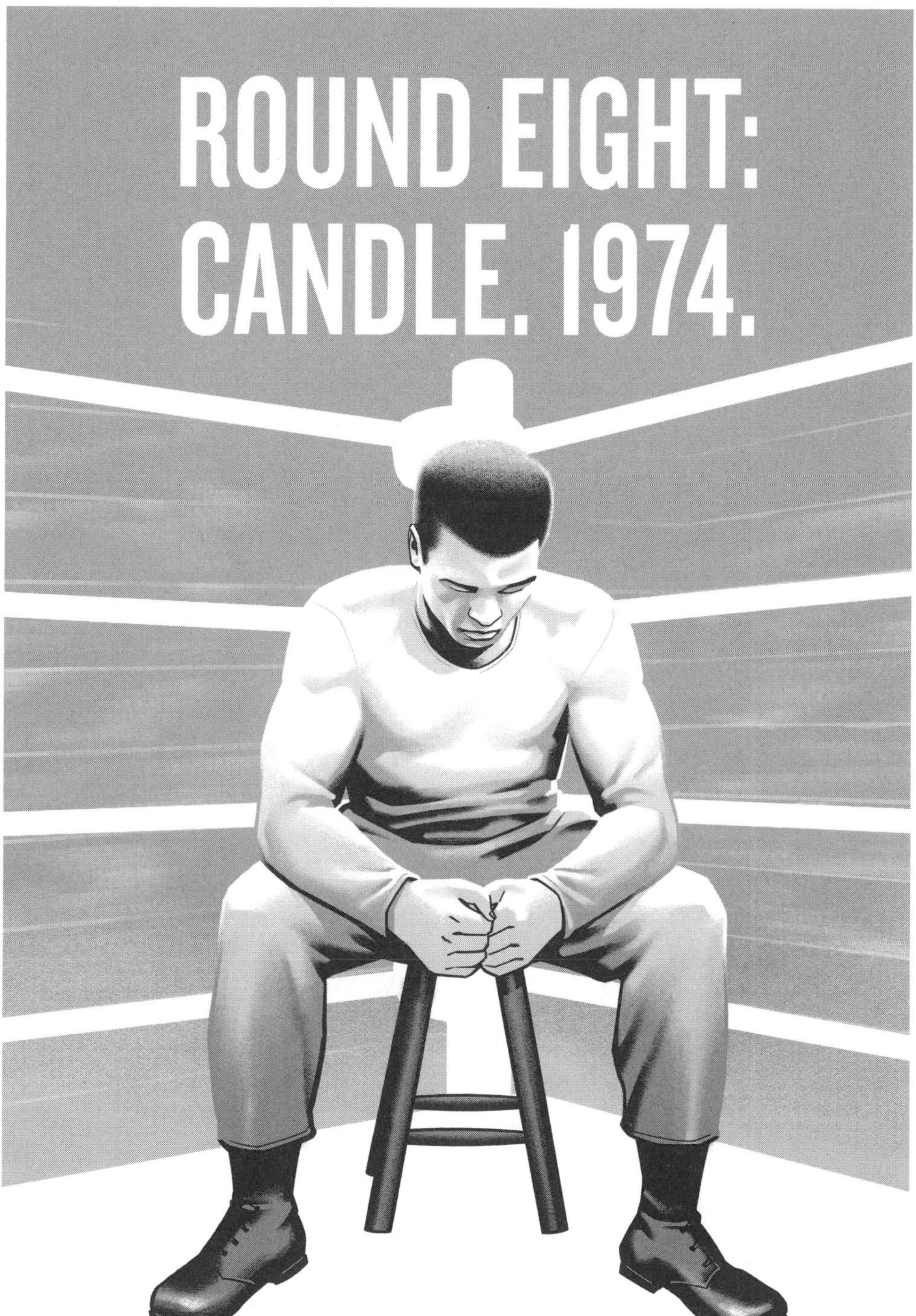

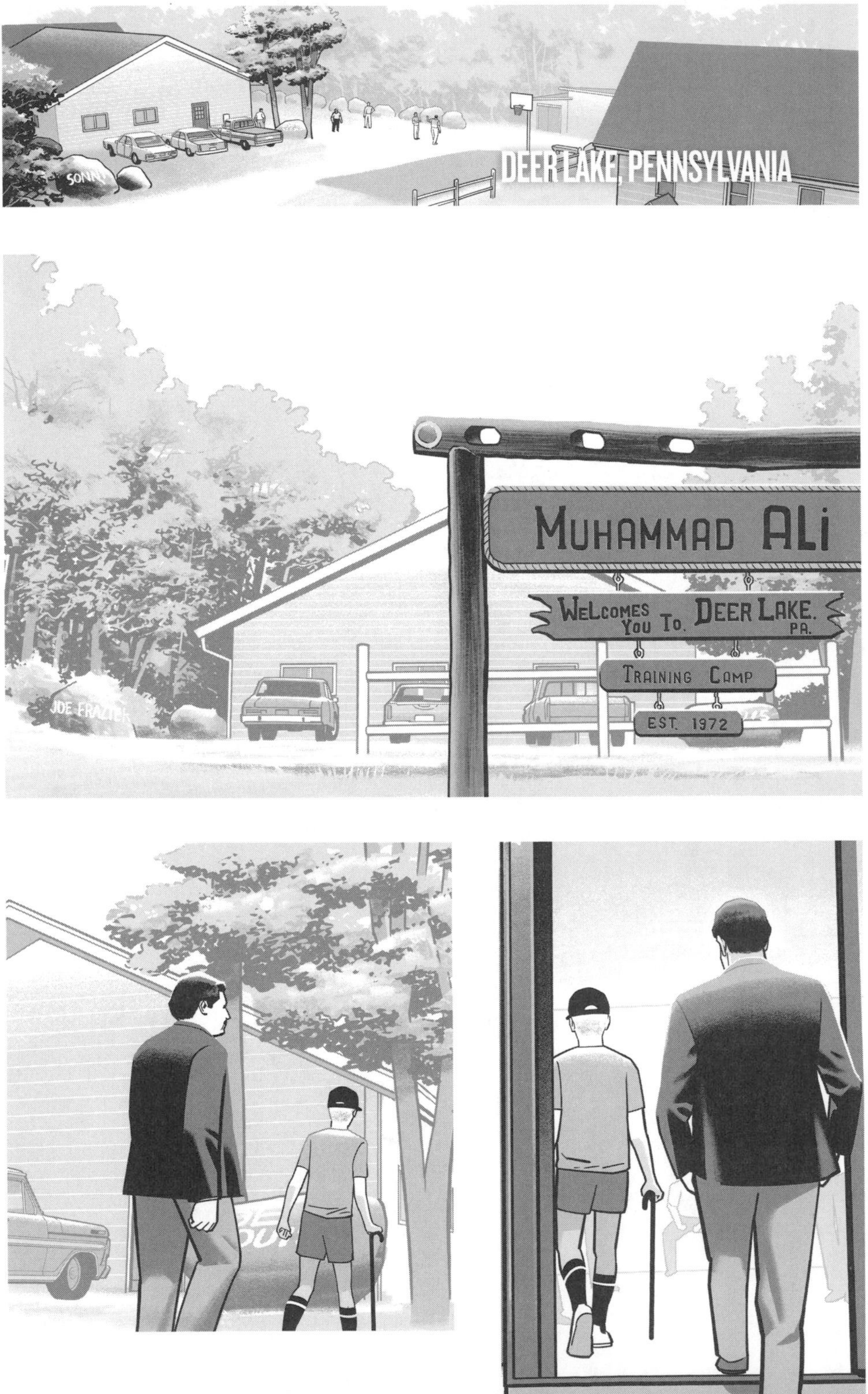
DEER LAKE, PENNSYLVANIA
MUHAMMAD ALi
WELcomes You To. DEER LAKE. PA.
TRAINING CAMP
EST. 1972

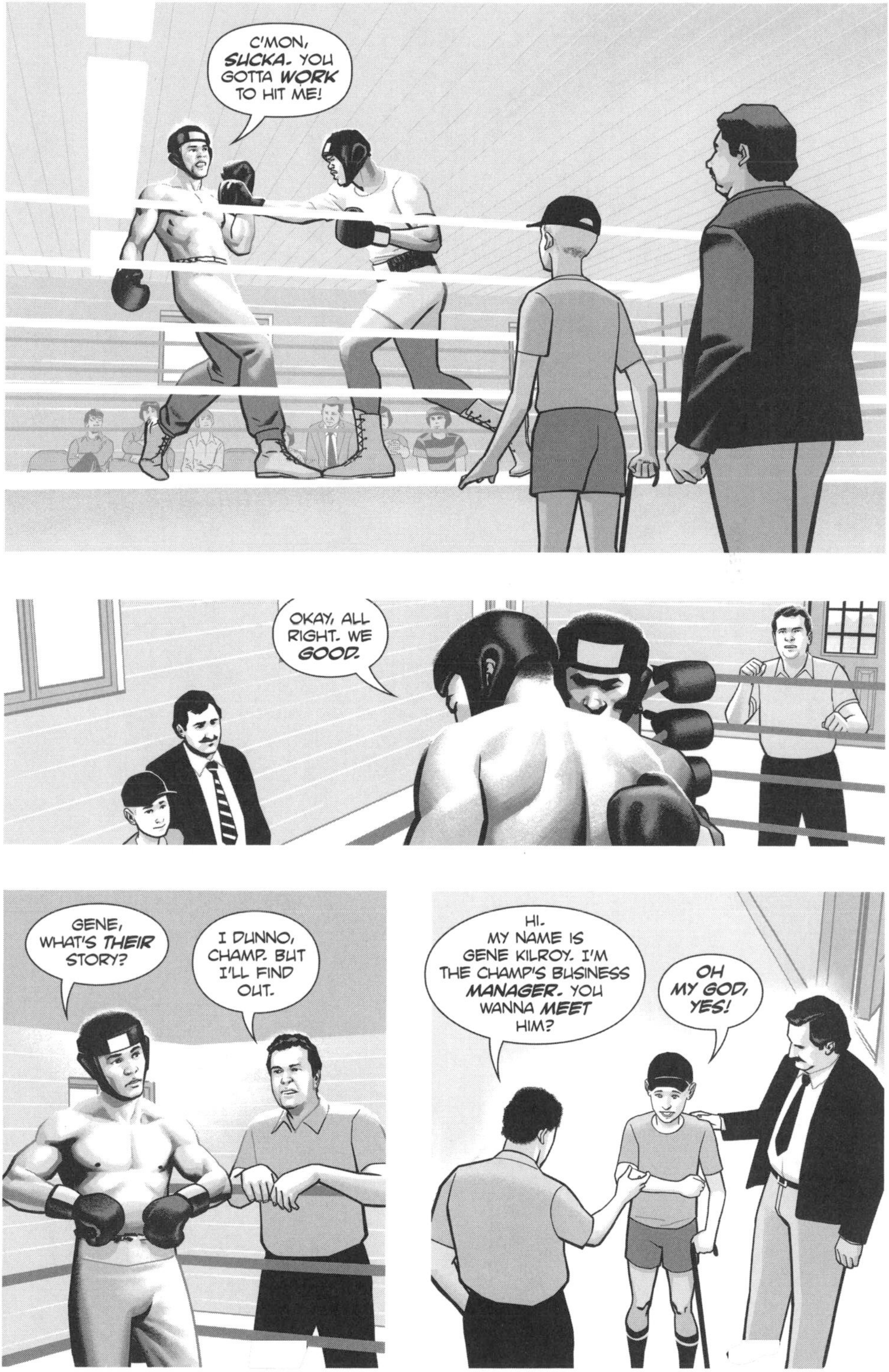
C'MON, SUCKA. YOU GOTTA WORK TO HIT ME!
OKAY, ALL RIGHT. WE GOOD.
GENE, WHAT'S THEIR STORY?
I DUNNO, CHAMP. BUT I'LL FIND OUT.
HI. MY NAME IS GENE KILROY. I'M THE CHAMP'S BUSINESS MANAGER. YOU WANNA MEET HIM?
OH MY GOD, YES!

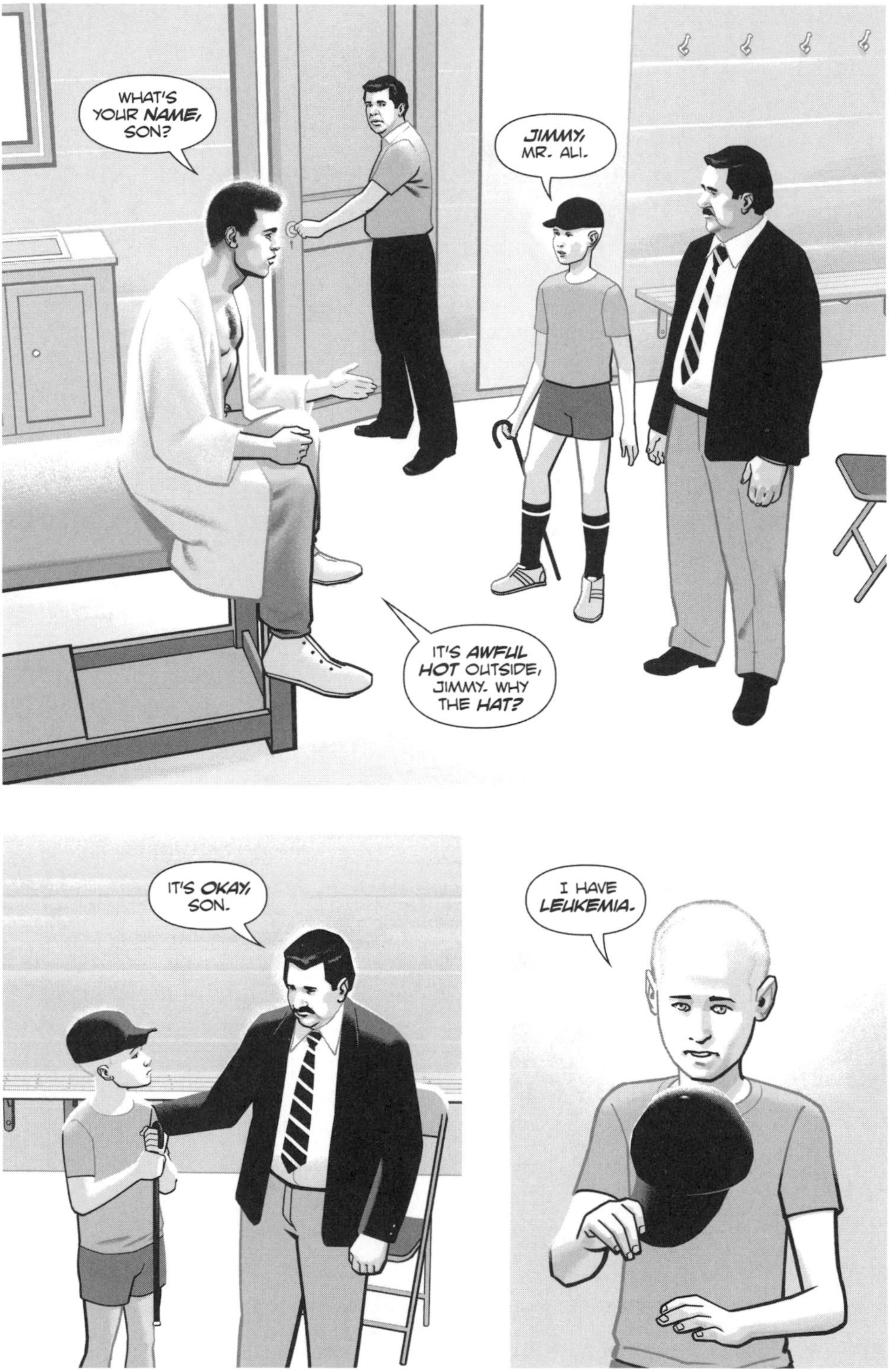
WHAT'S YOUR NAME, SON?
JIMMY, MR. ALI.
IT'S AWFUL HOT OUTSIDE, JIMMY. WHY THE HAT?
IT'S OKAY, SON.
I HAVE LEUKEMIA.

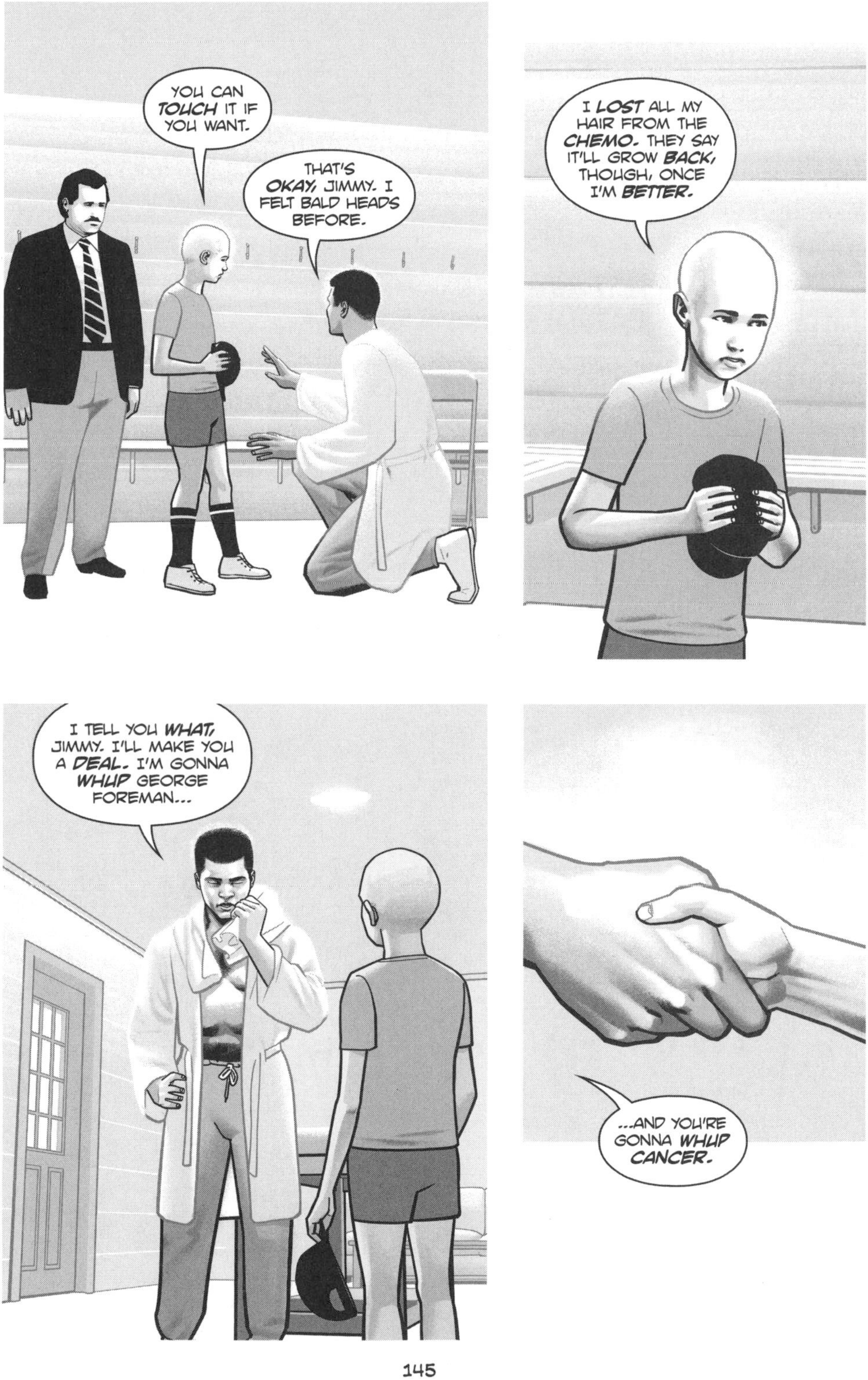
YOU CAN TOUCH IT IF YOU WANT.
THAT'S OKAY, JIMMY. I FELT BALD HEADS BEFORE.
I LOST ALL MY HAIR FROM THE CHEMO. THEY SAY IT'LL GROW BACK, THOUGH, ONCE I'M BETTER.
I TELL YOU WHAT, JIMMY. I'LL MAKE YOU A DEAL. I'M GONNA WHUP GEORGE FOREMAN...
...AND YOU'RE GONNA WHUP CANCER.

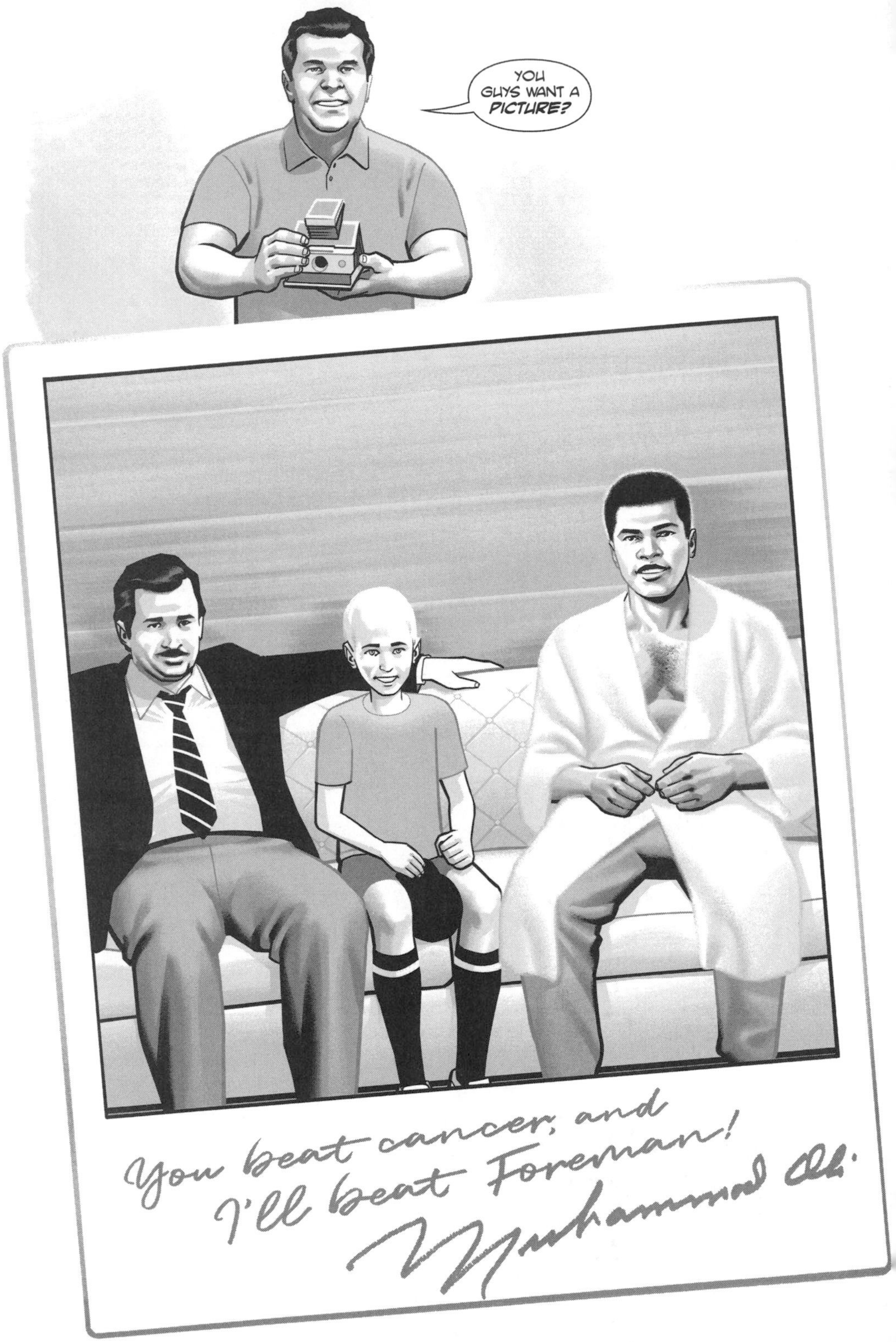
YOU GUYS WANT A PICTURE?
You beat cancer, and I'll beat Foreman!
Muhammad Ali

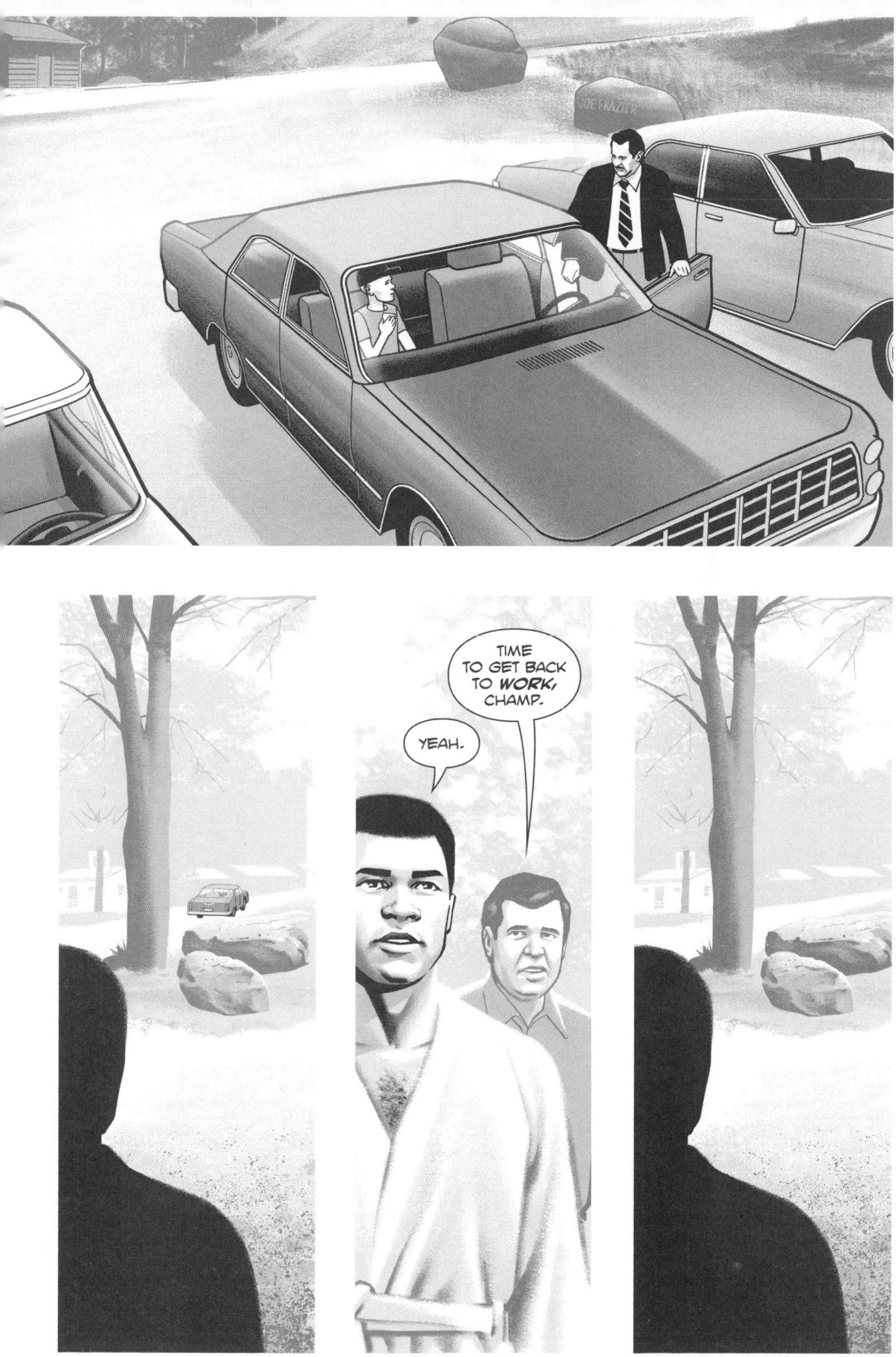
TIME TO GET BACK TO **WORK,** CHAMP.
YEAH.

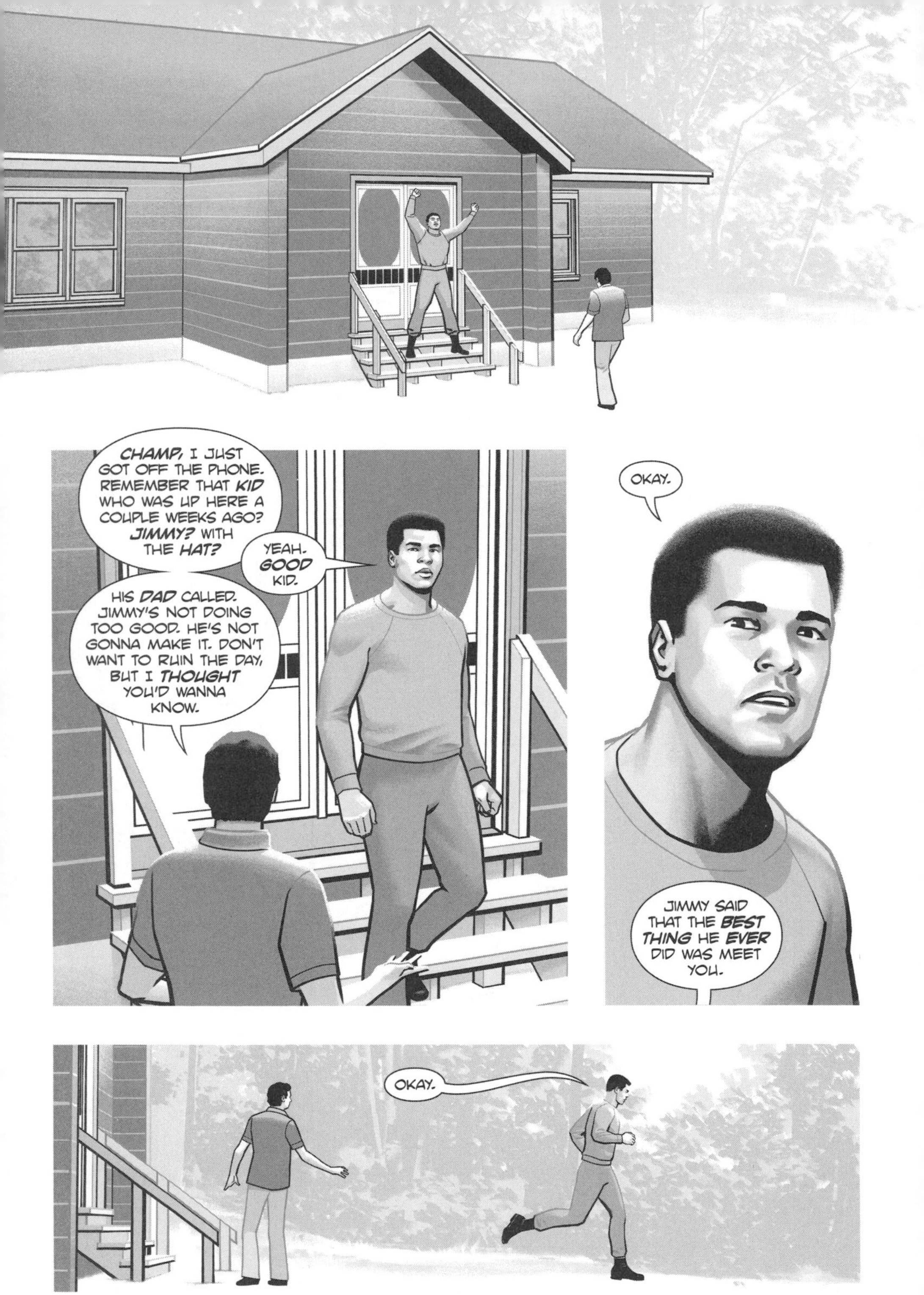
CHAMP, I JUST GOT OFF THE PHONE. REMEMBER THAT KID WHO WAS UP HERE A COUPLE WEEKS AGO? JIMMY? WITH THE HAT?
YEAH. GOOD KID.
HIS DAD CALLED. JIMMY'S NOT DOING TOO GOOD. HE'S NOT GONNA MAKE IT. DON'T WANT TO RUIN THE DAY, BUT I THOUGHT YOU'D WANNA KNOW.
OKAY.
JIMMY SAID THAT THE BEST THING HE EVER DID WAS MEET YOU.
OKAY.

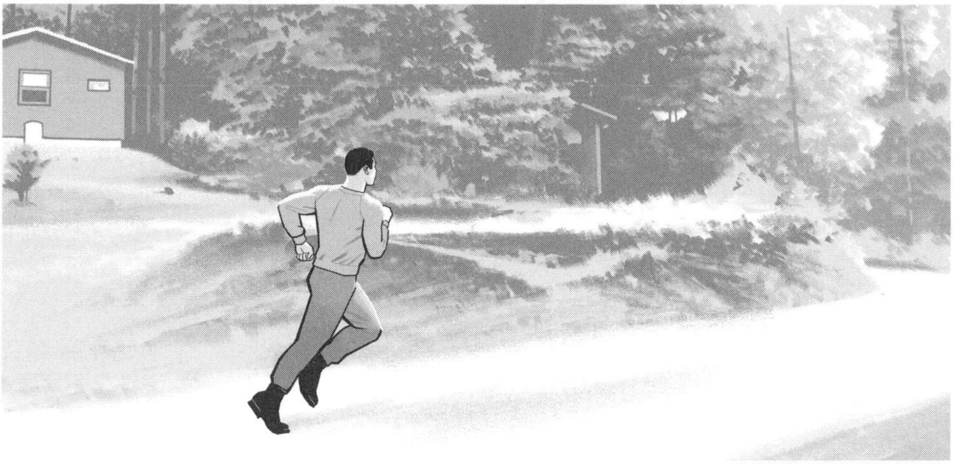

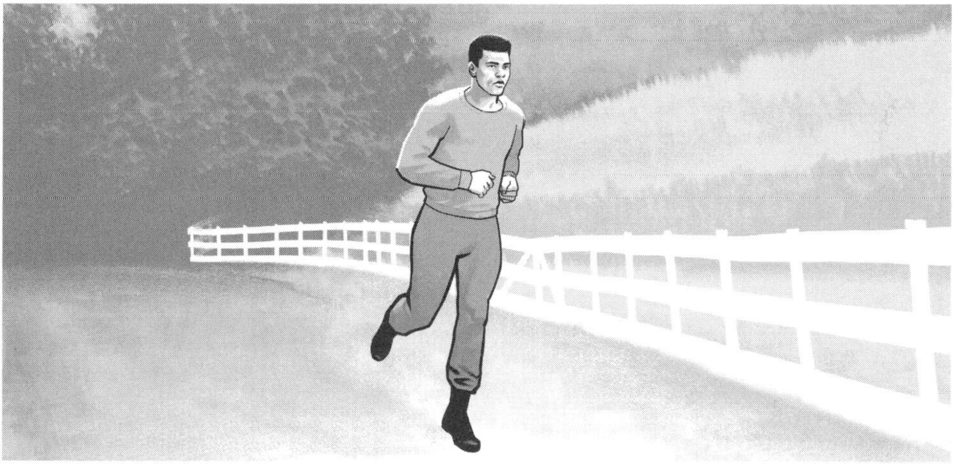

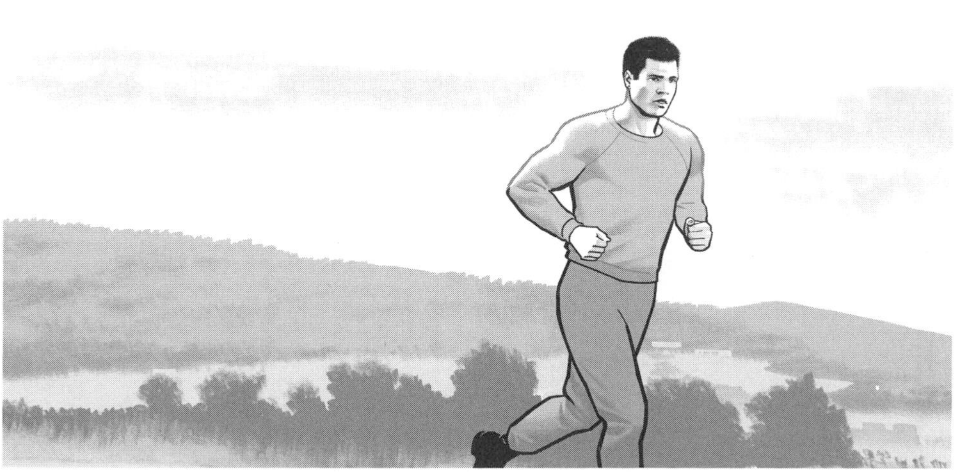

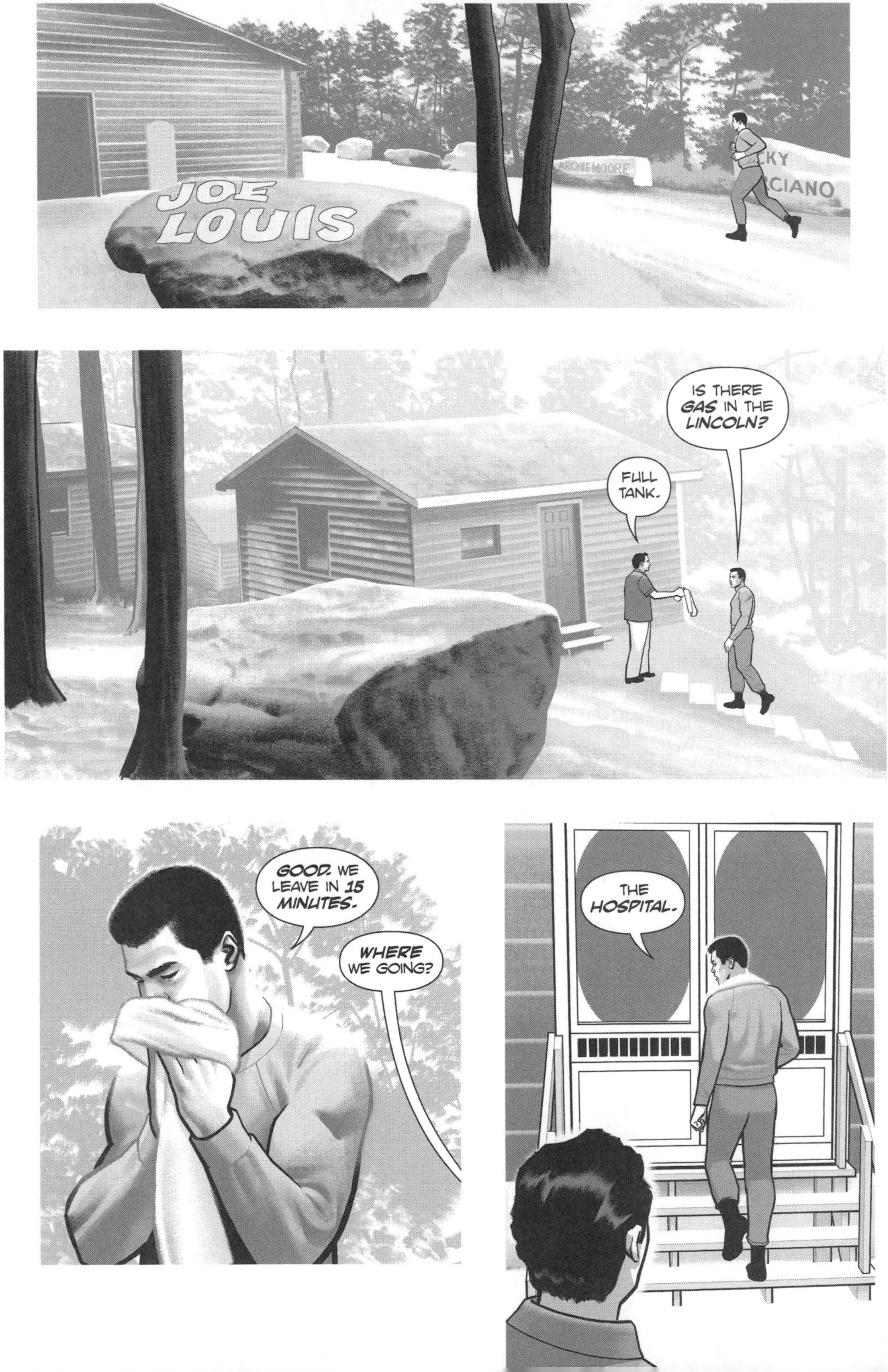
JOE LOUIS
ARCHIE MOORE
IS THERE GAS IN THE LINCOLN?
FULL TANK.
GOOD. WE LEAVE IN 15 MINUTES.
WHERE WE GOING?
THE HOSPITAL.

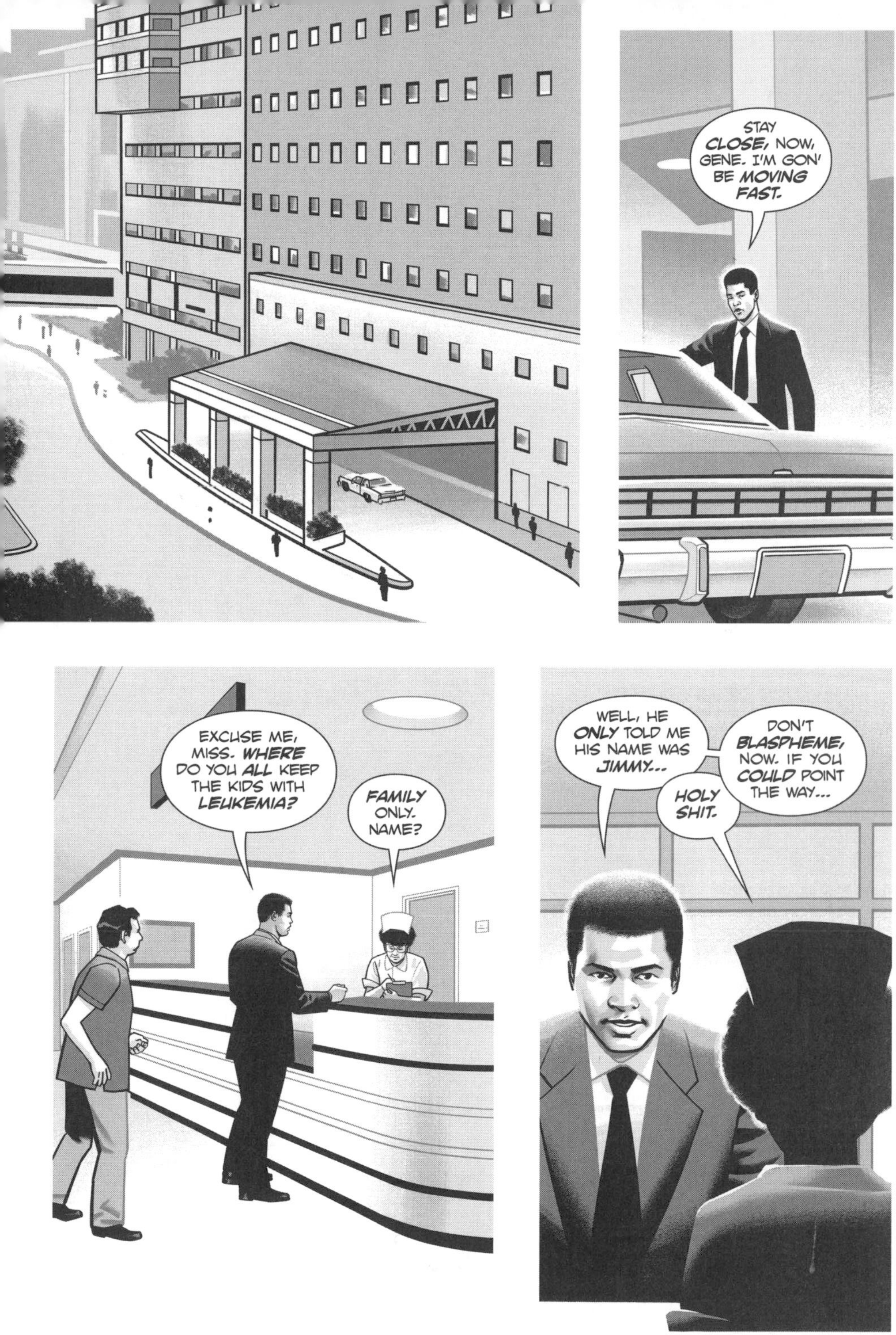
STAY CLOSE, NOW, GENE. I'M GON' BE MOVING FAST.
EXCUSE ME, MISS. WHERE DO YOU ALL KEEP THE KIDS WITH LEUKEMIA?
FAMILY ONLY. NAME?
WELL, HE ONLY TOLD ME HIS NAME WAS JIMMY...
HOLY SHIT.
DON'T BLASPHEME, NOW. IF YOU COULD POINT THE WAY...

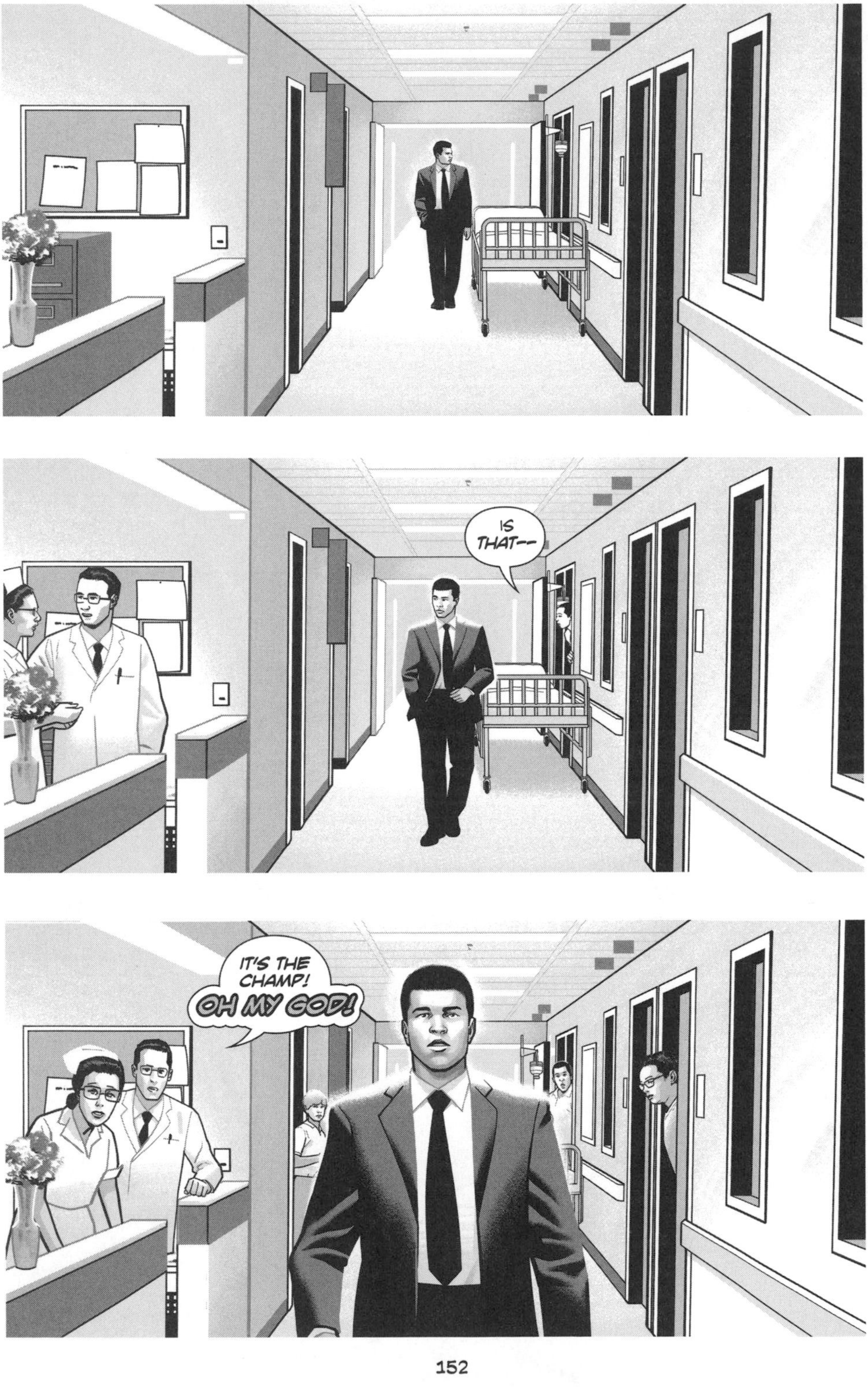
IS THAT--
IT'S THE CHAMP!
OH MY GOD!

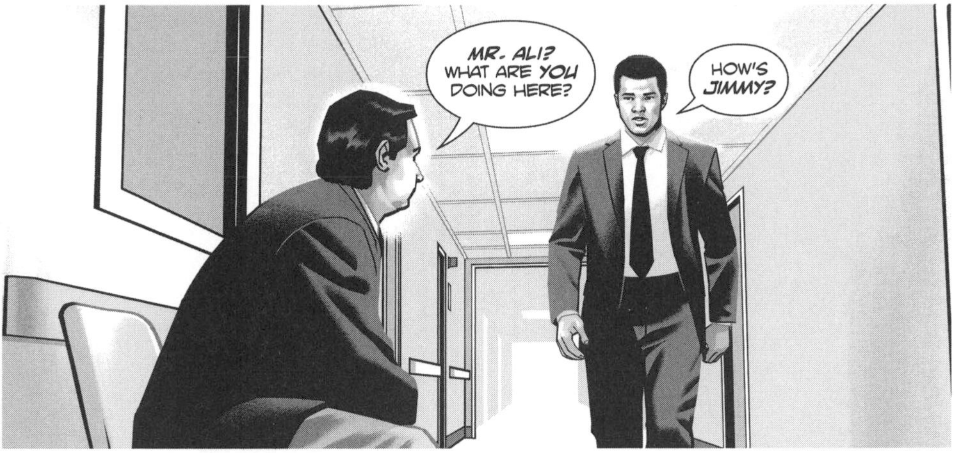
MR. ALI? WHAT ARE YOU DOING HERE?
HOW'S JIMMY?

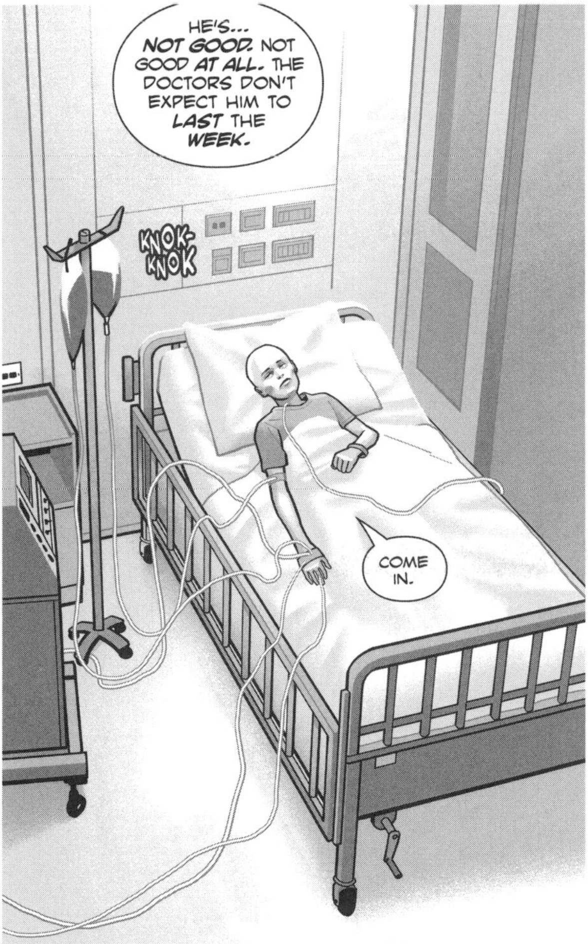
HE'S... NOT GOOD. NOT GOOD AT ALL. THE DOCTORS DON'T EXPECT HIM TO LAST THE WEEK.
KNOK-KNOK
COME IN.

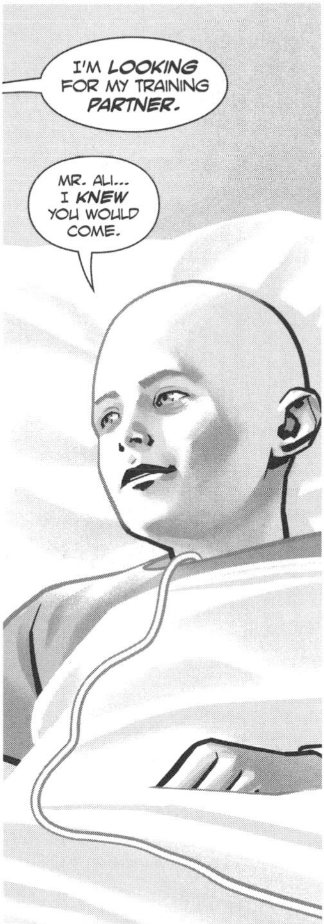
I'M LOOKING FOR MY TRAINING PARTNER.
MR. ALI... I KNEW YOU WOULD COME.

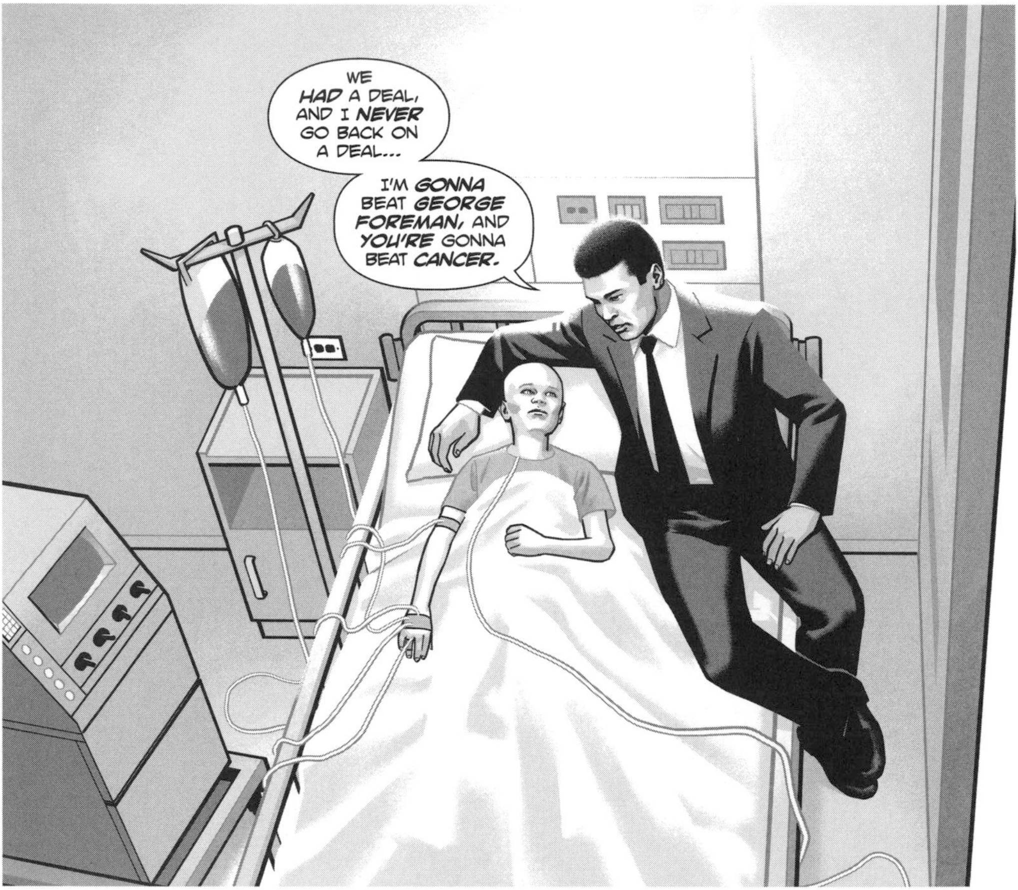
WE HAD A DEAL, AND I NEVER GO BACK ON A DEAL...
I'M GONNA BEAT GEORGE FOREMAN, AND YOU'RE GONNA BEAT CANCER.

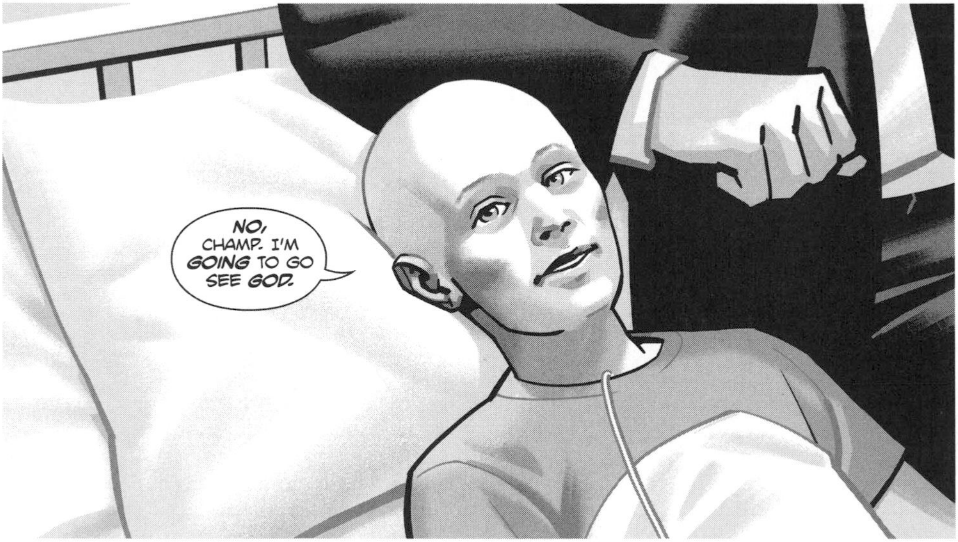
NO, CHAMP. I'M GOING TO GO SEE GOD.

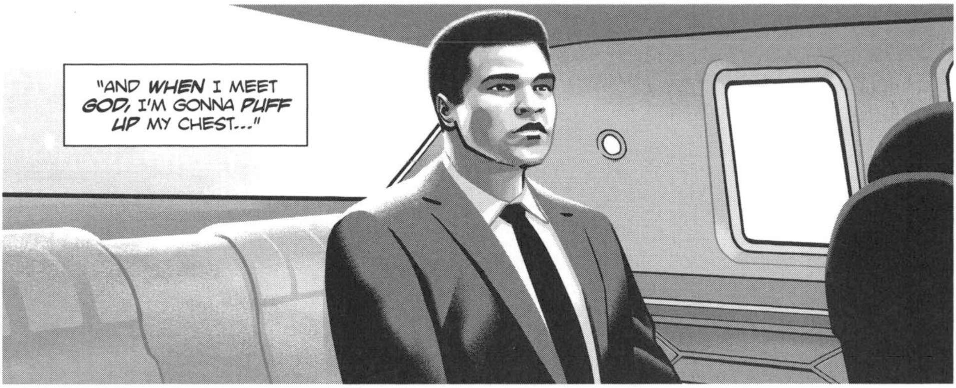
"AND WHEN I MEET GOD, I'M GONNA PUFF UP MY CHEST..."

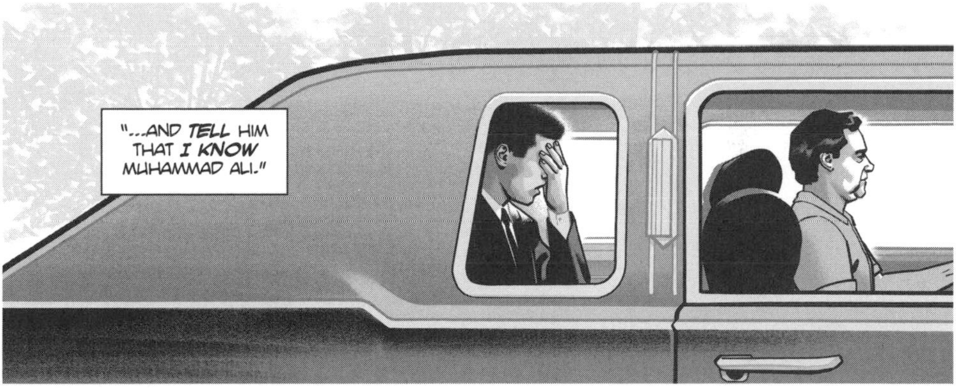
"...AND TELL HIM THAT I KNOW MUHAMMAD ALI."

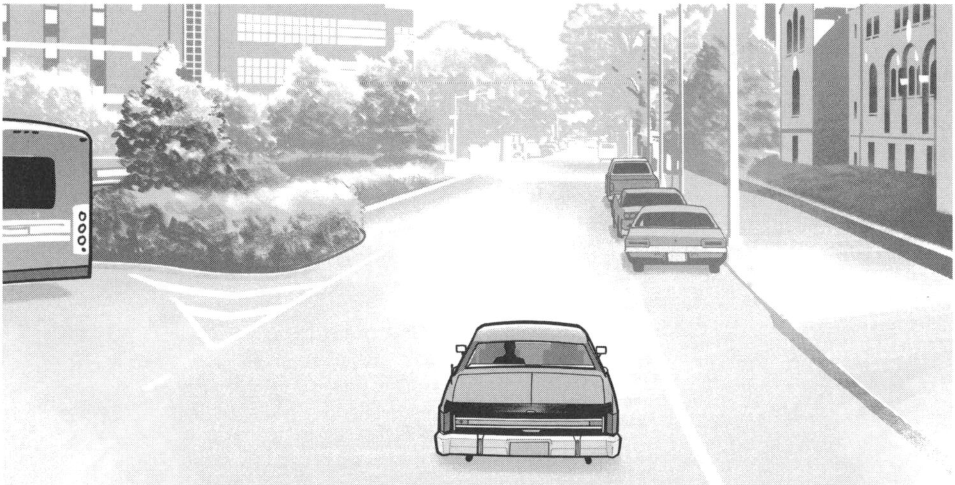

ROUND NINE: RUMBLE. 1974.

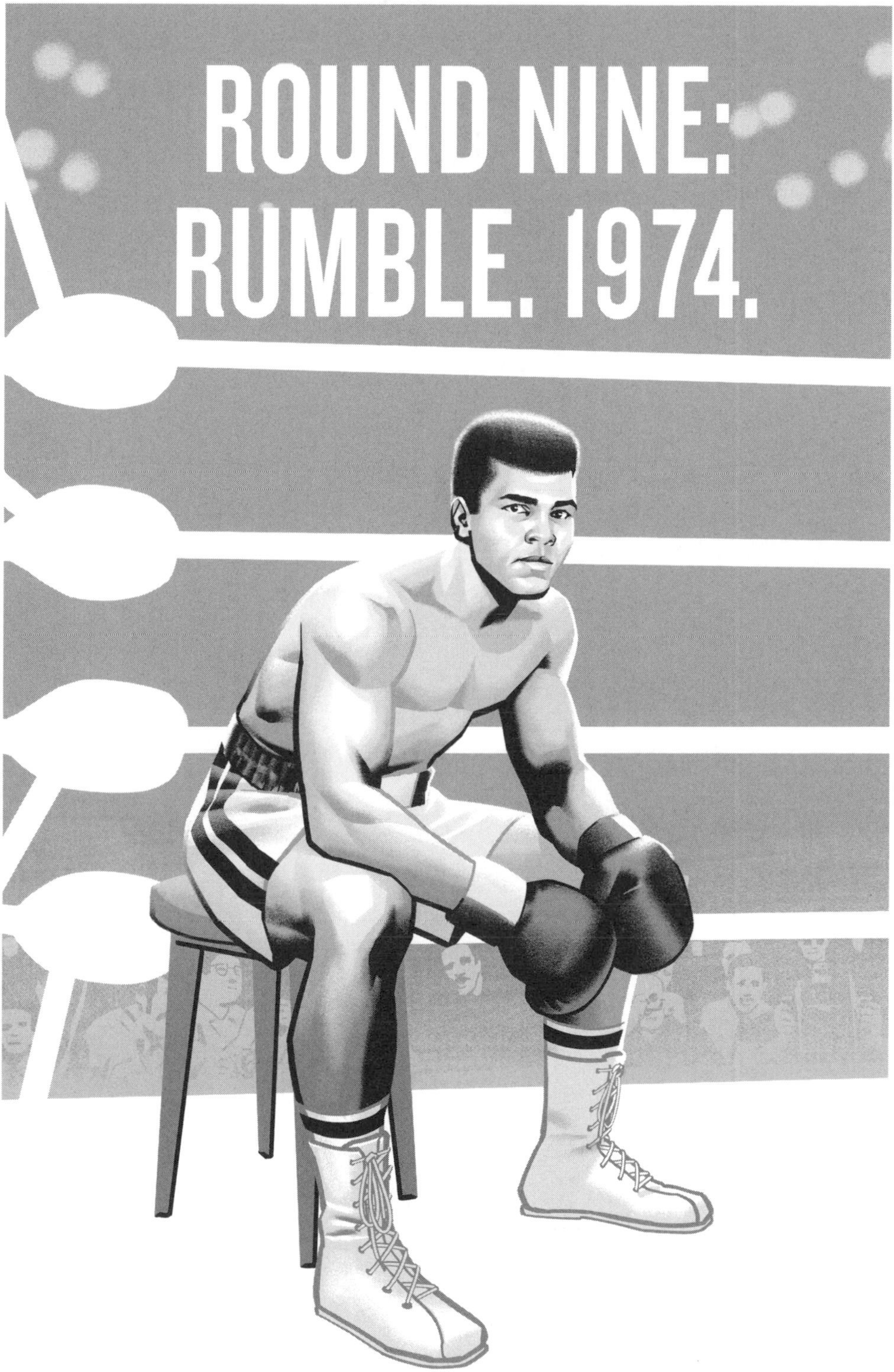

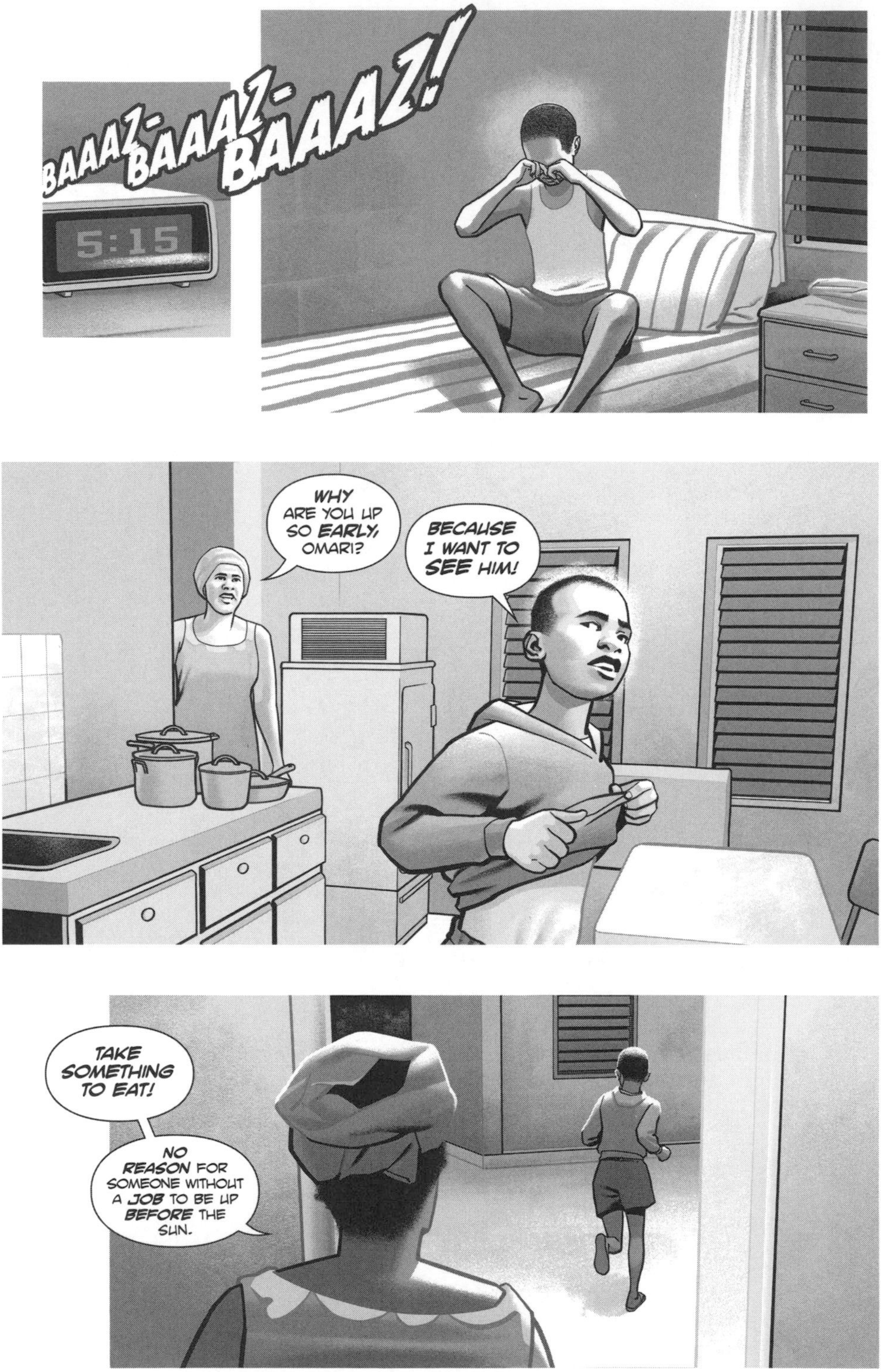
BAAAZ-BAAAZ-BAAAZ!
5:15
WHY ARE YOU UP SO EARLY, OMARI?
BECAUSE I WANT TO SEE HIM!
TAKE SOMETHING TO EAT!
NO REASON FOR SOMEONE WITHOUT A JOB TO BE UP BEFORE THE SUN.

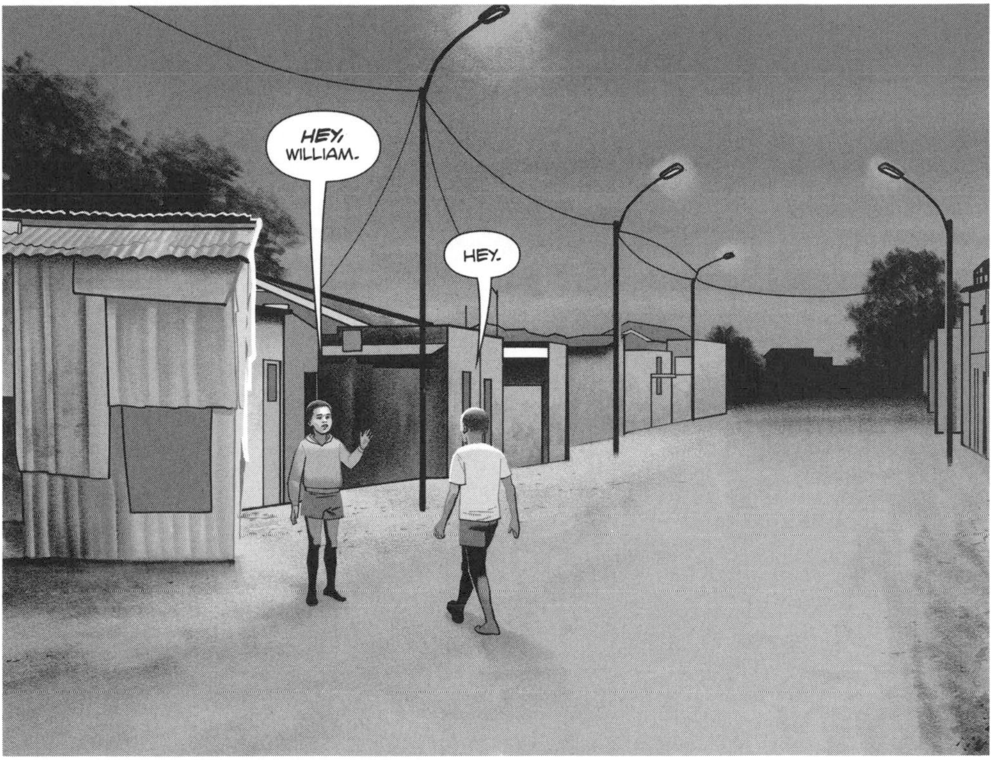
HEY, WILLIAM.
HEY.

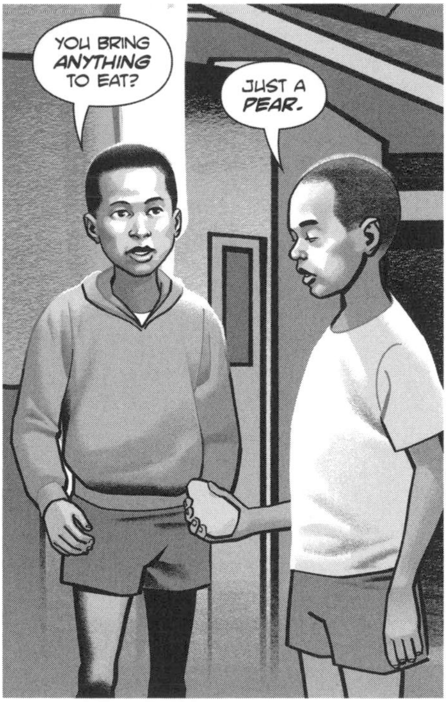
YOU BRING ANYTHING TO EAT?
JUST A PEAR.

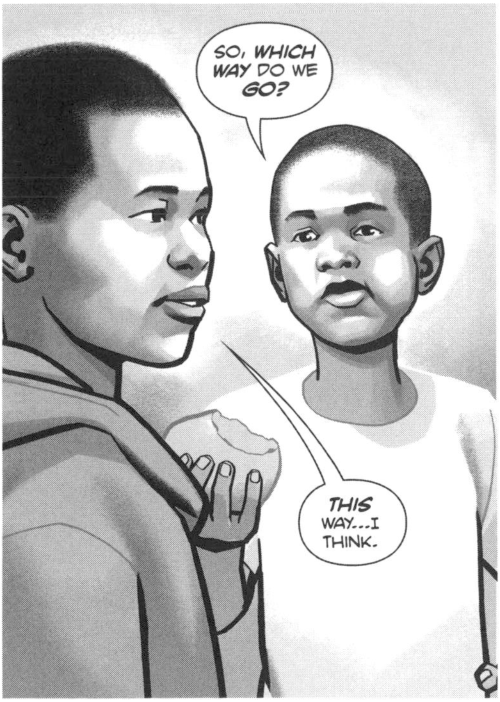
SO, WHICH WAY DO WE GO?
THIS WAY... I THINK.

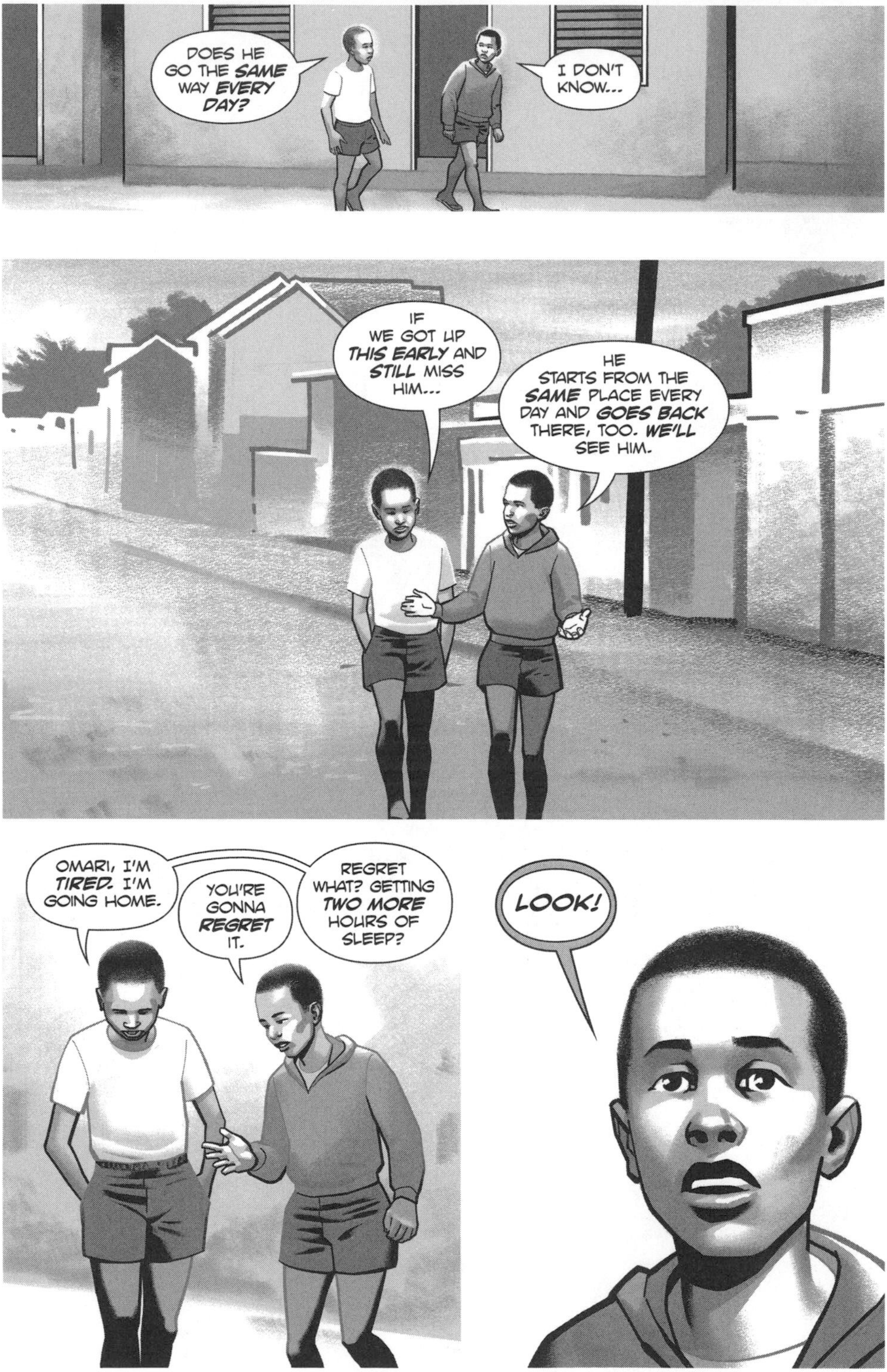
DOES HE GO THE SAME WAY EVERY DAY?
I DON'T KNOW...
IF WE GOT UP THIS EARLY AND STILL MISS HIM...
HE STARTS FROM THE SAME PLACE EVERY DAY AND GOES BACK THERE, TOO. WE'LL SEE HIM.
OMARI, I'M TIRED. I'M GOING HOME.
YOU'RE GONNA REGRET IT.
REGRET WHAT? GETTING TWO MORE HOURS OF SLEEP?
LOOK!

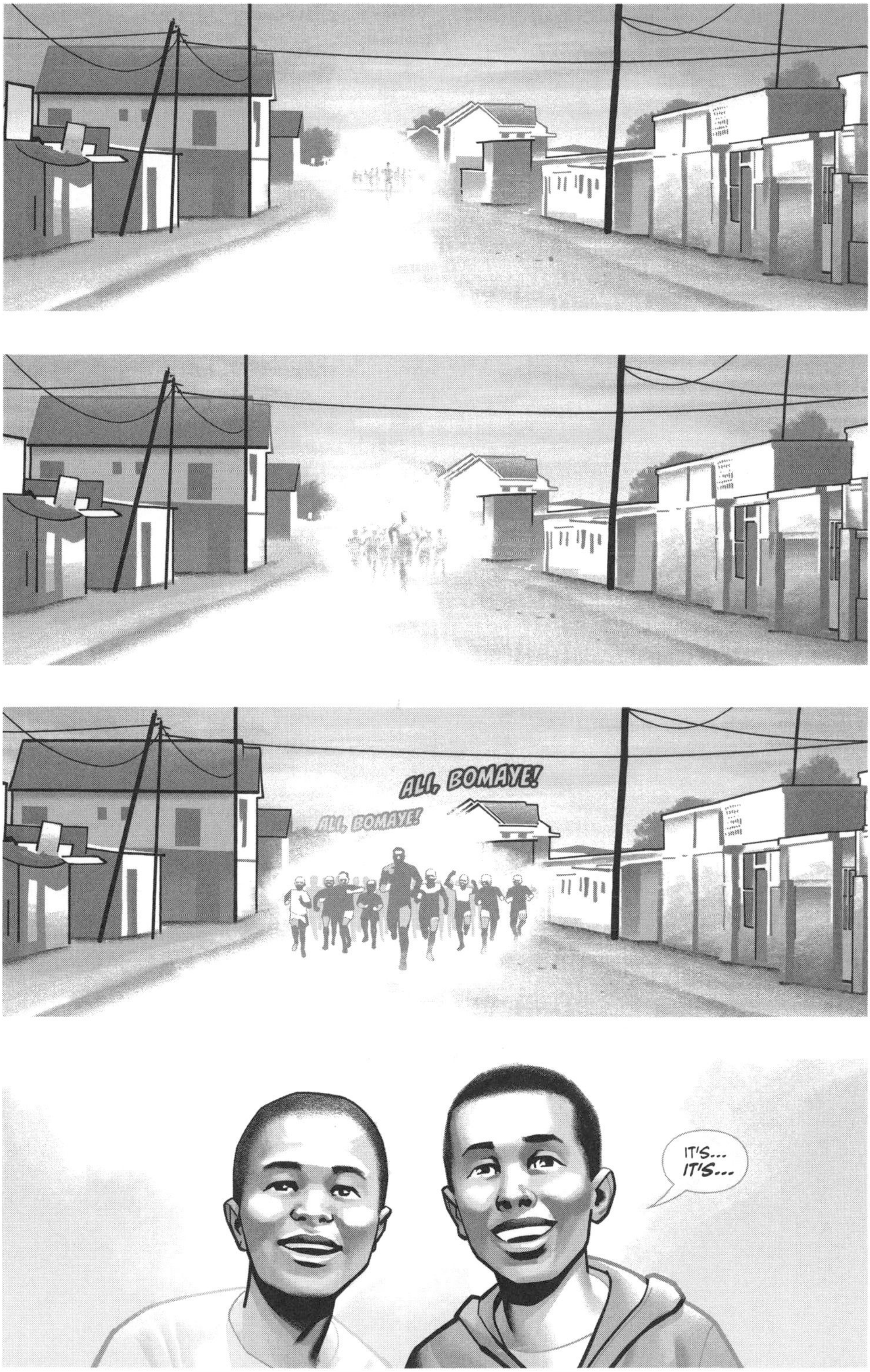
ALI, BOMAYE!
ALI, BOMAYE!
IT'S... IT'S...

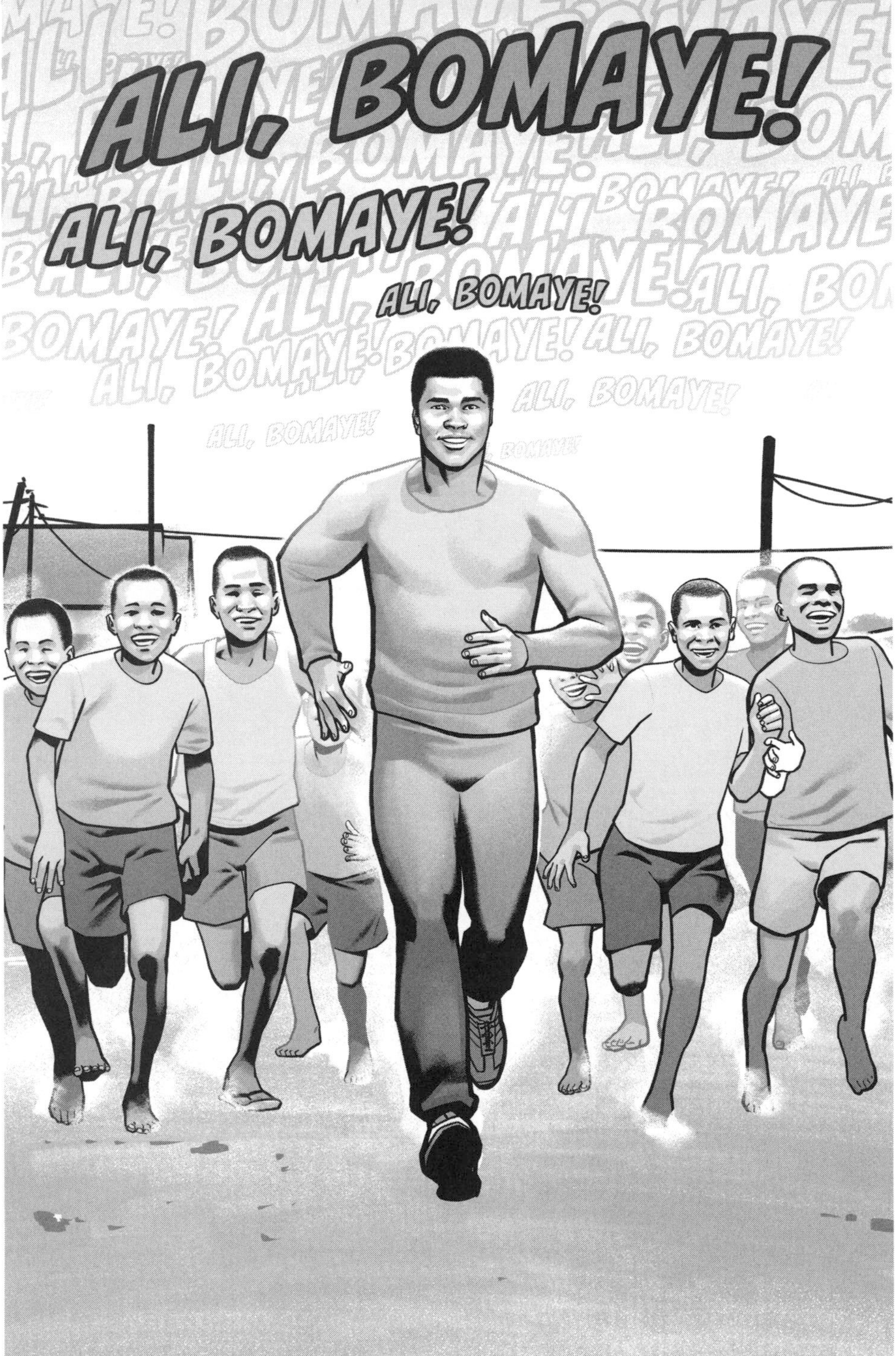
ALI, BOMAYE!
ALI, BOMAYE!
ALI, BOMAYE!
ALI, BOMAYE!
ALI, BOMAYE!

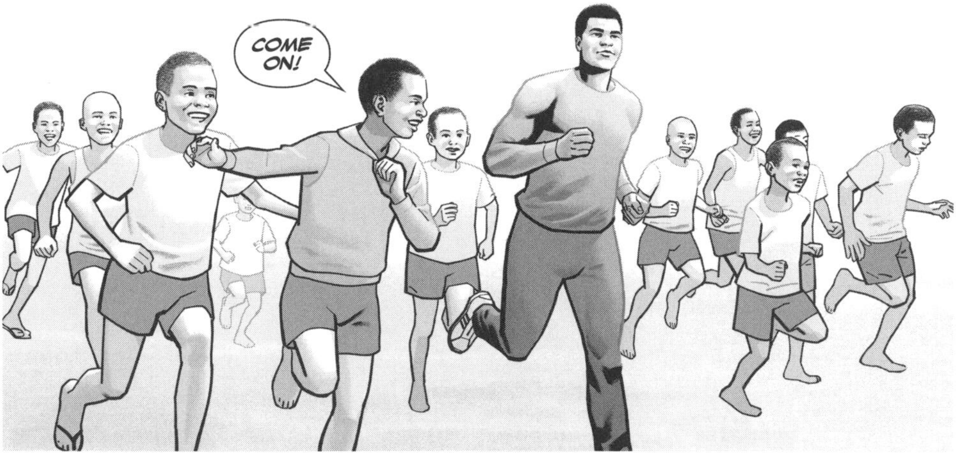
COME ON!

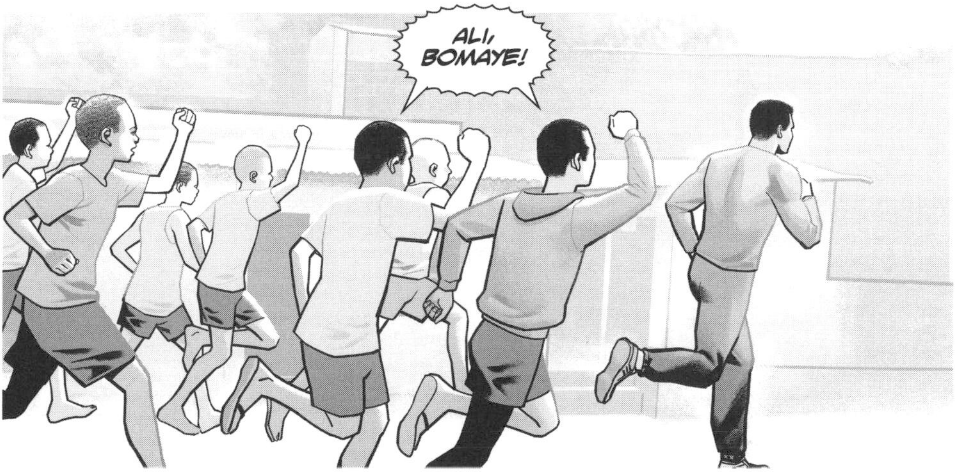
ALI, BOMAYE!

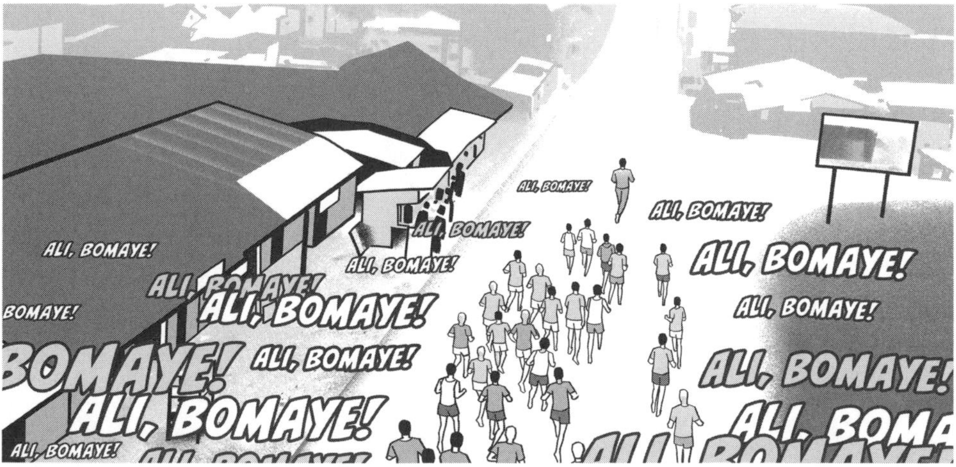
ALI, BOMAYE!
ALI, BOMAYE!
ALI, BOMAYE!
ALI, BOMAYE!
ALI, BOMAYE!
ALI, BOMAYE!
BOMAYE!
ALI, BOMAYE!
ALI, BOMAYE!
BOMAYE!
ALI, BOMAYE!
ALI, BOMAYE!
ALI, BOMAYE!
ALI, BOMAYE!
ALI, BOMA

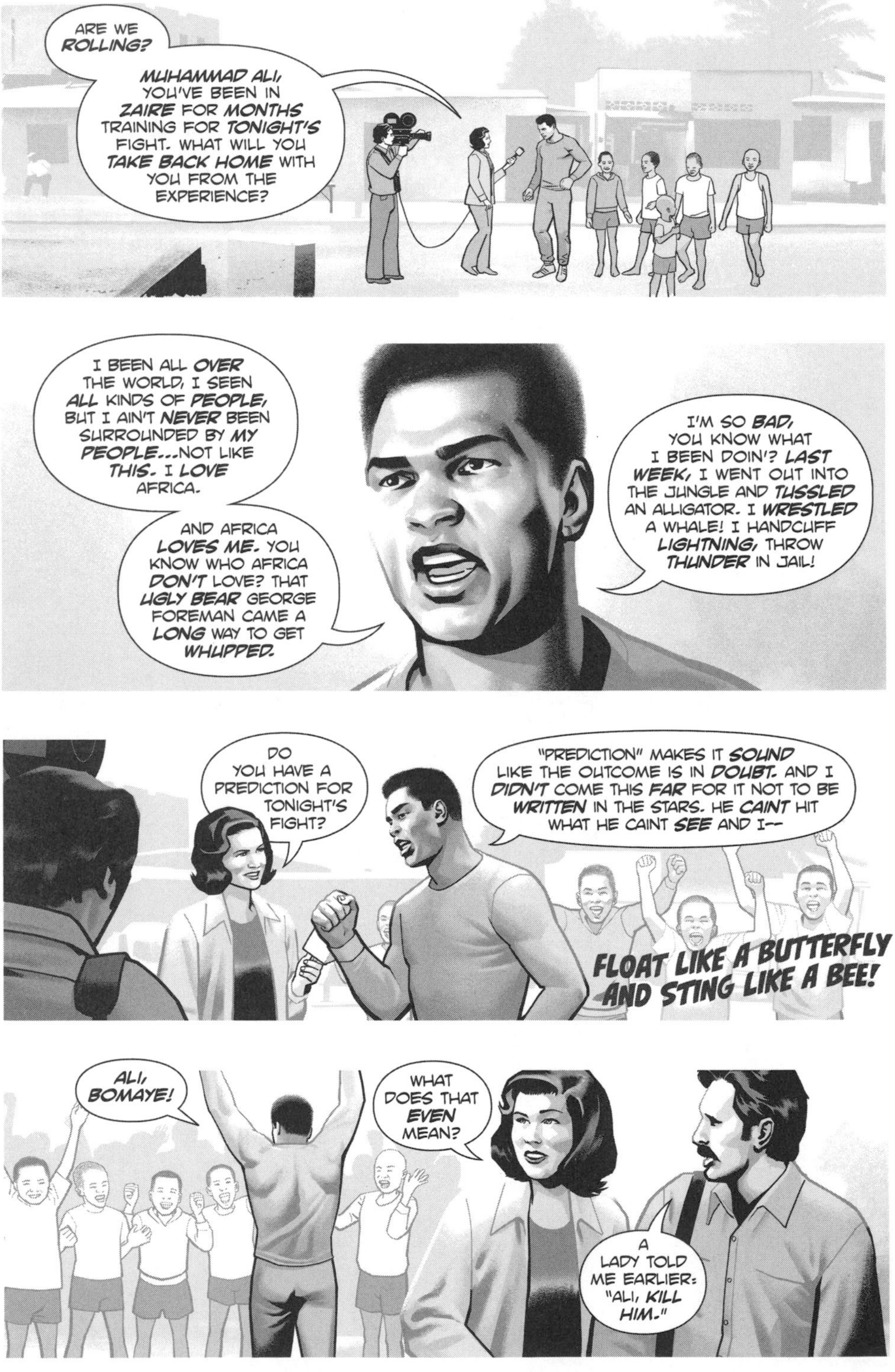
ARE WE ROLLING?
MUHAMMAD ALI, YOU'VE BEEN IN ZAIRE FOR MONTHS TRAINING FOR TONIGHT'S FIGHT. WHAT WILL YOU TAKE BACK HOME WITH YOU FROM THE EXPERIENCE?
I BEEN ALL OVER THE WORLD, I SEEN ALL KINDS OF PEOPLE, BUT I AIN'T NEVER BEEN SURROUNDED BY MY PEOPLE...NOT LIKE THIS. I LOVE AFRICA.
AND AFRICA LOVES ME. YOU KNOW WHO AFRICA DON'T LOVE? THAT UGLY BEAR GEORGE FOREMAN CAME A LONG WAY TO GET WHUPPED.
I'M SO BAD, YOU KNOW WHAT I BEEN DOIN'? LAST WEEK, I WENT OUT INTO THE JUNGLE AND TUSSLED AN ALLIGATOR. I WRESTLED A WHALE! I HANDCUFF LIGHTNING, THROW THUNDER IN JAIL!
DO YOU HAVE A PREDICTION FOR TONIGHT'S FIGHT?
"PREDICTION" MAKES IT SOUND LIKE THE OUTCOME IS IN DOUBT. AND I DIDN'T COME THIS FAR FOR IT NOT TO BE WRITTEN IN THE STARS. HE CAINT HIT WHAT HE CAINT SEE AND I--
FLOAT LIKE A BUTTERFLY AND STING LIKE A BEE!
ALI, BOMAYE!
WHAT DOES THAT EVEN MEAN?
A LADY TOLD ME EARLIER: "ALI, KILL HIM."

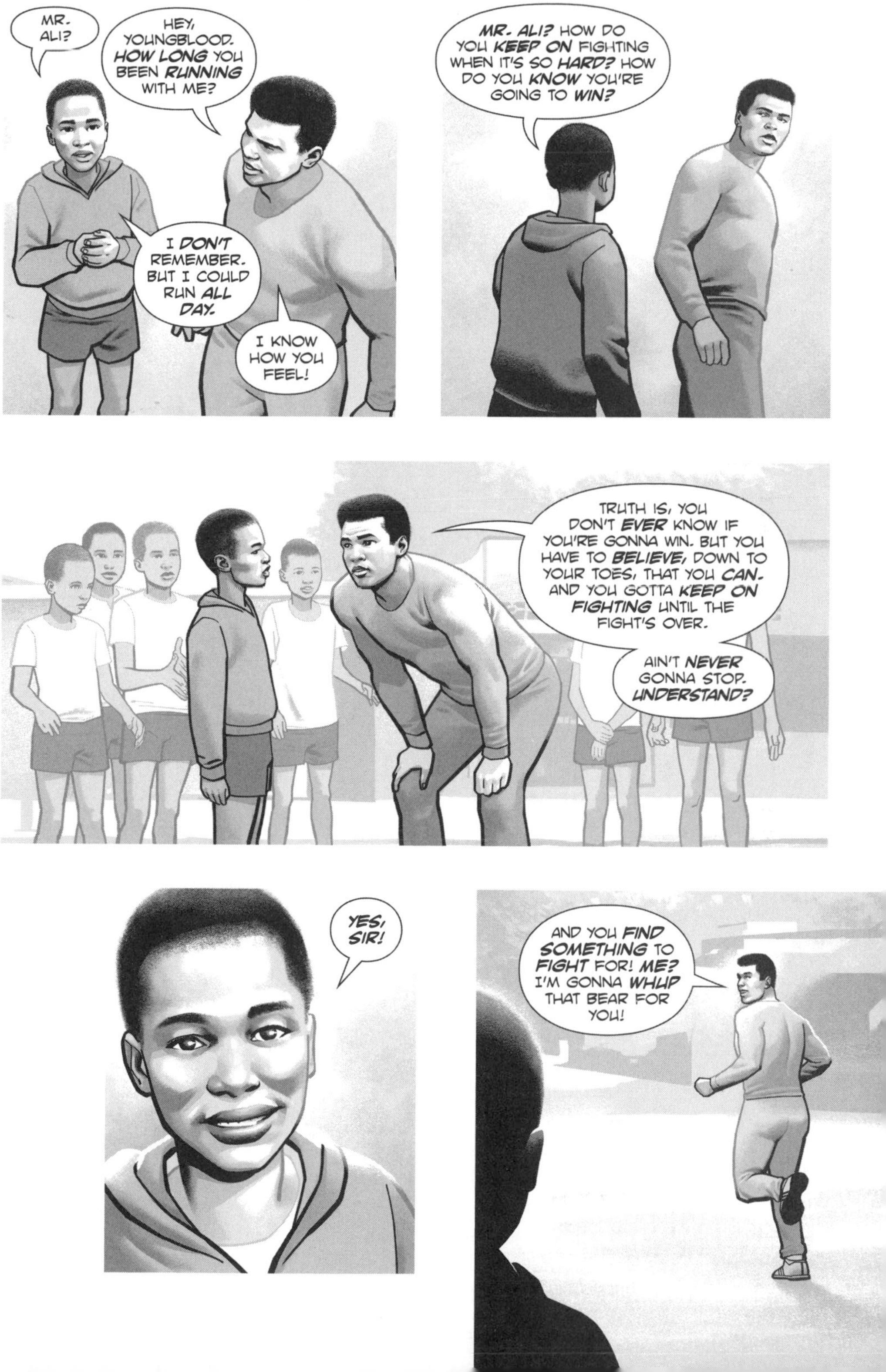
MR. ALI?
HEY, YOUNGBLOOD. HOW LONG YOU BEEN RUNNING WITH ME?
I DON'T REMEMBER. BUT I COULD RUN ALL DAY.
I KNOW HOW YOU FEEL!
MR. ALI? HOW DO YOU KEEP ON FIGHTING WHEN IT'S SO HARD? HOW DO YOU KNOW YOU'RE GOING TO WIN?
TRUTH IS, YOU DON'T EVER KNOW IF YOU'RE GONNA WIN. BUT YOU HAVE TO BELIEVE, DOWN TO YOUR TOES, THAT YOU CAN. AND YOU GOTTA KEEP ON FIGHTING UNTIL THE FIGHT'S OVER.
AIN'T NEVER GONNA STOP. UNDERSTAND?
YES, SIR!
AND YOU FIND SOMETHING TO FIGHT FOR! ME? I'M GONNA WHUP THAT BEAR FOR YOU!

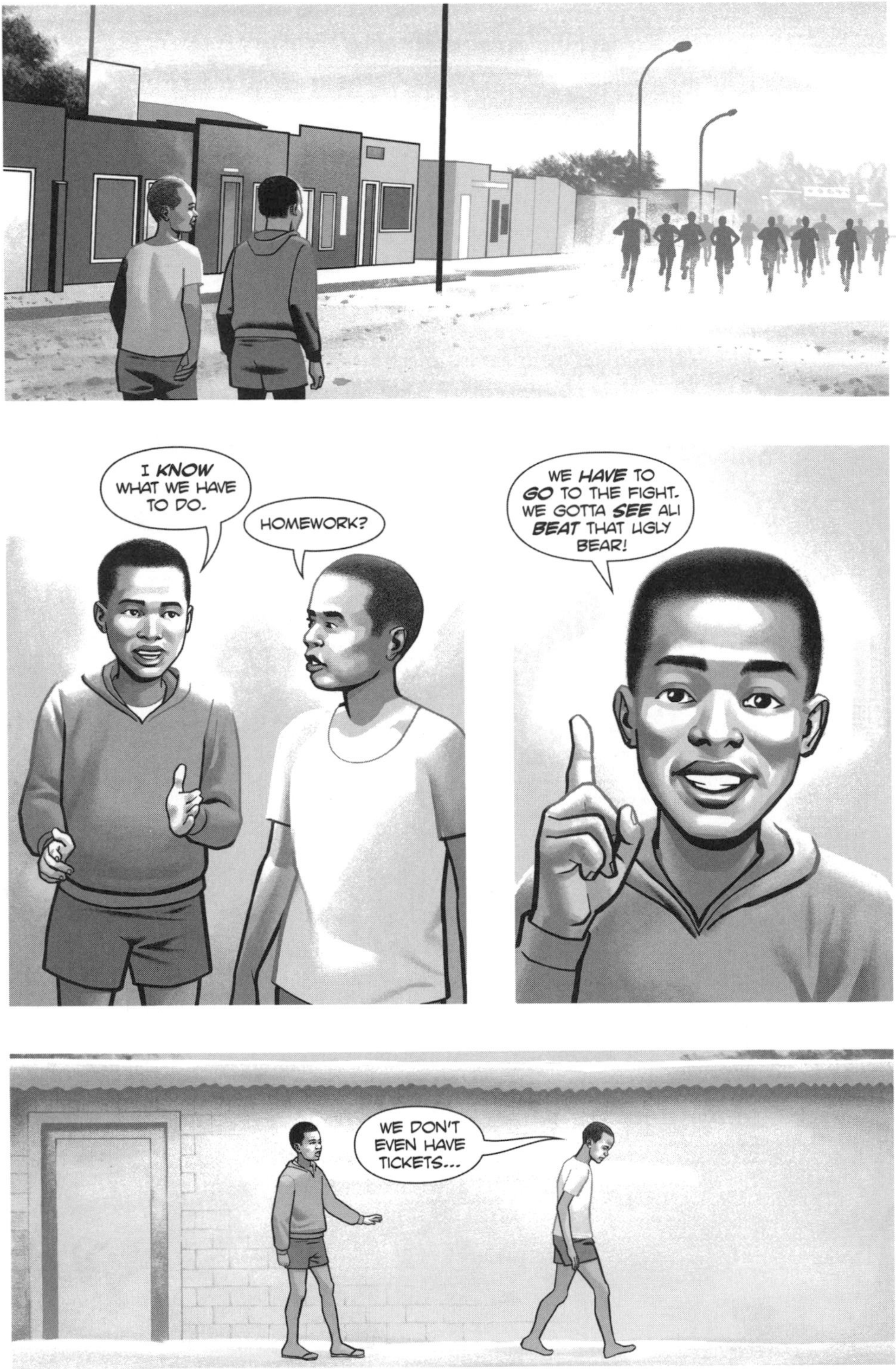
I KNOW WHAT WE HAVE TO DO.
HOMEWORK?
WE HAVE TO GO TO THE FIGHT. WE GOTTA SEE ALI BEAT THAT UGLY BEAR!
WE DON'T EVEN HAVE TICKETS...

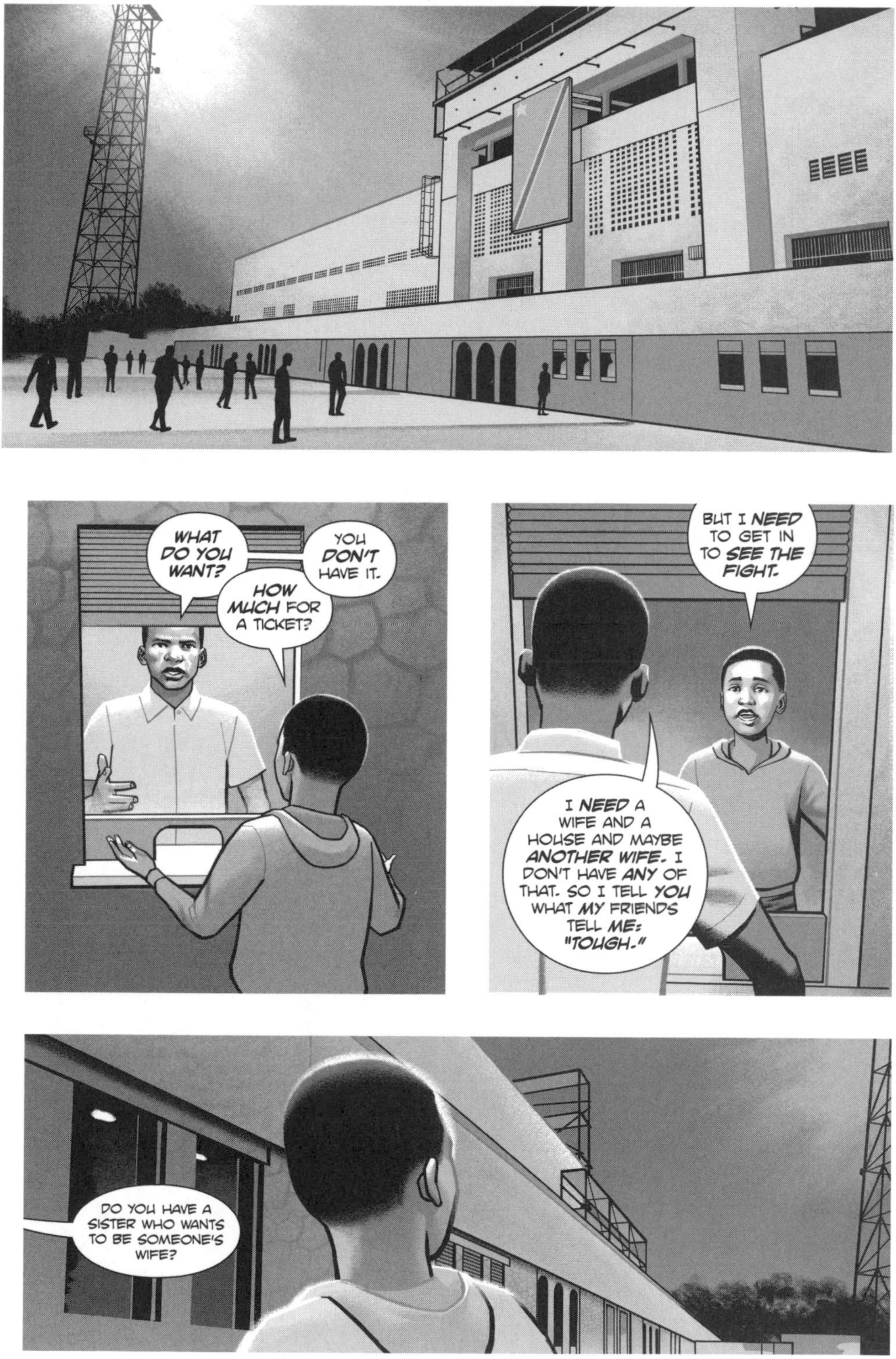
WHAT DO YOU WANT?
YOU DON'T HAVE IT.
HOW MUCH FOR A TICKET?
BUT I NEED TO GET IN TO SEE THE FIGHT.
I NEED A WIFE AND A HOUSE AND MAYBE ANOTHER WIFE. I DON'T HAVE ANY OF THAT. SO I TELL YOU WHAT MY FRIENDS TELL ME: "TOUGH."
DO YOU HAVE A SISTER WHO WANTS TO BE SOMEONE'S WIFE?

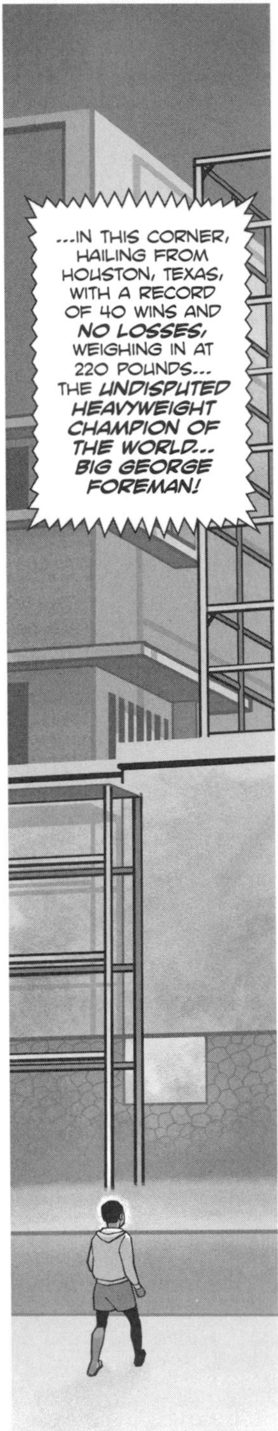
...IN THIS CORNER, HAILING FROM HOUSTON, TEXAS, WITH A RECORD OF 40 WINS AND NO LOSSES, WEIGHING IN AT 220 POUNDS... THE UNDISPUTED HEAVYWEIGHT CHAMPION OF THE WORLD... BIG GEORGE FOREMAN!

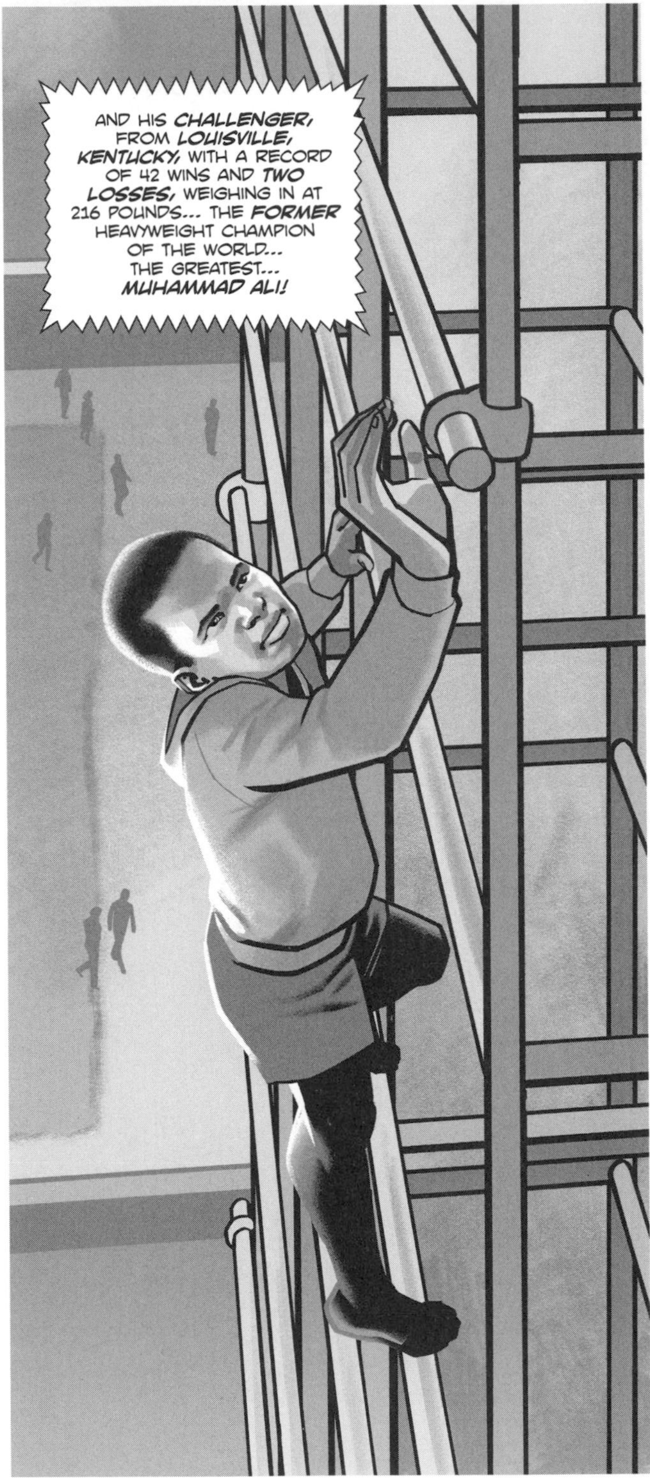
AND HIS CHALLENGER, FROM LOUISVILLE, KENTUCKY, WITH A RECORD OF 42 WINS AND TWO LOSSES, WEIGHING IN AT 216 POUNDS... THE FORMER HEAVYWEIGHT CHAMPION OF THE WORLD... THE GREATEST... MUHAMMAD ALI!

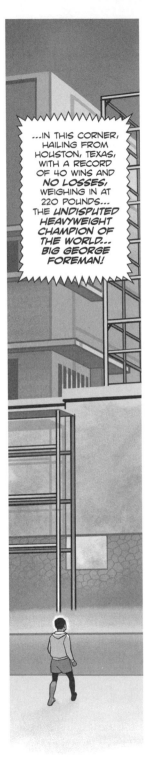

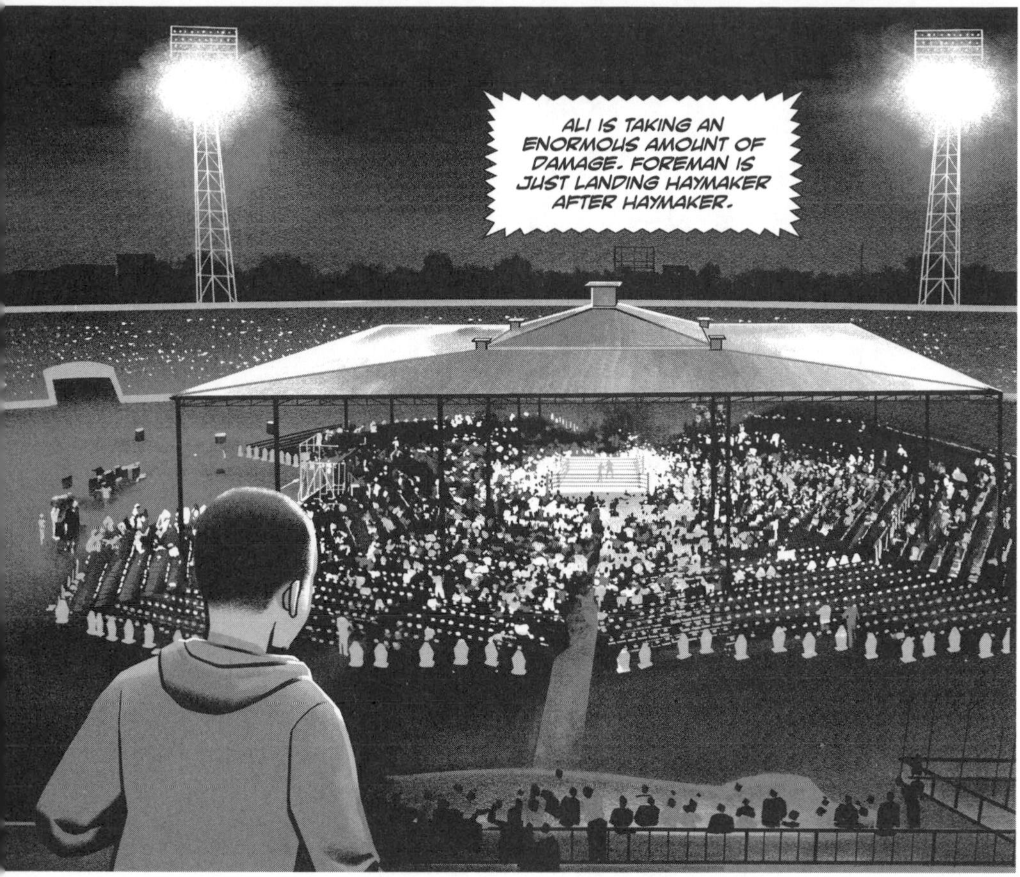
ALI IS TAKING AN ENORMOUS AMOUNT OF DAMAGE. FOREMAN IS JUST LANDING HAYMAKER AFTER HAYMAKER.

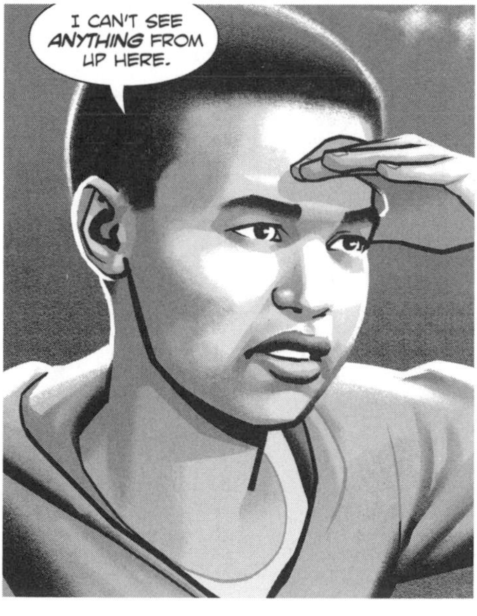
I CAN'T SEE ANYTHING FROM UP HERE.

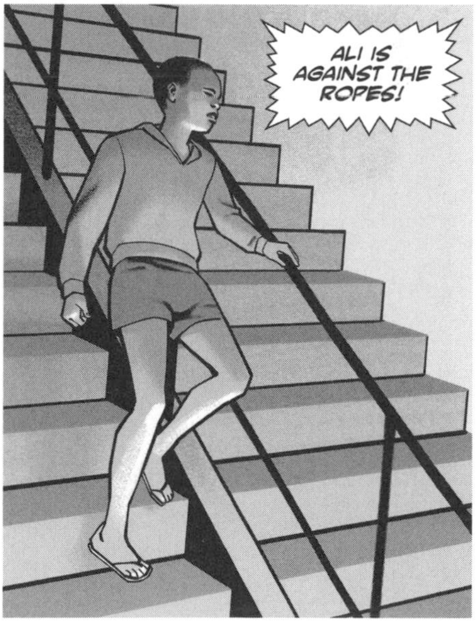
ALI IS AGAINST THE ROPES!

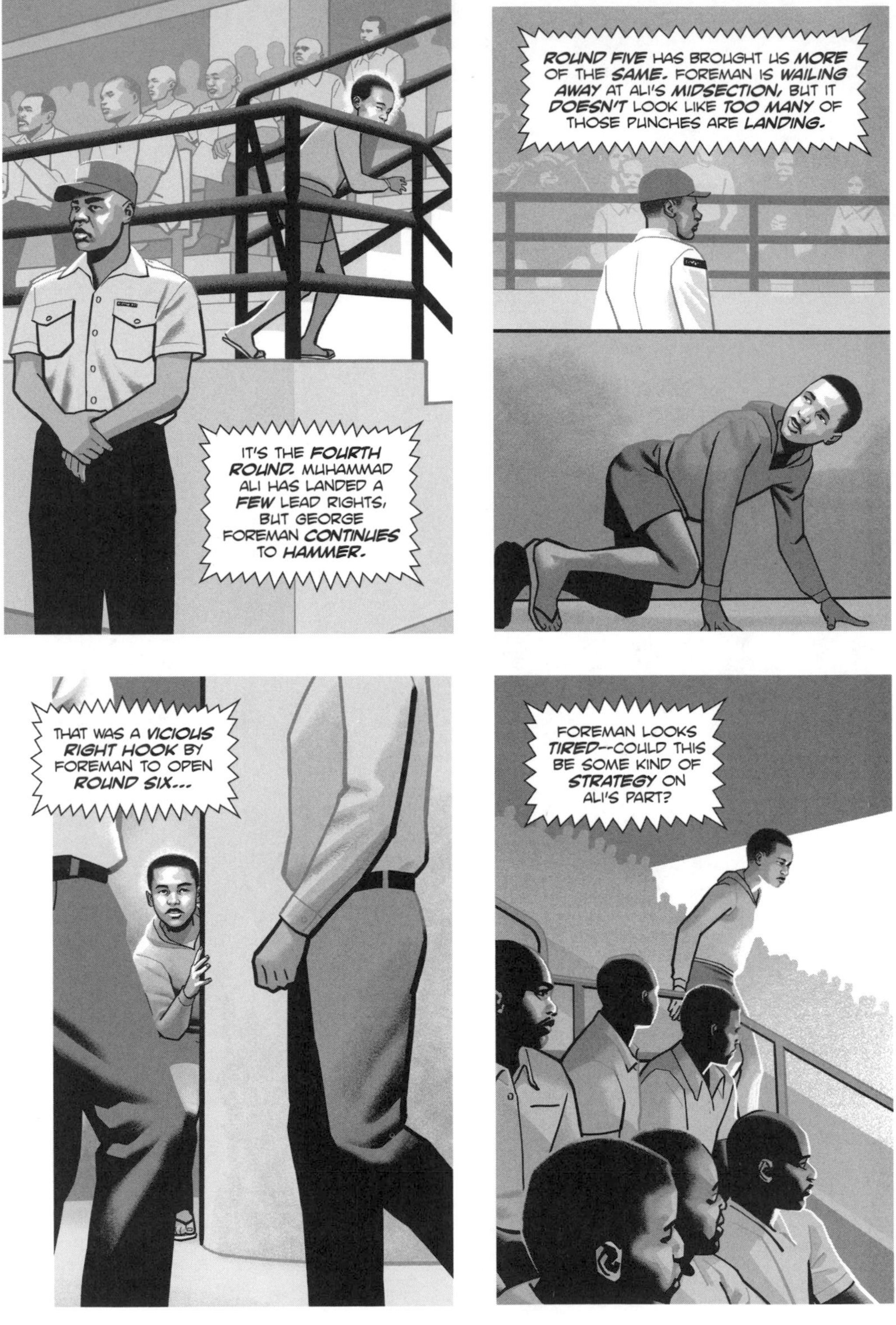
IT'S THE FOURTH ROUND. MUHAMMAD ALI HAS LANDED A FEW LEAD RIGHTS, BUT GEORGE FOREMAN CONTINUES TO HAMMER.
ROUND FIVE HAS BROUGHT US MORE OF THE SAME. FOREMAN IS WAILING AWAY AT ALI'S MIDSECTION, BUT IT DOESN'T LOOK LIKE TOO MANY OF THOSE PUNCHES ARE LANDING.
THAT WAS A VICIOUS RIGHT HOOK BY FOREMAN TO OPEN ROUND SIX...
FOREMAN LOOKS TIRED--COULD THIS BE SOME KIND OF STRATEGY ON ALI'S PART?

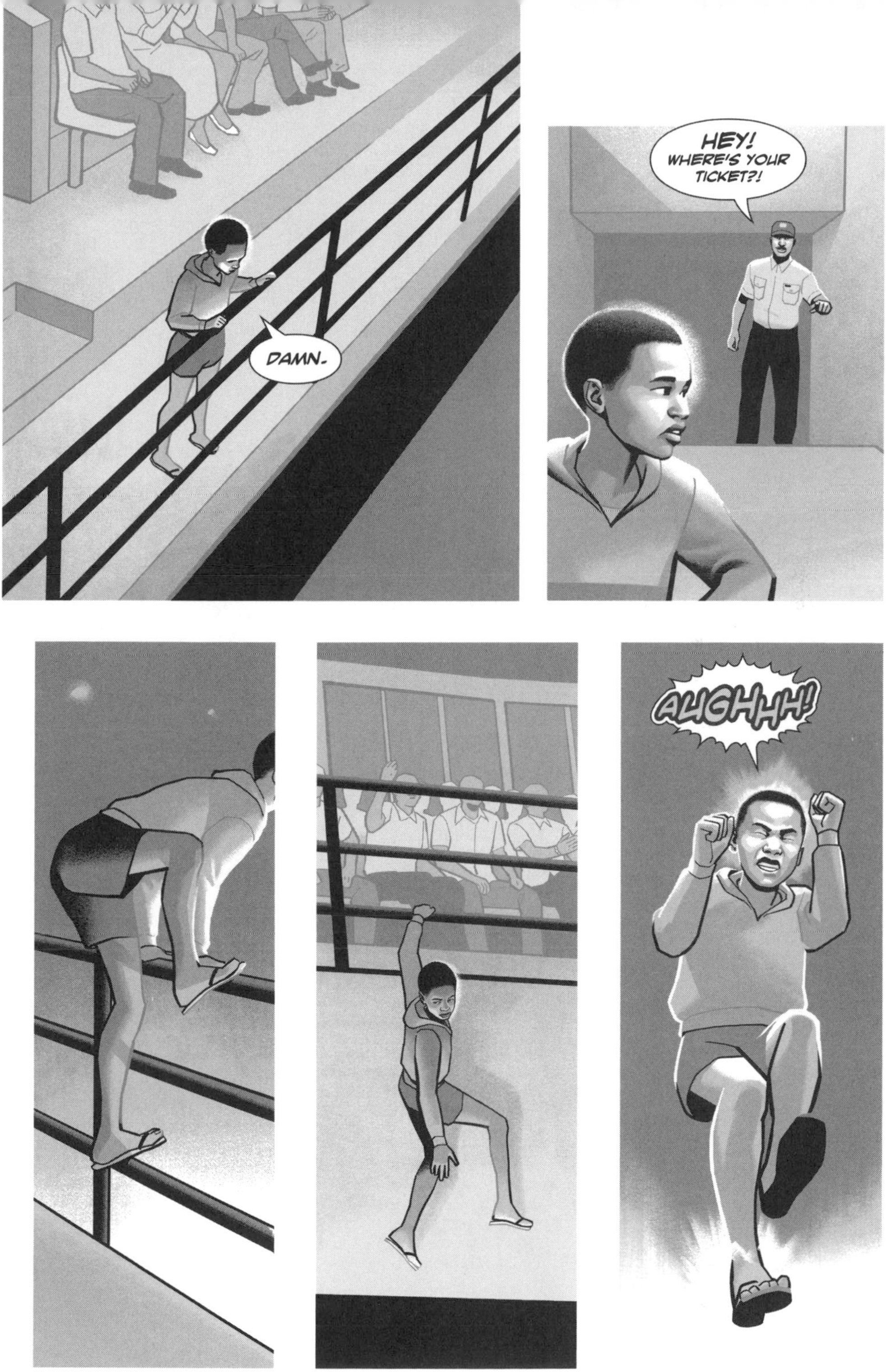
DAMN.
HEY! WHERE'S YOUR TICKET?!
AUGHHH!

ALI IS GETTING *KILLED.* I CAN'T BELIEVE I *WASTED* MY MONEY ON *THIS.*

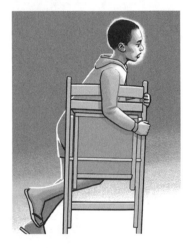

WE'RE COMING TO *THE END* OF THE *SEVENTH ROUND.* ALI LOOKS SHAKEN, *BATTERED.*

NOOOOOOO!

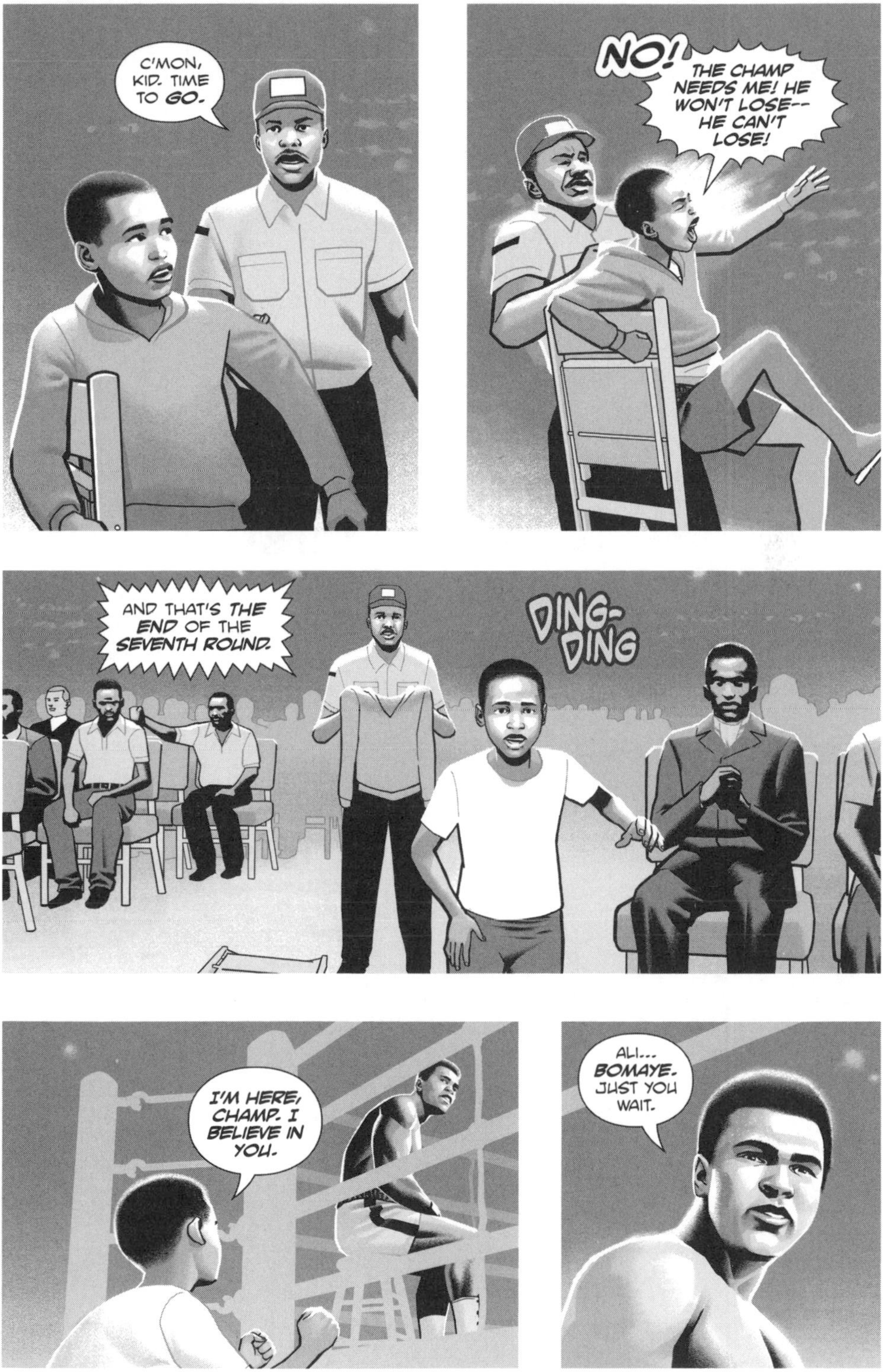
C'MON, KID. TIME TO GO.
NO!
THE CHAMP NEEDS ME! HE WON'T LOSE-- HE CAN'T LOSE!
AND THAT'S THE END OF THE SEVENTH ROUND.
DING-DING
I'M HERE, CHAMP. I BELIEVE IN YOU.
ALI... BOMAYE. JUST YOU WAIT.

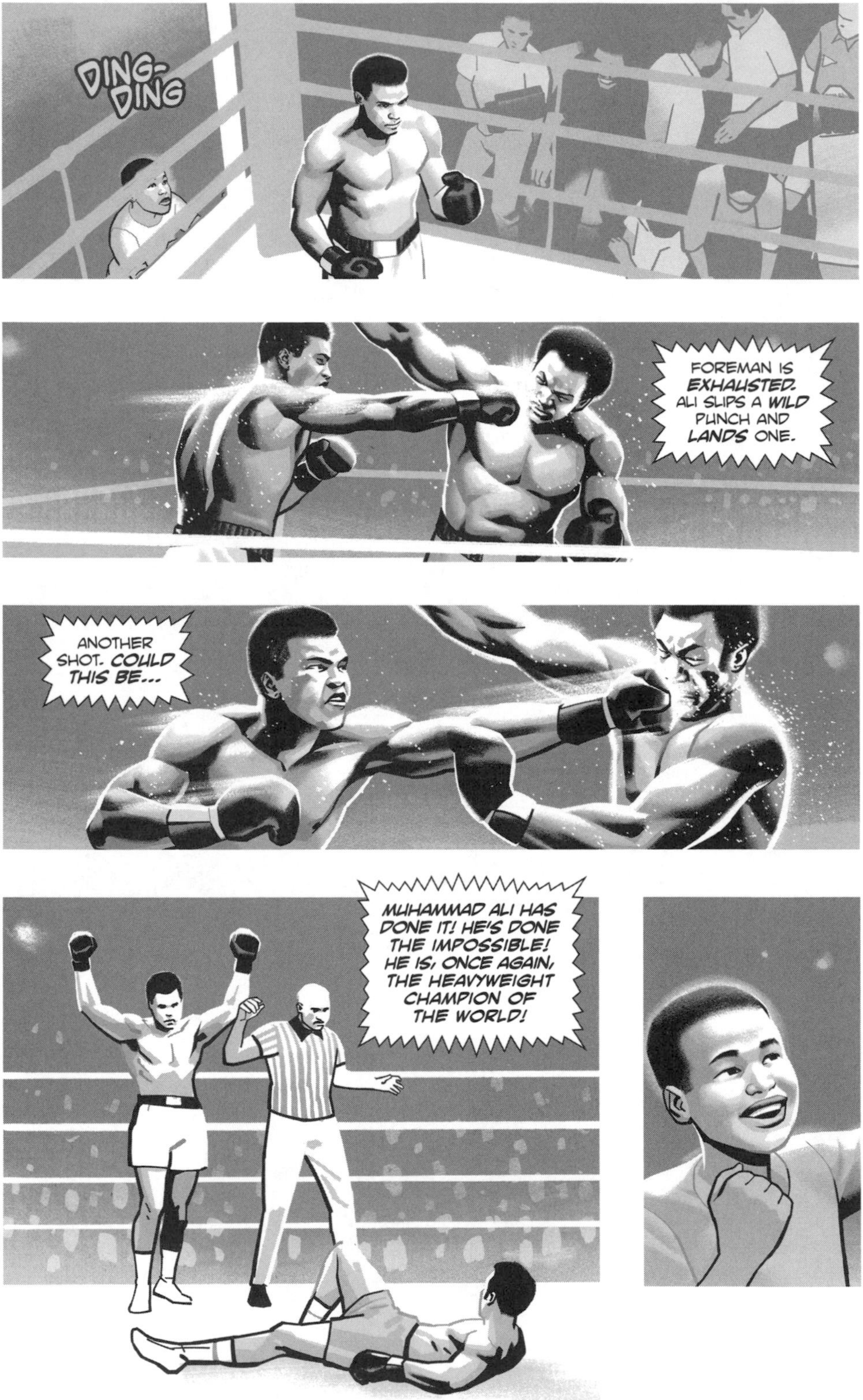
DING-DING
FOREMAN IS EXHAUSTED. ALI SLIPS A WILD PUNCH AND LANDS ONE.
ANOTHER SHOT. COULD THIS BE...
MUHAMMAD ALI HAS DONE IT! HE'S DONE THE IMPOSSIBLE! HE IS, ONCE AGAIN, THE HEAVYWEIGHT CHAMPION OF THE WORLD!

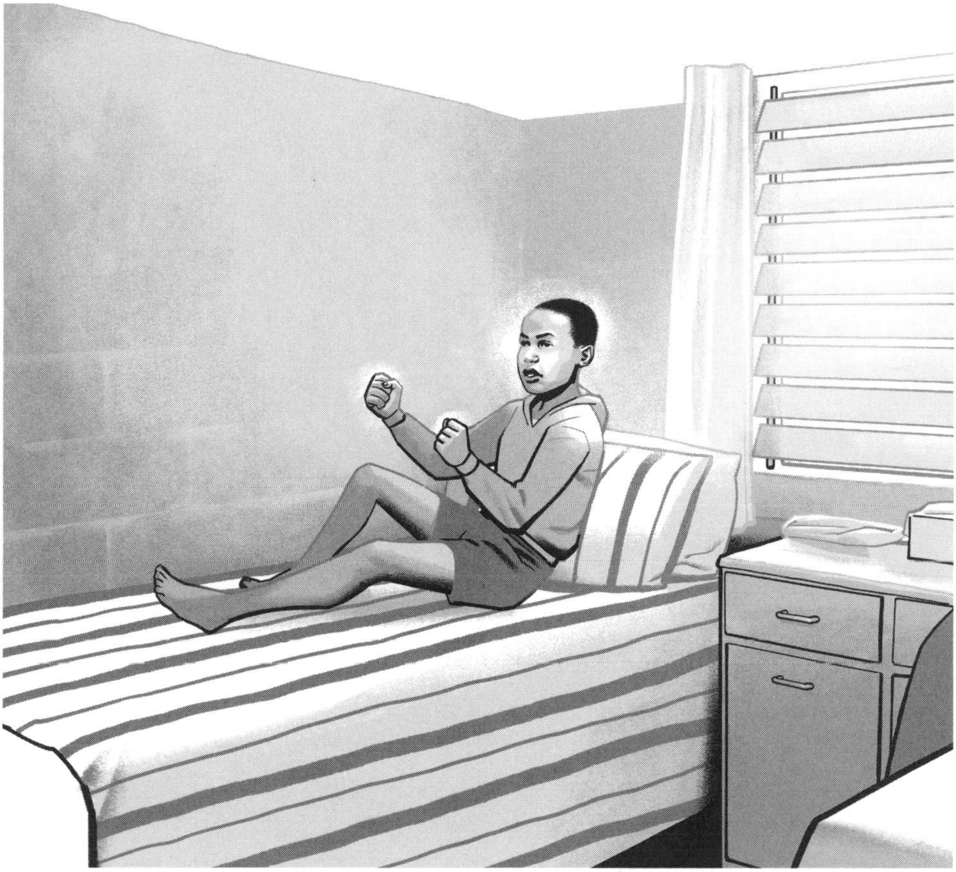

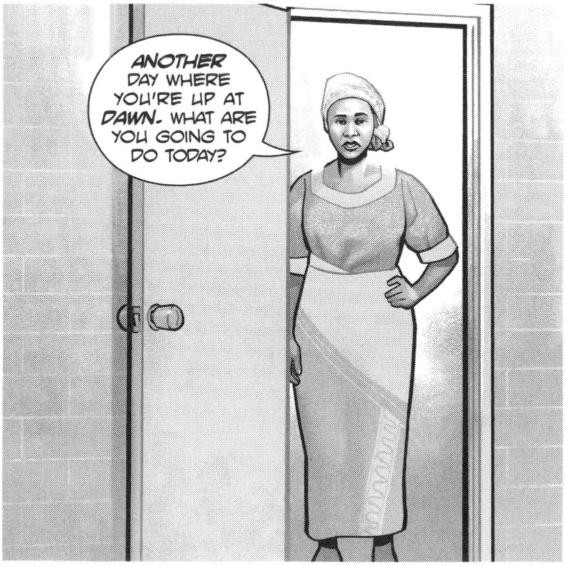
ANOTHER DAY WHERE YOU'RE UP AT DAWN. WHAT ARE YOU GOING TO DO TODAY?

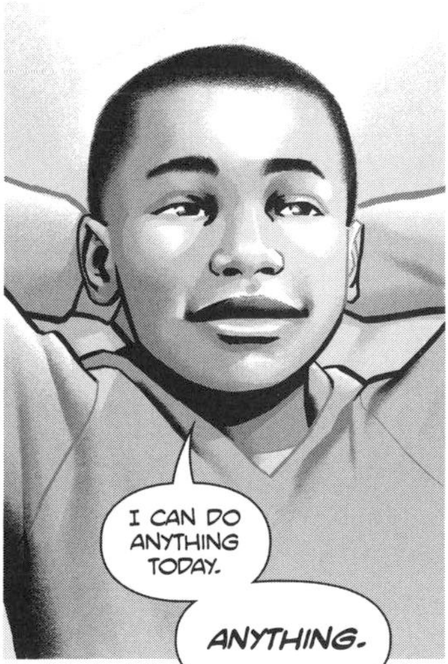
I CAN DO ANYTHING TODAY.
ANYTHING.

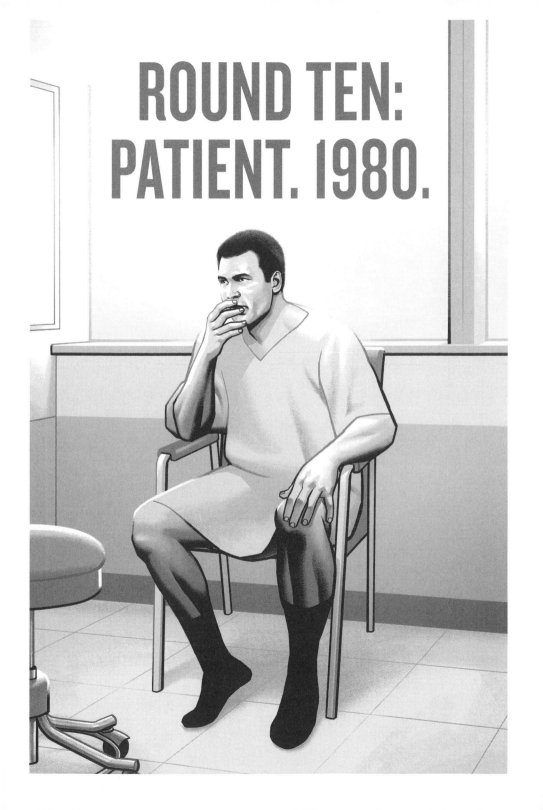

ROUND TEN:
PATIENT. 1980.

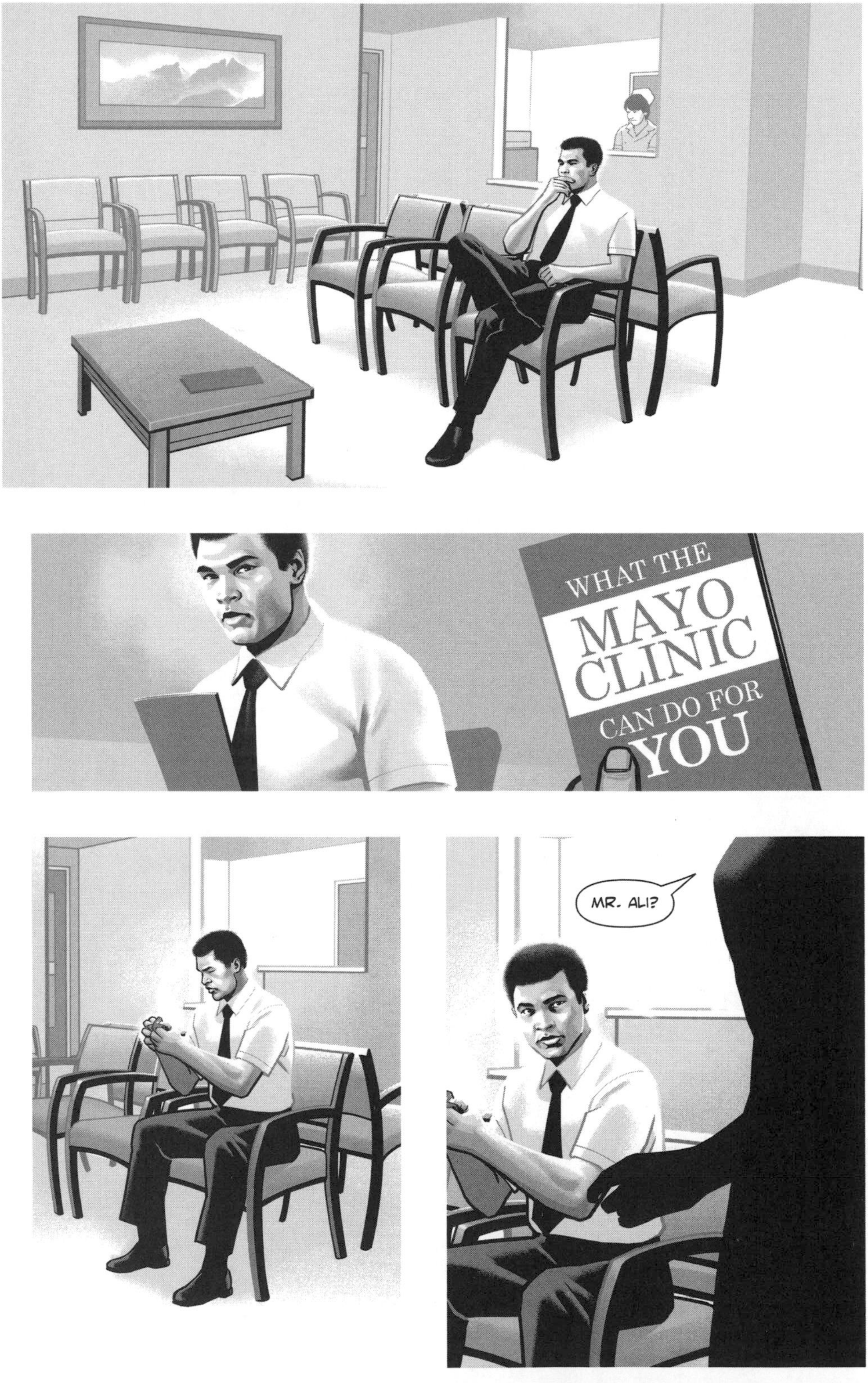
WHAT THE
MAYO CLINIC
CAN DO FOR YOU
MR. ALI?

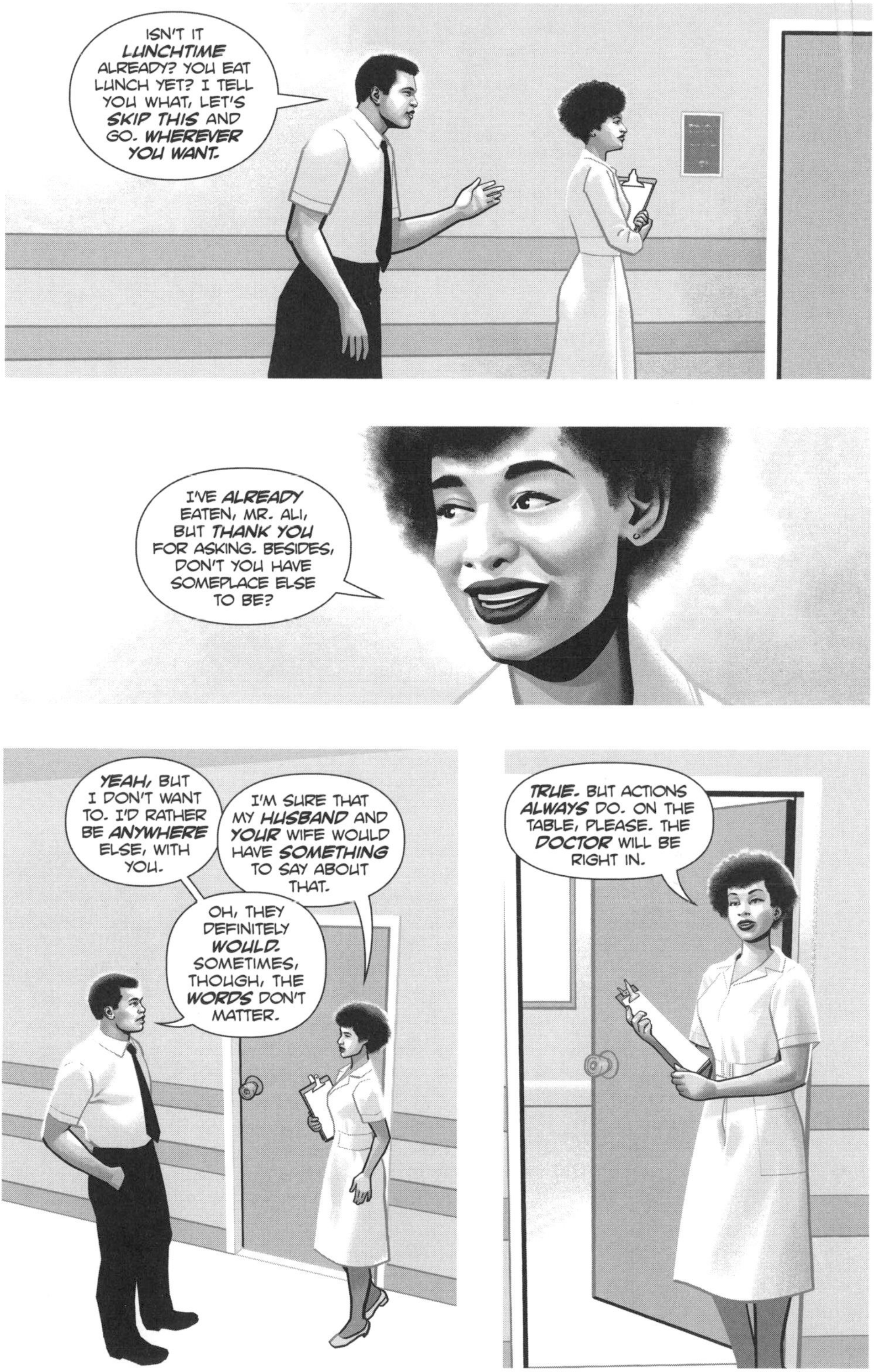
ISN'T IT LUNCHTIME ALREADY? YOU EAT LUNCH YET? I TELL YOU WHAT, LET'S SKIP THIS AND GO. WHEREVER YOU WANT.
I'VE ALREADY EATEN, MR. ALI, BUT THANK YOU FOR ASKING. BESIDES, DON'T YOU HAVE SOMEPLACE ELSE TO BE?
YEAH, BUT I DON'T WANT TO. I'D RATHER BE ANYWHERE ELSE, WITH YOU.
I'M SURE THAT MY HUSBAND AND YOUR WIFE WOULD HAVE SOMETHING TO SAY ABOUT THAT.
OH, THEY DEFINITELY WOULD. SOMETIMES, THOUGH, THE WORDS DON'T MATTER.
TRUE. BUT ACTIONS ALWAYS DO. ON THE TABLE, PLEASE. THE DOCTOR WILL BE RIGHT IN.

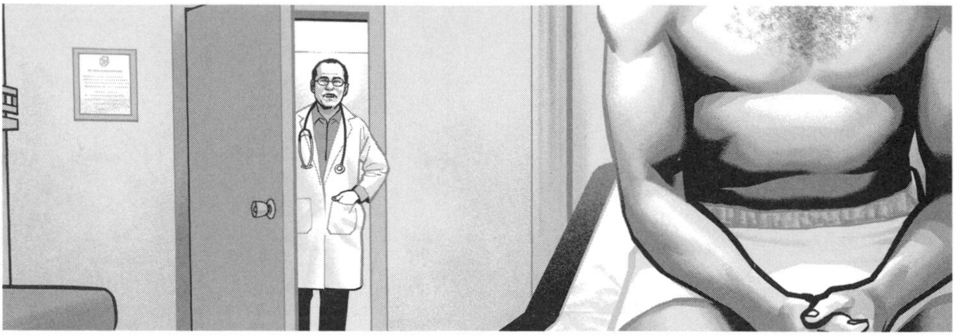

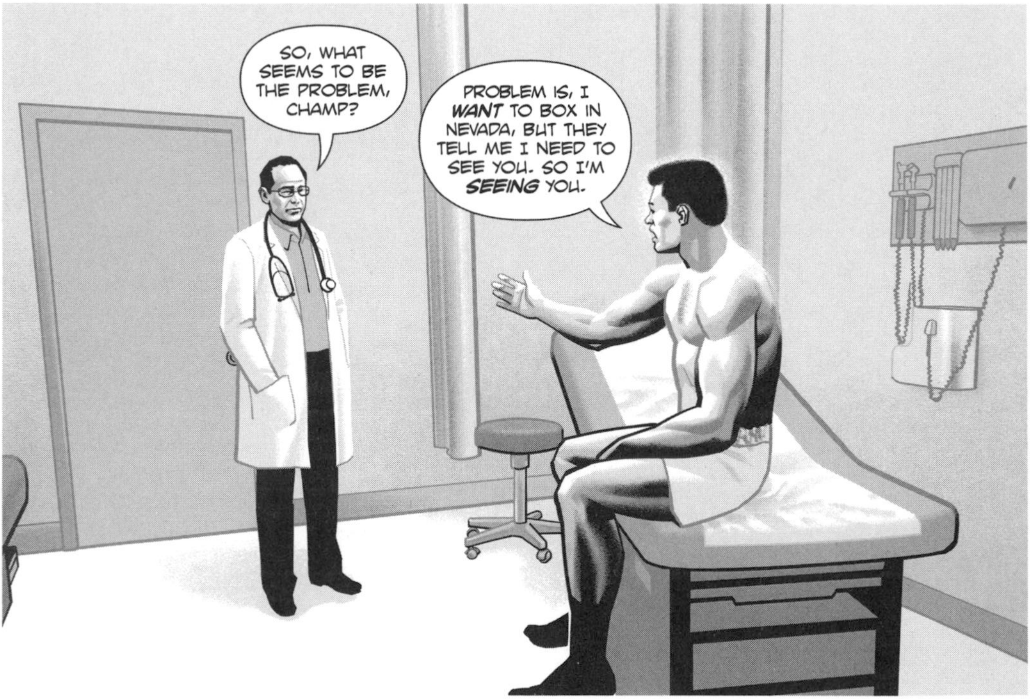
SO, WHAT SEEMS TO BE THE PROBLEM, CHAMP?
PROBLEM IS, I WANT TO BOX IN NEVADA, BUT THEY TELL ME I NEED TO SEE YOU. SO I'M SEEING YOU.

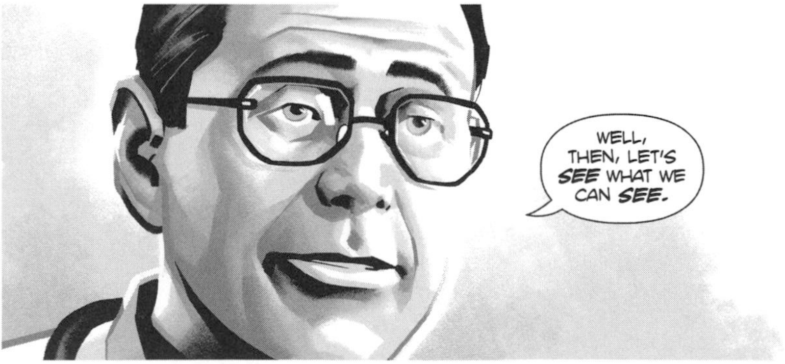
WELL, THEN, LET'S SEE WHAT WE CAN SEE.

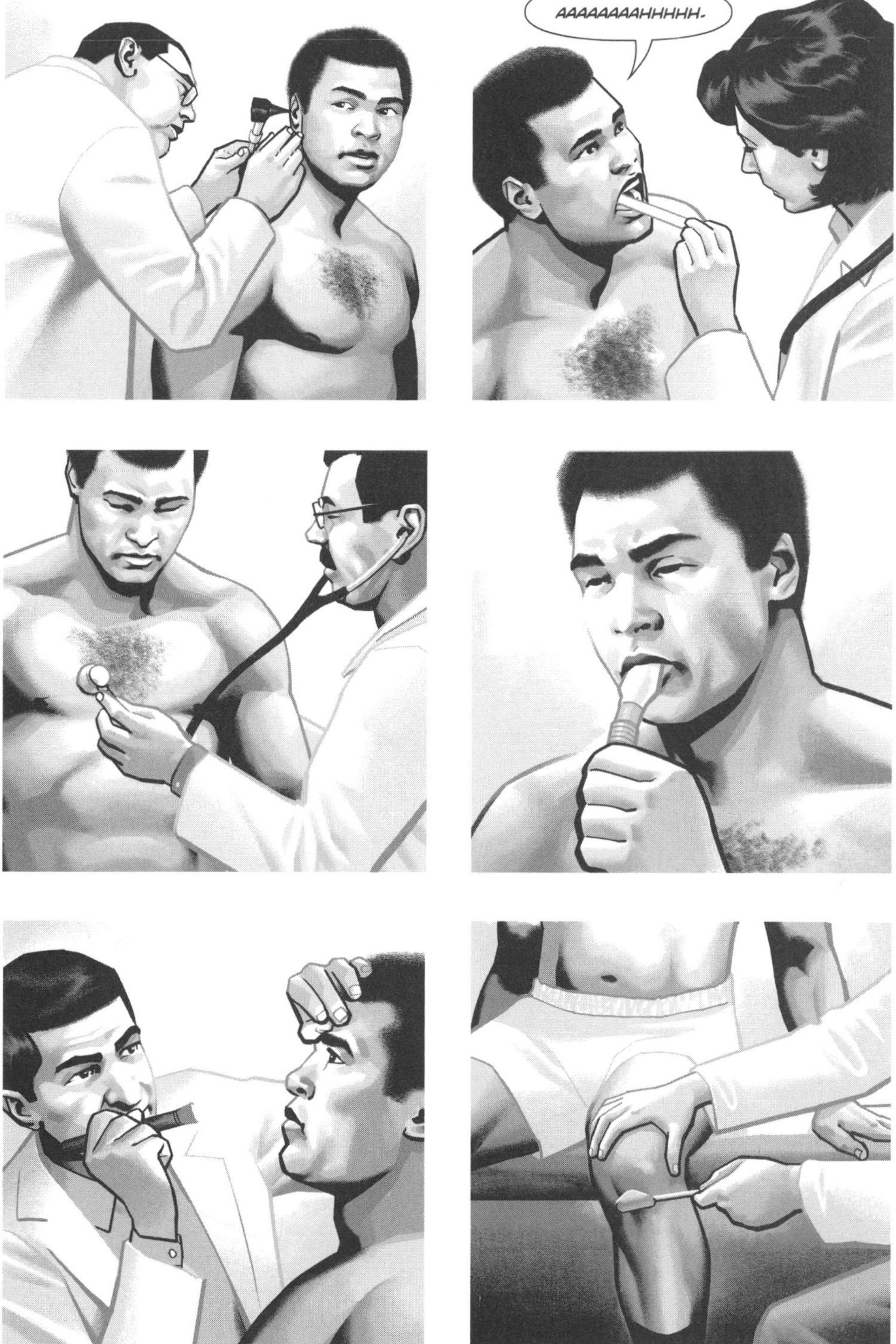
AAAAAAAAHHHHH.

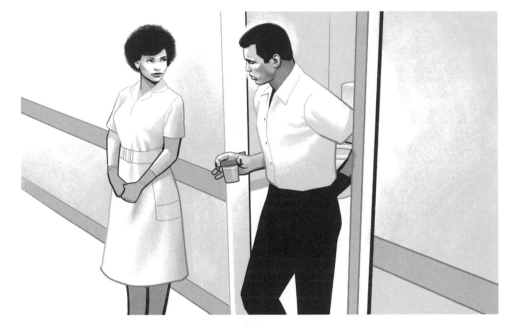

DON'T SAY I NEVER GAVE YOU NOTHING.

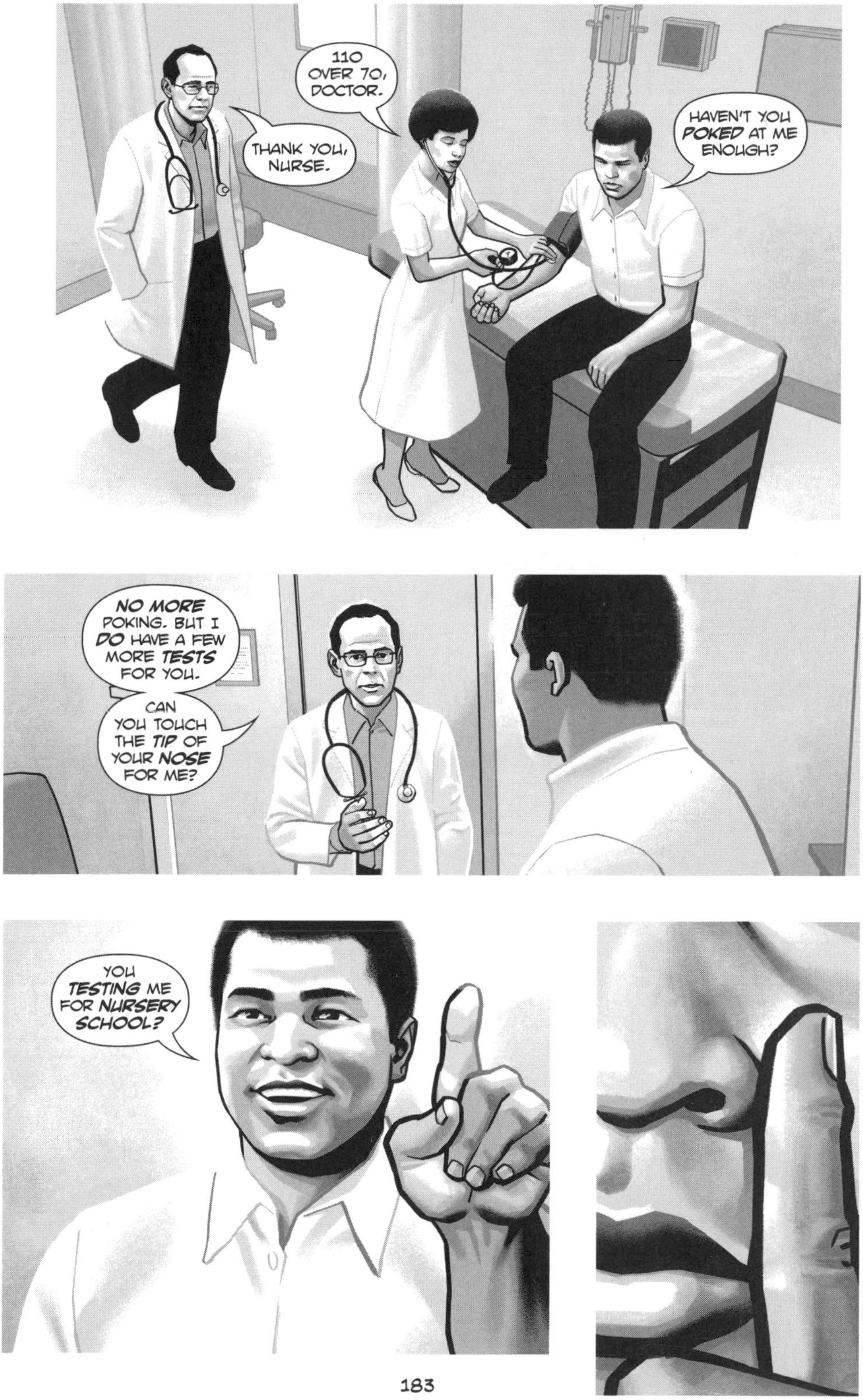
110 OVER 70, DOCTOR.
THANK YOU, NURSE.
HAVEN'T YOU *POKED* AT ME ENOUGH?
NO MORE POKING. BUT I *DO* HAVE A FEW MORE *TESTS* FOR YOU.
CAN YOU TOUCH THE *TIP* OF YOUR *NOSE* FOR ME?
YOU *TESTING* ME FOR *NURSERY SCHOOL?*

OKAY, STAND UP, PLEASE.

I'D LIKE YOU TO *HOP* ON *ONE* FOOT.

YOU'RE *NOT* GONNA GIVE ME ANY *ROPE* TO JUMP?

NOT *TODAY.*

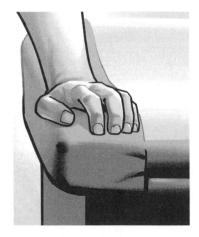

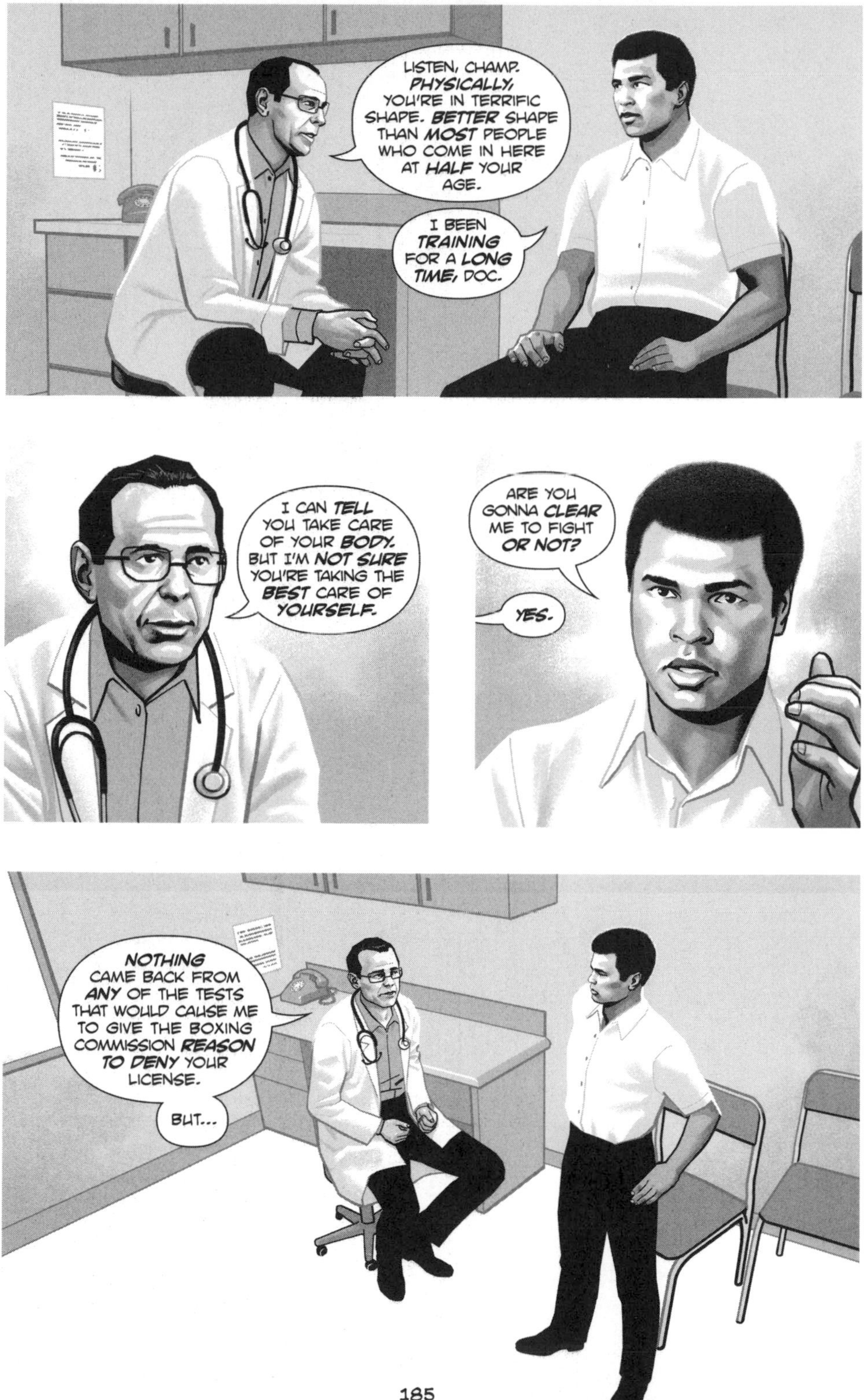
LISTEN, CHAMP. PHYSICALLY, YOU'RE IN TERRIFIC SHAPE. BETTER SHAPE THAN MOST PEOPLE WHO COME IN HERE AT HALF YOUR AGE.
I BEEN TRAINING FOR A LONG TIME, DOC.
I CAN TELL YOU TAKE CARE OF YOUR BODY. BUT I'M NOT SURE YOU'RE TAKING THE BEST CARE OF YOURSELF.
ARE YOU GONNA CLEAR ME TO FIGHT OR NOT?
YES.
NOTHING CAME BACK FROM ANY OF THE TESTS THAT WOULD CAUSE ME TO GIVE THE BOXING COMMISSION REASON TO DENY YOUR LICENSE.
BUT...

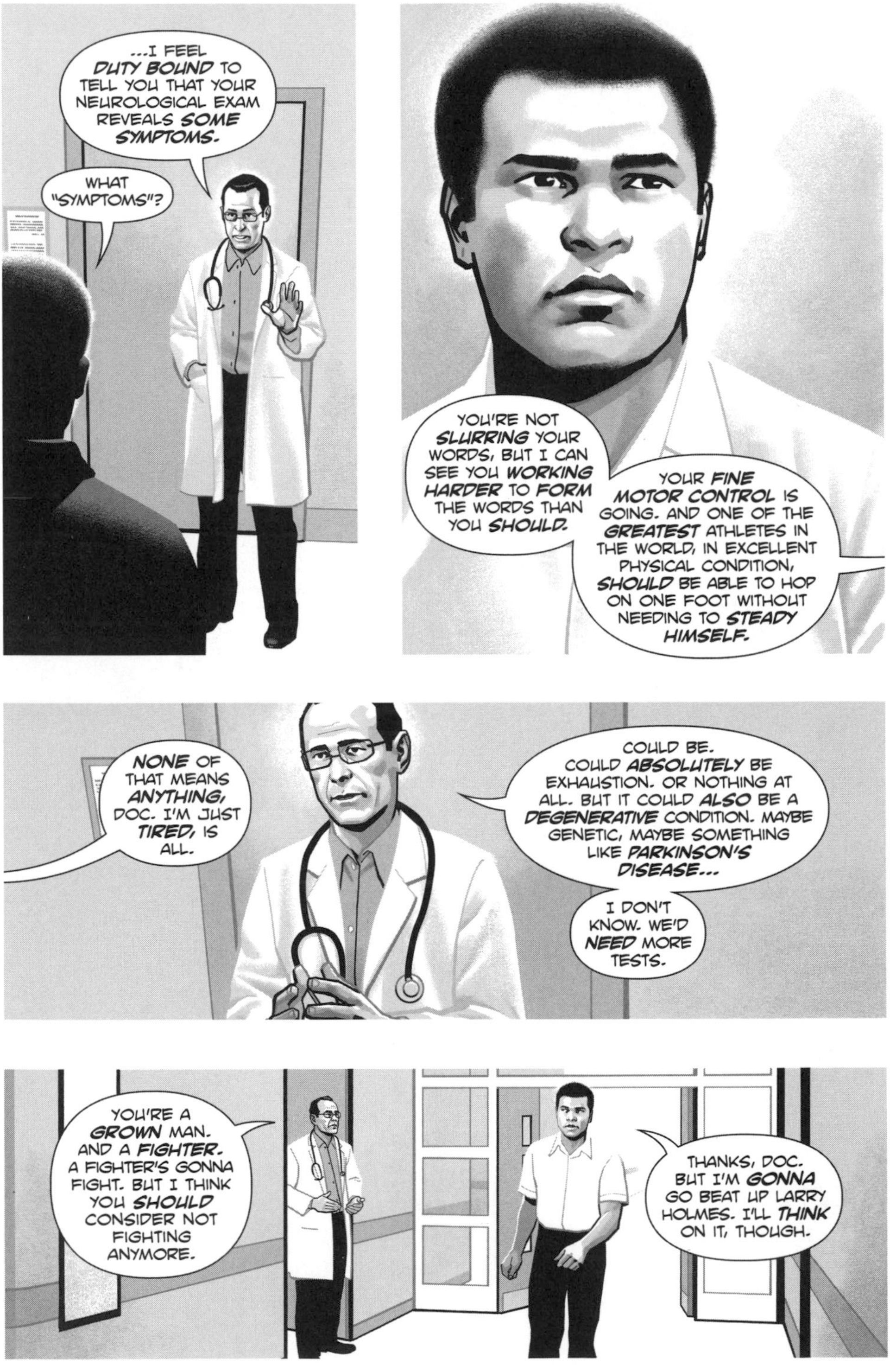
...I FEEL DUTY BOUND TO TELL YOU THAT YOUR NEUROLOGICAL EXAM REVEALS SOME SYMPTOMS.
WHAT "SYMPTOMS"?
YOU'RE NOT SLURRING YOUR WORDS, BUT I CAN SEE YOU WORKING HARDER TO FORM THE WORDS THAN YOU SHOULD.
YOUR FINE MOTOR CONTROL IS GOING. AND ONE OF THE GREATEST ATHLETES IN THE WORLD, IN EXCELLENT PHYSICAL CONDITION, SHOULD BE ABLE TO HOP ON ONE FOOT WITHOUT NEEDING TO STEADY HIMSELF.
NONE OF THAT MEANS ANYTHING, DOC. I'M JUST TIRED, IS ALL.
COULD BE. COULD ABSOLUTELY BE EXHAUSTION. OR NOTHING AT ALL. BUT IT COULD ALSO BE A DEGENERATIVE CONDITION. MAYBE GENETIC, MAYBE SOMETHING LIKE PARKINSON'S DISEASE...
I DON'T KNOW. WE'D NEED MORE TESTS.
YOU'RE A GROWN MAN. AND A FIGHTER. A FIGHTER'S GONNA FIGHT. BUT I THINK YOU SHOULD CONSIDER NOT FIGHTING ANYMORE.
THANKS, DOC. BUT I'M GONNA GO BEAT UP LARRY HOLMES. I'LL THINK ON IT, THOUGH.

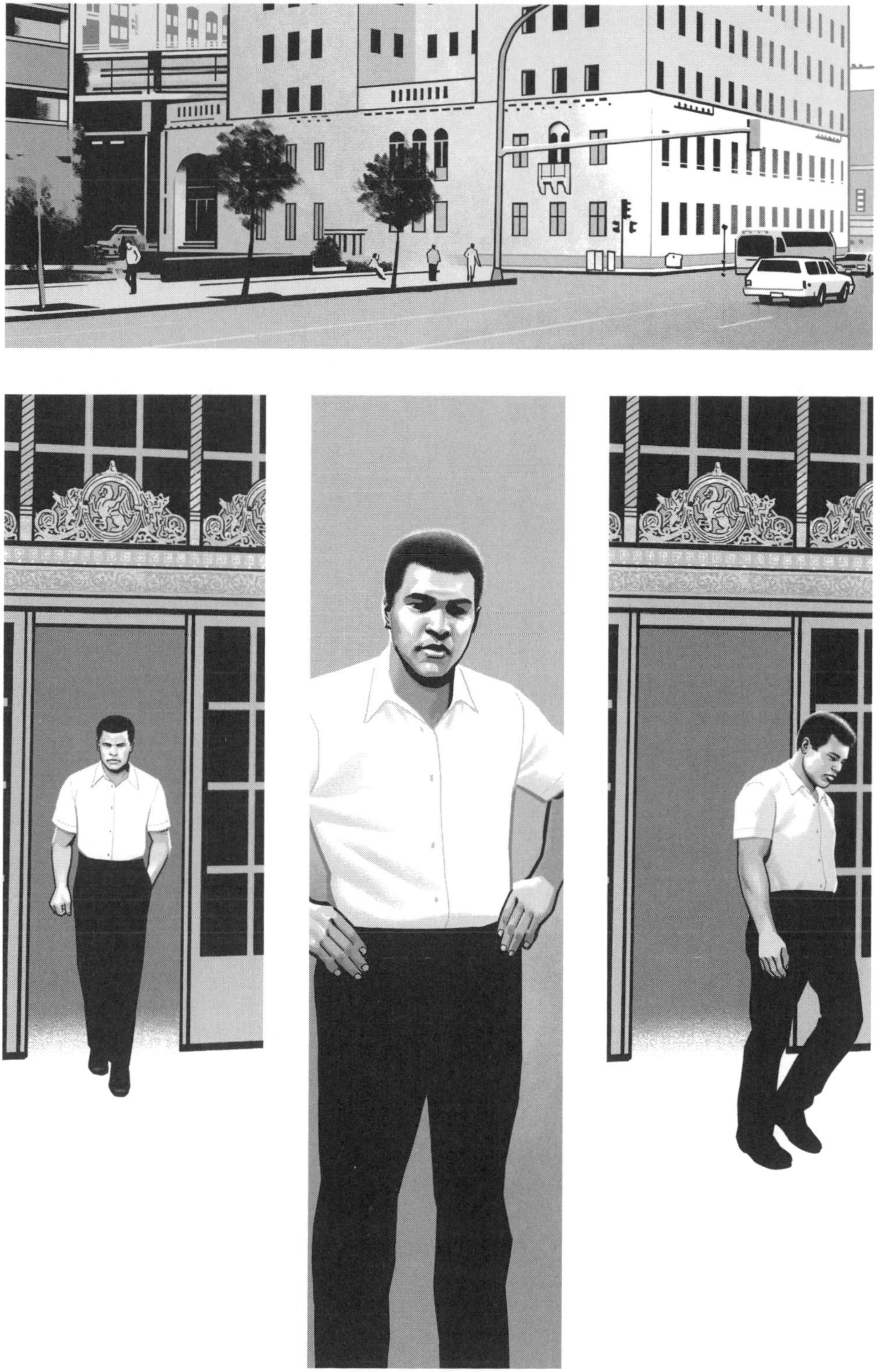

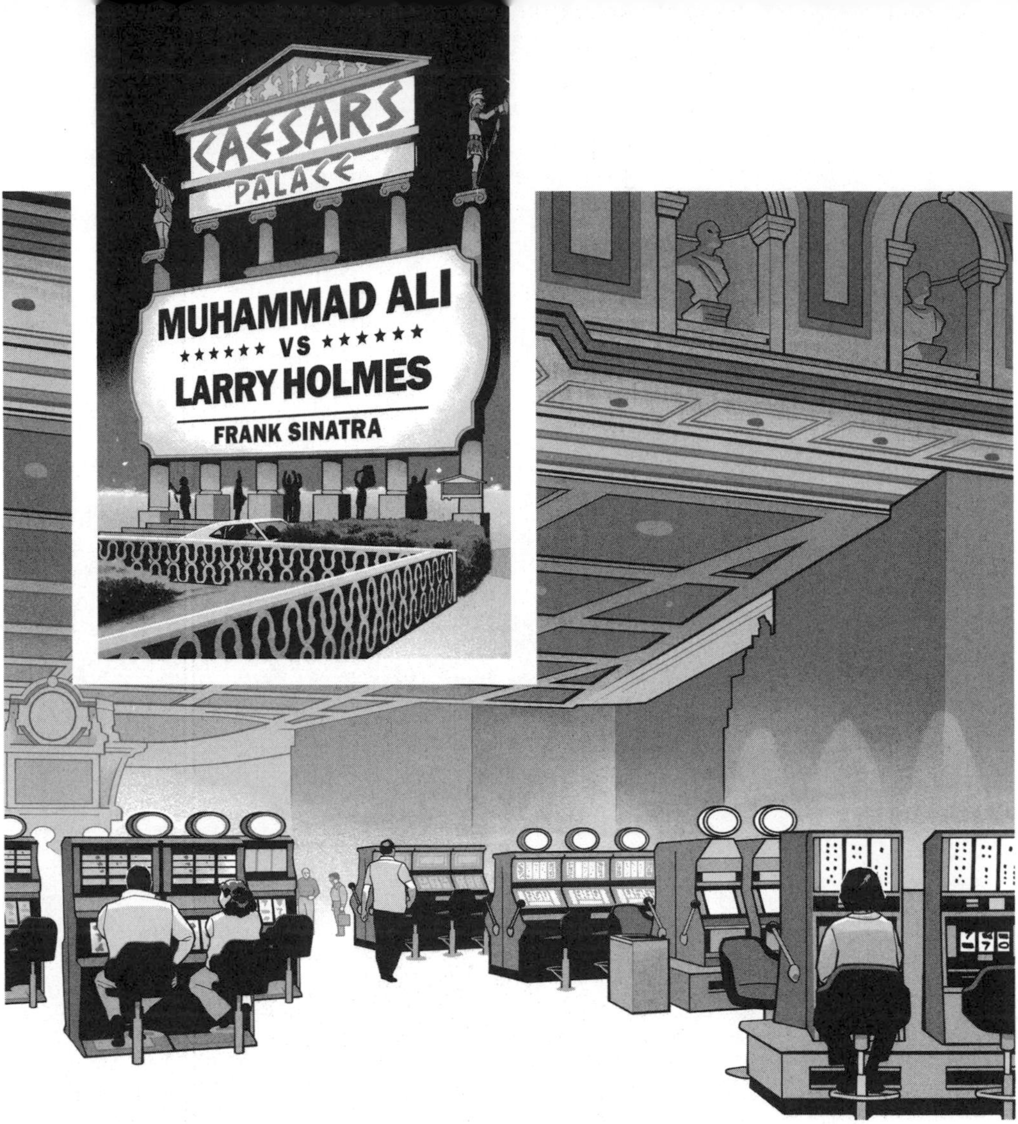
CAESARS
PALACE
MUHAMMAD ALI
VS
LARRY HOLMES
FRANK SINATRA

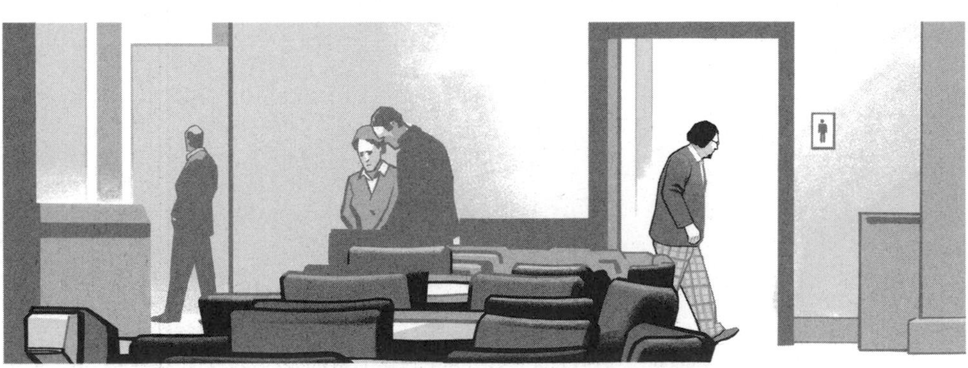

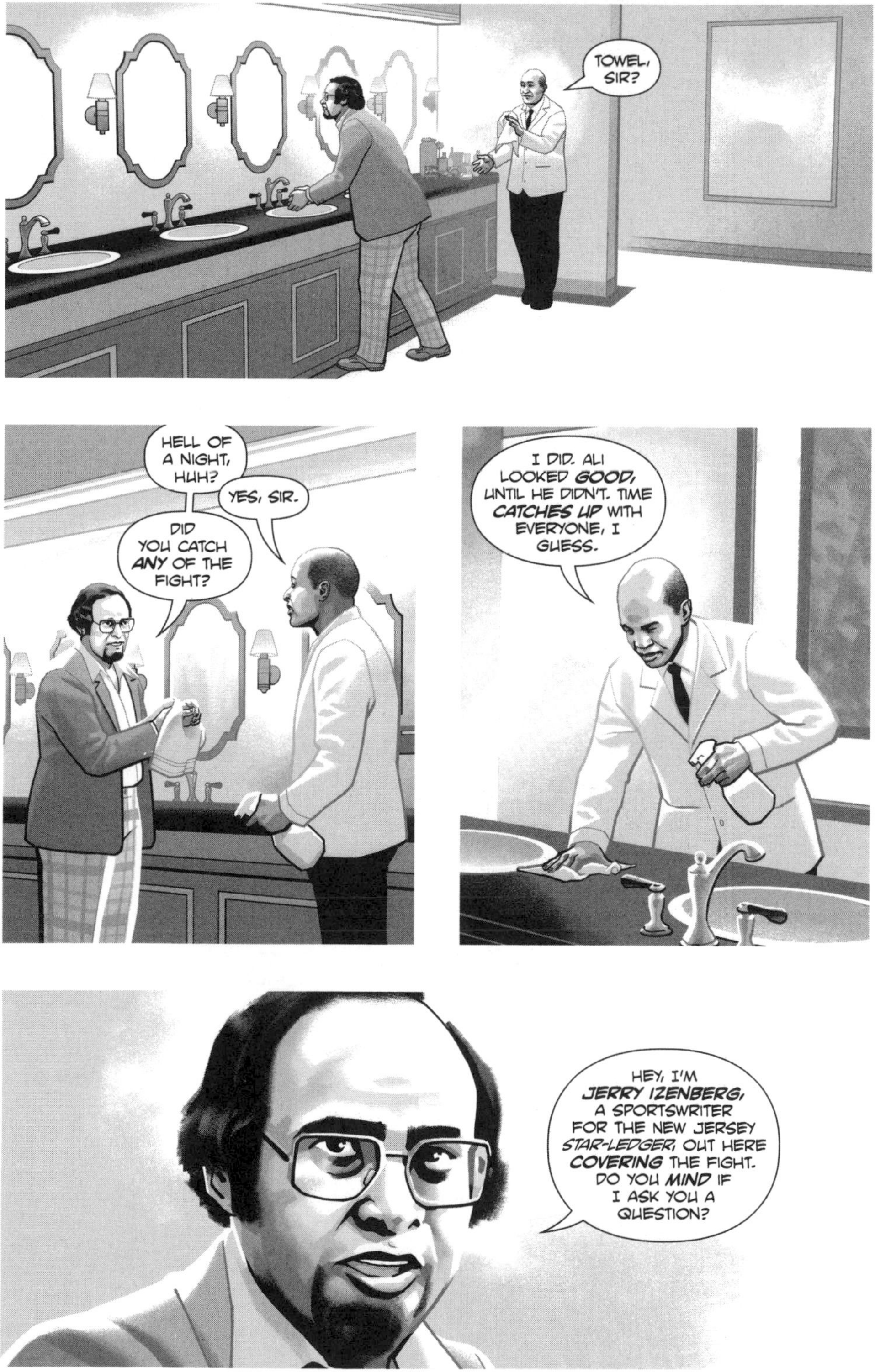
TOWEL, SIR?
HELL OF A NIGHT, HUH?
YES, SIR.
DID YOU CATCH ANY OF THE FIGHT?
I DID. ALI LOOKED GOOD, UNTIL HE DIDN'T. TIME CATCHES UP WITH EVERYONE, I GUESS.
HEY, I'M JERRY IZENBERG, A SPORTSWRITER FOR THE NEW JERSEY STAR-LEDGER, OUT HERE COVERING THE FIGHT. DO YOU MIND IF I ASK YOU A QUESTION?

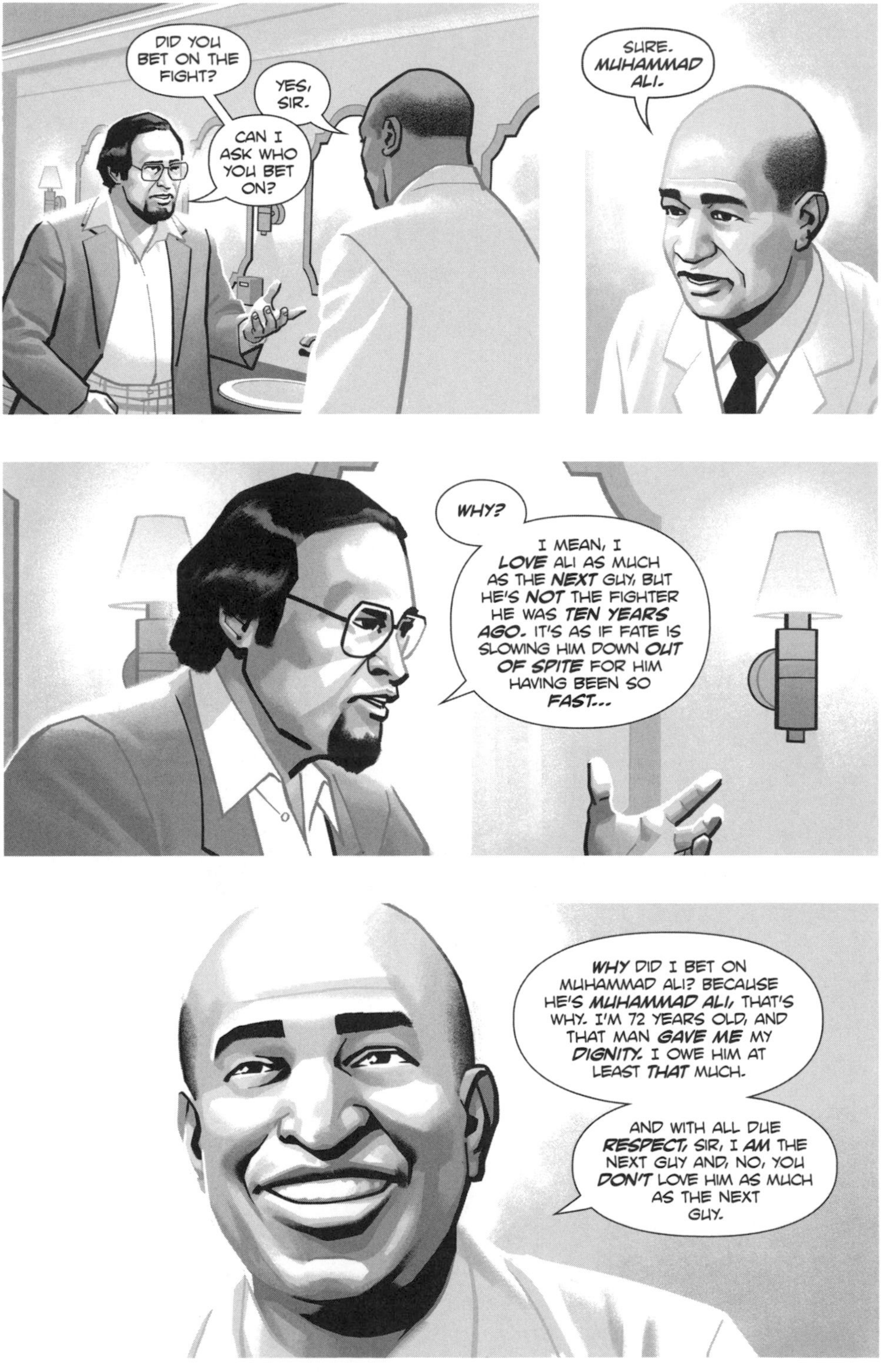
DID YOU BET ON THE FIGHT?
YES, SIR.
CAN I ASK WHO YOU BET ON?
SURE. MUHAMMAD ALI.
WHY?
I MEAN, I LOVE ALI AS MUCH AS THE NEXT GUY, BUT HE'S NOT THE FIGHTER HE WAS TEN YEARS AGO. IT'S AS IF FATE IS SLOWING HIM DOWN OUT OF SPITE FOR HIM HAVING BEEN SO FAST...
WHY DID I BET ON MUHAMMAD ALI? BECAUSE HE'S MUHAMMAD ALI, THAT'S WHY. I'M 72 YEARS OLD, AND THAT MAN GAVE ME MY DIGNITY. I OWE HIM AT LEAST THAT MUCH.
AND WITH ALL DUE RESPECT, SIR, I AM THE NEXT GUY AND, NO, YOU DON'T LOVE HIM AS MUCH AS THE NEXT GUY.

ROUND ELEVEN: SHEPHERD. 1990.

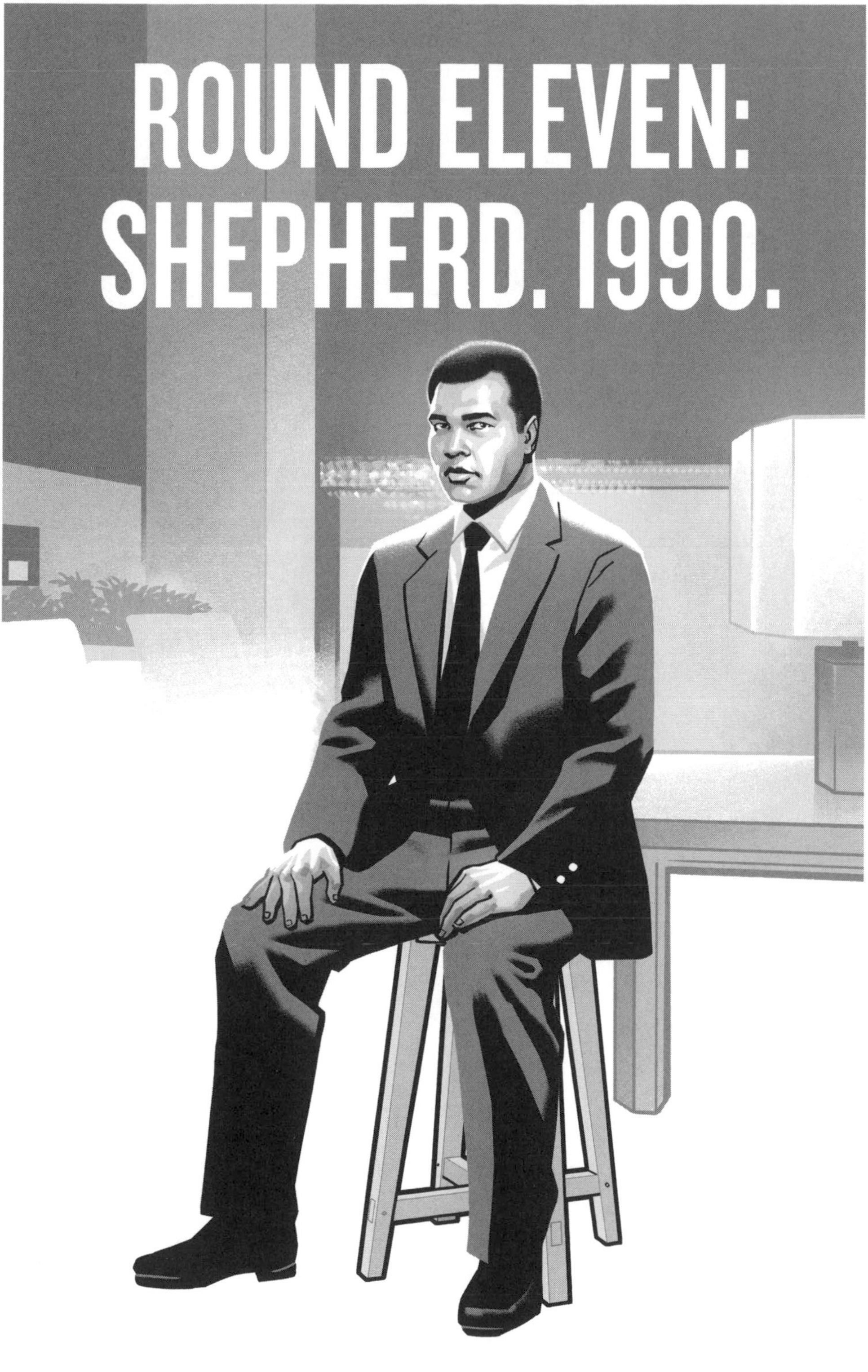

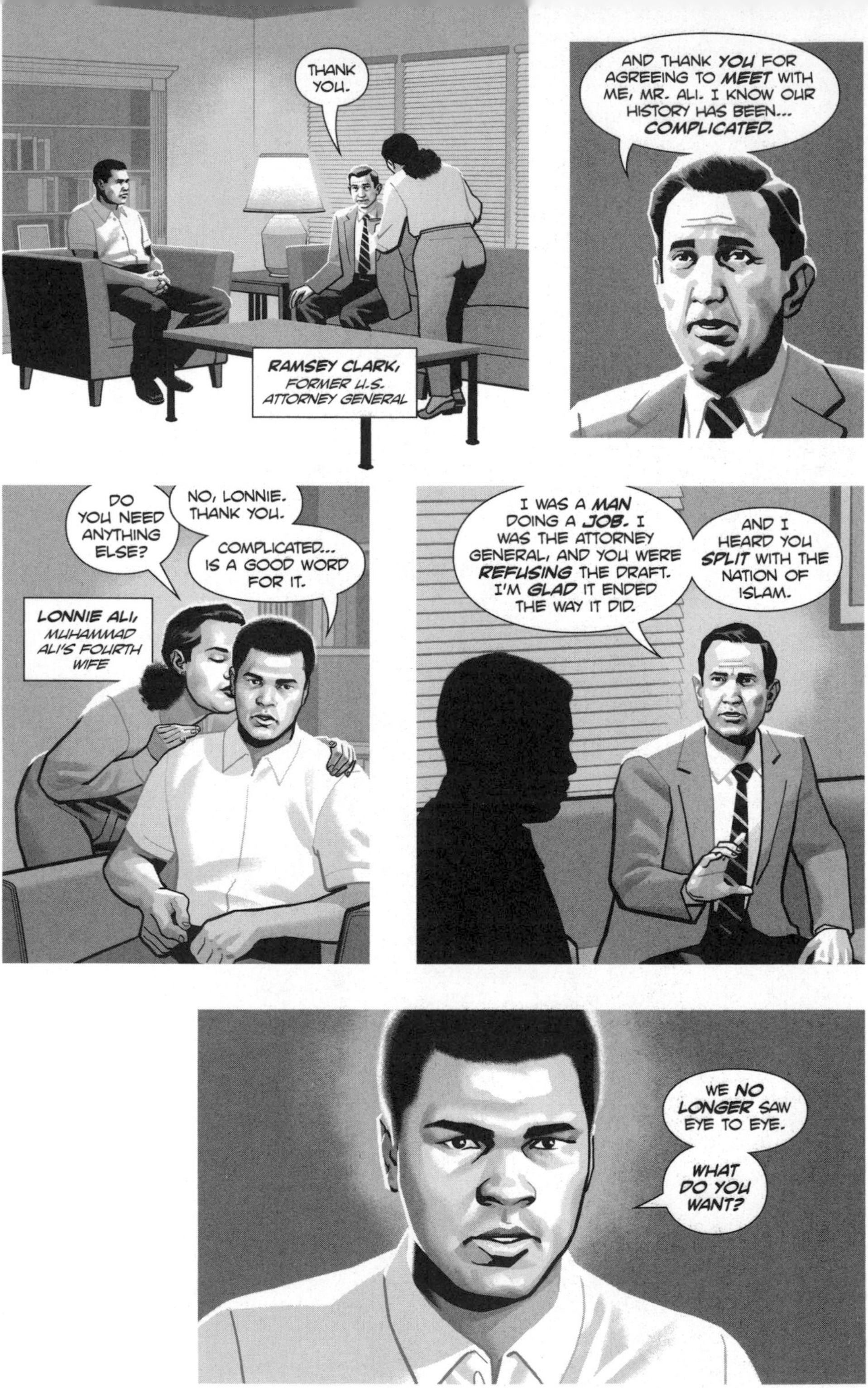
THANK YOU.
AND THANK YOU FOR AGREEING TO MEET WITH ME, MR. ALI. I KNOW OUR HISTORY HAS BEEN... COMPLICATED.
RAMSEY CLARK, FORMER U.S. ATTORNEY GENERAL
DO YOU NEED ANYTHING ELSE?
NO, LONNIE. THANK YOU.
COMPLICATED... IS A GOOD WORD FOR IT.
LONNIE ALI, MUHAMMAD ALI'S FOURTH WIFE
I WAS A MAN DOING A JOB. I WAS THE ATTORNEY GENERAL, AND YOU WERE REFUSING THE DRAFT. I'M GLAD IT ENDED THE WAY IT DID.
AND I HEARD YOU SPLIT WITH THE NATION OF ISLAM.
WE NO LONGER SAW EYE TO EYE.
WHAT DO YOU WANT?

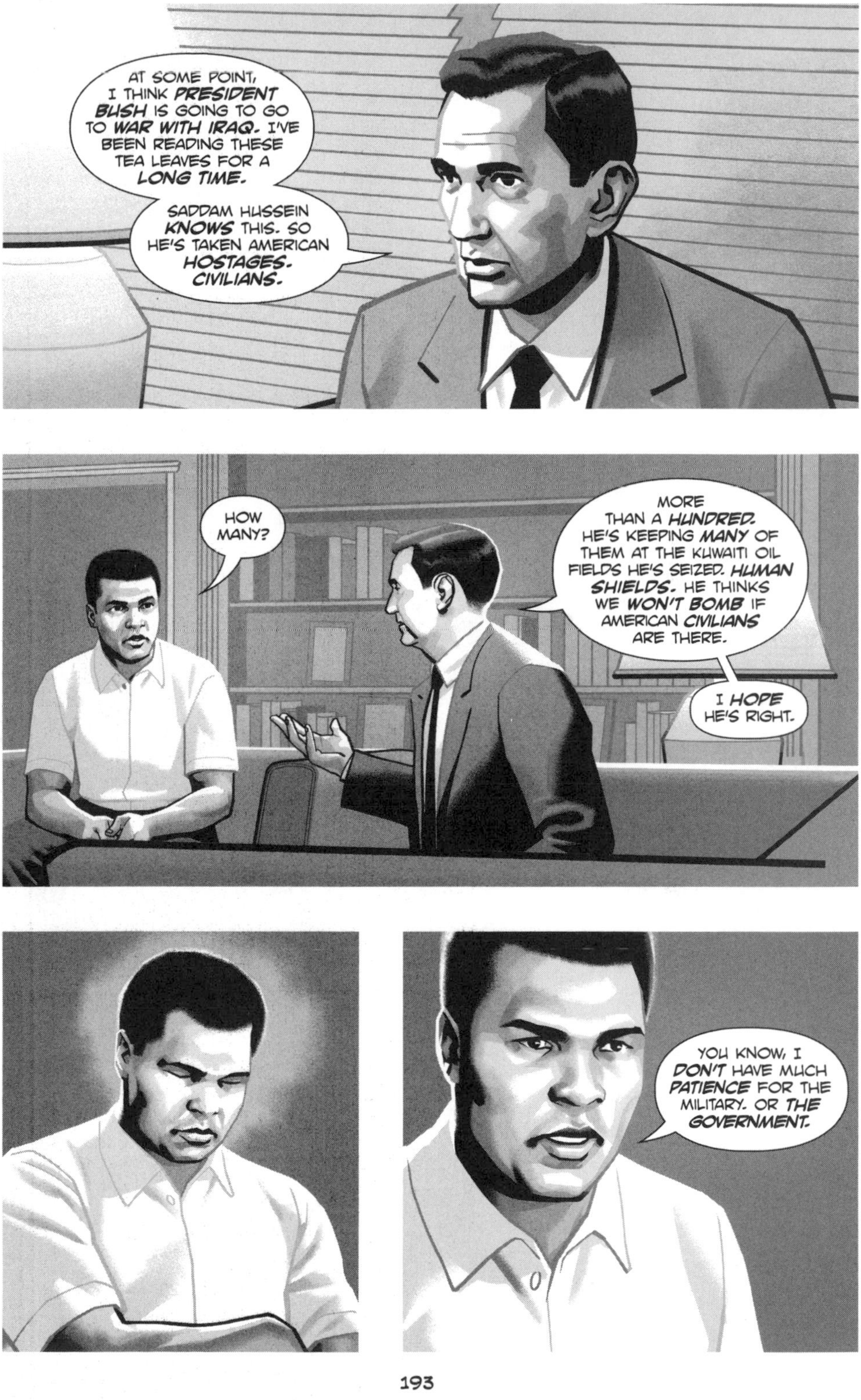
AT SOME POINT, I THINK PRESIDENT BUSH IS GOING TO GO TO WAR WITH IRAQ. I'VE BEEN READING THESE TEA LEAVES FOR A LONG TIME.
SADDAM HUSSEIN KNOWS THIS. SO HE'S TAKEN AMERICAN HOSTAGES. CIVILIANS.
HOW MANY?
MORE THAN A HUNDRED. HE'S KEEPING MANY OF THEM AT THE KUWAITI OIL FIELDS HE'S SEIZED. HUMAN SHIELDS. HE THINKS WE WON'T BOMB IF AMERICAN CIVILIANS ARE THERE.
I HOPE HE'S RIGHT.
YOU KNOW, I DON'T HAVE MUCH PATIENCE FOR THE MILITARY. OR THE GOVERNMENT.

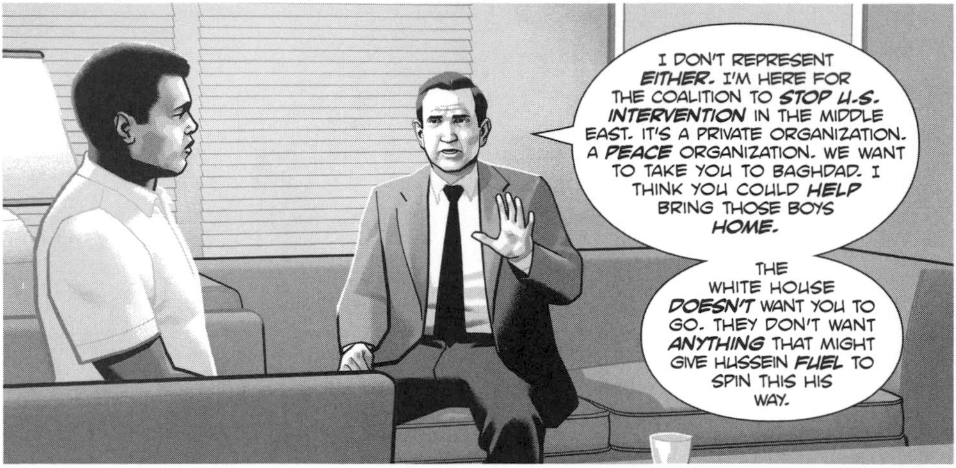
I DON'T REPRESENT EITHER. I'M HERE FOR THE COALITION TO STOP U.S. INTERVENTION IN THE MIDDLE EAST. IT'S A PRIVATE ORGANIZATION. A PEACE ORGANIZATION. WE WANT TO TAKE YOU TO BAGHDAD. I THINK YOU COULD HELP BRING THOSE BOYS HOME.
THE WHITE HOUSE DOESN'T WANT YOU TO GO. THEY DON'T WANT ANYTHING THAT MIGHT GIVE HUSSEIN FUEL TO SPIN THIS HIS WAY.

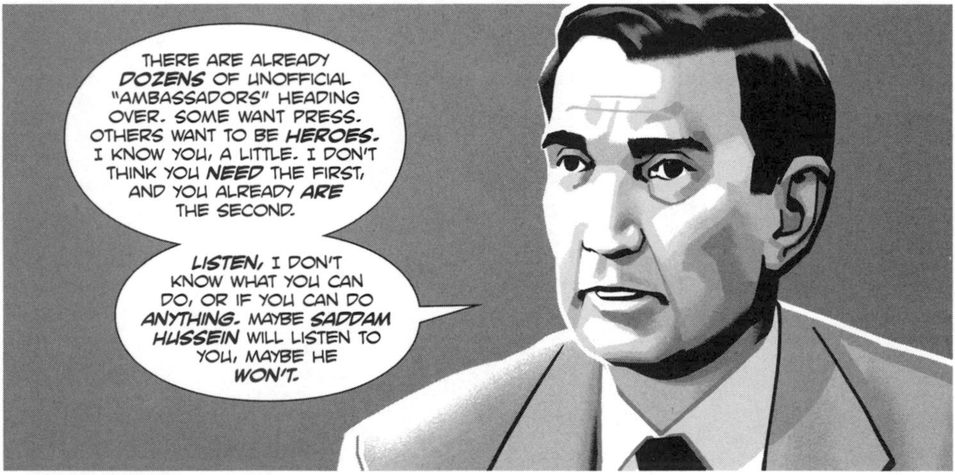
THERE ARE ALREADY DOZENS OF UNOFFICIAL "AMBASSADORS" HEADING OVER. SOME WANT PRESS. OTHERS WANT TO BE HEROES. I KNOW YOU, A LITTLE. I DON'T THINK YOU NEED THE FIRST, AND YOU ALREADY ARE THE SECOND.
LISTEN, I DON'T KNOW WHAT YOU CAN DO, OR IF YOU CAN DO ANYTHING. MAYBE SADDAM HUSSEIN WILL LISTEN TO YOU, MAYBE HE WON'T.

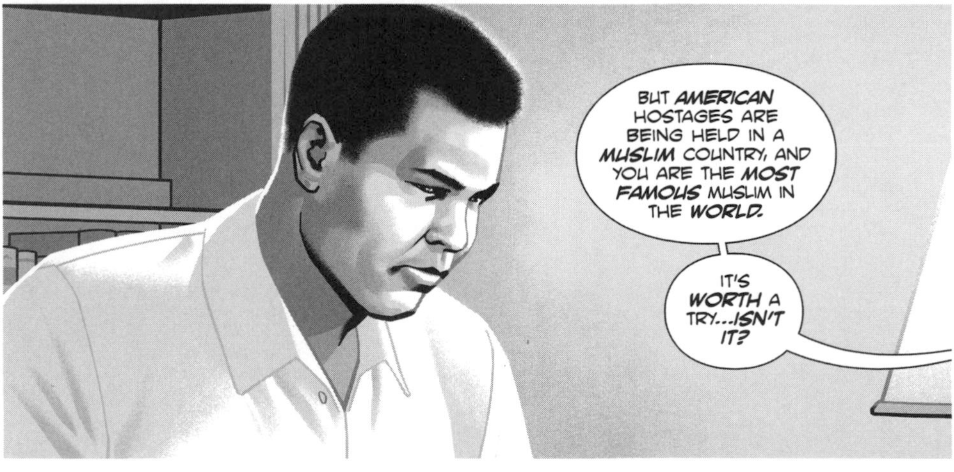
BUT AMERICAN HOSTAGES ARE BEING HELD IN A MUSLIM COUNTRY, AND YOU ARE THE MOST FAMOUS MUSLIM IN THE WORLD.
IT'S WORTH A TRY...ISN'T IT?

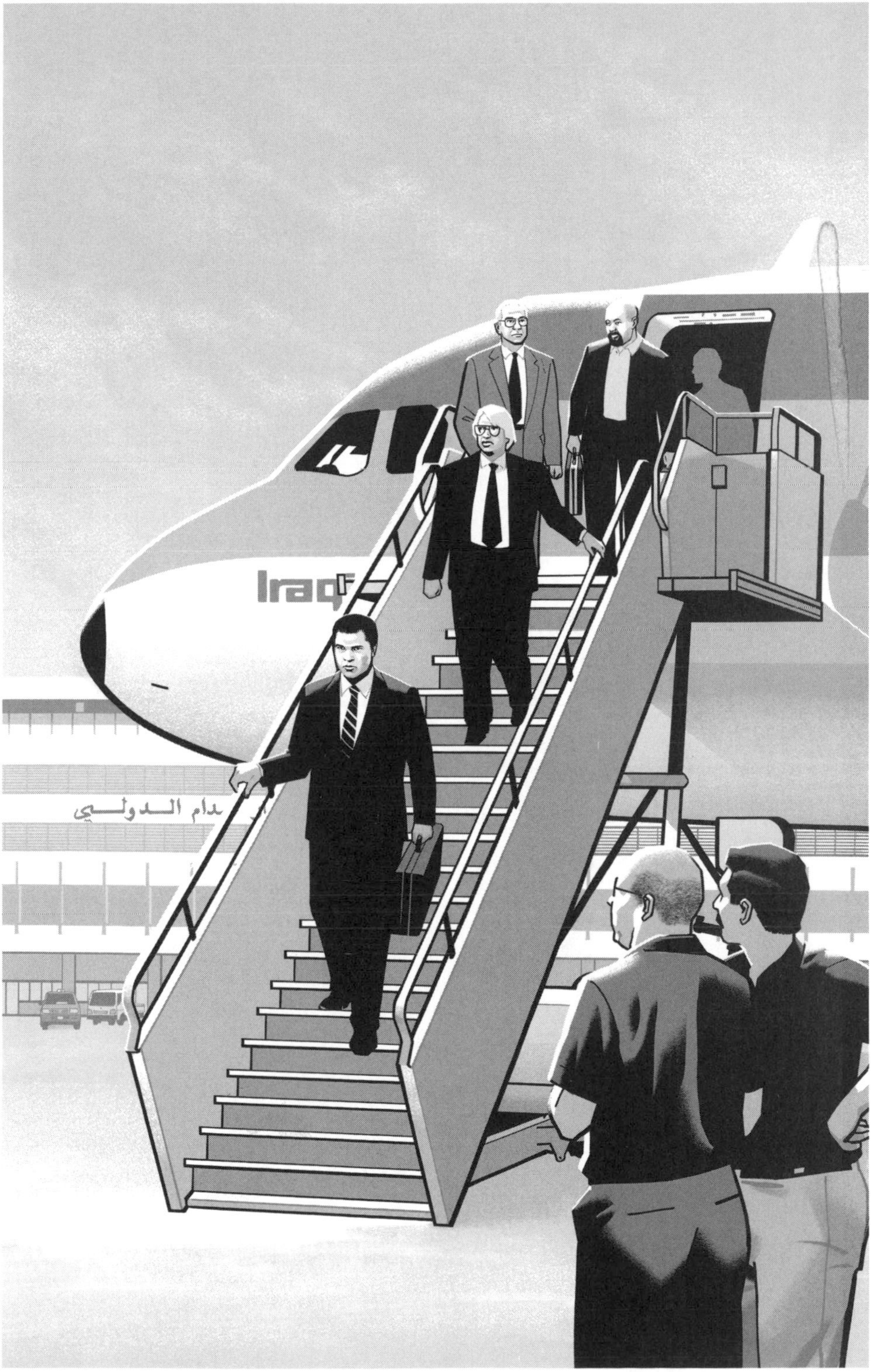
Iraq

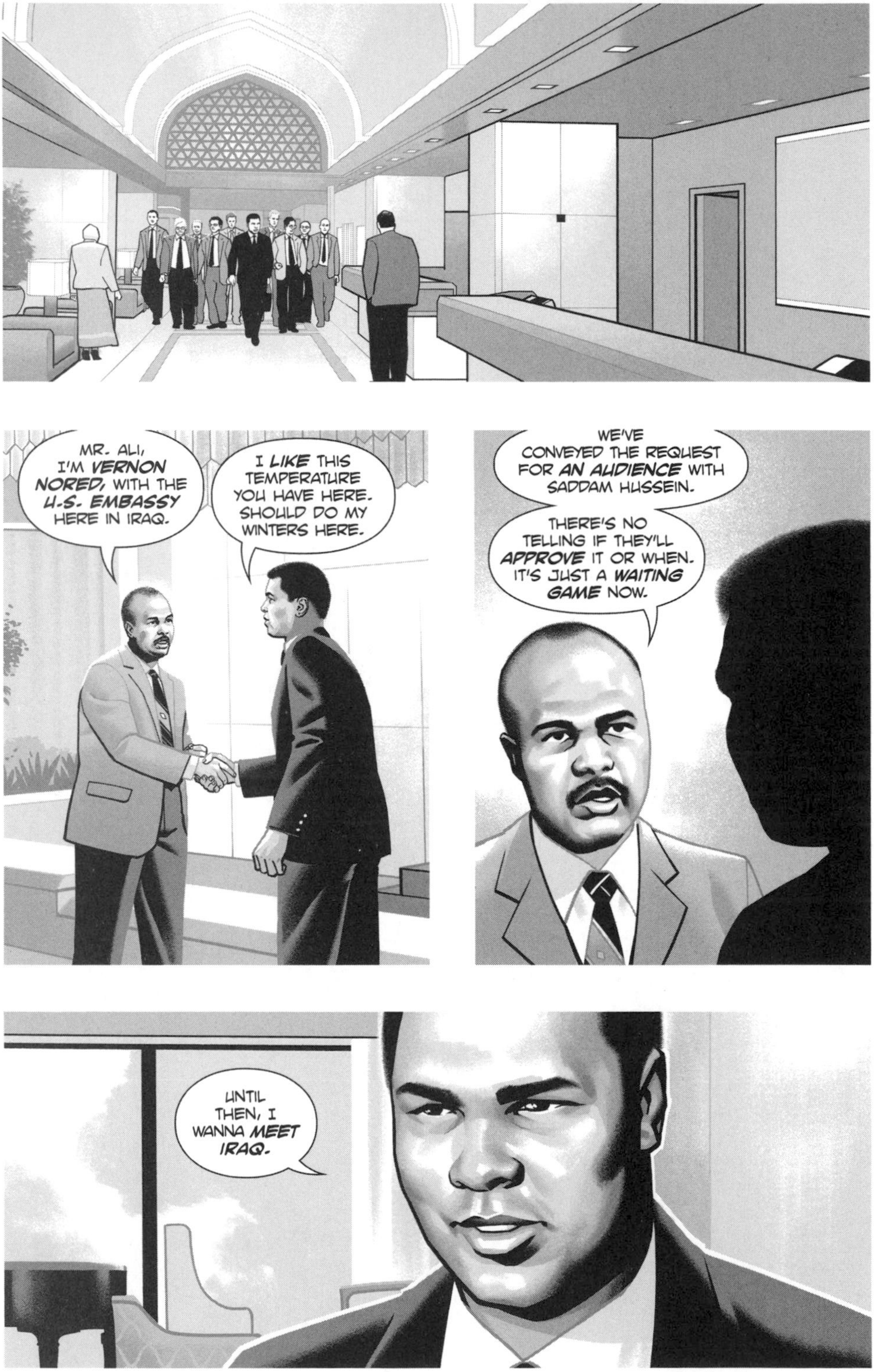
MR. ALI, I'M VERNON NORED, WITH THE U.S. EMBASSY HERE IN IRAQ.
I LIKE THIS TEMPERATURE YOU HAVE HERE. SHOULD DO MY WINTERS HERE.
WE'VE CONVEYED THE REQUEST FOR AN AUDIENCE WITH SADDAM HUSSEIN.
THERE'S NO TELLING IF THEY'LL APPROVE IT OR WHEN. IT'S JUST A WAITING GAME NOW.
UNTIL THEN, I WANNA MEET IRAQ.

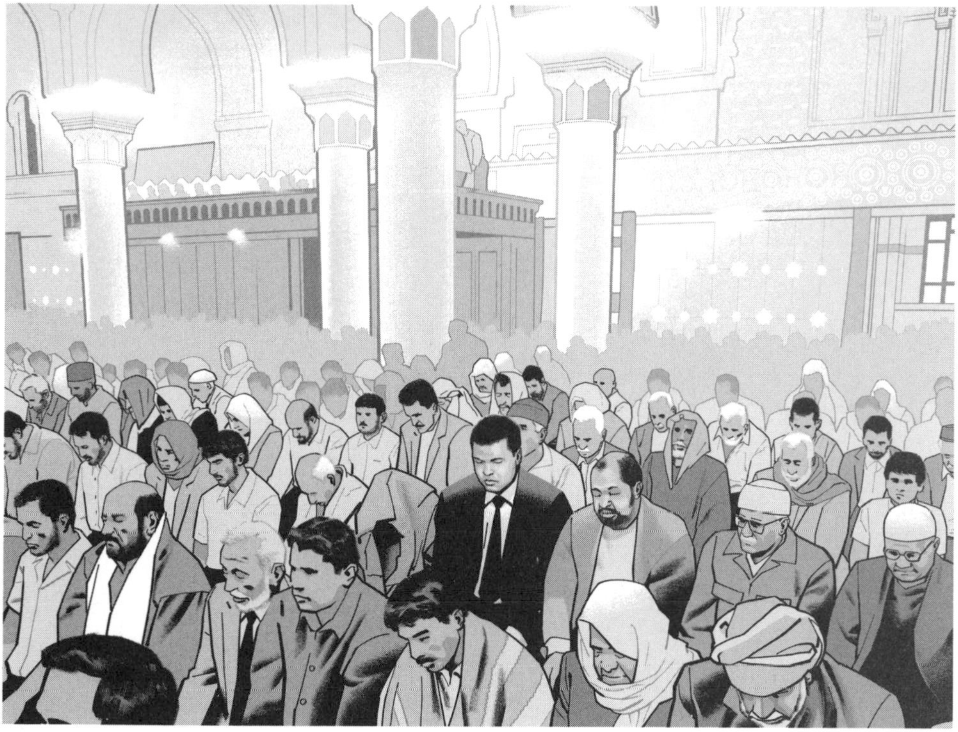

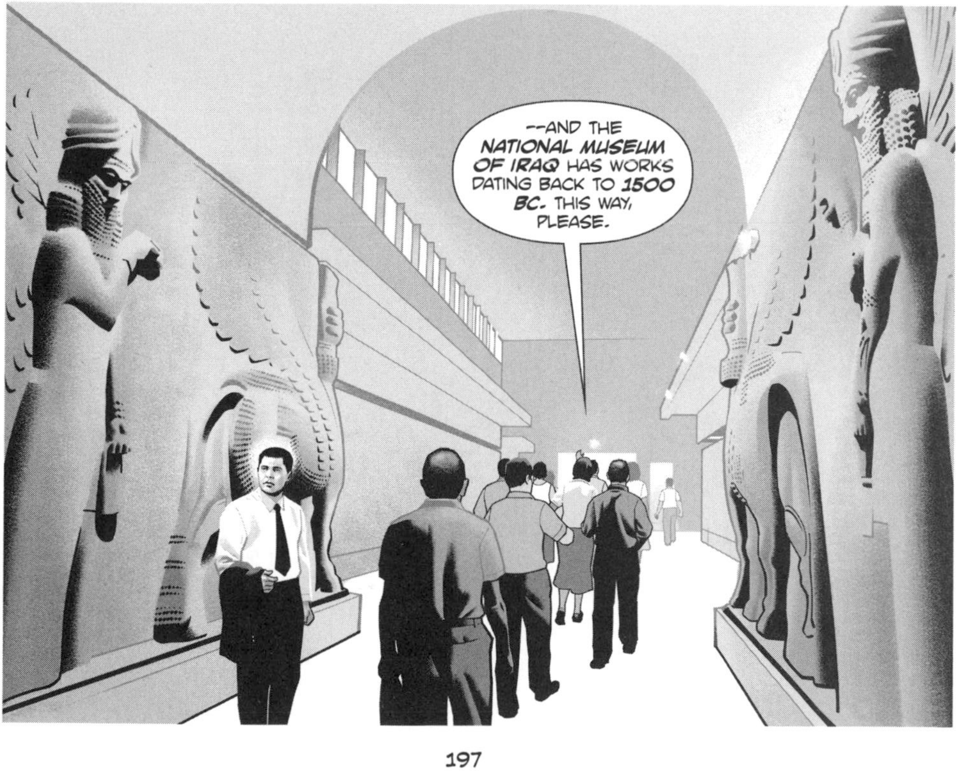
--AND THE NATIONAL MUSEUM OF IRAQ HAS WORKS DATING BACK TO 1500 BC. THIS WAY, PLEASE.

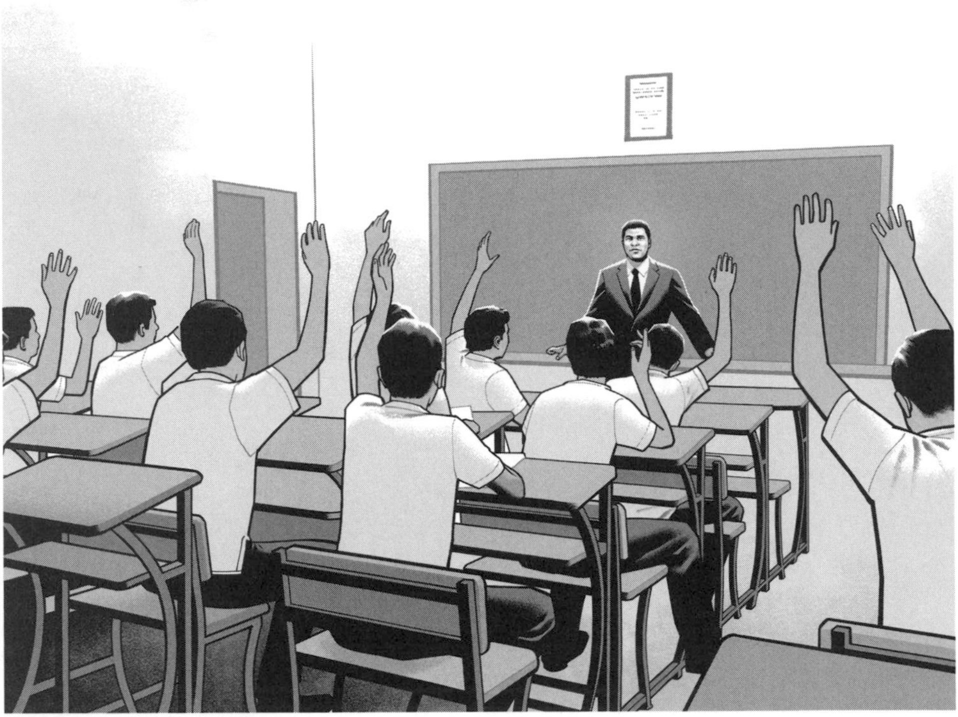

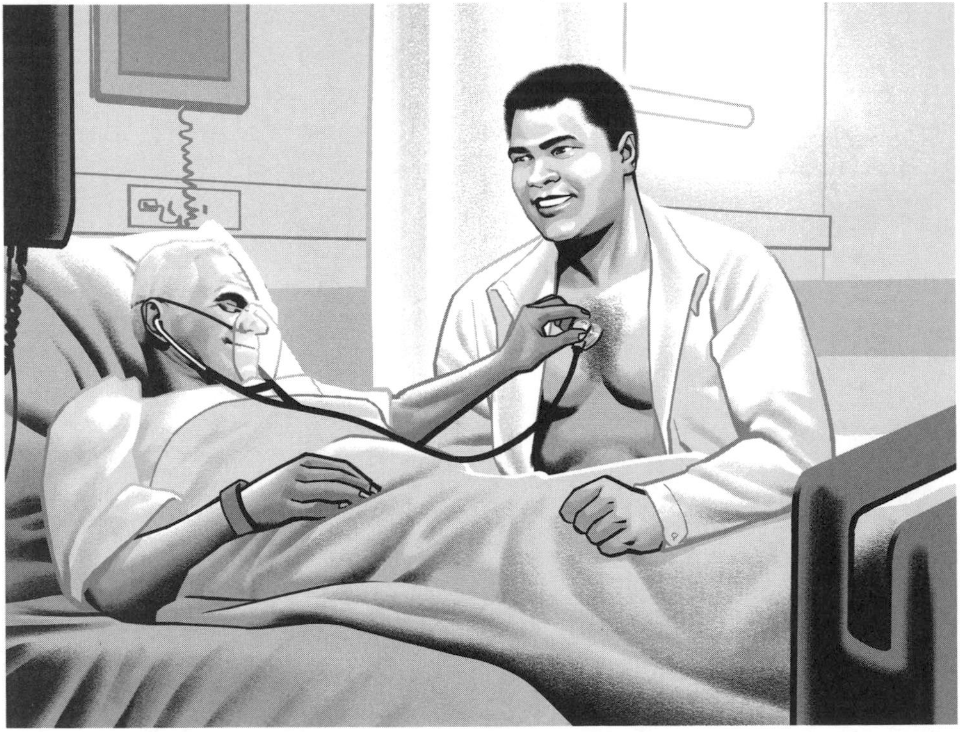

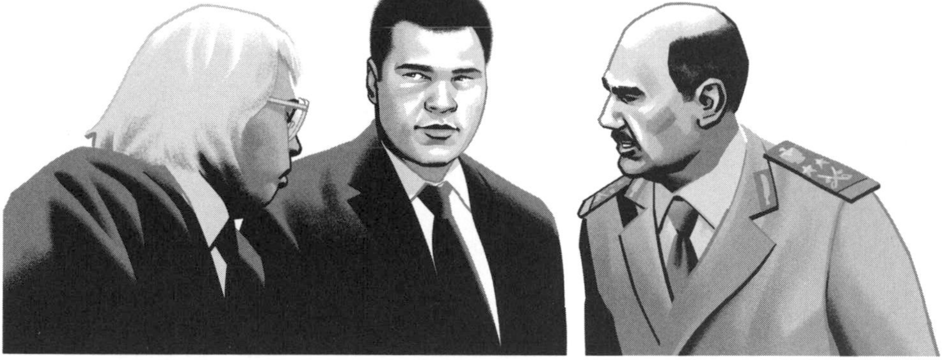

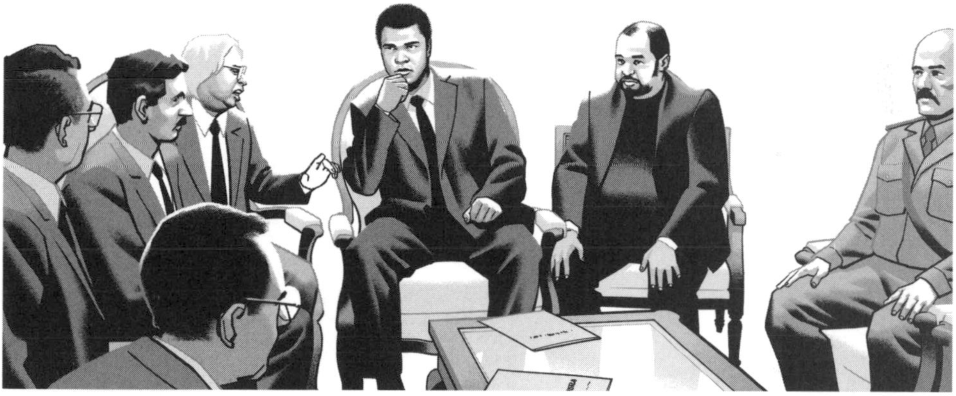

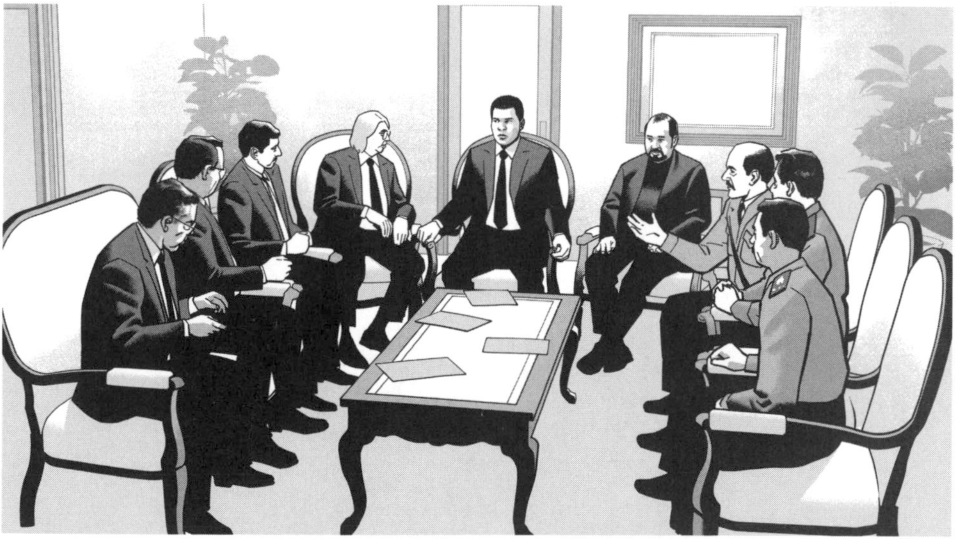

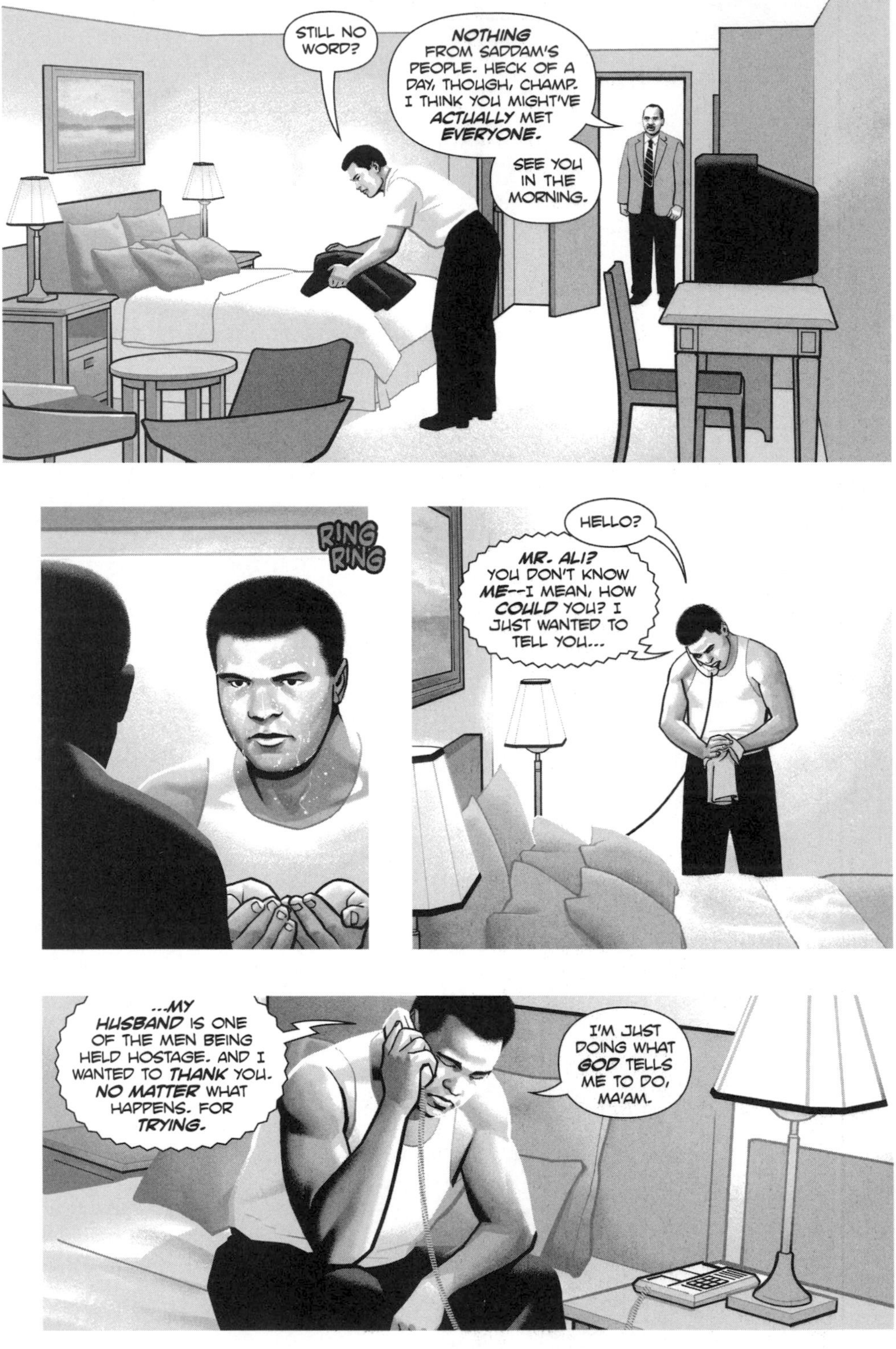
STILL NO WORD?
NOTHING FROM SADDAM'S PEOPLE. HECK OF A DAY, THOUGH, CHAMP. I THINK YOU MIGHT'VE ACTUALLY MET EVERYONE.
SEE YOU IN THE MORNING.
RING RING
HELLO?
MR. ALI? YOU DON'T KNOW ME--I MEAN, HOW COULD YOU? I JUST WANTED TO TELL YOU...
...MY HUSBAND IS ONE OF THE MEN BEING HELD HOSTAGE. AND I WANTED TO THANK YOU. NO MATTER WHAT HAPPENS. FOR TRYING.
I'M JUST DOING WHAT GOD TELLS ME TO DO, MA'AM.

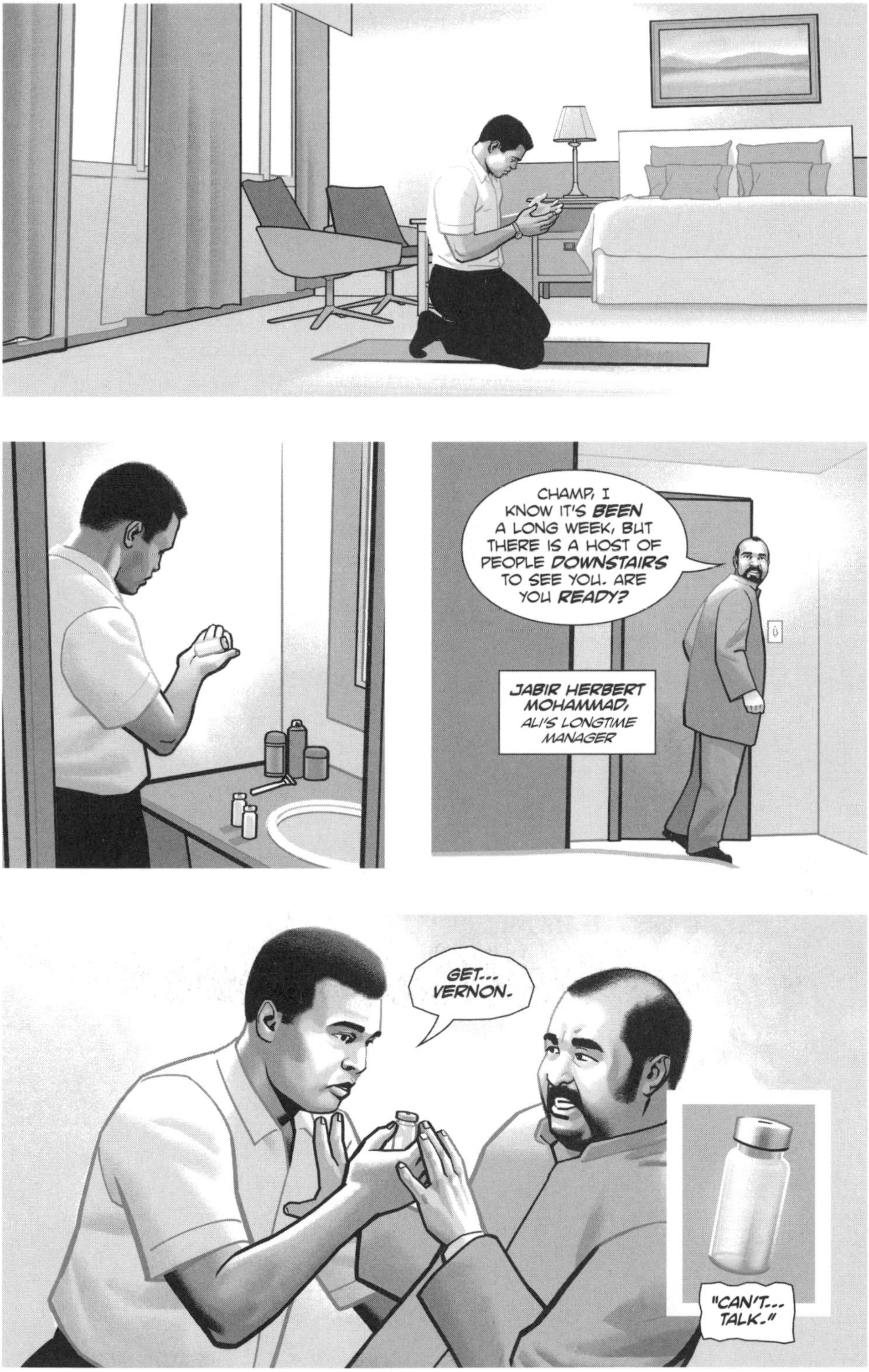
CHAMP, I KNOW IT'S BEEN A LONG WEEK, BUT THERE IS A HOST OF PEOPLE DOWNSTAIRS TO SEE YOU. ARE YOU READY?
JABIR HERBERT MOHAMMAD, ALI'S LONGTIME MANAGER
GET... VERNON.
"CAN'T... TALK."

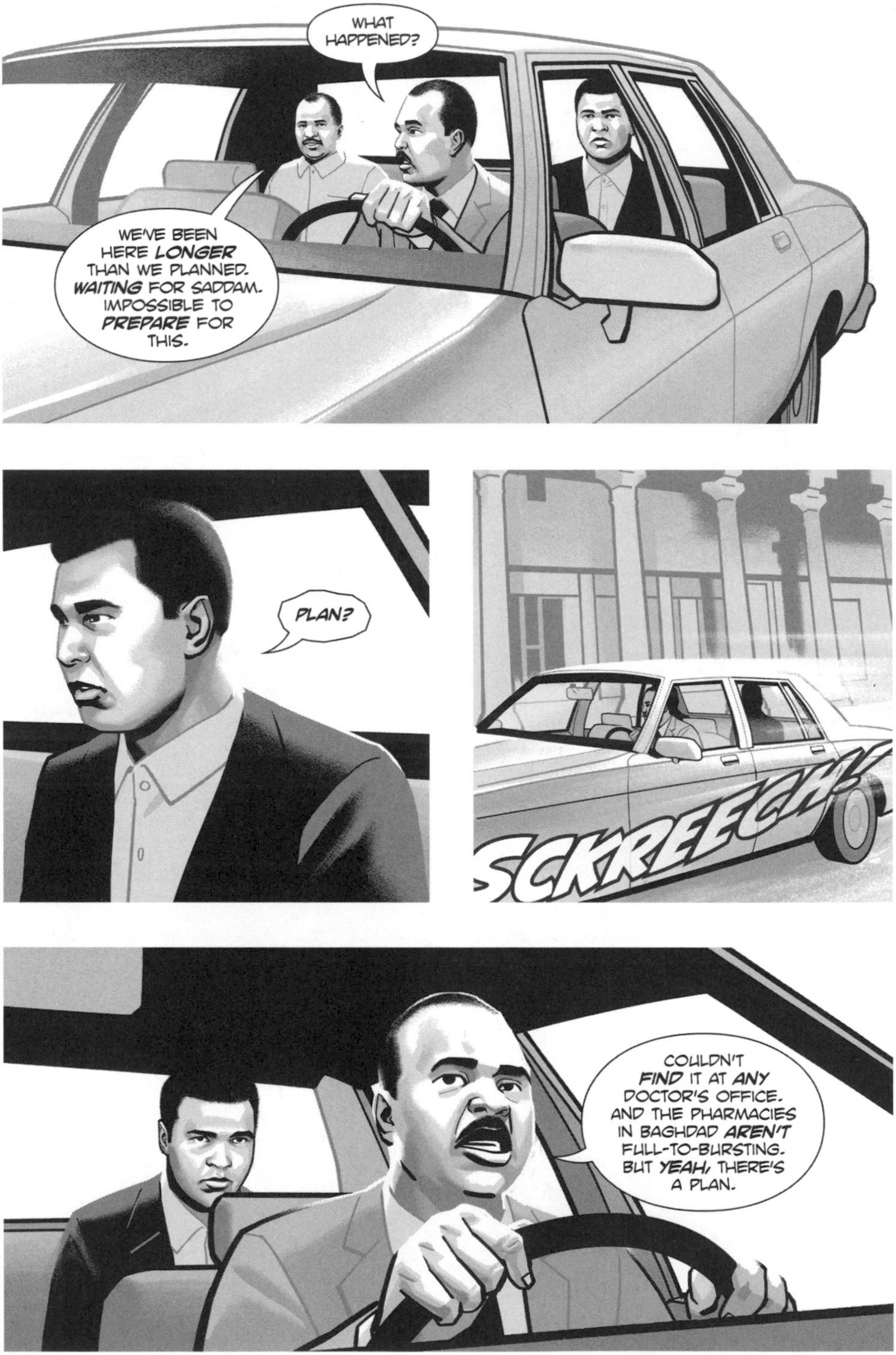
WHAT HAPPENED?
WE'VE BEEN HERE LONGER THAN WE PLANNED. WAITING FOR SADDAM. IMPOSSIBLE TO PREPARE FOR THIS.
PLAN?
SCKREEECH!
COULDN'T FIND IT AT ANY DOCTOR'S OFFICE. AND THE PHARMACIES IN BAGHDAD AREN'T FULL-TO-BURSTING. BUT YEAH, THERE'S A PLAN.

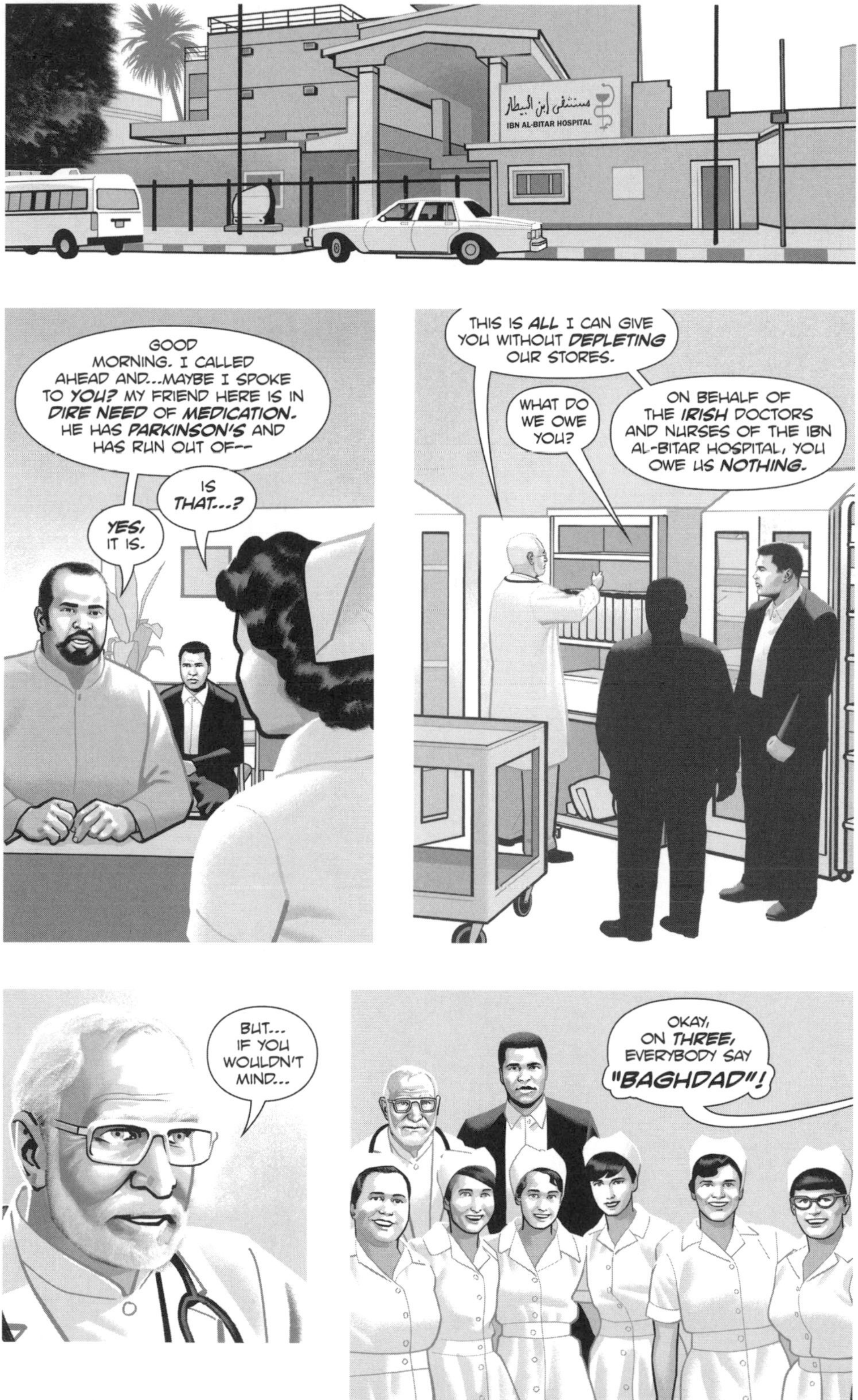

مستشفى إبن البيطار
IBN AL-BITAR HOSPITAL
GOOD MORNING. I CALLED AHEAD AND...MAYBE I SPOKE TO *YOU?* MY FRIEND HERE IS IN *DIRE NEED* OF *MEDICATION.* HE HAS *PARKINSON'S* AND HAS RUN OUT OF--
IS *THAT...?*
YES, IT IS.
THIS IS *ALL* I CAN GIVE YOU WITHOUT *DEPLETING* OUR STORES.
WHAT DO WE OWE YOU?
ON BEHALF OF THE *IRISH* DOCTORS AND NURSES OF THE IBN AL-BITAR HOSPITAL, YOU OWE US *NOTHING.*
BUT... IF YOU WOULDN'T MIND...
OKAY, ON *THREE,* EVERYBODY SAY *"BAGHDAD"!*

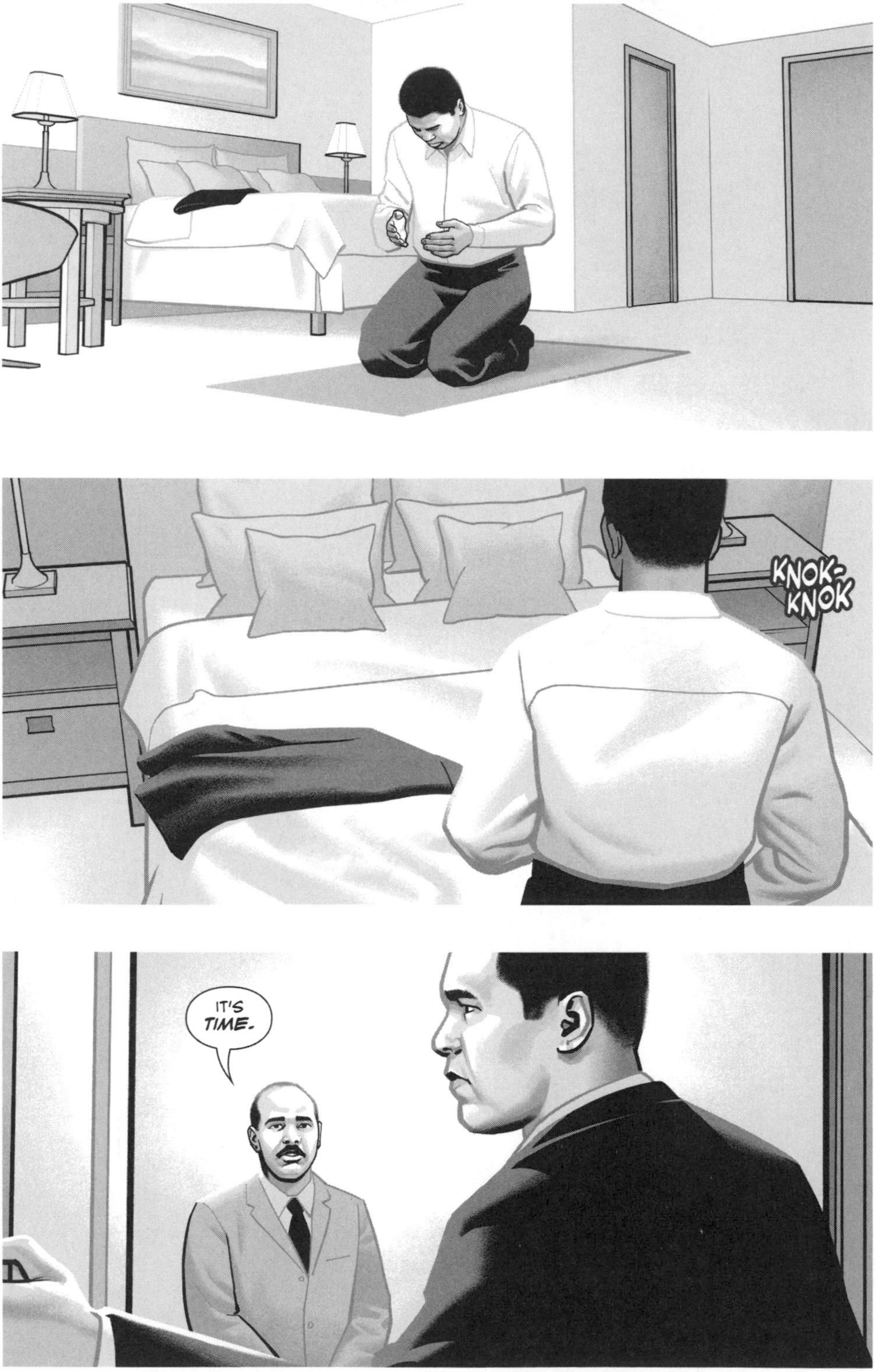
KNOK-KNOK
IT'S TIME.

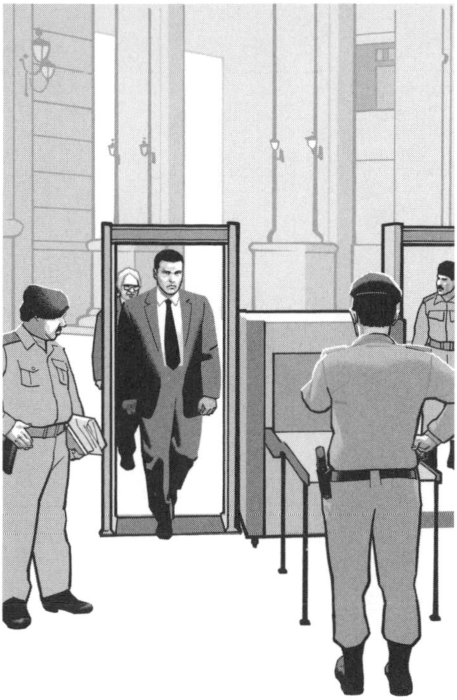
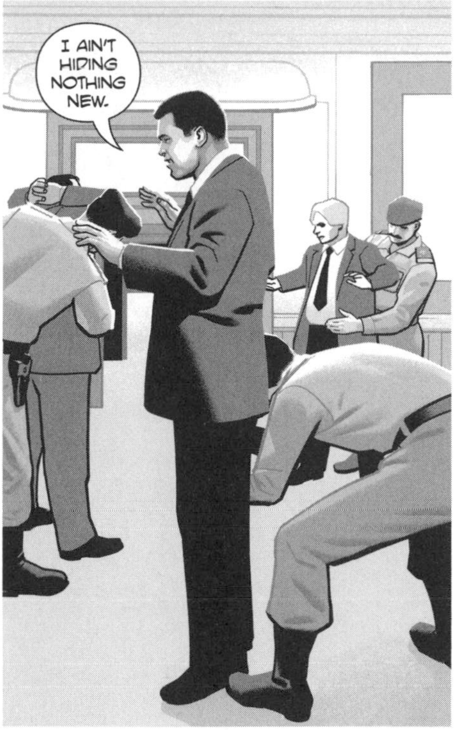
I AIN'T HIDING NOTHING NEW.
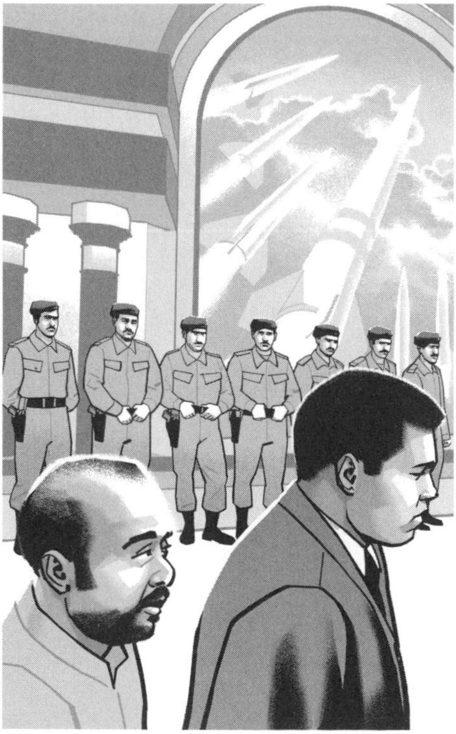
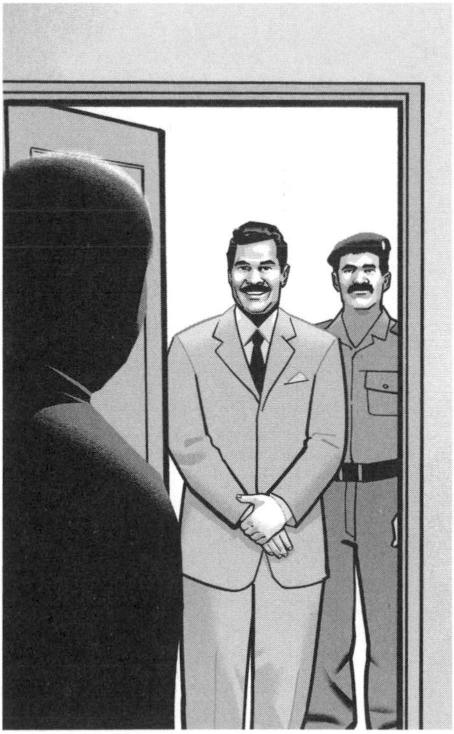

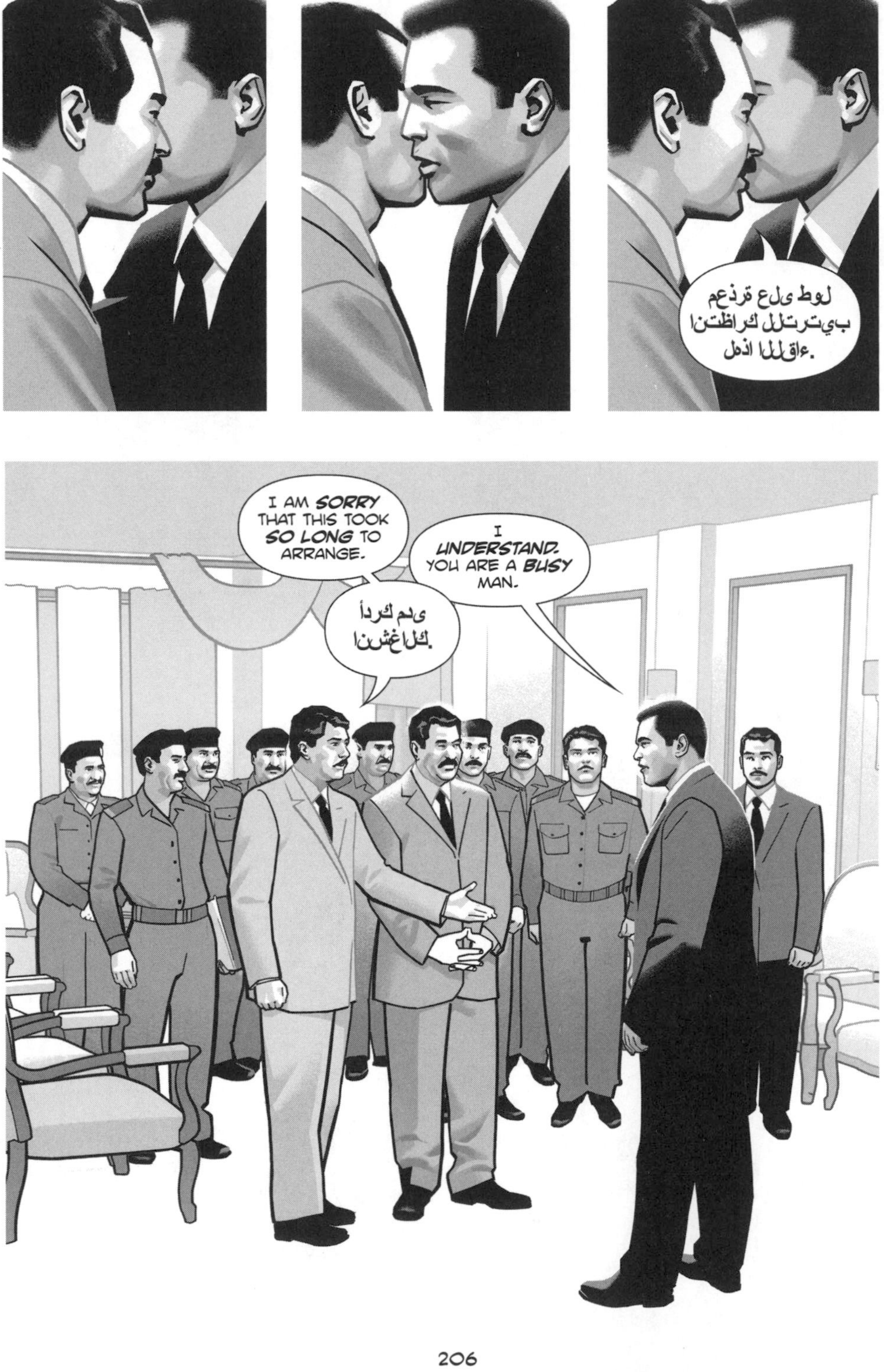
لوط ىلع ةرذعم
بيترتلل كراظتنا
ءاقللا اذهل.
I AM SORRY THAT THIS TOOK SO LONG TO ARRANGE.
ىدم كردأ
كلاغشنا.
I UNDERSTAND. YOU ARE A BUSY MAN.

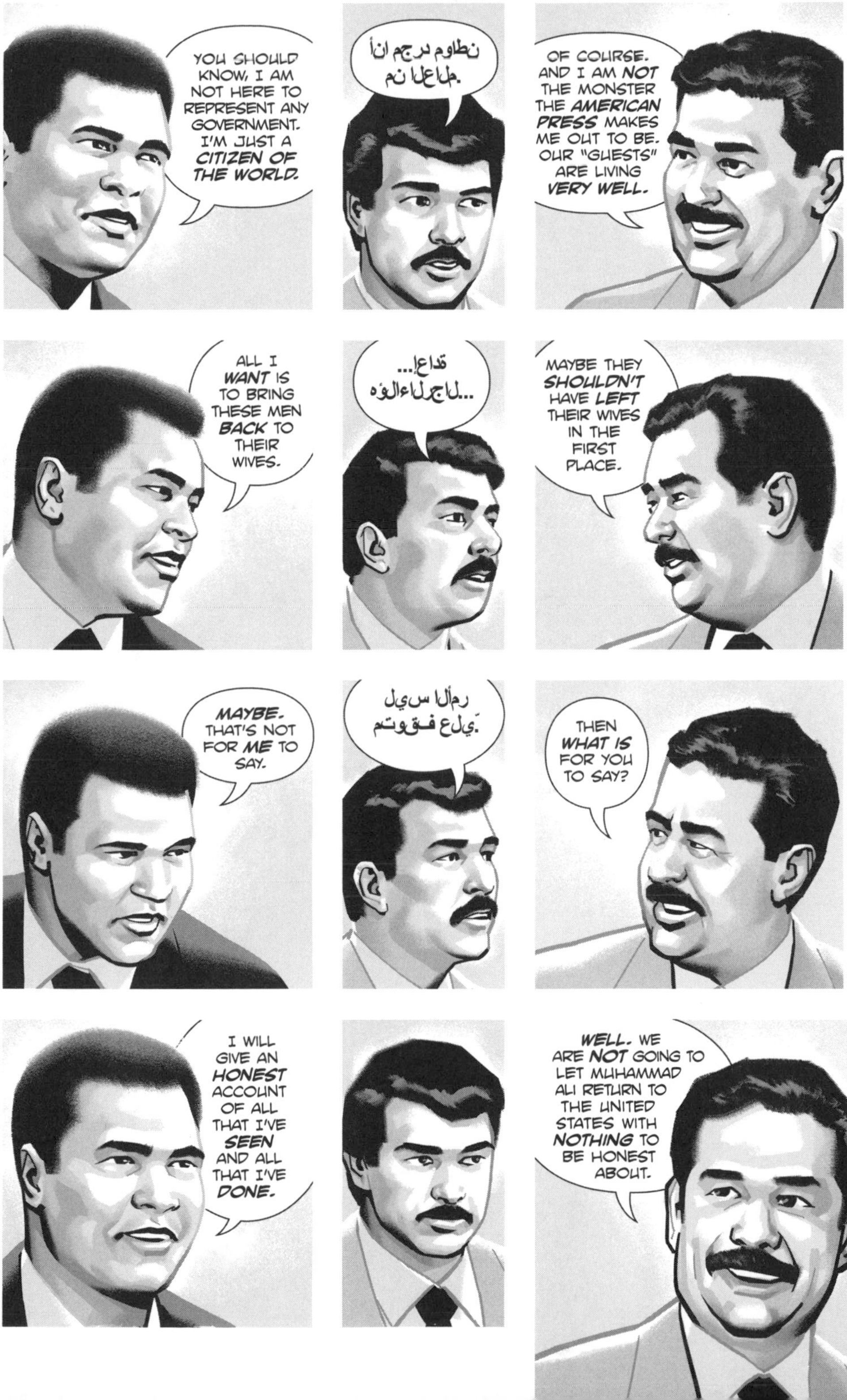

YOU SHOULD KNOW, I AM NOT HERE TO REPRESENT ANY GOVERNMENT. I'M JUST A **CITIZEN OF THE WORLD.**
OF COURSE. AND I AM **NOT** THE MONSTER THE **AMERICAN PRESS** MAKES ME OUT TO BE. OUR "GUESTS" ARE LIVING **VERY WELL.**
ALL I **WANT** IS TO BRING THESE MEN **BACK** TO THEIR WIVES.
MAYBE THEY **SHOULDN'T** HAVE **LEFT** THEIR WIVES IN THE FIRST PLACE.
MAYBE. THAT'S NOT FOR **ME** TO SAY.
THEN **WHAT IS** FOR YOU TO SAY?
I WILL GIVE AN **HONEST** ACCOUNT OF ALL THAT I'VE **SEEN** AND ALL THAT I'VE **DONE.**
WELL. WE ARE **NOT** GOING TO LET MUHAMMAD ALI RETURN TO THE UNITED STATES WITH **NOTHING** TO BE HONEST ABOUT.

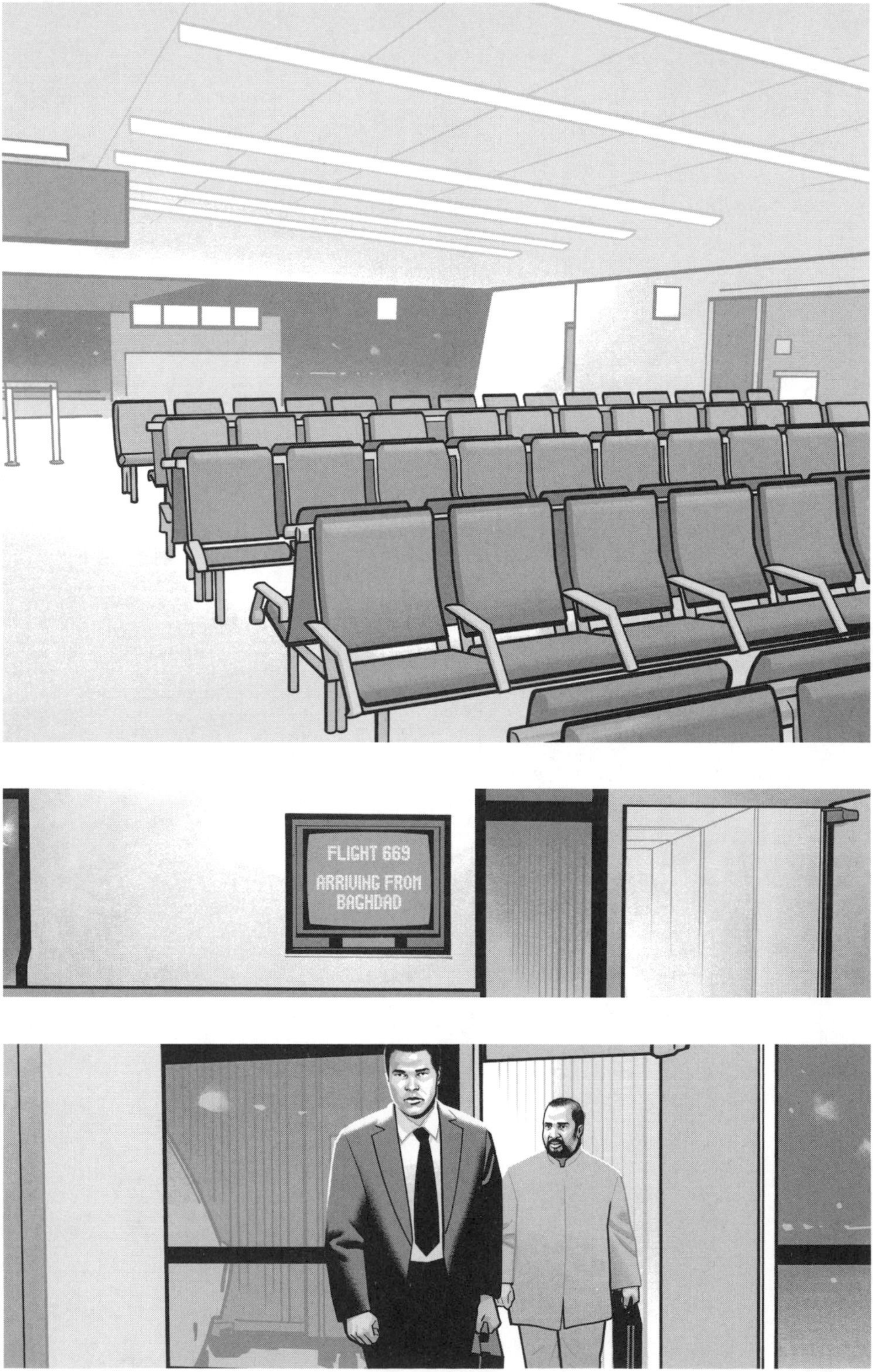
FLIGHT 669
ARRIVING FROM BAGHDAD

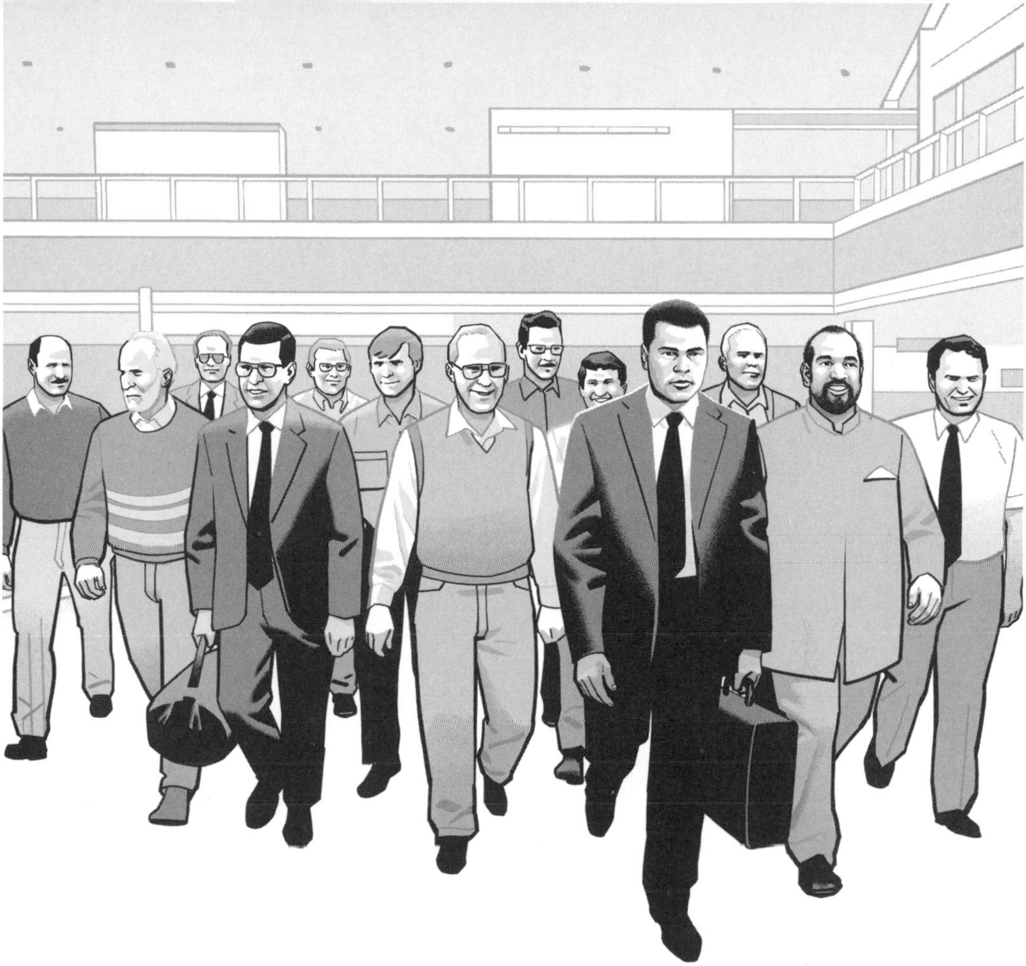

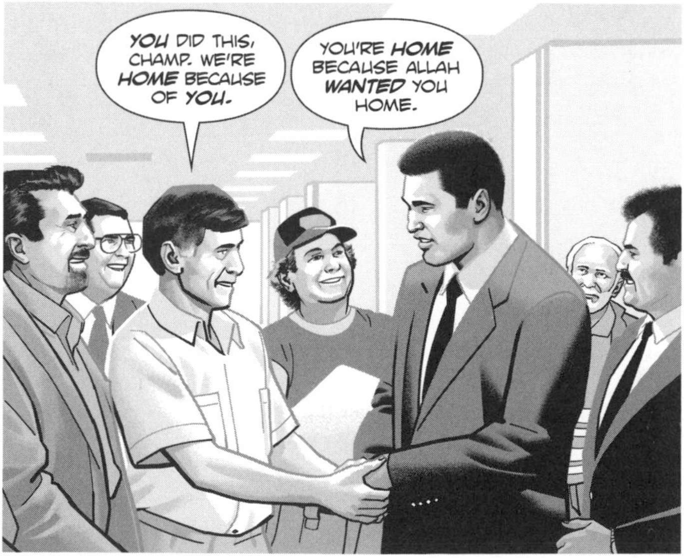
YOU DID THIS, CHAMP. WE'RE HOME BECAUSE OF YOU.
YOU'RE HOME BECAUSE ALLAH WANTED YOU HOME.

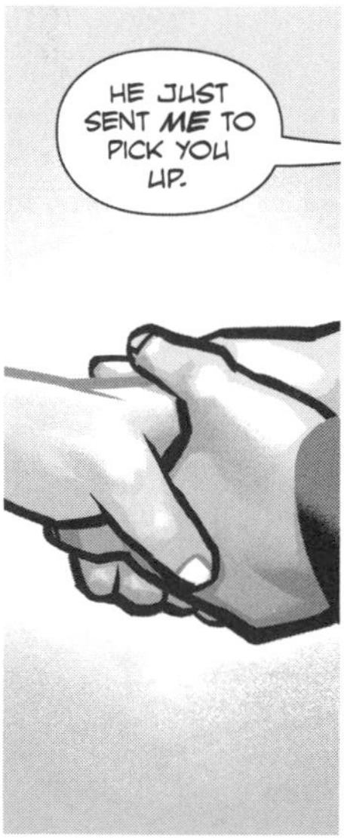
HE JUST SENT ME TO PICK YOU UP.

ROUND TWELVE: SURVIVOR. 1996.

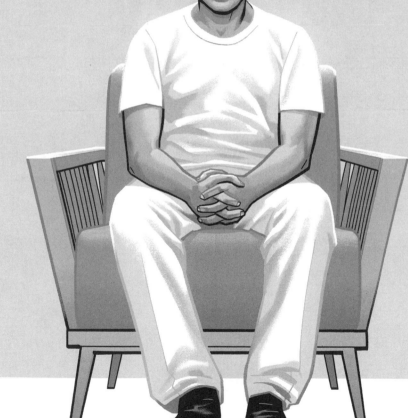

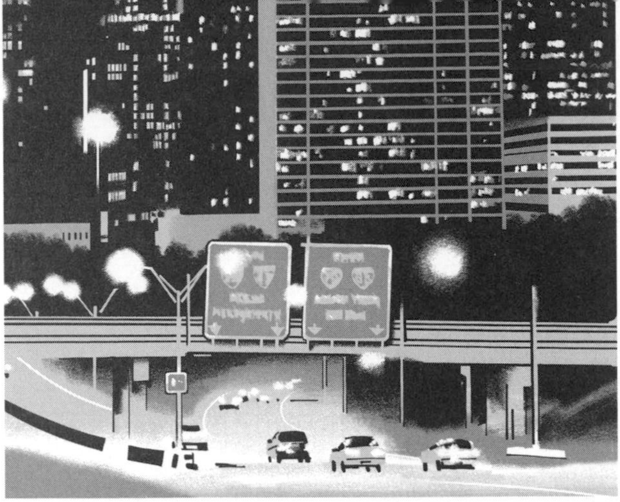

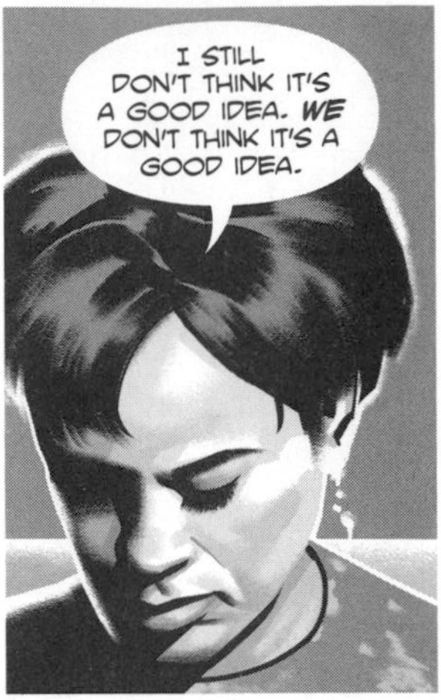
I STILL DON'T THINK IT'S A GOOD IDEA. **WE** DON'T THINK IT'S A GOOD IDEA.

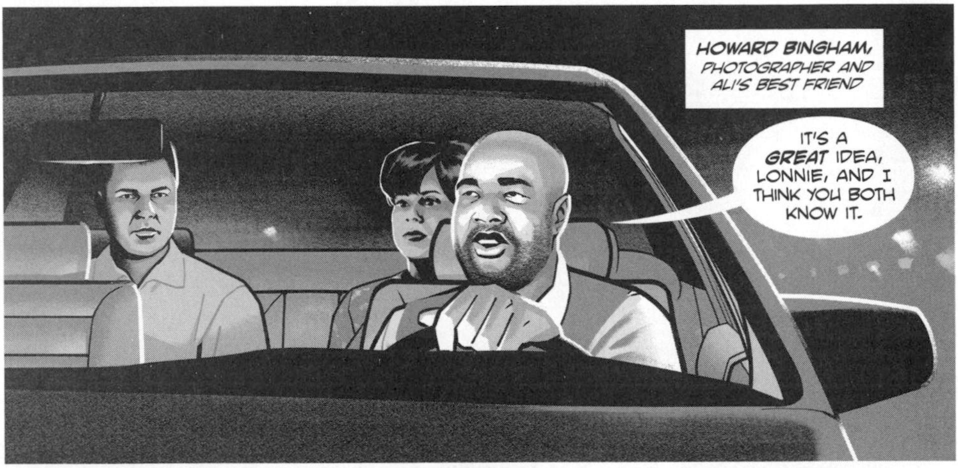
HOWARD BINGHAM, PHOTOGRAPHER AND ALI'S BEST FRIEND
IT'S A **GREAT** IDEA, LONNIE, AND I THINK YOU BOTH KNOW IT.

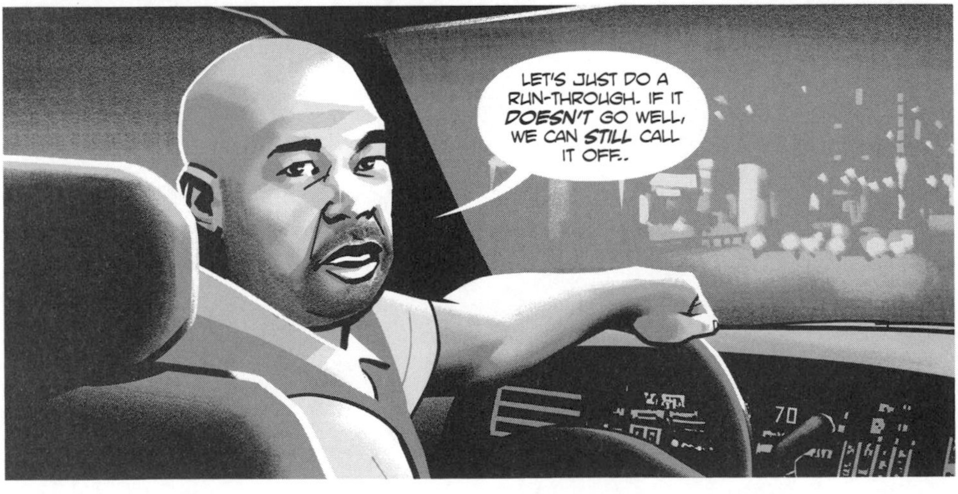
LET'S JUST DO A RUN-THROUGH. IF IT **DOESN'T** GO WELL, WE CAN **STILL** CALL IT OFF..

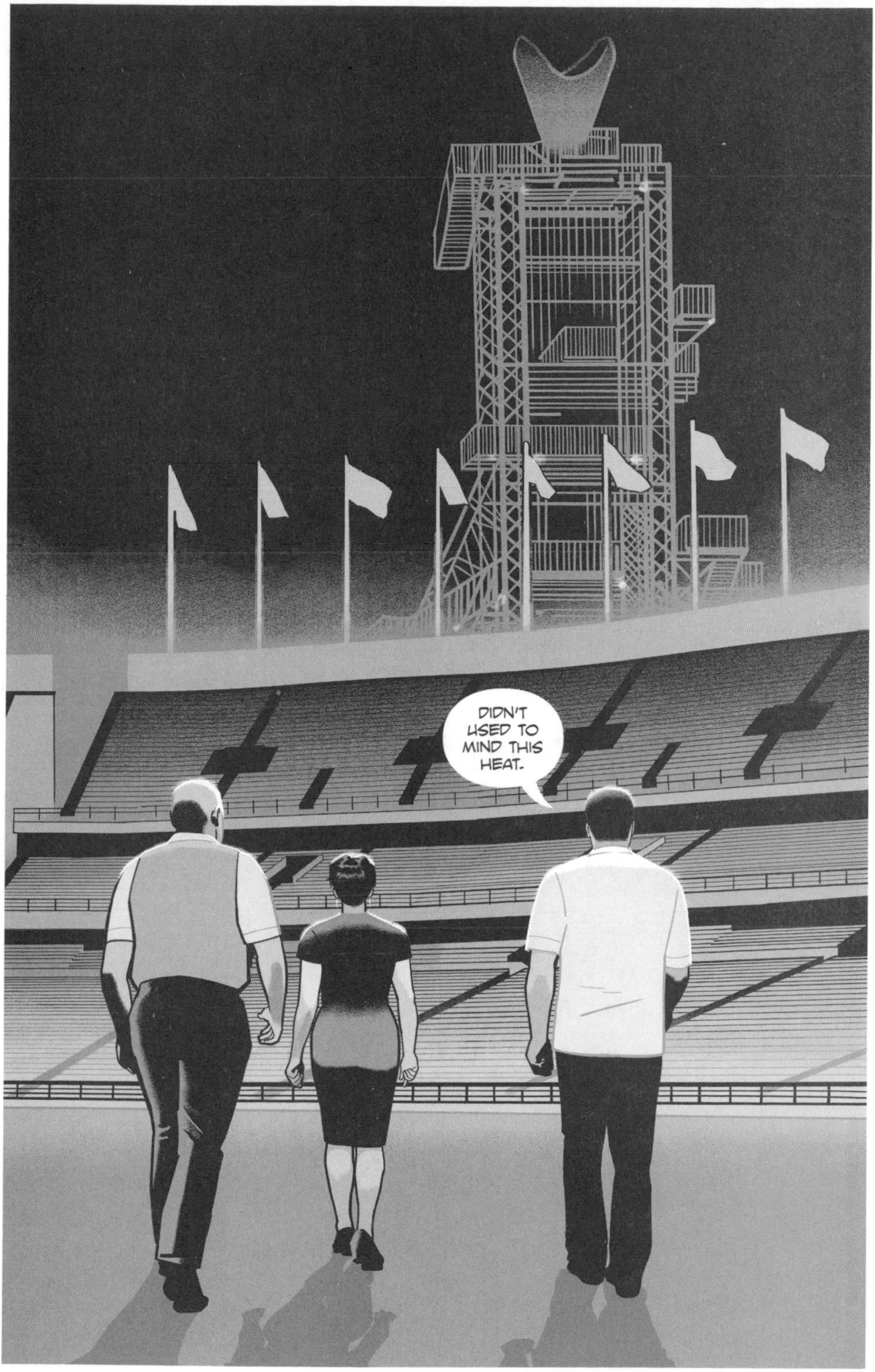
DIDN'T USED TO MIND THIS HEAT.

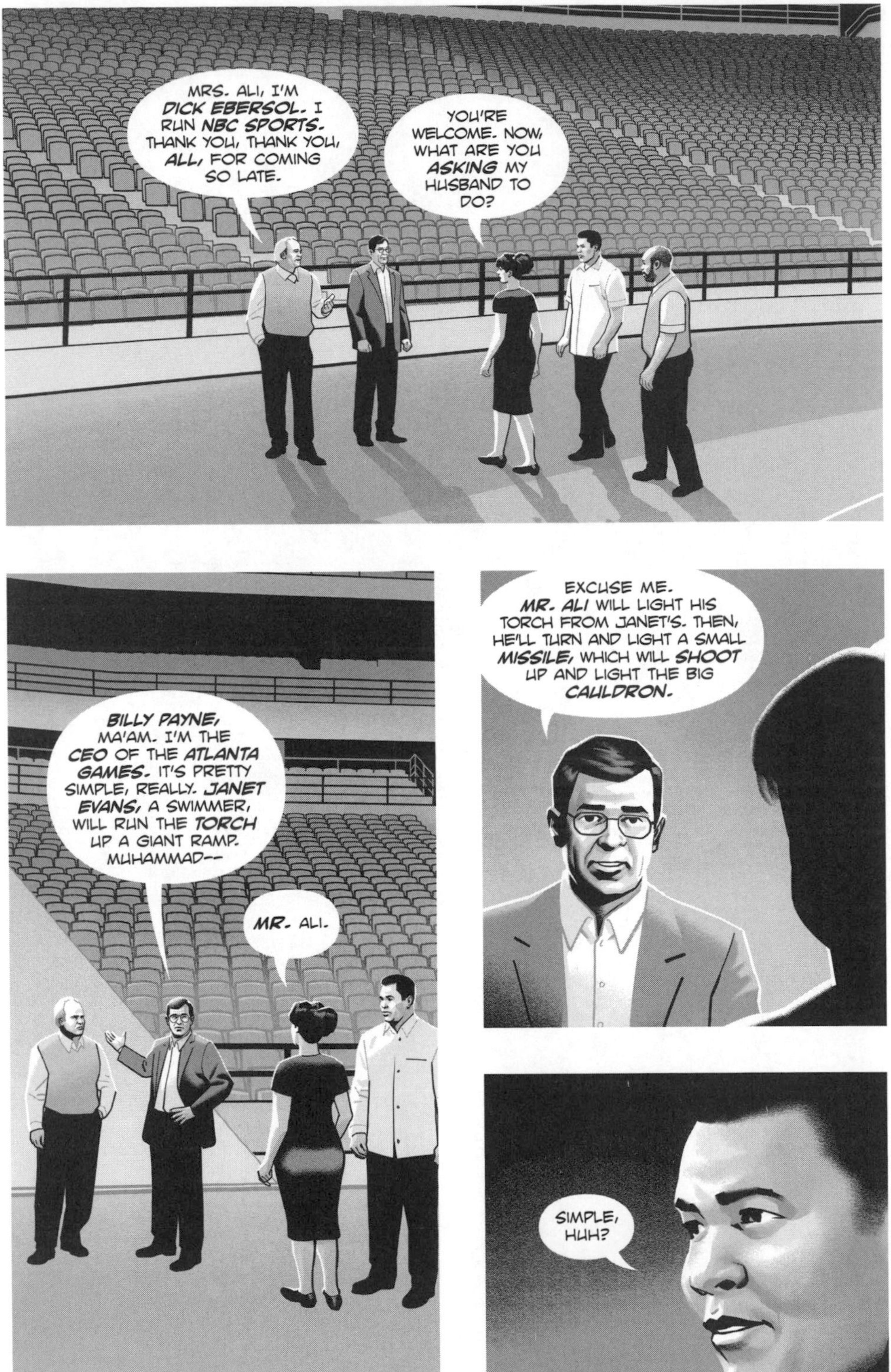
MRS. ALI, I'M DICK EBERSOL. I RUN NBC SPORTS. THANK YOU, THANK YOU, ALL, FOR COMING SO LATE.
YOU'RE WELCOME. NOW, WHAT ARE YOU ASKING MY HUSBAND TO DO?
BILLY PAYNE, MA'AM. I'M THE CEO OF THE ATLANTA GAMES. IT'S PRETTY SIMPLE, REALLY. JANET EVANS, A SWIMMER, WILL RUN THE TORCH UP A GIANT RAMP. MUHAMMAD--
MR. ALI.
EXCUSE ME. MR. ALI WILL LIGHT HIS TORCH FROM JANET'S. THEN, HE'LL TURN AND LIGHT A SMALL MISSILE, WHICH WILL SHOOT UP AND LIGHT THE BIG CAULDRON.
SIMPLE, HUH?

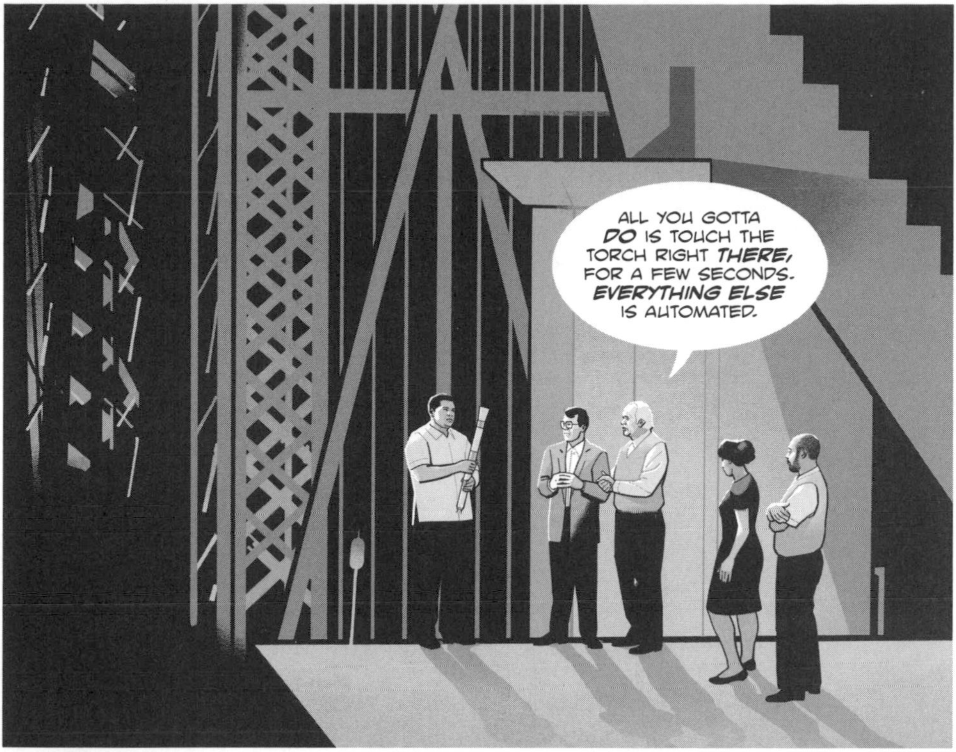
ALL YOU GOTTA DO IS TOUCH THE TORCH RIGHT THERE, FOR A FEW SECONDS. EVERYTHING ELSE IS AUTOMATED.

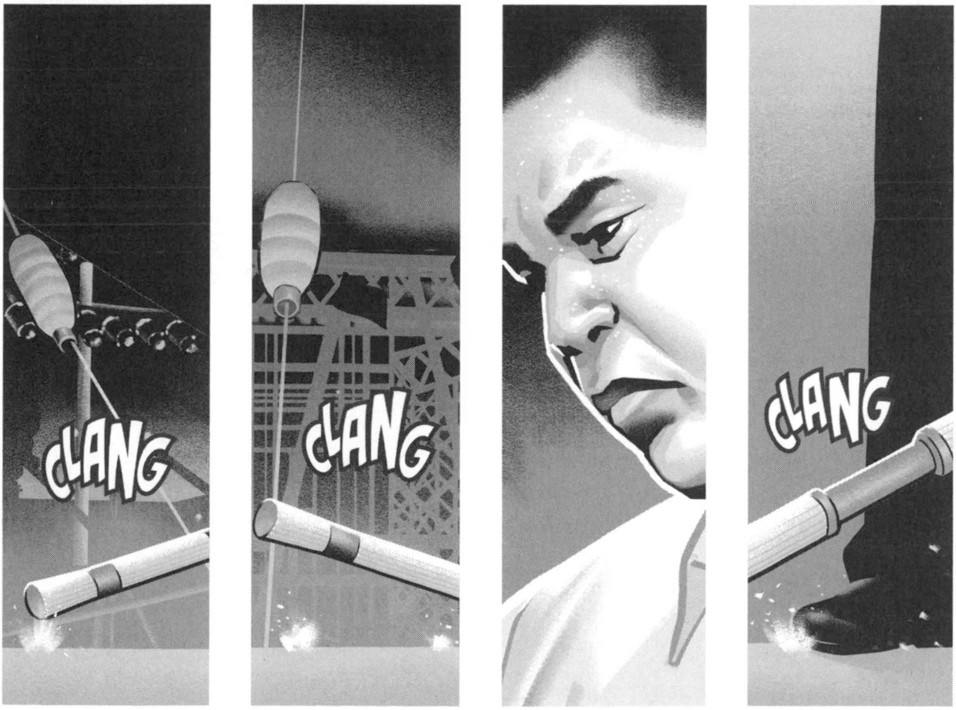
CLANG
CLANG
CLANG

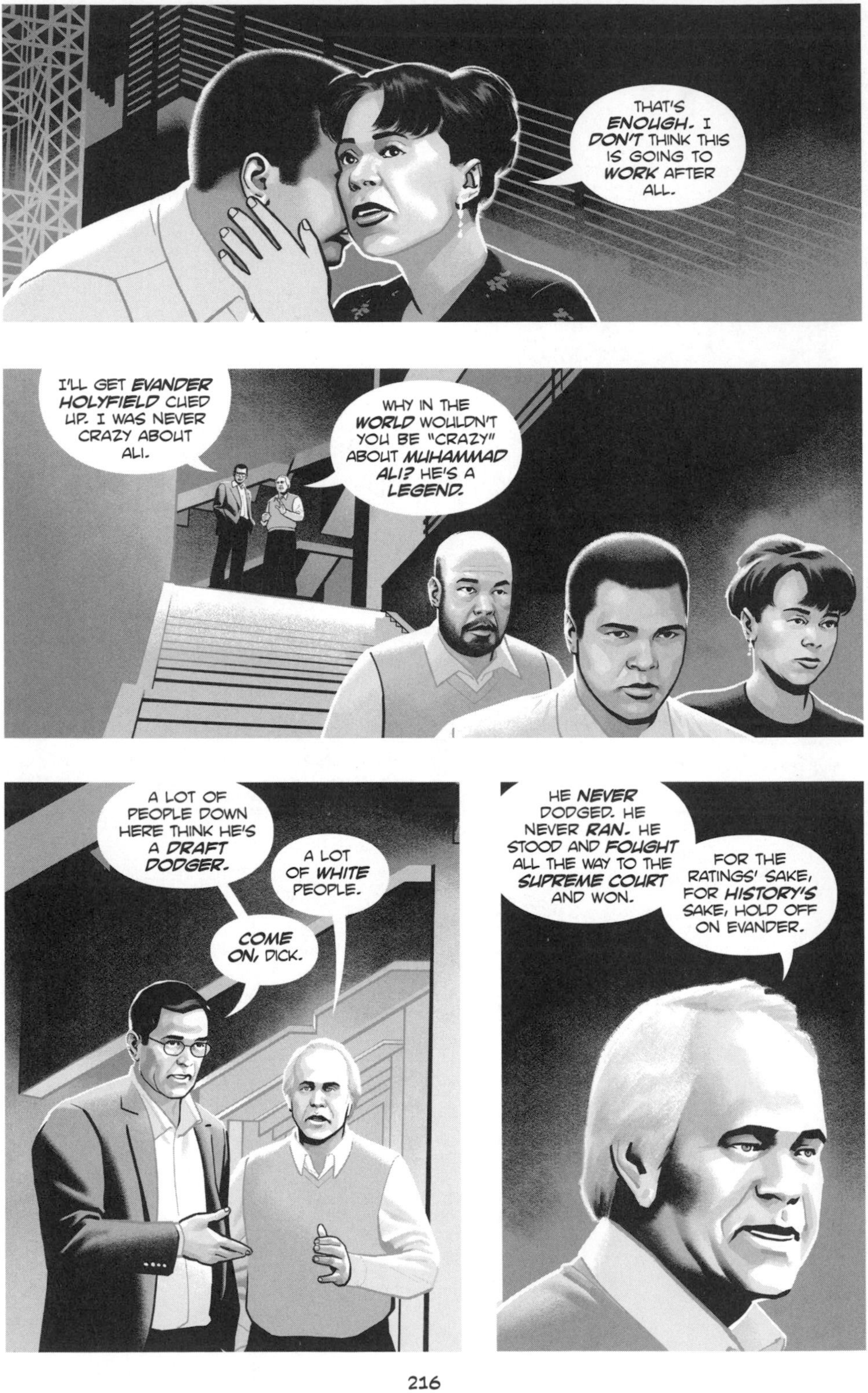
THAT'S ENOUGH. I DON'T THINK THIS IS GOING TO WORK AFTER ALL.
I'LL GET EVANDER HOLYFIELD CUED UP. I WAS NEVER CRAZY ABOUT ALI.
WHY IN THE WORLD WOULDN'T YOU BE "CRAZY" ABOUT MUHAMMAD ALI? HE'S A LEGEND.
A LOT OF PEOPLE DOWN HERE THINK HE'S A DRAFT DODGER.
A LOT OF WHITE PEOPLE.
COME ON, DICK.
HE NEVER DODGED. HE NEVER RAN. HE STOOD AND FOUGHT ALL THE WAY TO THE SUPREME COURT AND WON.
FOR THE RATINGS' SAKE, FOR HISTORY'S SAKE, HOLD OFF ON EVANDER.

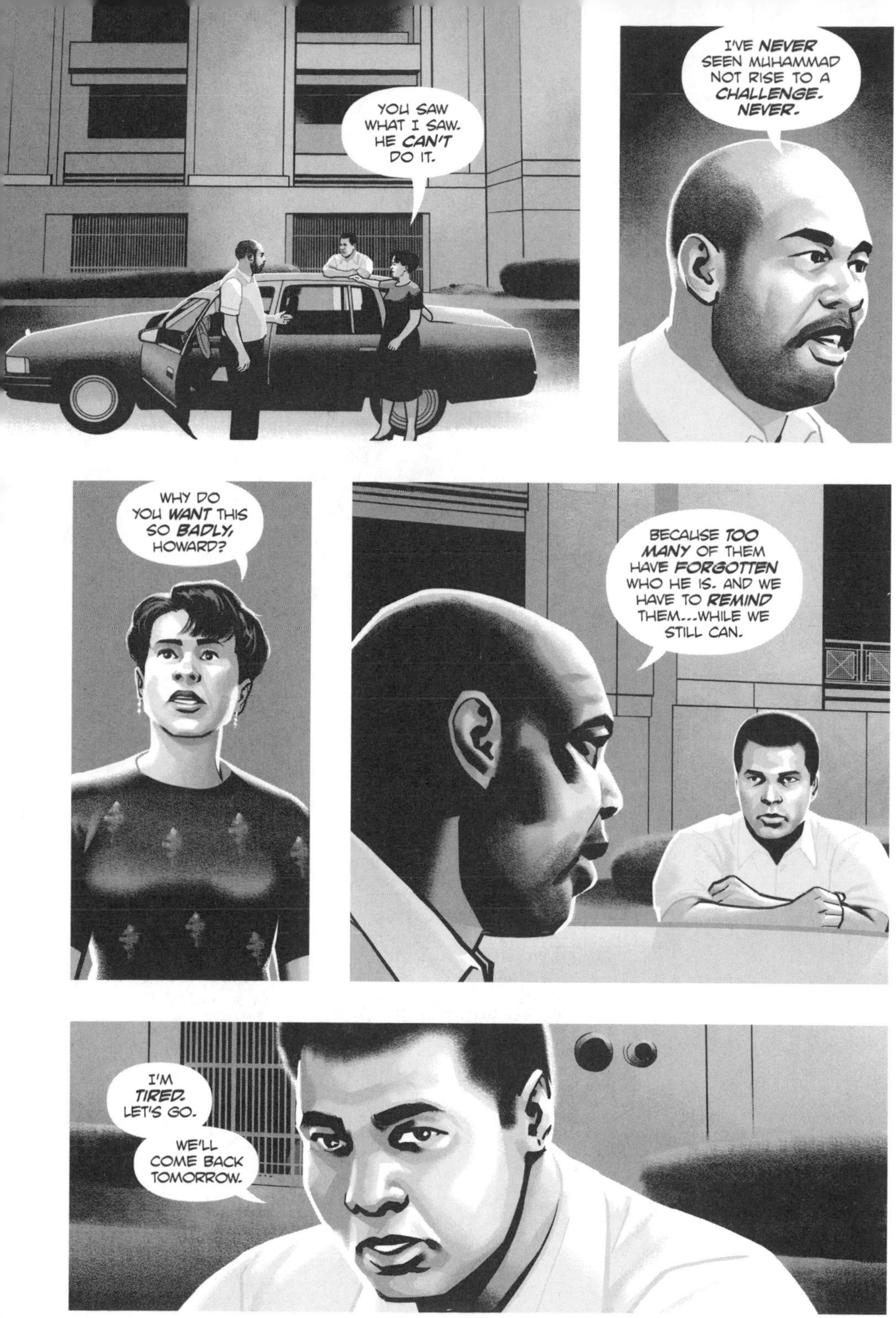
YOU SAW WHAT I SAW. HE CAN'T DO IT.
I'VE NEVER SEEN MUHAMMAD NOT RISE TO A CHALLENGE. NEVER.
WHY DO YOU WANT THIS SO BADLY, HOWARD?
BECAUSE TOO MANY OF THEM HAVE FORGOTTEN WHO HE IS. AND WE HAVE TO REMIND THEM...WHILE WE STILL CAN.
I'M TIRED. LET'S GO.
WE'LL COME BACK TOMORROW.

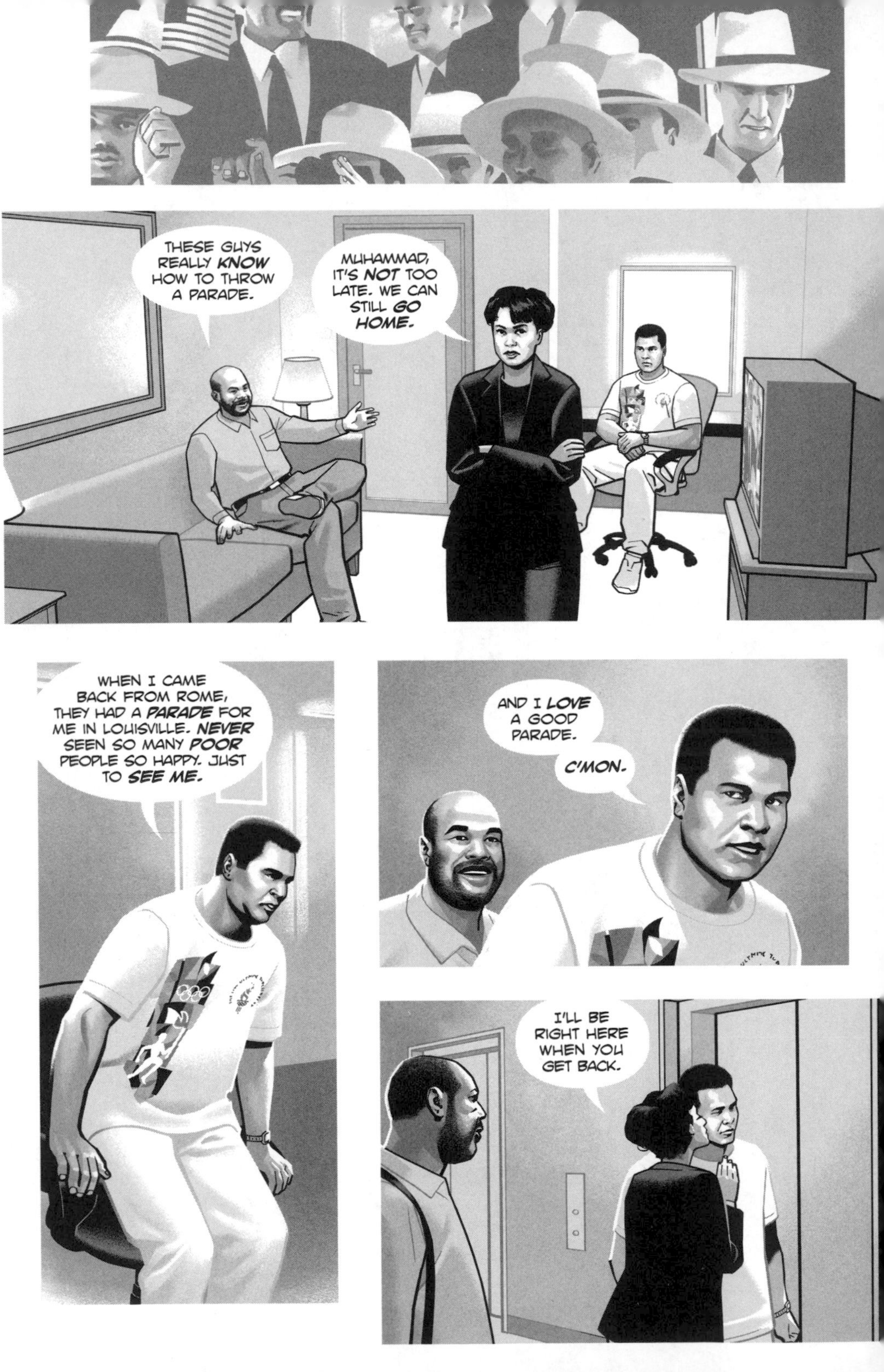
THESE GUYS REALLY KNOW HOW TO THROW A PARADE.
MUHAMMAD, IT'S NOT TOO LATE. WE CAN STILL GO HOME.
WHEN I CAME BACK FROM ROME, THEY HAD A PARADE FOR ME IN LOUISVILLE. NEVER SEEN SO MANY POOR PEOPLE SO HAPPY. JUST TO SEE ME.
AND I LOVE A GOOD PARADE.
C'MON.
I'LL BE RIGHT HERE WHEN YOU GET BACK.

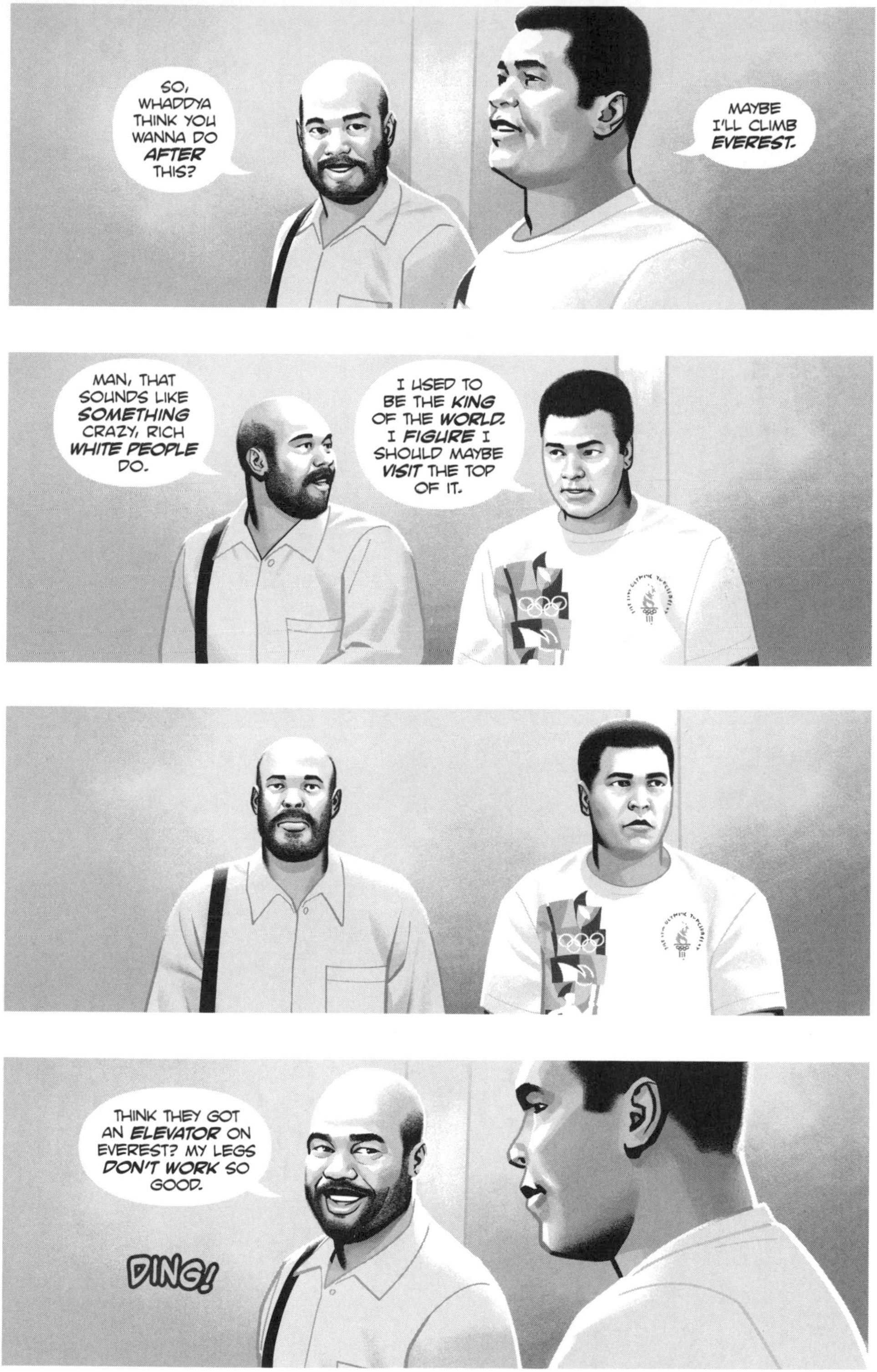
SO, WHADDYA THINK YOU WANNA DO AFTER THIS?
MAYBE I'LL CLIMB EVEREST.
MAN, THAT SOUNDS LIKE SOMETHING CRAZY, RICH WHITE PEOPLE DO.
I USED TO BE THE KING OF THE WORLD. I FIGURE I SHOULD MAYBE VISIT THE TOP OF IT.
THINK THEY GOT AN ELEVATOR ON EVEREST? MY LEGS DON'T WORK SO GOOD.
DING!

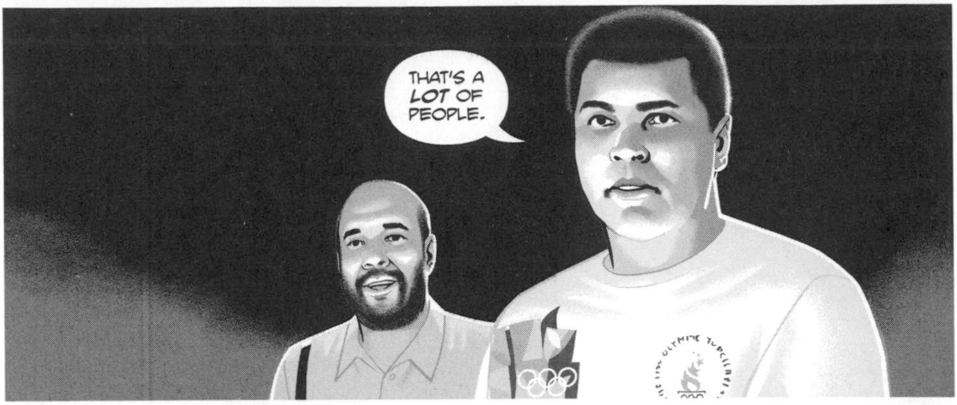
THAT'S A LOT OF PEOPLE.

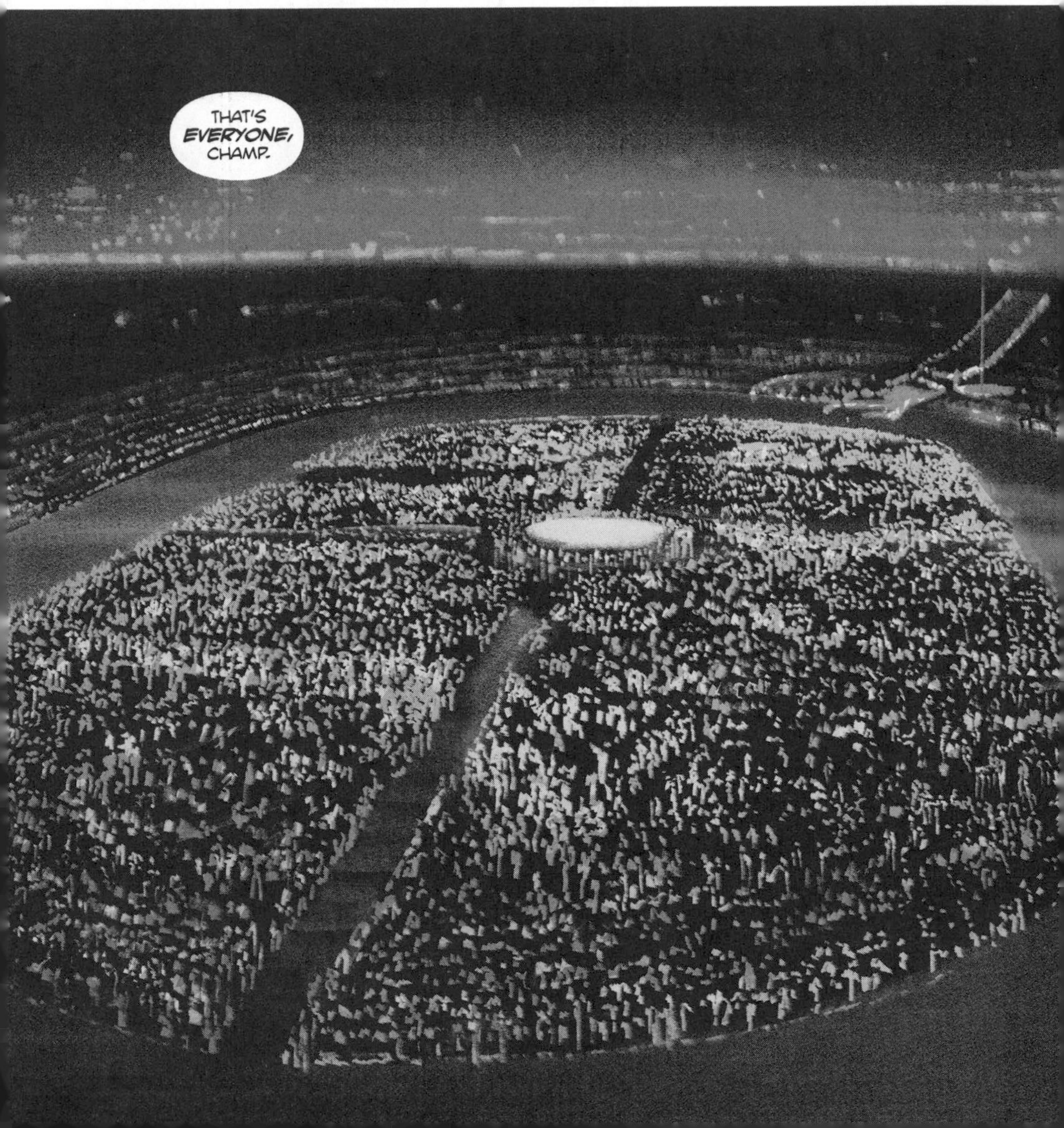
THAT'S EVERYONE, CHAMP.

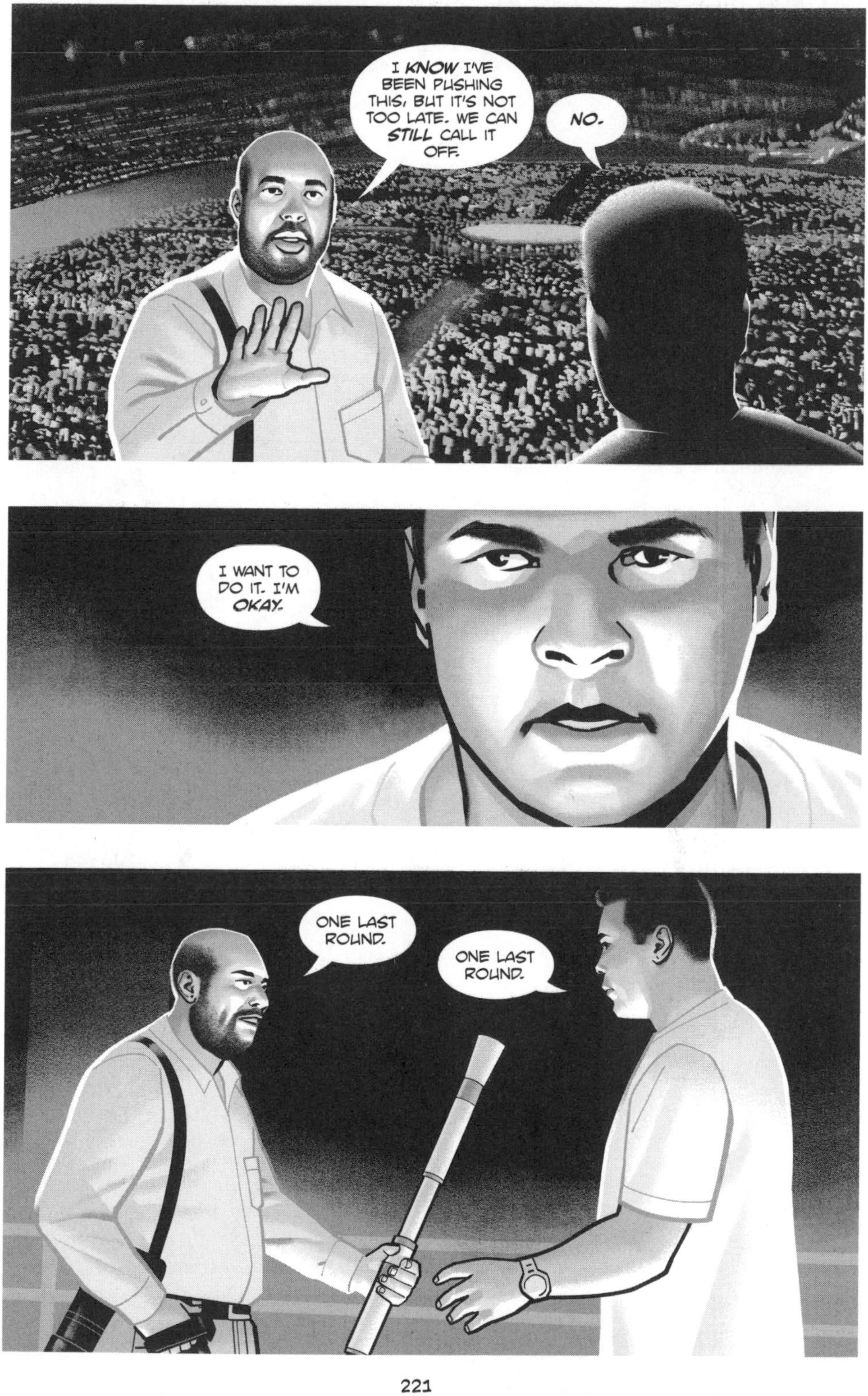
I KNOW I'VE BEEN PUSHING THIS, BUT IT'S NOT TOO LATE. WE CAN STILL CALL IT OFF.
NO.
I WANT TO DO IT. I'M OKAY.
ONE LAST ROUND.
ONE LAST ROUND.

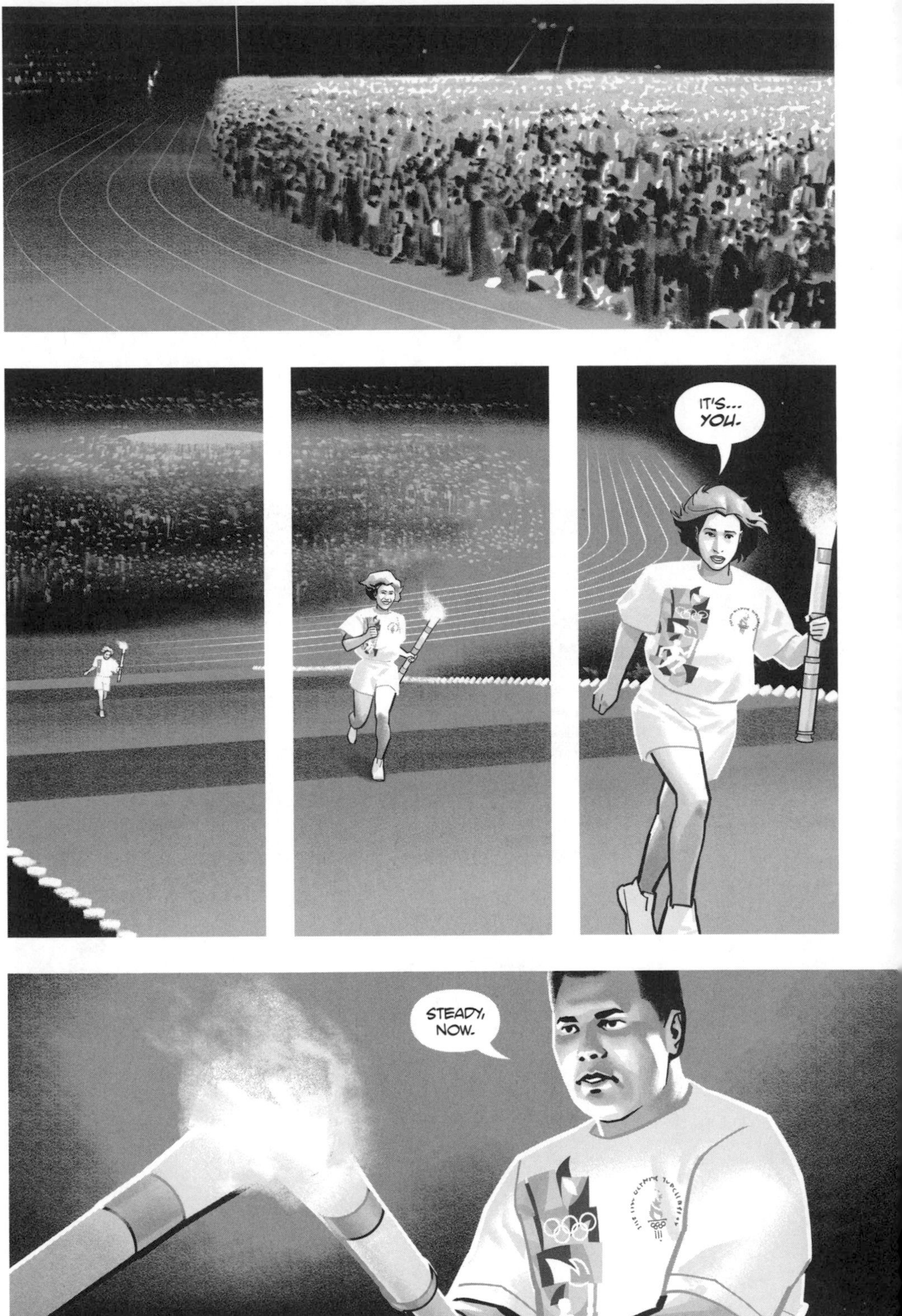
IT'S... YOU.
STEADY, NOW.

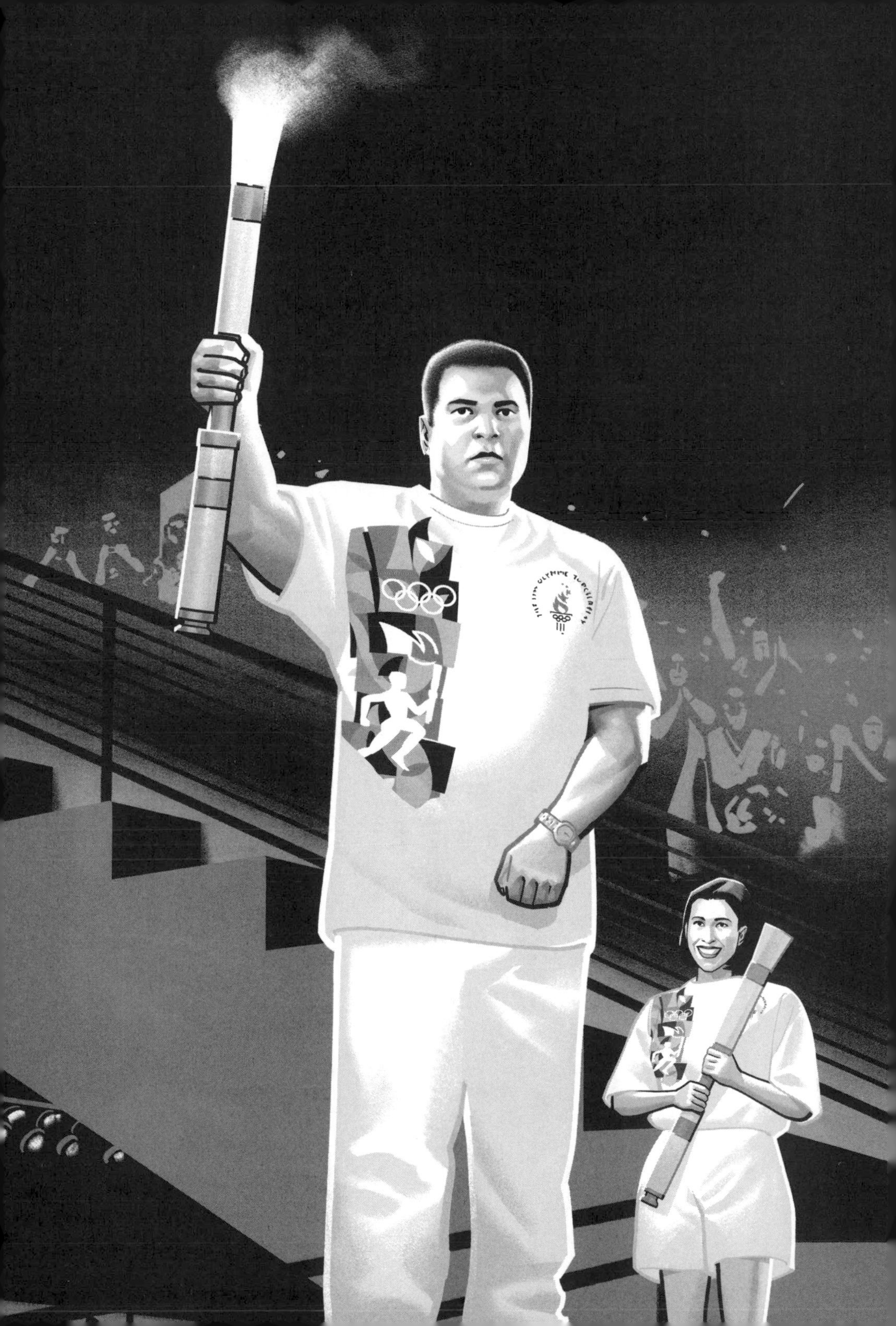

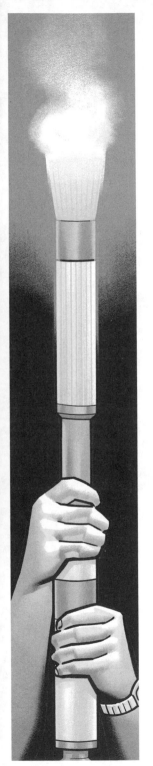

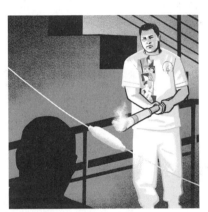

WHY WON'T IT *LIGHT?!*

FWOOOSH

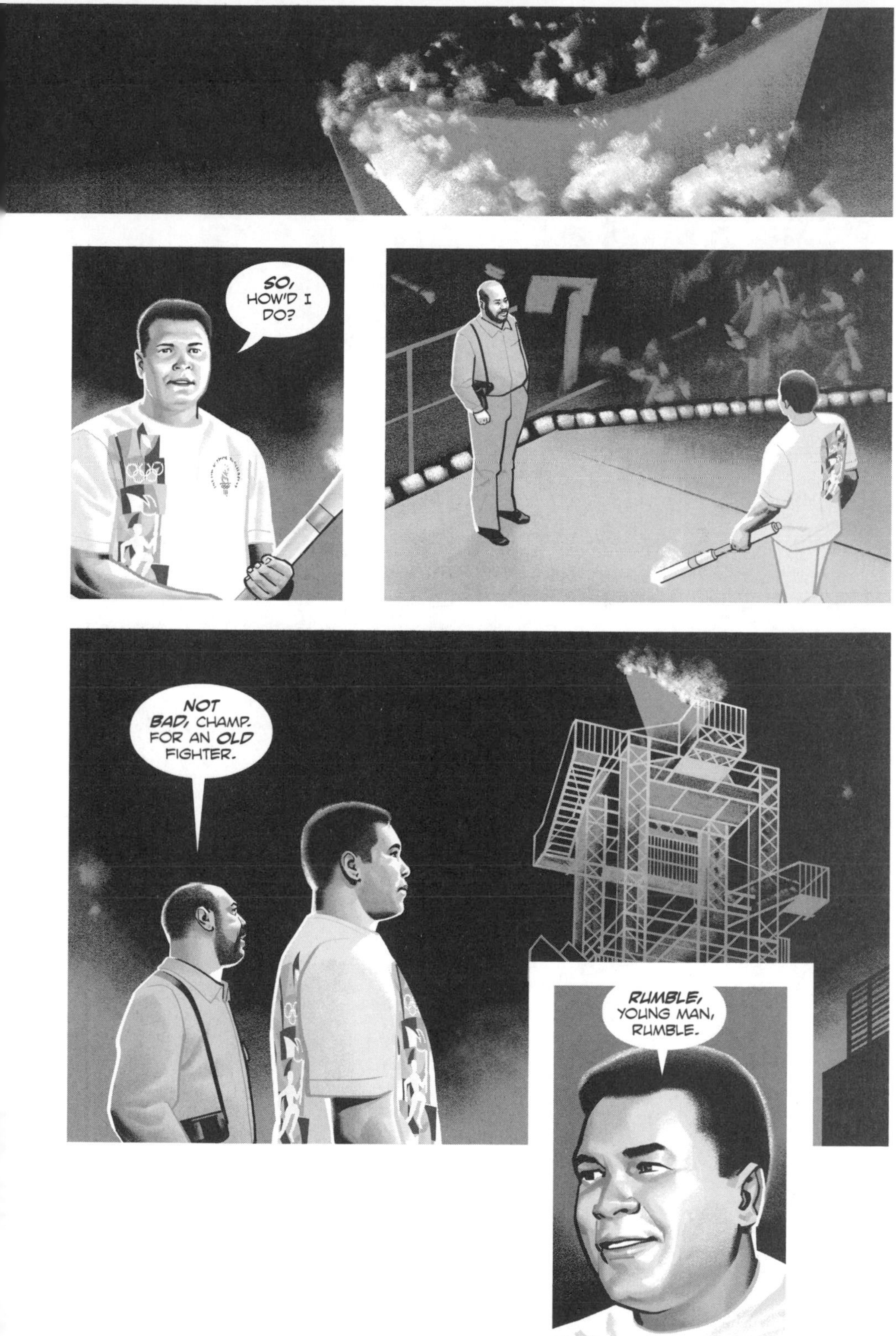
SO, HOW'D I DO?
NOT BAD, CHAMP. FOR AN OLD FIGHTER.
RUMBLE, YOUNG MAN, RUMBLE.

BIBLIOGRAPHY

ARTICLES

BECKER, BRIAN. "I Was with Muhammad Ali on His Hostage-Release Trip to Iraq—and the Media Has It All Wrong." Answer Coalition. June 10, 2016. https://www.answercoalition.org/i_was_with_muhammad_ali_on _his_hostage_release_trip_to_iraq_and_the_media_has_it_all_wrong.

BERKOW, IRA. "Joe Elsby Martin, 80, Muhammad Ali's First Boxing Teacher." *New York Times.* September 17, 1996. https://www.nytimes. com/1996/09/17/sports/joe-elsby-martin-80-muhammad-ali-s-first -boxing-teacher.html.

BOREN, CINDY. "The Iconic Moment Muhammad Ali Lit Olympic Flame in Atlanta Almost Didn't Happen." *The Washington Post.* June 4, 2016. https://www.washingtonpost.com/news/early-lead/wp/2016/06/04 /the-iconic-moment-muhammad-ali-lit-olympic-torch-in-atlanta -almost-didnt-happen.

CARLSON, HEATHER J. "Ali's Mayo Visit: 'Me, Hurt?'" *Post Bulletin.* June 6, 2016. https://www.postbulletin.com/newsmd/alis-mayo-visit-me-hurt.

GRIERSON, TIM. "How Muhammad Ali's Iconic 'Esquire' Cover Helped Cement a Legend." *Rolling Stone.* June 5, 2016. https://www .rollingstone.com/cultureculturefeatures/how-muhammad-alis-iconic -esquire-cover-helped-cement-a-legend-69404.

IZENBERG, JERRY. "Muhammad Ali: Why They Called him 'The Greatest' and Why I Called Him My Friend." *The Star-Ledger.* June 4, 2016. https://www.nj.com/sports/2016/06/former_heavyweight_champ _muhmmad_ali_dies_the_gre.html.

REGALDO, SAMUEL O. *"Clay, aka Ali v. United States* (1971): Muhammad Ali, Precedent, and the Burger Court." *Journal of Sport History* 34, no. 2 (Summer 2007): 169–182. https://www.jstor.org/stable/43610014.

REMNICK, DAVID. "American Hunger." *The New Yorker.* October 12, 1998. https://www.newyorker.com/magazine/1998/10/12/american-hunger.

SILVER, MICHAEL. "Where Were You on March 8, 1971?" ESPN Classic. November 19, 2003. https://www.espn.com/classic/s/silver_ali_frazier.html.

BOOKS

MARANISS, DAVID. *Rome 1960: The Olympics That Changed the World.* New York: Simon & Schuster, 2008.

REMNICK, DAVID. *King of the World: Muhammad Ali and the Rise of an American Hero.* New York: Penguin Random House, 1998.

FILMED MEDIA

30 FOR 30 SHORTS. "Ali: The Mission." ESPN, 14:02. January 16, 2013. https://www.espn.com/espnplus/collections/9410/30-for-30-shorts.

FREARS, STEPHEN. *Muhammad Ali's Greatest Fight.* Sakura Films, Rainmark Films, 2013. 1 hr., 37 min. https://www.amazon.com /Muhammad-Greatest-Fight-Christopher-Plummer/dp B00G6UET3C.

GAST, LEON. *When We Were Kings.* PolyGram Film Entertainment, 1996. 1 hr., 29 min. https://www.amazon.com/When-Were-Kings-Leon-Gast /dp/B07TPDBFFI.

KILROY, GENE. "Gene Kilroy | Muhammad Ali's business manager on life with 'The Greatest.'" Interview by Shane Hannon. May 31, 2020. Video, 57:27. https://www.youtube.com/watch?v=u7xpDm8HrpE.

SIEGEL, BILL. *The Trials of Muhammad Ali.* Kartemquin Films, 2013. 1 hr., 26 min. https://www.amazon.com/Trials-Muhammad -Ali/dp/B00HZ7EYYO.

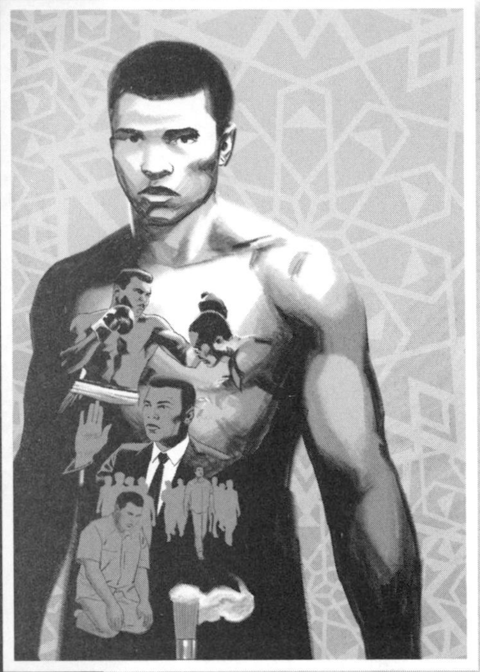

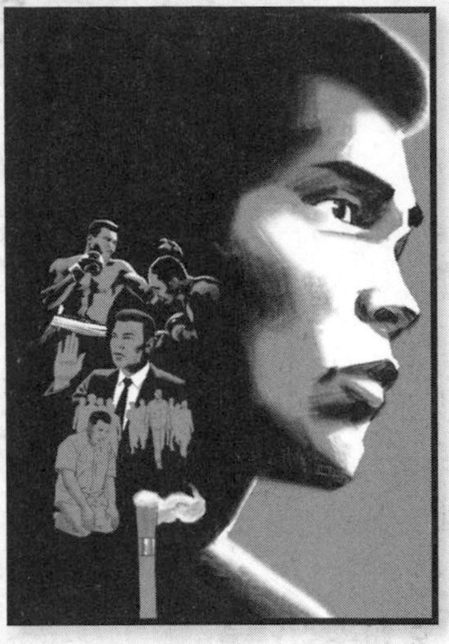

Muhammad Ali

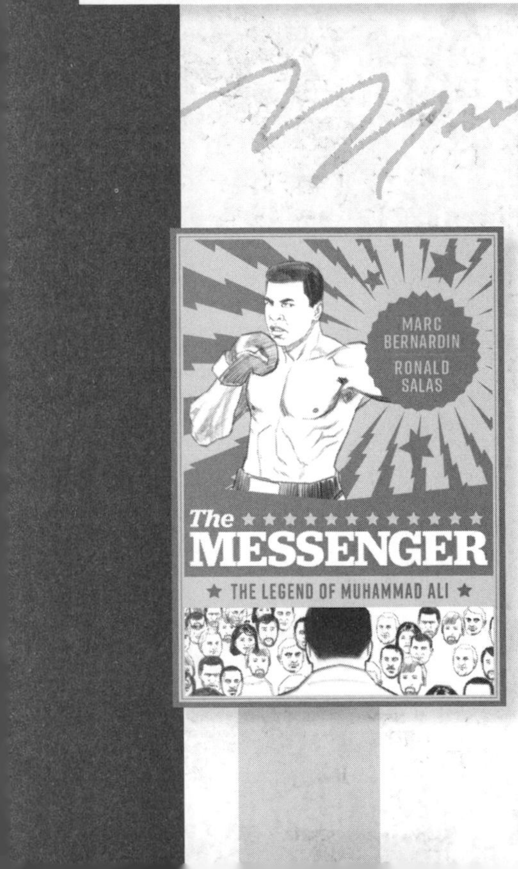
MARC
BERNARDIN
RONALD
SALAS
The
MESSENGER
THE LEGEND OF MUHAMMAD ALI

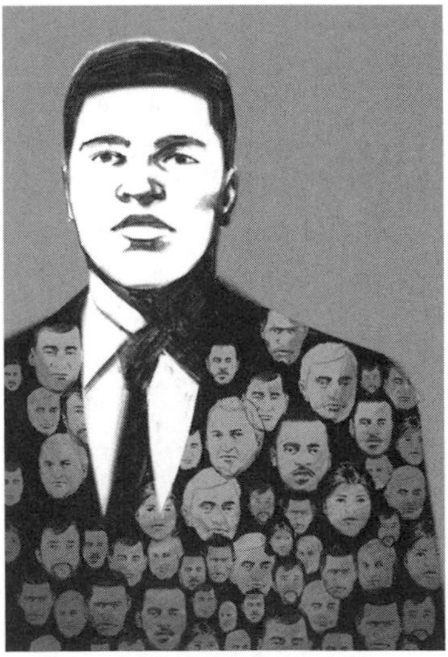

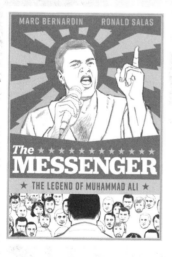

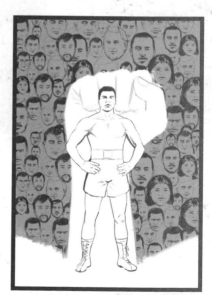

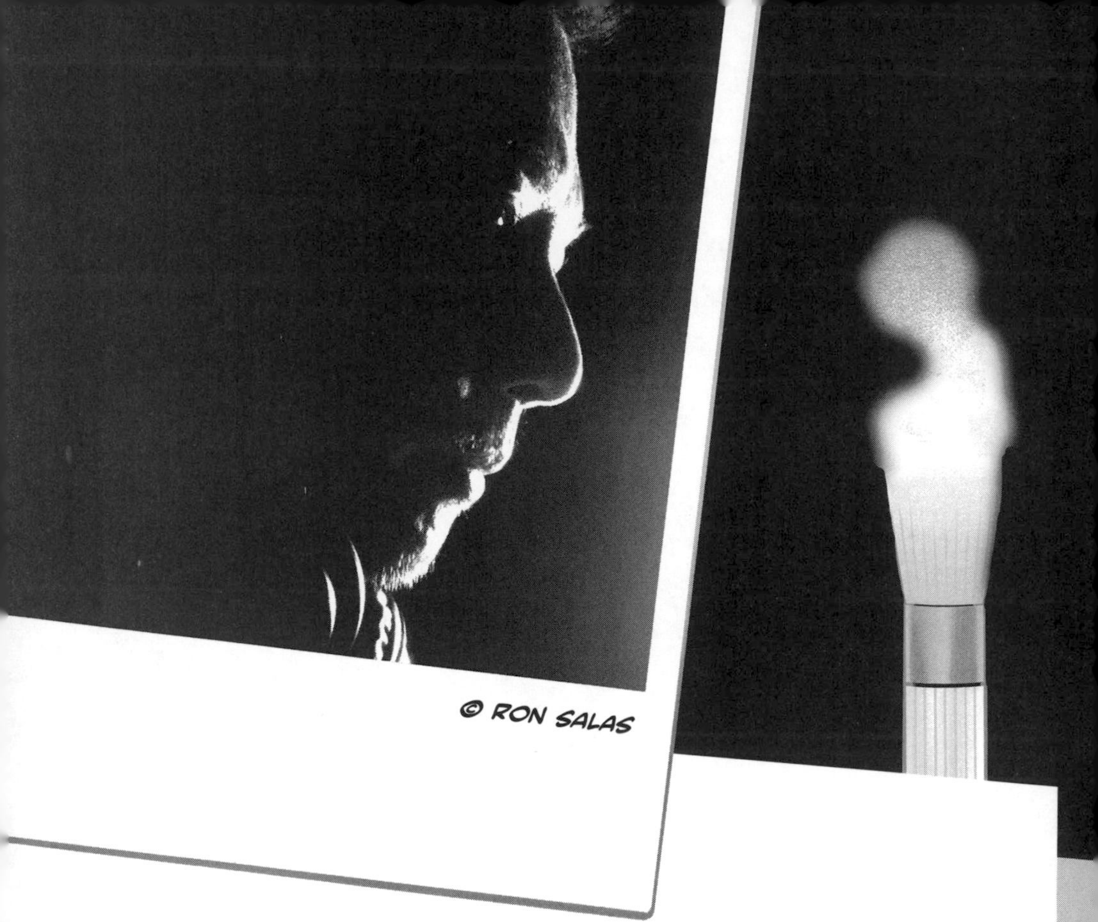
© RON SALAS

RON SALAS is a Philippine-born illustrator and comic book artist. He grew up in the suburbs of Toronto and moved to the US in 2002. He has worked as an illustrator and designer for companies such as Disney, Universal, Hard Rock Cafe, Planet Hollywood, and *Playboy.* He has also worked as a branding/marketing designer for a number of brands. He currently works as a freelance illustrator whose previously published work includes *Spider-Man*, *Prince Valiant*, and *28 Days Later*.

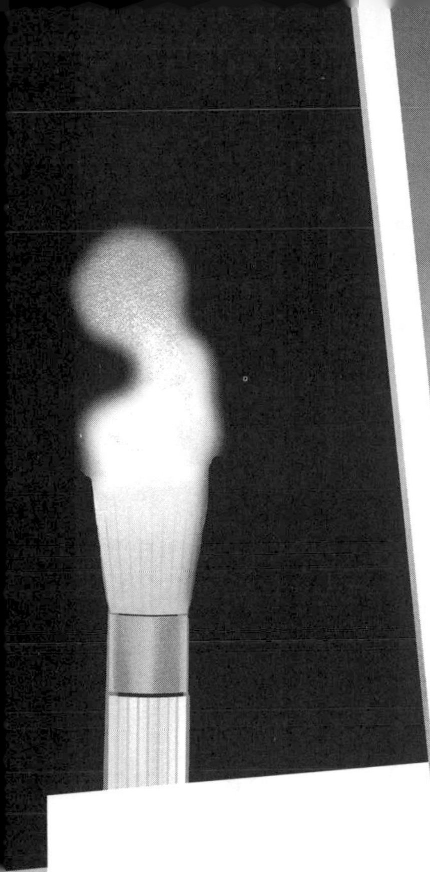

MARC BERNARDIN is a WGA Award–winning television writer-producer who has worked on *Star Trek: Picard*, *The Continental*, *Carnival Row*, *Treadstone*, *Castle Rock*, *Critical Role: The Legend of Vox Machina*, *Masters of the Universe: Revelations*, and *Alphas*. In an earlier life, he was a journalist for the *Los Angeles Times*, the *Hollywood Reporter*, *Playboy*, and *Entertainment Weekly*. In comics, he's an Eisner Award–nominated writer of *Adora and the Distance*, *Peter Parker: The Amazing Shutterbug*, *Genius*, *The Highwaymen*, and *Monster Attack Network*. And he cohosts the *Fat Man Beyond* podcast with Kevin Smith.

GRAPHIC NOVELS THAT BELONG ON EVERYONE'S BOOKSHELF

ANDREW S. WEISS
"ABSORBING AND VISUALLY STUNNING."
—MADELEINE K. ALBRIGHT
BRIAN "BOX" BROWN
ACCIDENTAL CZAR
THE LIFE AND LIES OF VLADIMIR PUTIN

ACCIDENTAL CZAR
by Andrew S. Weiss and Brian "Box" Brown

FROM SMALL STEPS TO GREAT LEAPS
Dragon Hoops
NEW YORK TIMES–BESTSELLING AUTHOR
GENE LUEN YANG

DRAGON HOOPS
by Gene Luen Yang

SO MUCH FOR LOVE
How I Survived a Toxic Relationship
SOPHIE LAMBDA

SO MUCH FOR LOVE
by Sophie Lambda

PHILIPPE SQUARZONI
HOMICIDE
THE GRAPHIC NOVEL PART ONE
BASED ON THE BOOK BY
DAVID SIMON

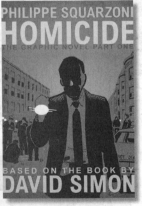

HOMICIDE: THE GRAPHIC NOVEL, PART ONE
by David Simon and Philippe Squarzoni

AUTHOR OF THE #1 NEW YORK TIMES BESTSELLER FEYNMAN
OTTAVIANI & DYE
EINSTEIN

EINSTEIN
by Jim Ottaviani and Jerel Dye

Ronald WIMBERLY
Brahm REVEL
NOW LET ME FLY

NOW LET ME FLY
by Ronald Wimberly and Brahm Revel